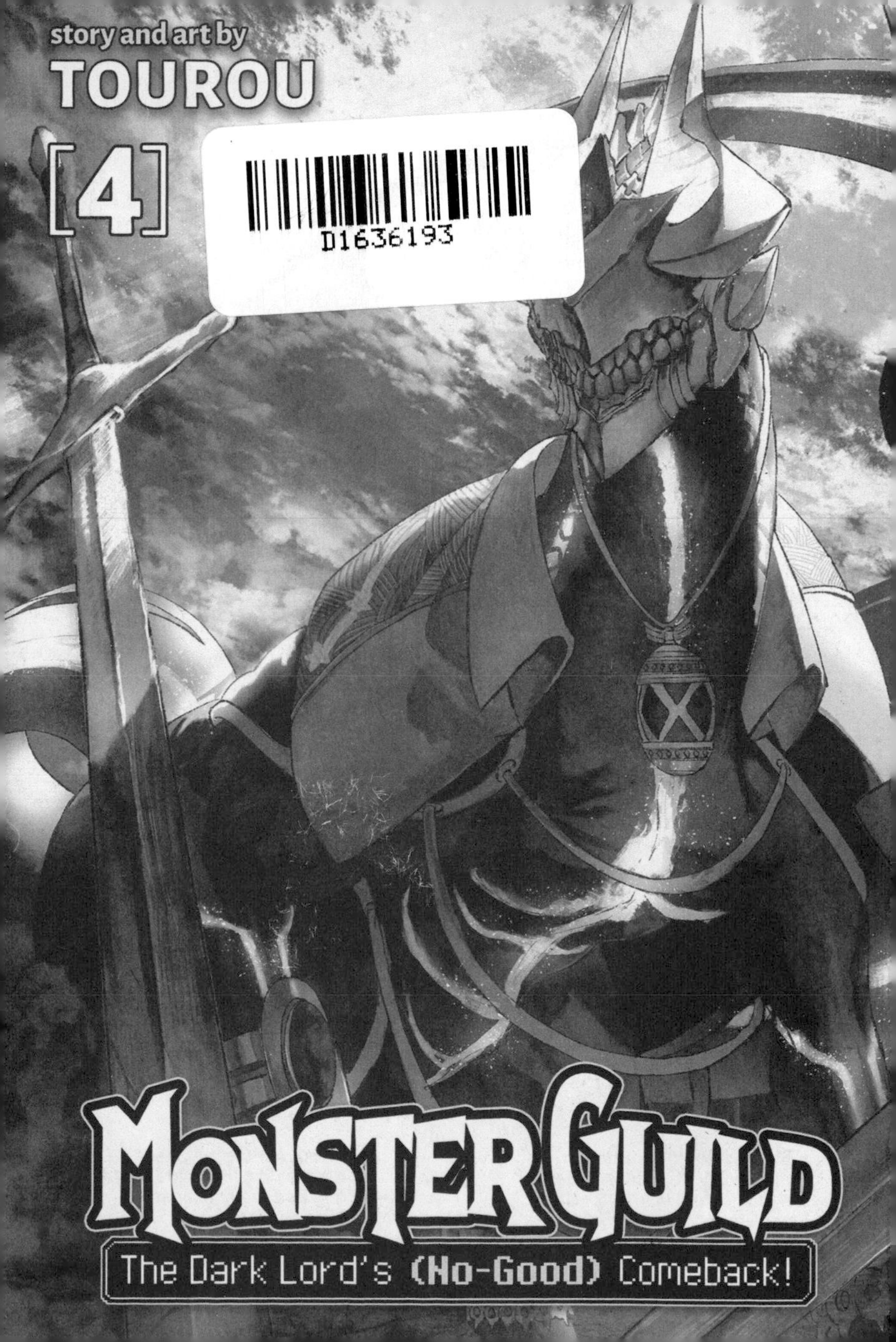
story and art by
TOUROU
[4]
MONSTER GUILD
The Dark Lord's (No-Good) Comeback!

Character Introduction

after
before

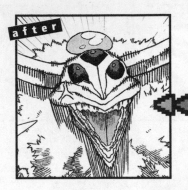

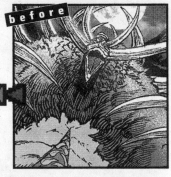

THE DARK LORD OF AGNIIN

The former the king of evil and tyranny. He barely recovered after his defeat at the hands of the hero, and he's now barely a threat. He travels the world in an attempt to regain his reign over Agniin. There's something mysterious about his staff...

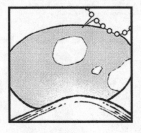

SLIME

A slime who is always cheerful and optimistic. Despite his outer arrogance, he is loyal. The Dark Lord describes him as his "first minion" and Slime calls him his "best friend."

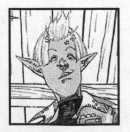

CREATIVE MASTER

A kindhearted elf craftsman from the Dark Elf Village. Has a soft spot for his grandmother. Frivolous but talented. His real name is Gimlet.

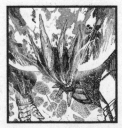

HELLFIRE

A kind-hearted monster who teaches Orcs muscle building. His race is still unknown. He has many aliases including "The Ancient Fire," "Ishkarinoa's Bullet," and "Ifrit." When his body gets cold, he stops being able to think clearly.

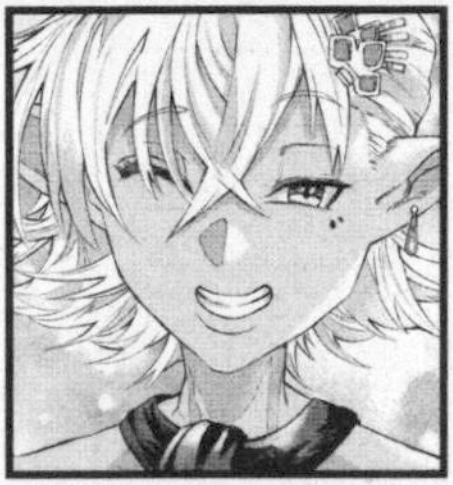

Daughter of a Dark Elf

A girl who lives in the Dark Elf Village.

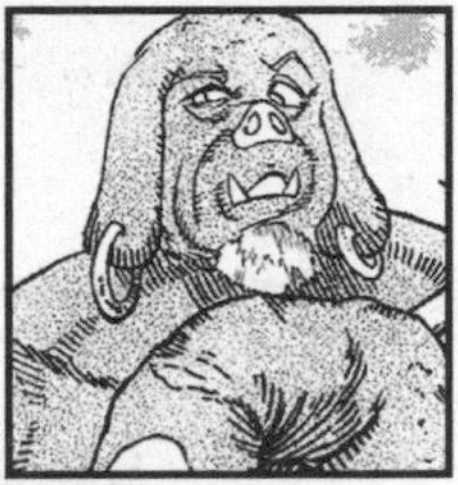

Orc

The Orc who saved the Dark Lord and Slime from the kidnapper. He is good at taking care of people.

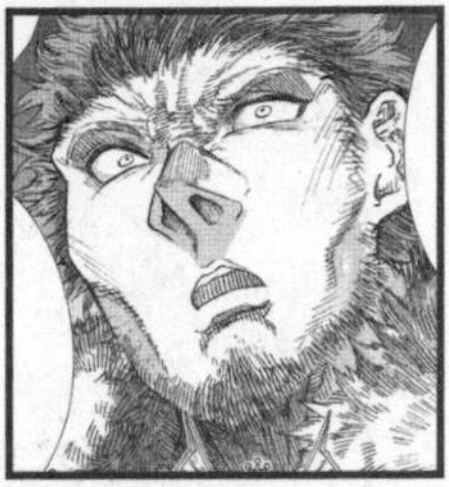

Luminary • Virgoski

A Knight of the United Kingdoms' Graft and West Tomalia's Holy King. Also called "The Blazing Lion," he is a relentless monster-slayer.

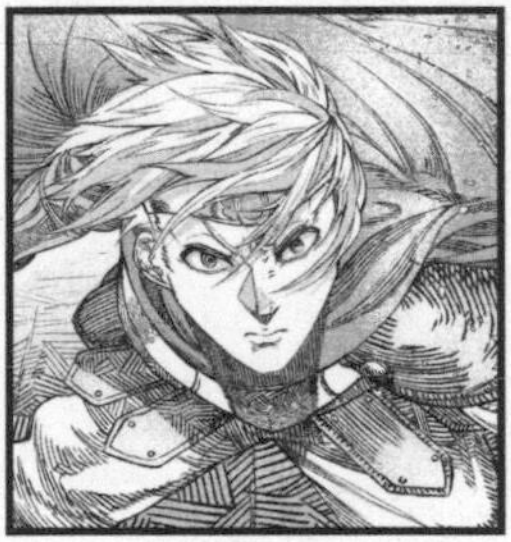

Hero

The enemy of the Dark Lord. Always resurrects, no matter how many times he is defeated. Is it his divine protection?

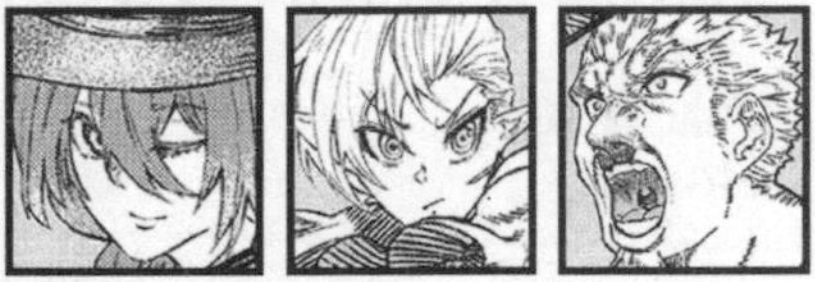

The Hero's Party

The hero's friends.

The adventure so far:

The Dark Lord of Agniin was the ultimate tyrant, but the hero's endless resurrections eventually outpaced the Dark Lord's ability to kill his nemesis. Time and magic revived him, but after almost being erased from existence and losing everything, the Dark Lord has nothing left to show for his once great power. Embracing a fresh start, he set out on a journey to expand his knowledge, accompanied by his slime friend. After experiencing the warmth of orcs and dark elves and the grief of death, the Dark Lord begins to change bit by bit...

The Dark Lord's group is captured by the humans when they raid the Fortress of Concealment. While escaping, they search for Alicia, the sister of the queen, who was also captive. They find her, but the queen's magic goes berserk at the sight of her sister's corpse and the humans are awakened. The Dark Lord sacrifices himself to save Slime and the queen, but only narrowly wins against the Luminary•Virgoski and loses consciousness shortly after...

CONTENTS

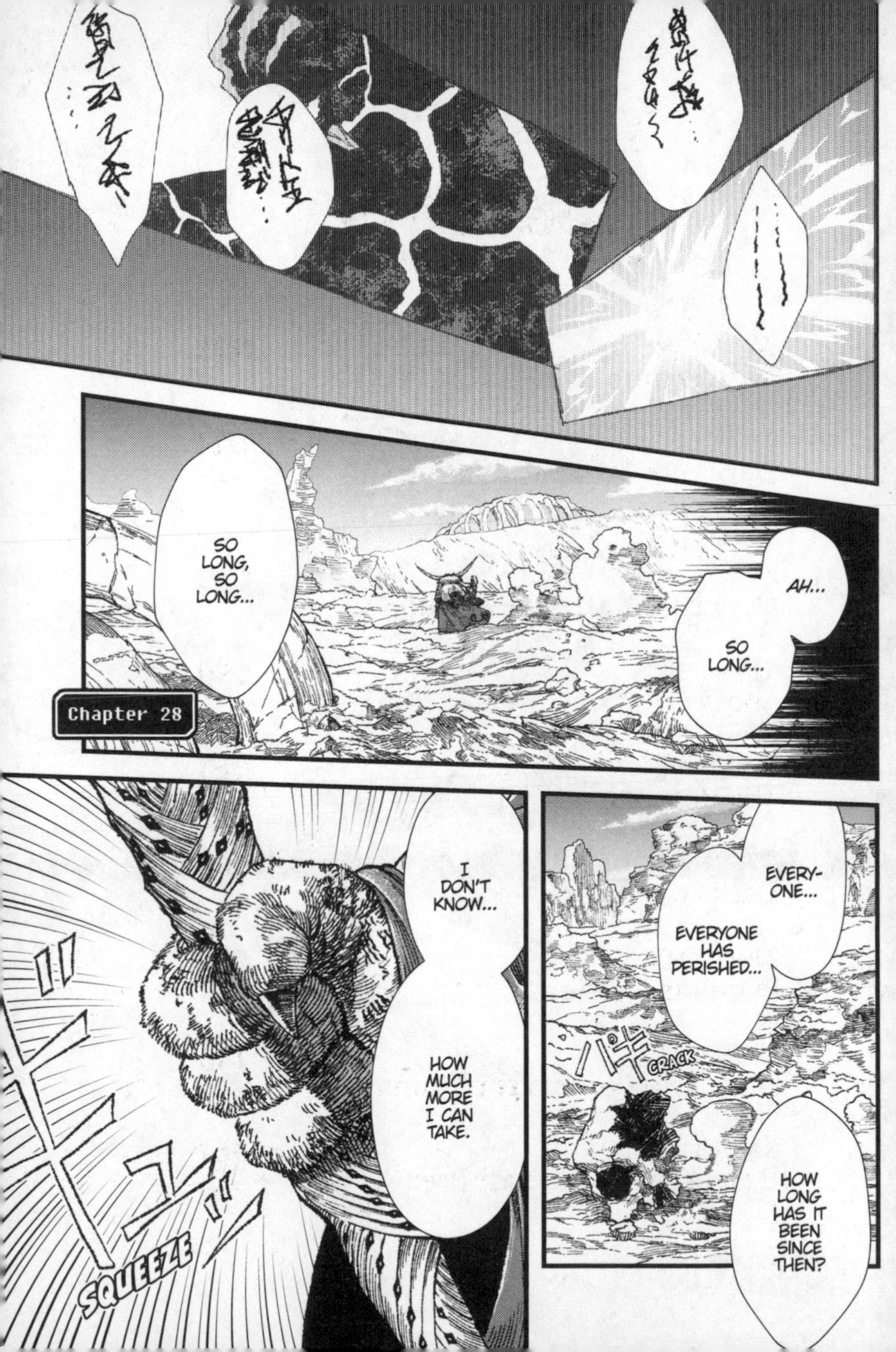

AH...
SO LONG...
SO LONG, SO LONG...
Chapter 28
EVERY-ONE...
EVERYONE HAS PERISHED...
CRACK
HOW LONG HAS IT BEEN SINCE THEN?
I DON'T KNOW...
HOW MUCH MORE I CAN TAKE.
SQUEEZE

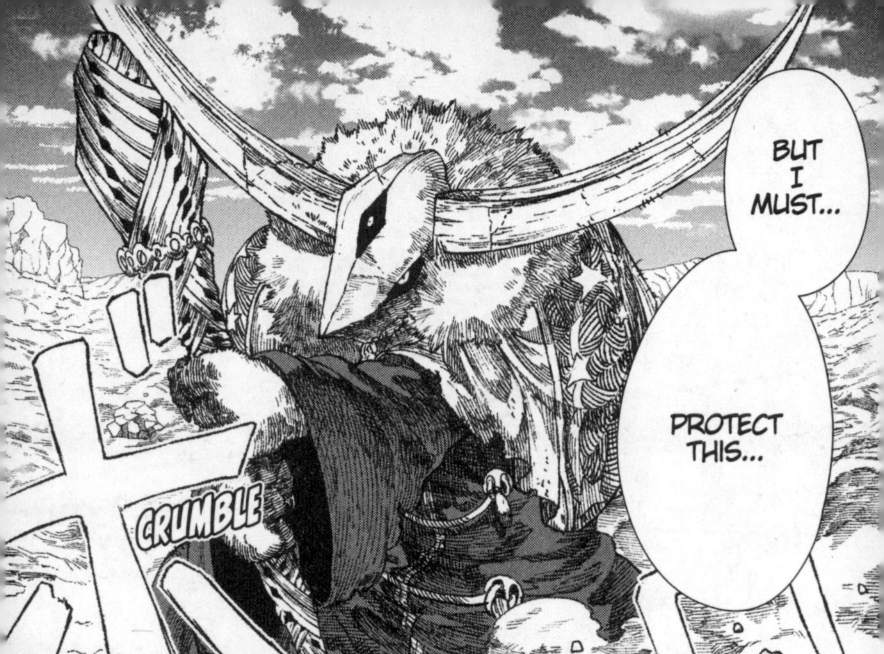
BUT I MUST...
PROTECT THIS...
CRUMBLE

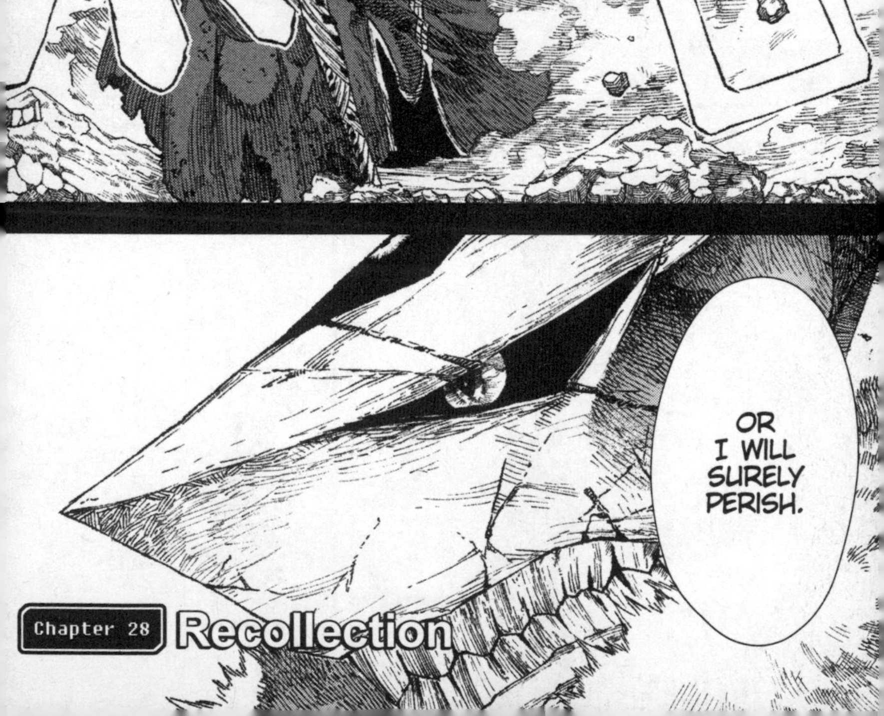
OR I WILL SURELY PERISH.

Chapter 28 Recollection

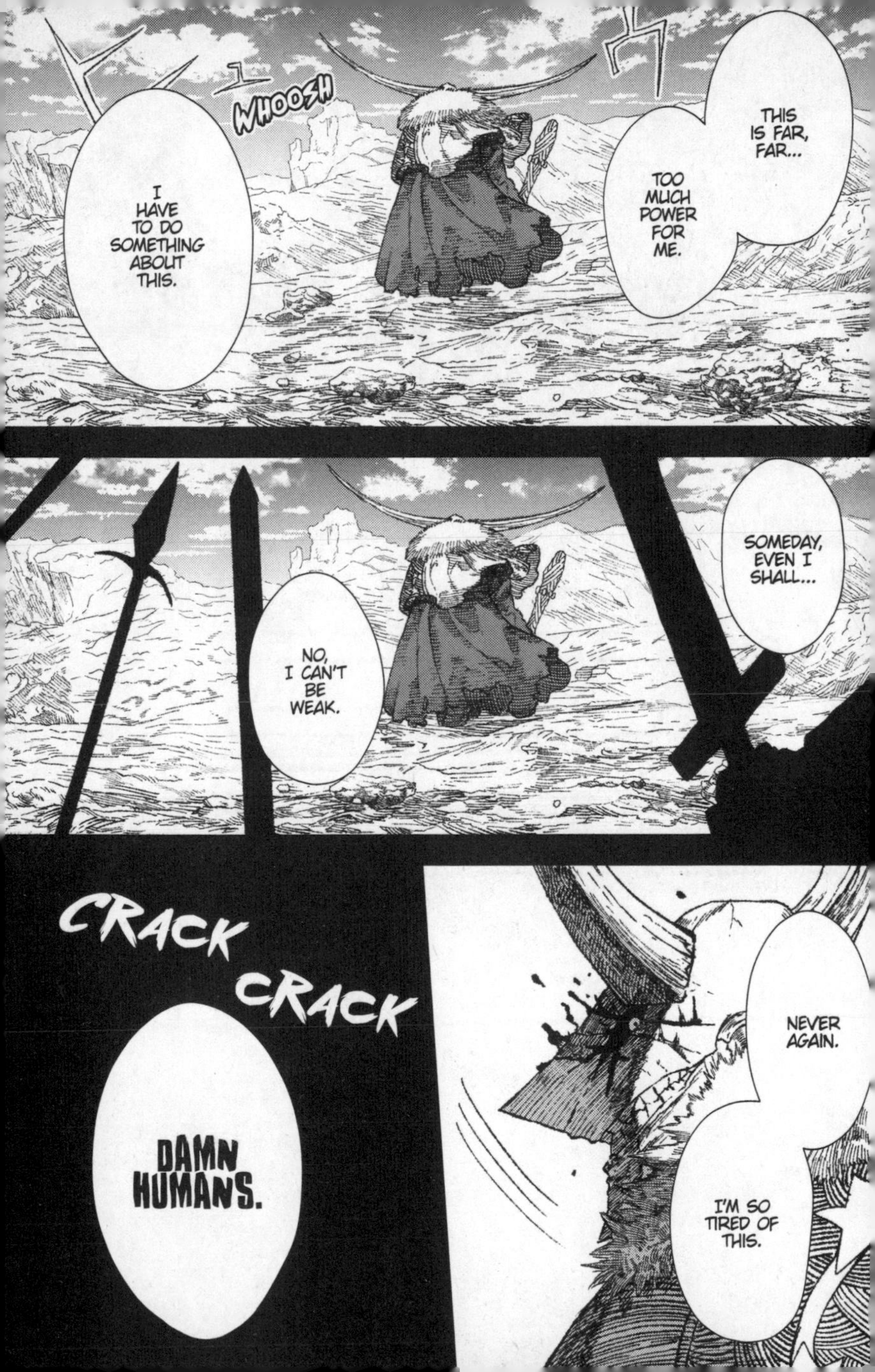
THIS IS FAR, FAR...
TOO MUCH POWER FOR ME.
WHOOSH
I HAVE TO DO SOMETHING ABOUT THIS.
SOMEDAY, EVEN I SHALL...
NO, I CAN'T BE WEAK.
NEVER AGAIN.
I'M SO TIRED OF THIS.
CRACK
CRACK
DAMN HUMANS.

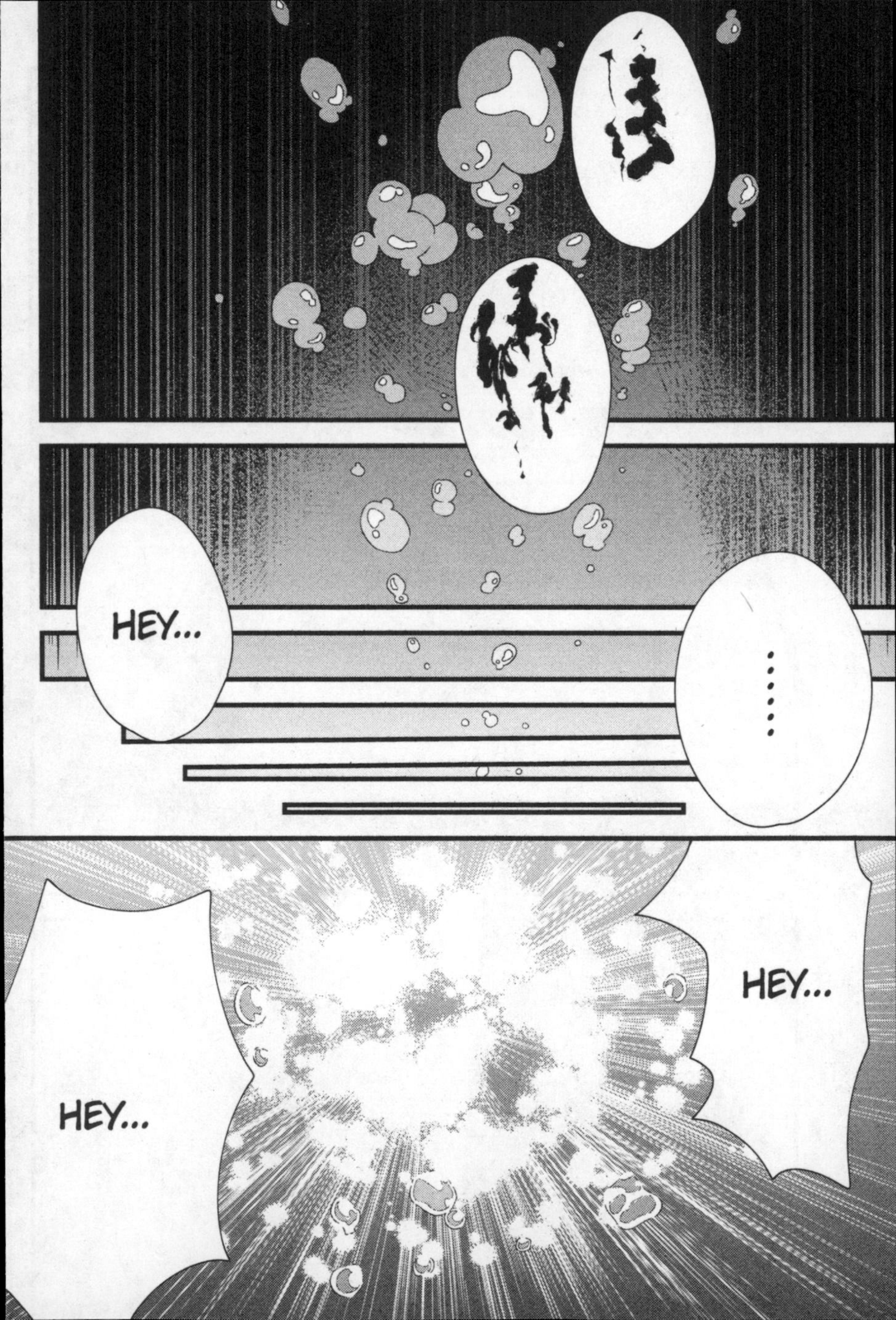
......
HEY...
HEY...
HEY...

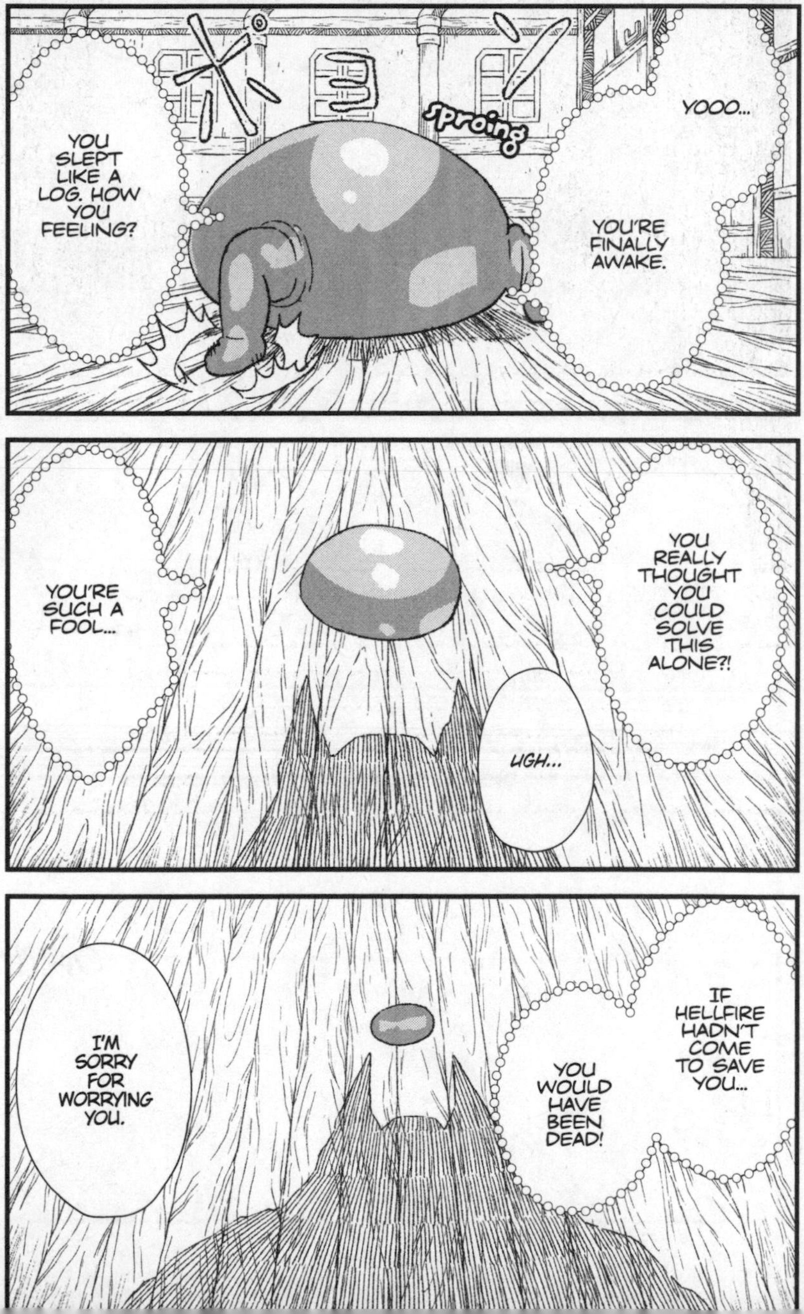
YOOO...
sproing
YOU'RE FINALLY AWAKE.
YOU SLEPT LIKE A LOG. HOW YOU FEELING?
YOU REALLY THOUGHT YOU COULD SOLVE THIS ALONE?!
UGH...
YOU'RE SUCH A FOOL...
IF HELLFIRE HADN'T COME TO SAVE YOU...
YOU WOULD HAVE BEEN DEAD!
I'M SORRY FOR WORRYING YOU.

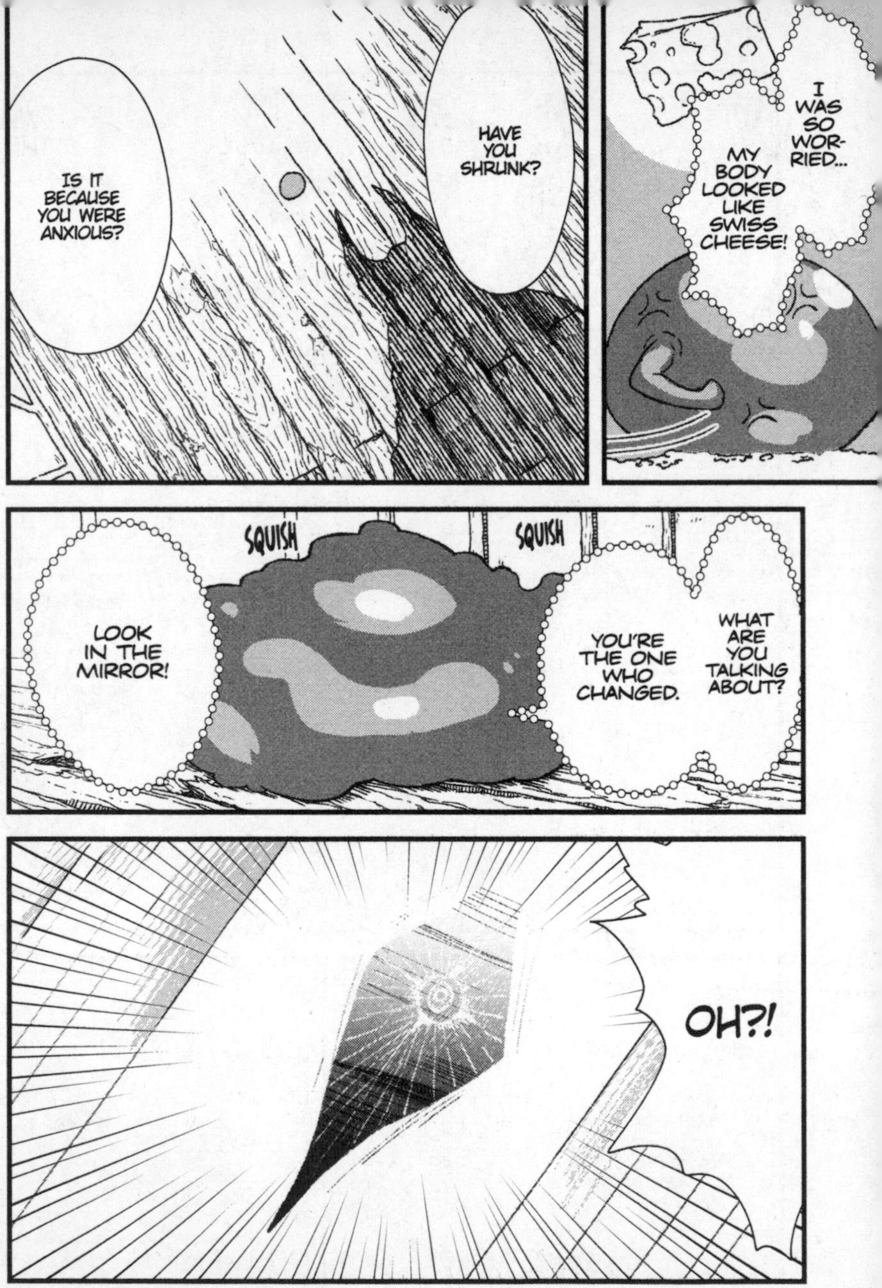
I WAS SO WORRIED...
MY BODY LOOKED LIKE SWISS CHEESE!
HAVE YOU SHRUNK?
IS IT BECAUSE YOU WERE ANXIOUS?
WHAT ARE YOU TALKING ABOUT?
YOU'RE THE ONE WHO CHANGED.
SQUISH
SQUISH
LOOK IN THE MIRROR!
OH?!

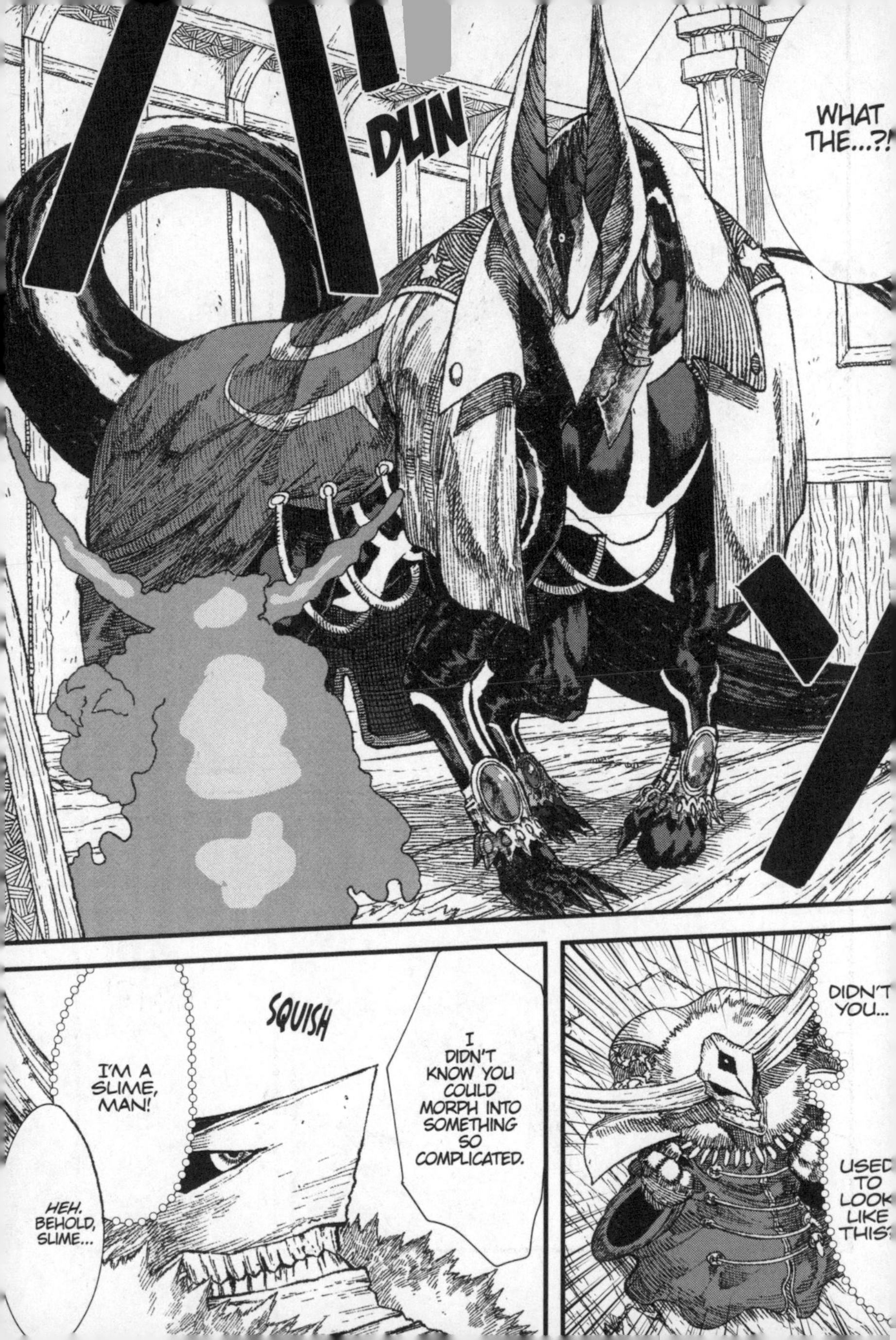
WHAT THE...?!
DUN
DIDN'T YOU...
USED TO LOOK LIKE THIS?
I DIDN'T KNOW YOU COULD MORPH INTO SOMETHING SO COMPLICATED.
SQUISH
I'M A SLIME, MAN!
HEH. BEHOLD, SLIME...

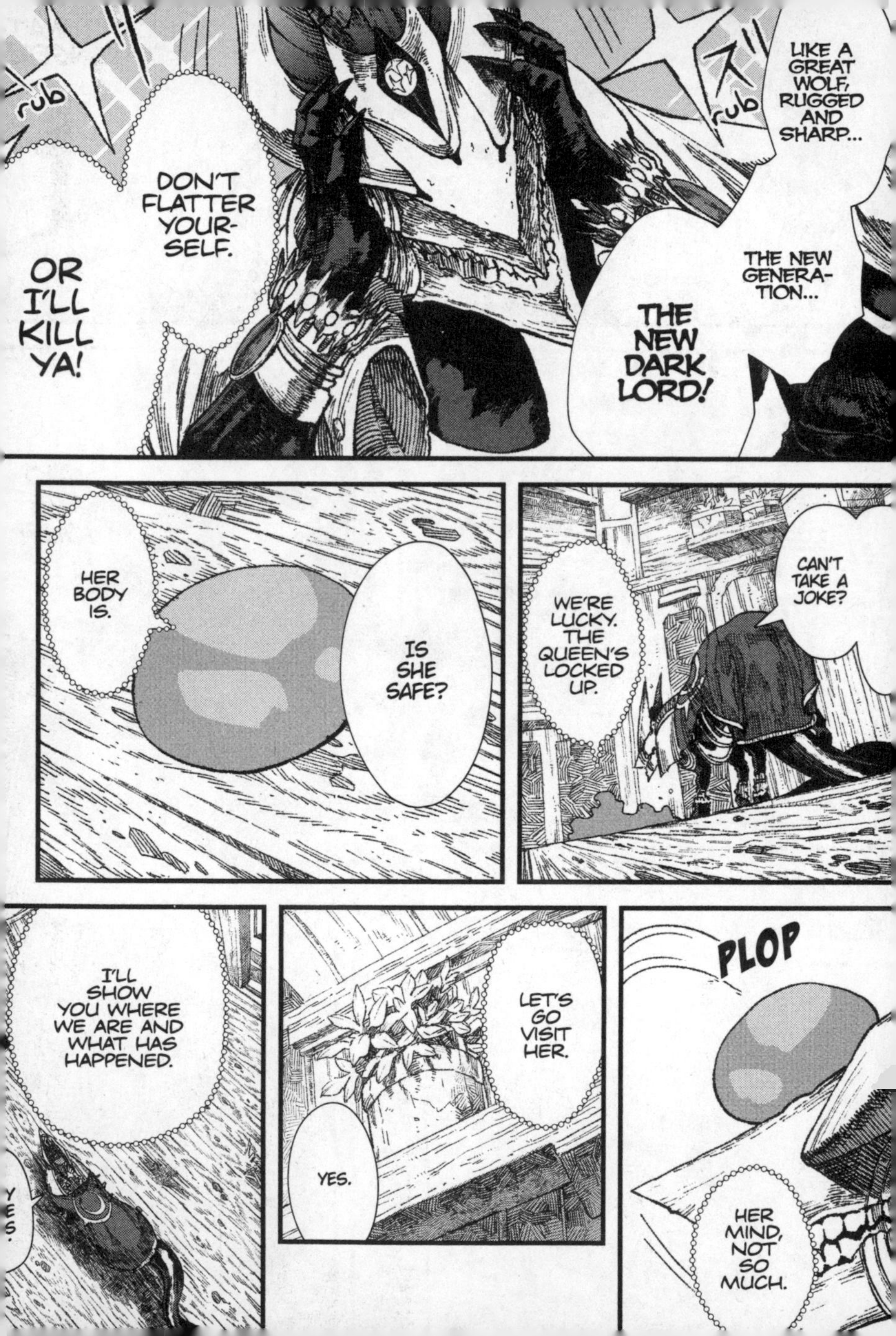
rub
LIKE A GREAT WOLF, RUGGED AND SHARP...
THE NEW GENERATION...
THE NEW DARK LORD!
rub
DON'T FLATTER YOURSELF.
OR I'LL KILL YA!
CAN'T TAKE A JOKE?
WE'RE LUCKY. THE QUEEN'S LOCKED UP.
IS SHE SAFE?
HER BODY IS.
PLOP
HER MIND, NOT SO MUCH.
LET'S GO VISIT HER.
YES.
I'LL SHOW YOU WHERE WE ARE AND WHAT HAS HAPPENED.
YES.

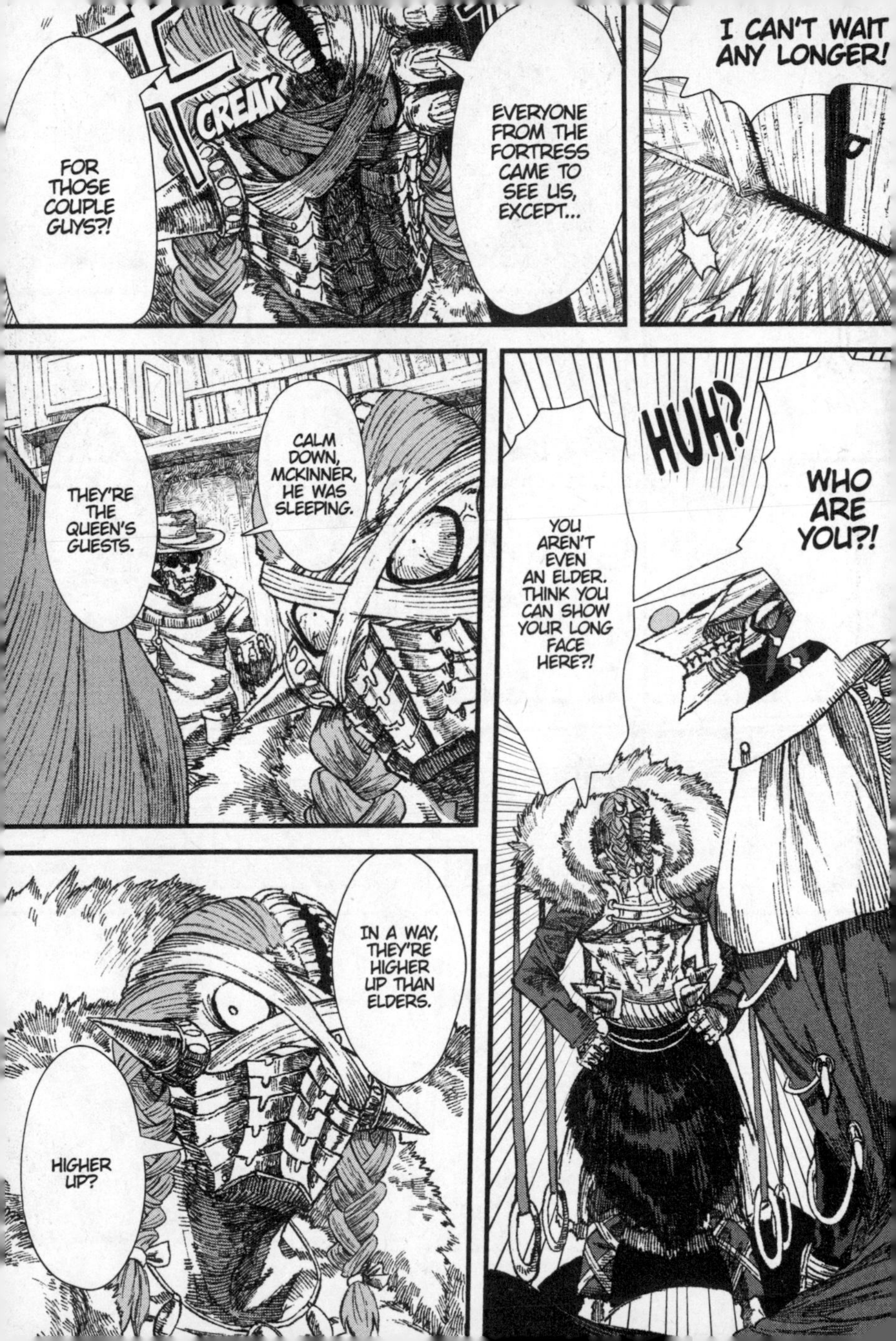
I CAN'T WAIT ANY LONGER!
EVERYONE FROM THE FORTRESS CAME TO SEE US, EXCEPT...
CREAK
FOR THOSE COUPLE GUYS?!
HUH?
WHO ARE YOU?!
YOU AREN'T EVEN AN ELDER. THINK YOU CAN SHOW YOUR LONG FACE HERE?!
CALM DOWN, MCKINNER, HE WAS SLEEPING.
THEY'RE THE QUEEN'S GUESTS.
IN A WAY, THEY'RE HIGHER UP THAN ELDERS.
HIGHER UP?

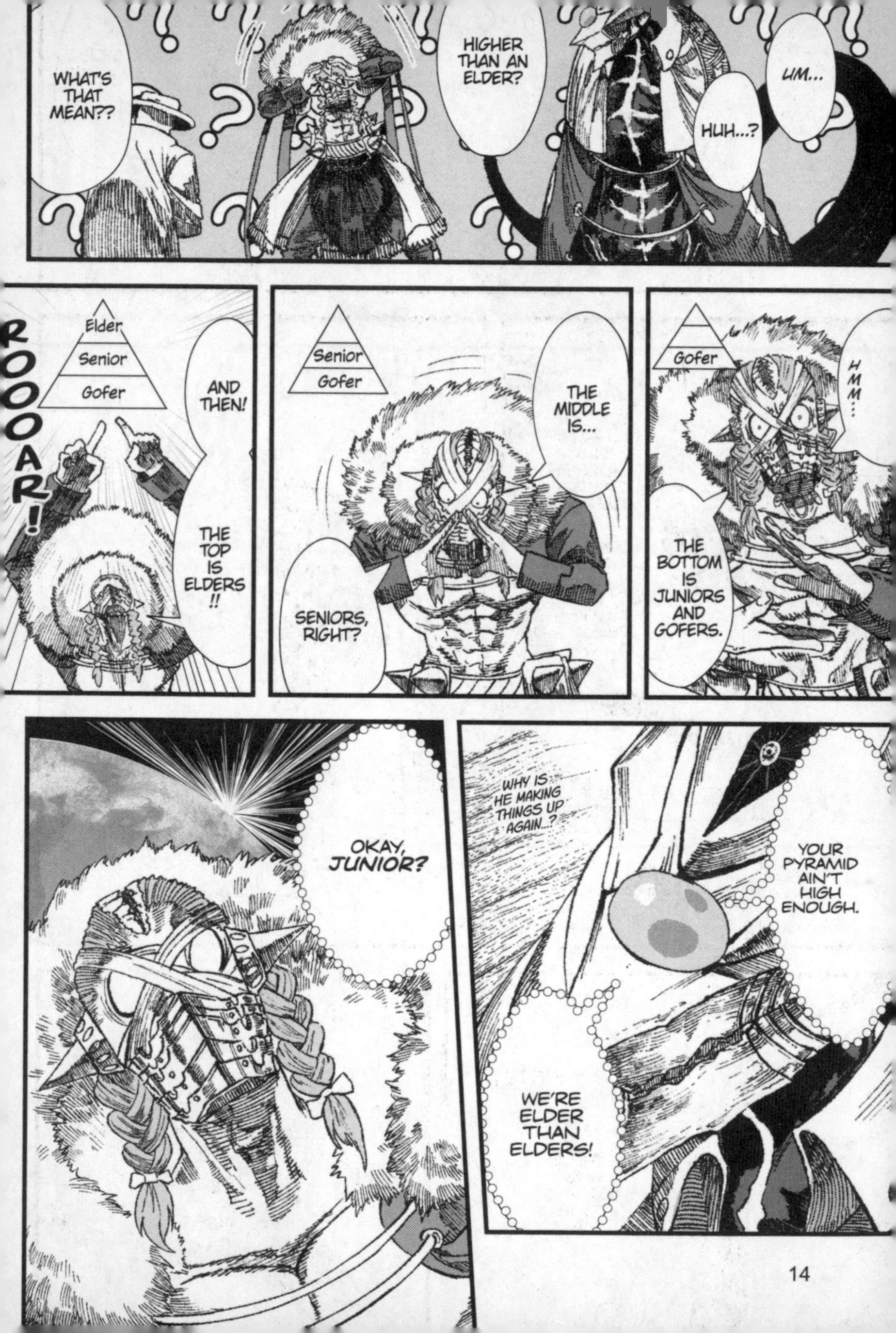
UM...
HUH...?
HIGHER THAN AN ELDER?
WHAT'S THAT MEAN??
HMM...
Gofer
THE BOTTOM IS JUNIORS AND GOFERS.
Senior
Gofer
THE MIDDLE IS...
SENIORS, RIGHT?
Elder
Senior
Gofer
AND THEN!
THE TOP IS ELDERS!!
ROOOOAR!
YOUR PYRAMID AIN'T HIGH ENOUGH.
WHY IS HE MAKING THINGS UP AGAIN...?
WE'RE ELDER THAN ELDERS!
OKAY, JUNIOR?

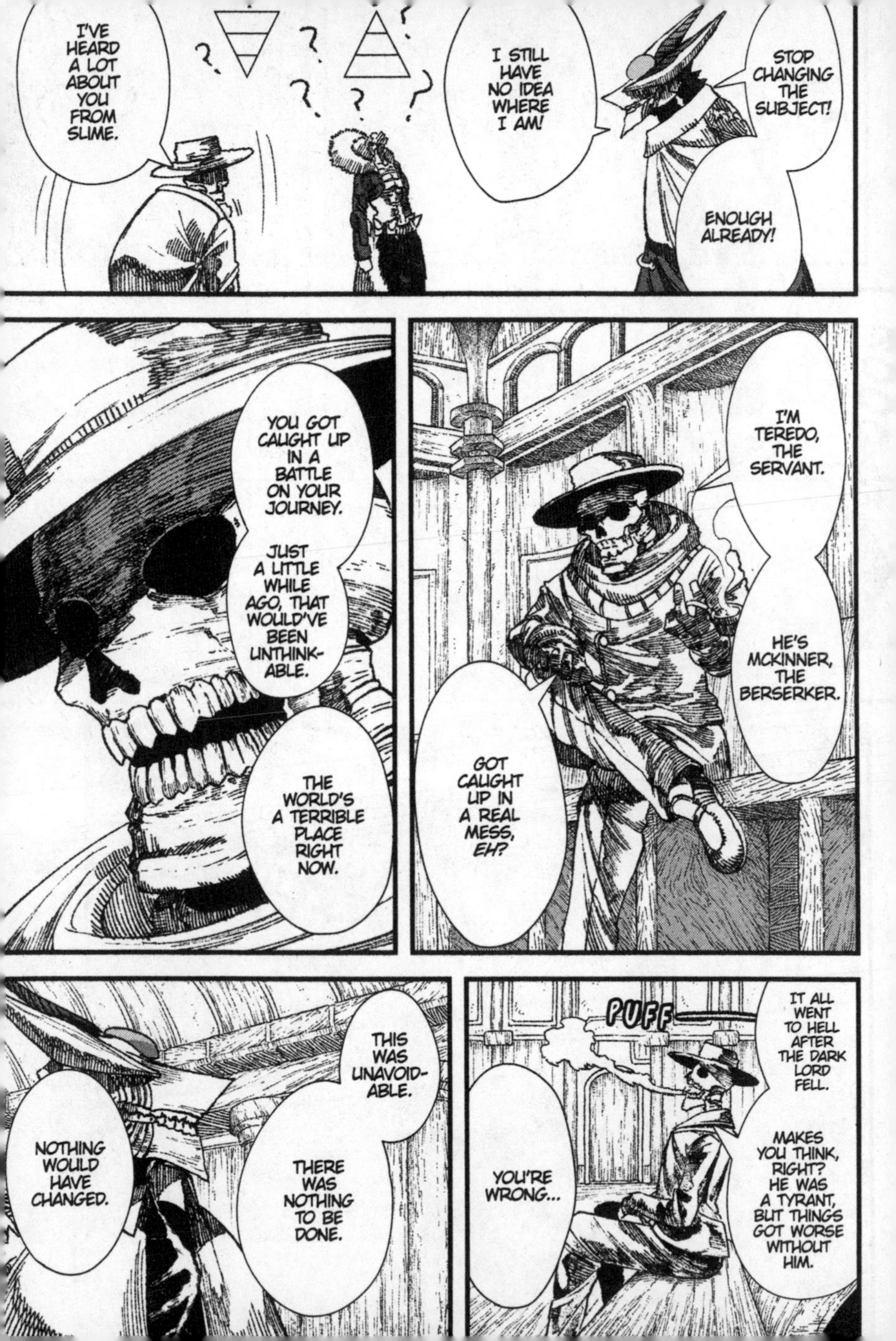
STOP CHANGING THE SUBJECT!
ENOUGH ALREADY!
I STILL HAVE NO IDEA WHERE I AM!
I'VE HEARD A LOT ABOUT YOU FROM SLIME.
I'M TEREDO, THE SERVANT.
HE'S MCKINNER, THE BERSERKER.
GOT CAUGHT UP IN A REAL MESS, EH?
YOU GOT CAUGHT UP IN A BATTLE ON YOUR JOURNEY.
JUST A LITTLE WHILE AGO, THAT WOULD'VE BEEN UNTHINKABLE.
THE WORLD'S A TERRIBLE PLACE RIGHT NOW.
PUFF
IT ALL WENT TO HELL AFTER THE DARK LORD FELL.
MAKES YOU THINK, RIGHT? HE WAS A TYRANT, BUT THINGS GOT WORSE WITHOUT HIM.
YOU'RE WRONG...
THIS WAS UNAVOIDABLE.
THERE WAS NOTHING TO BE DONE.
NOTHING WOULD HAVE CHANGED.

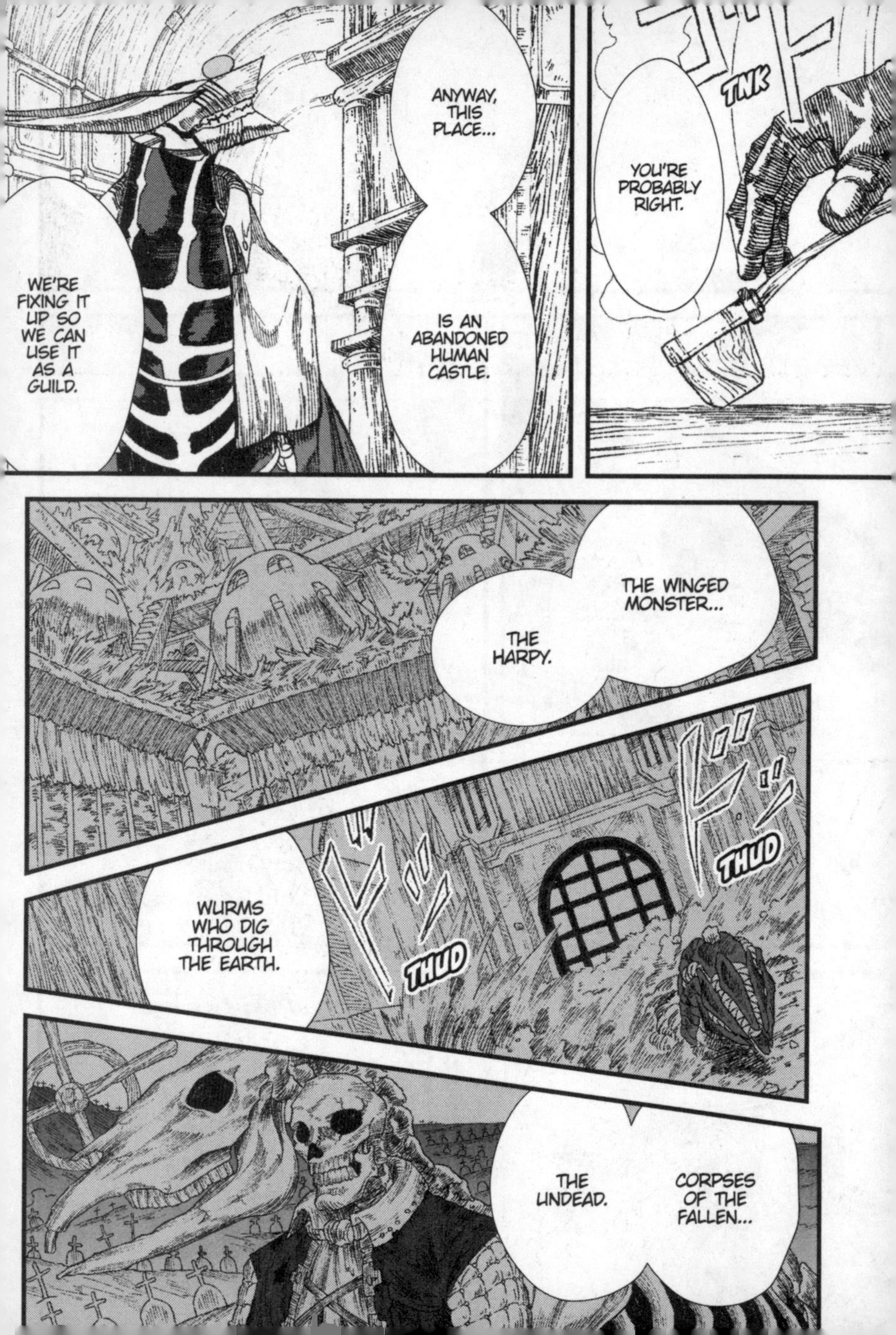
TNK
YOU'RE PROBABLY RIGHT.
ANYWAY, THIS PLACE...
IS AN ABANDONED HUMAN CASTLE.
WE'RE FIXING IT UP SO WE CAN USE IT AS A GUILD.
THE WINGED MONSTER...
THE HARPY.
THUD
WURMS WHO DIG THROUGH THE EARTH.
THUD
CORPSES OF THE FALLEN...
THE UNDEAD.

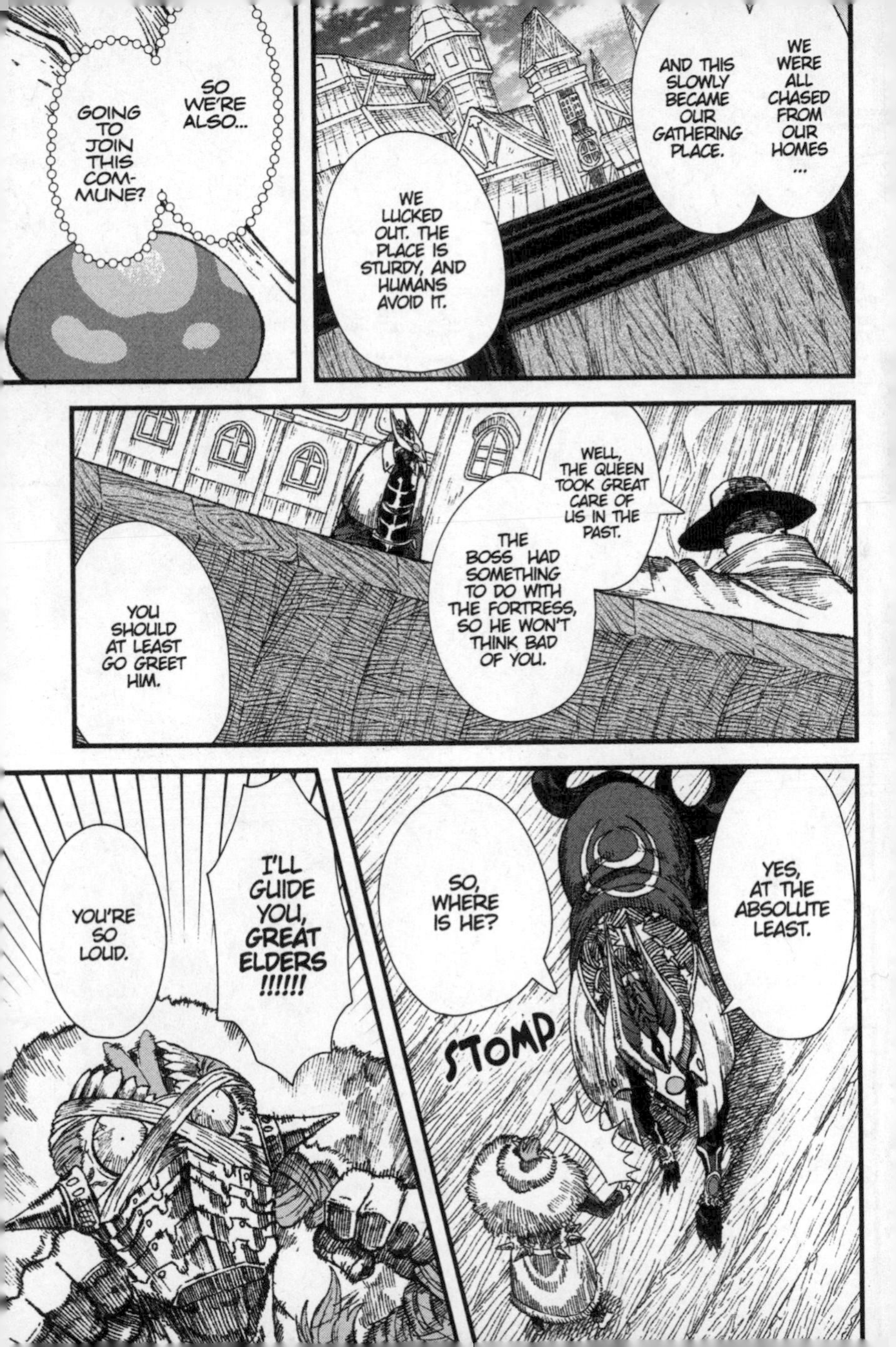
WE WERE ALL CHASED FROM OUR HOMES...
AND THIS SLOWLY BECAME OUR GATHERING PLACE.
WE LUCKED OUT. THE PLACE IS STURDY, AND HUMANS AVOID IT.
SO WE'RE ALSO...
GOING TO JOIN THIS COM-MUNE?
WELL, THE QUEEN TOOK GREAT CARE OF US IN THE PAST.
THE BOSS HAD SOMETHING TO DO WITH THE FORTRESS, SO HE WON'T THINK BAD OF YOU.
YOU SHOULD AT LEAST GO GREET HIM.
YES, AT THE ABSOLUTE LEAST.
SO, WHERE IS HE?
STOMP
I'LL GUIDE YOU, GREAT ELDERS!!!!!!
YOU'RE SO LOUD.

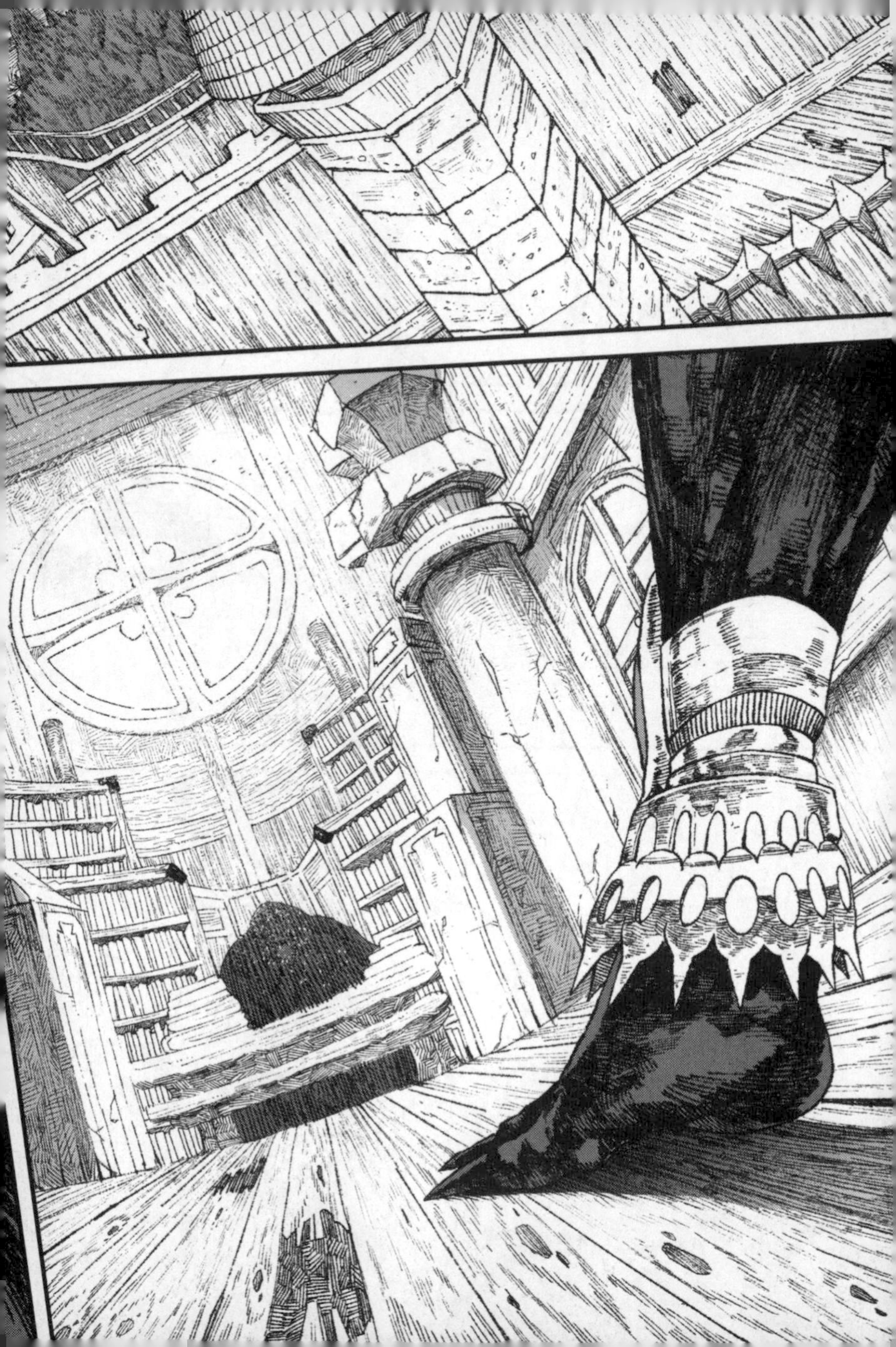

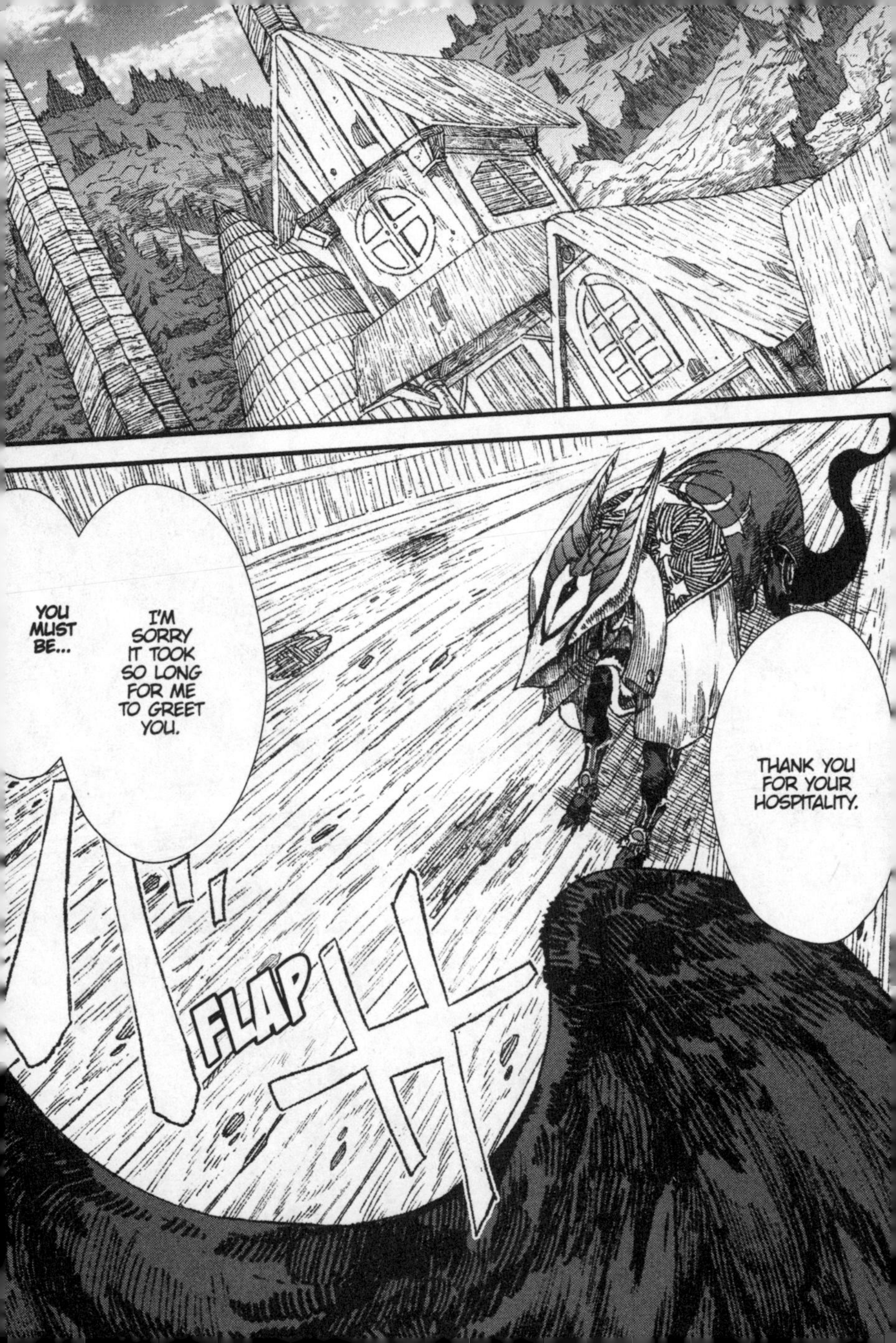
THANK YOU FOR YOUR HOSPITALITY.
I'M SORRY IT TOOK SO LONG FOR ME TO GREET YOU.
YOU MUST BE...
FLAP

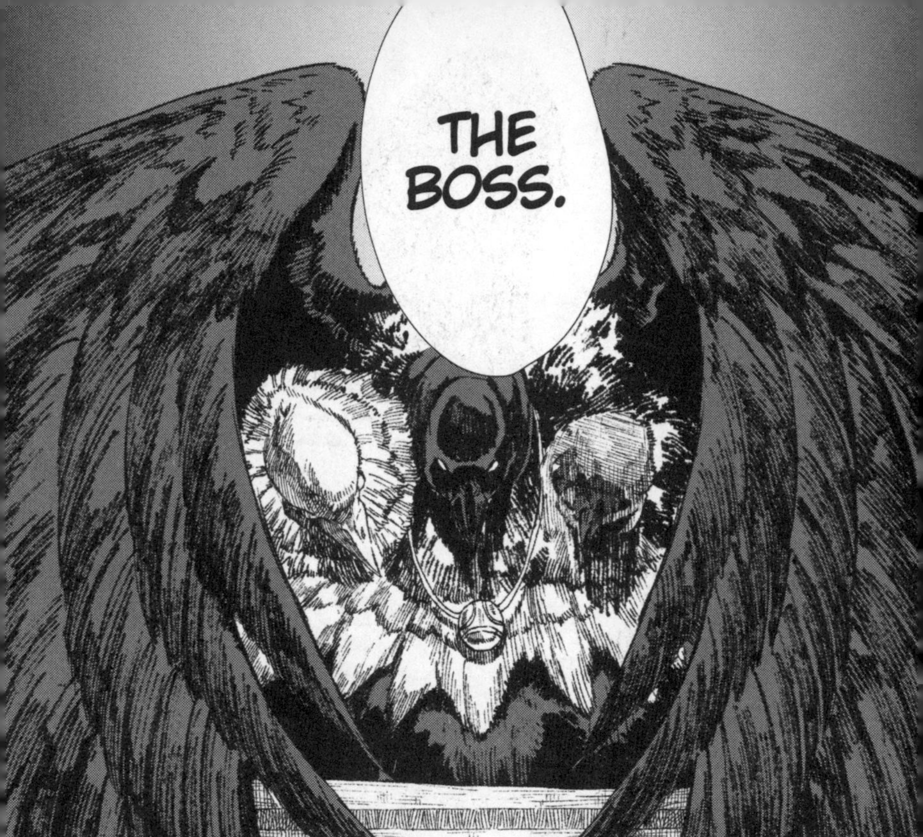
THE BOSS.
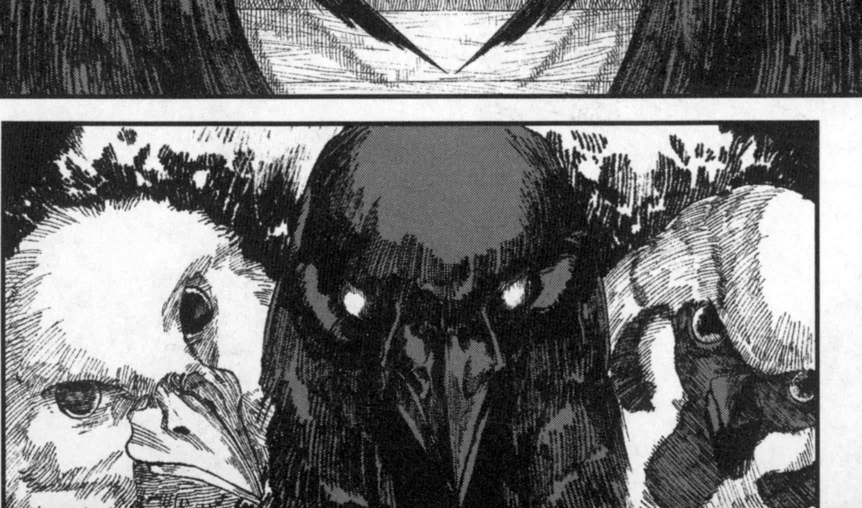

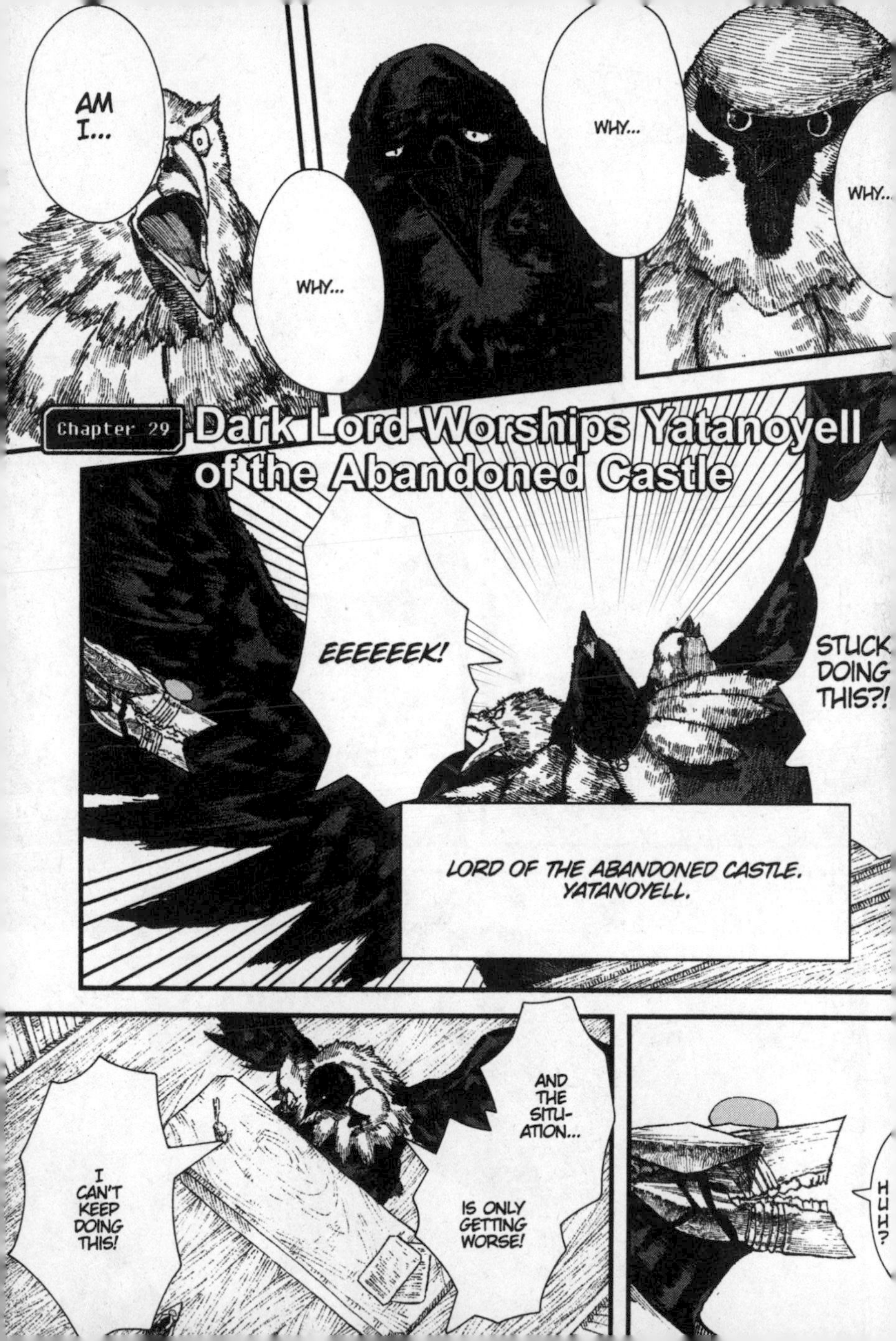
WHY...
WHY...
WHY...
AM I...
Chapter 29 Dark Lord Worships Yatanoyell of the Abandoned Castle
STUCK DOING THIS?!
EEEEEEK!
LORD OF THE ABANDONED CASTLE. YATANOYELL.
HUH?
AND THE SITU-ATION...
IS ONLY GETTING WORSE!
I CAN'T KEEP DOING THIS!

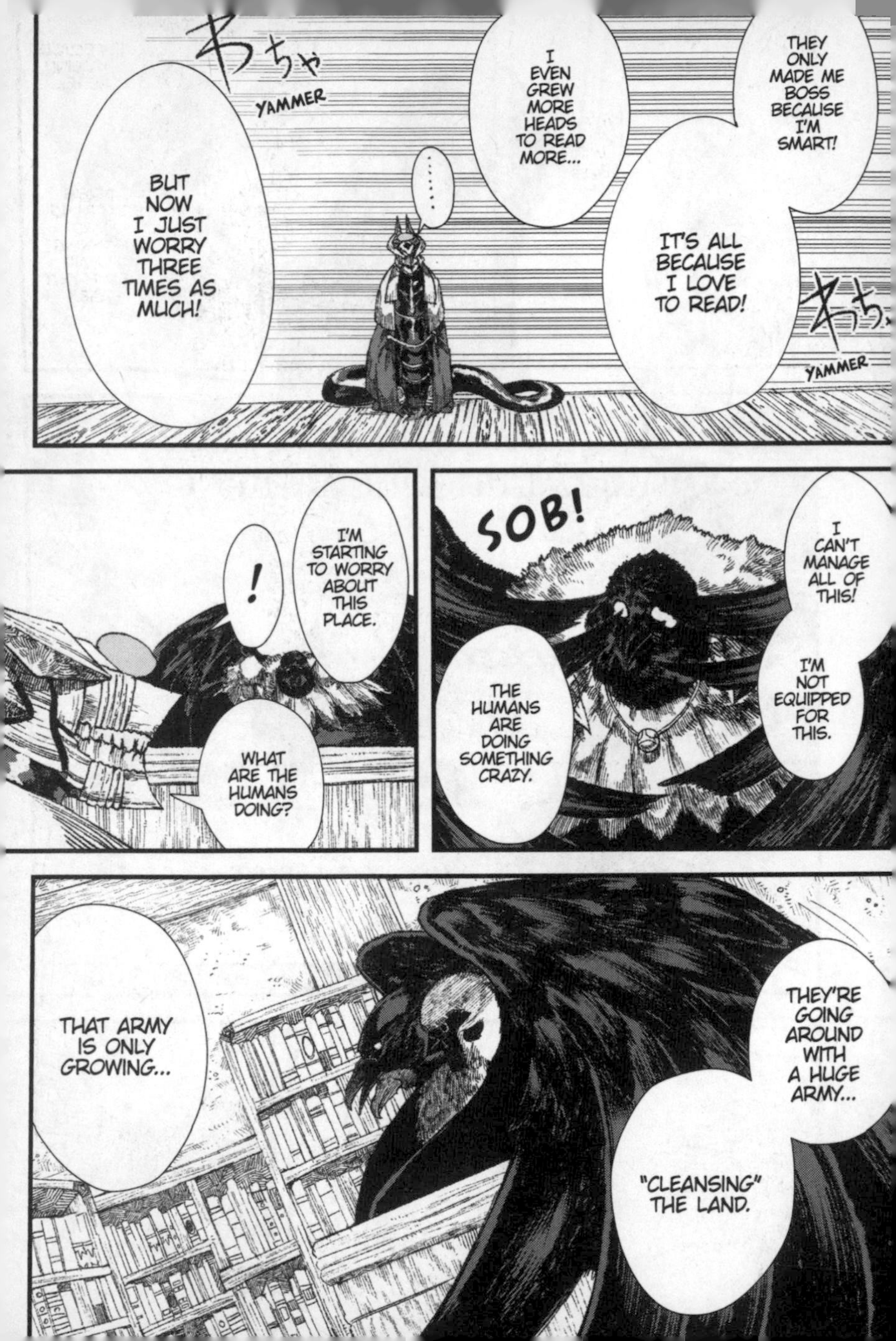
THEY ONLY MADE ME BOSS BECAUSE I'M SMART!
IT'S ALL BECAUSE I LOVE TO READ!
YAMMER
I EVEN GREW MORE HEADS TO READ MORE...
......
YAMMER
BUT NOW I JUST WORRY THREE TIMES AS MUCH!
SOB!
I CAN'T MANAGE ALL OF THIS!
I'M NOT EQUIPPED FOR THIS.
THE HUMANS ARE DOING SOMETHING CRAZY.
I'M STARTING TO WORRY ABOUT THIS PLACE.
!
WHAT ARE THE HUMANS DOING?
THEY'RE GOING AROUND WITH A HUGE ARMY...
"CLEANSING" THE LAND.
THAT ARMY IS ONLY GROWING...

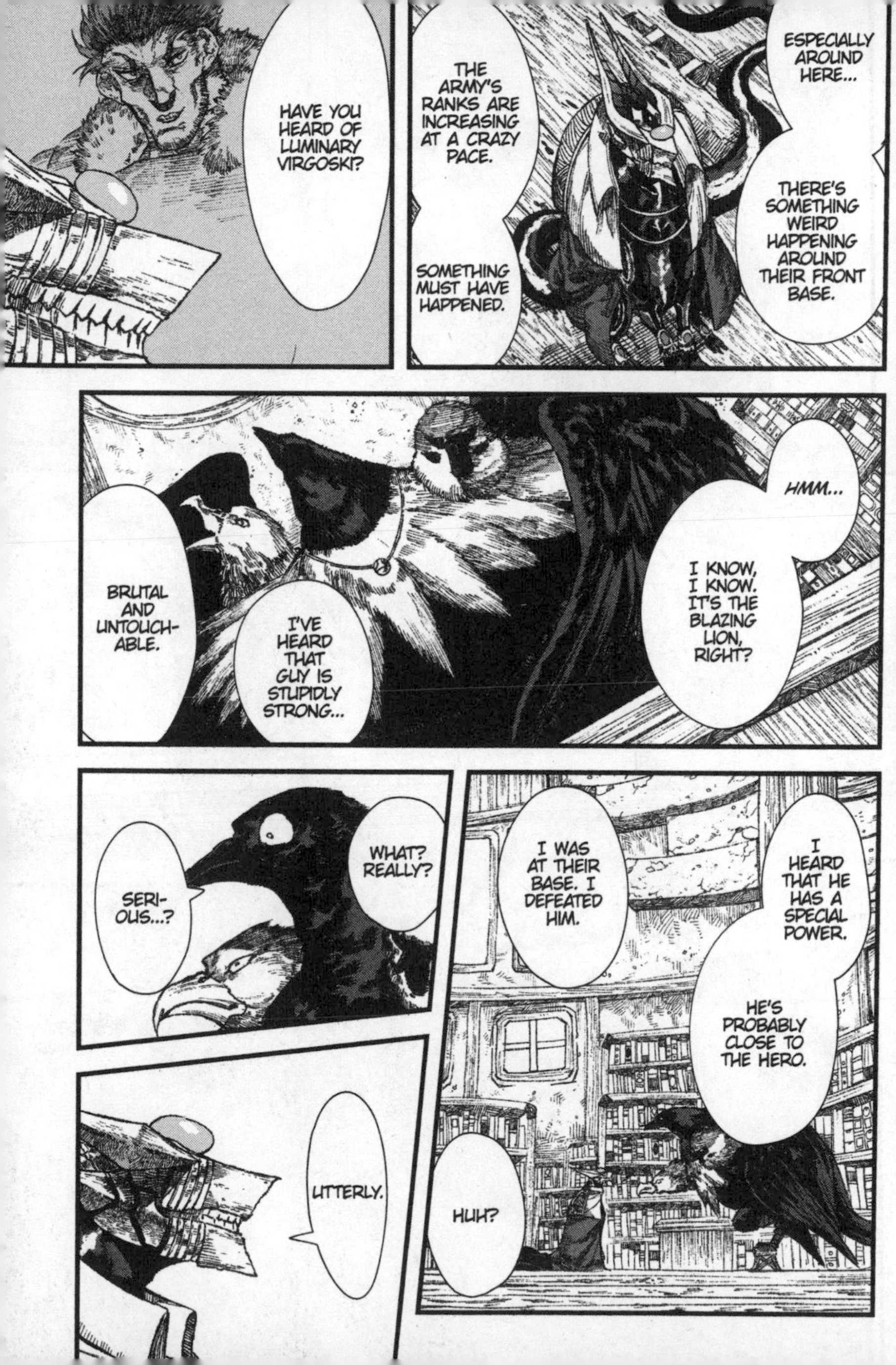
ESPECIALLY AROUND HERE...
THERE'S SOMETHING WEIRD HAPPENING AROUND THEIR FRONT BASE.
THE ARMY'S RANKS ARE INCREASING AT A CRAZY PACE.
SOMETHING MUST HAVE HAPPENED.
HAVE YOU HEARD OF LUMINARY VIRGOSKI?
HMM...
I KNOW, I KNOW. IT'S THE BLAZING LION, RIGHT?
I'VE HEARD THAT GUY IS STUPIDLY STRONG...
BRUTAL AND UNTOUCHABLE.
I HEARD THAT HE HAS A SPECIAL POWER.
HE'S PROBABLY CLOSE TO THE HERO.
I WAS AT THEIR BASE. I DEFEATED HIM.
HUH?
WHAT? REALLY?
SERI-OUS...?
UTTERLY.

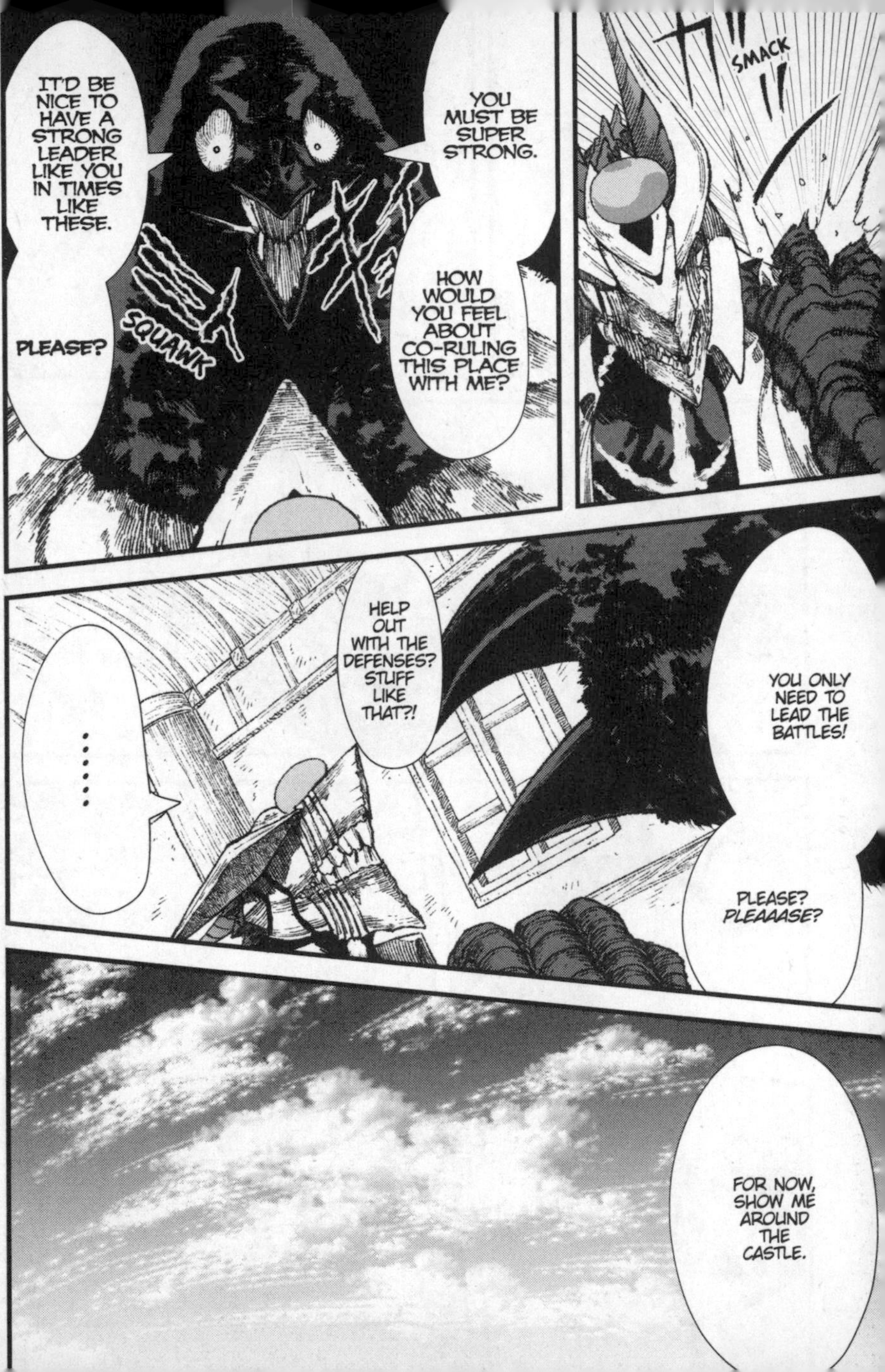
SMACK
YOU MUST BE SUPER STRONG.
IT'D BE NICE TO HAVE A STRONG LEADER LIKE YOU IN TIMES LIKE THESE.
HOW WOULD YOU FEEL ABOUT CO-RULING THIS PLACE WITH ME?
SQUAWK
PLEASE?
YOU ONLY NEED TO LEAD THE BATTLES!
PLEASE? PLEAAASE?
HELP OUT WITH THE DEFENSES? STUFF LIKE THAT?!
......
FOR NOW, SHOW ME AROUND THE CASTLE.

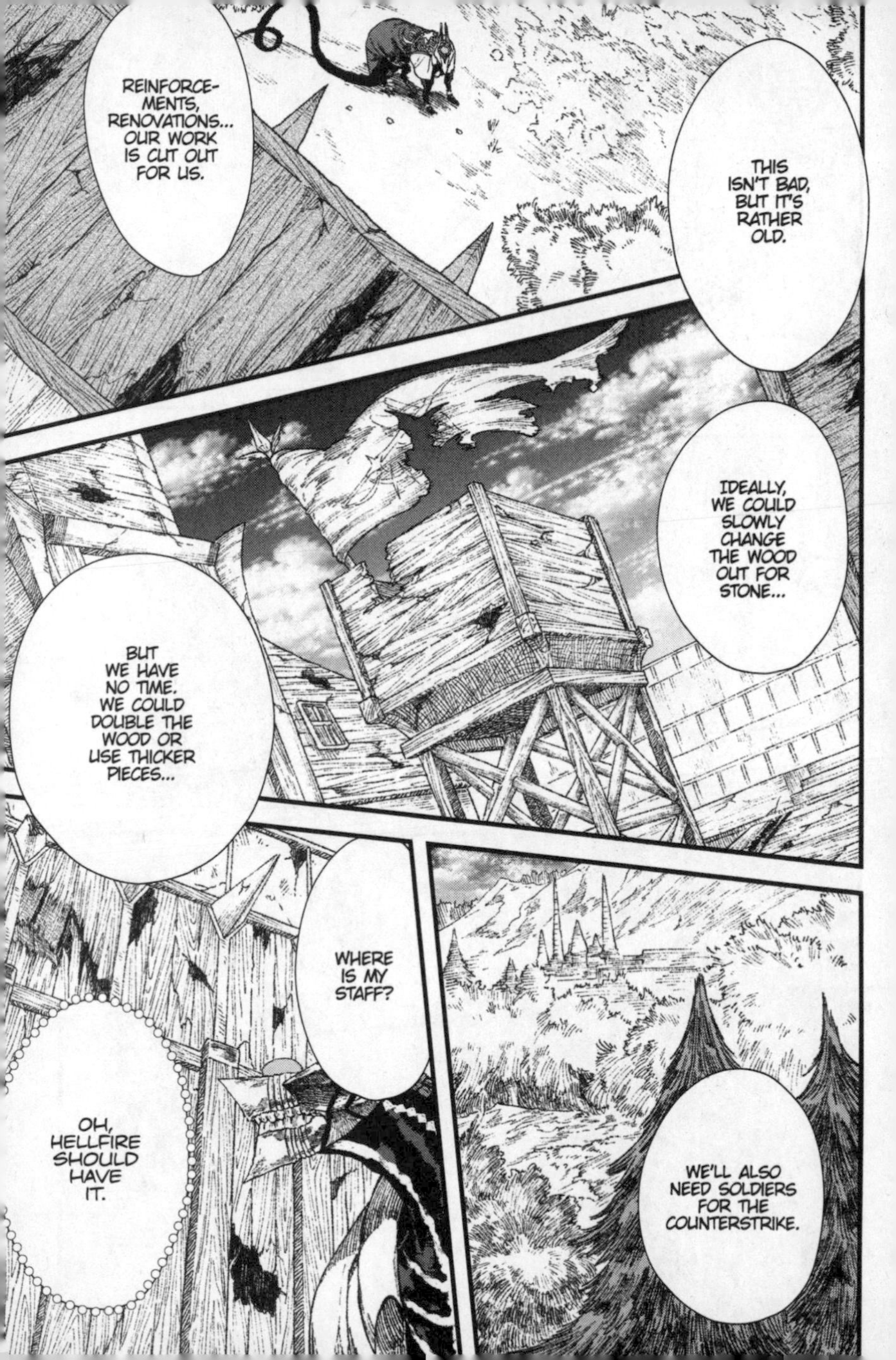
THIS ISN'T BAD, BUT IT'S RATHER OLD.
REINFORCEMENTS, RENOVATIONS... OUR WORK IS CUT OUT FOR US.
IDEALLY, WE COULD SLOWLY CHANGE THE WOOD OUT FOR STONE...
BUT WE HAVE NO TIME. WE COULD DOUBLE THE WOOD OR USE THICKER PIECES...
WE'LL ALSO NEED SOLDIERS FOR THE COUNTERSTRIKE.
WHERE IS MY STAFF?
OH, HELLFIRE SHOULD HAVE IT.

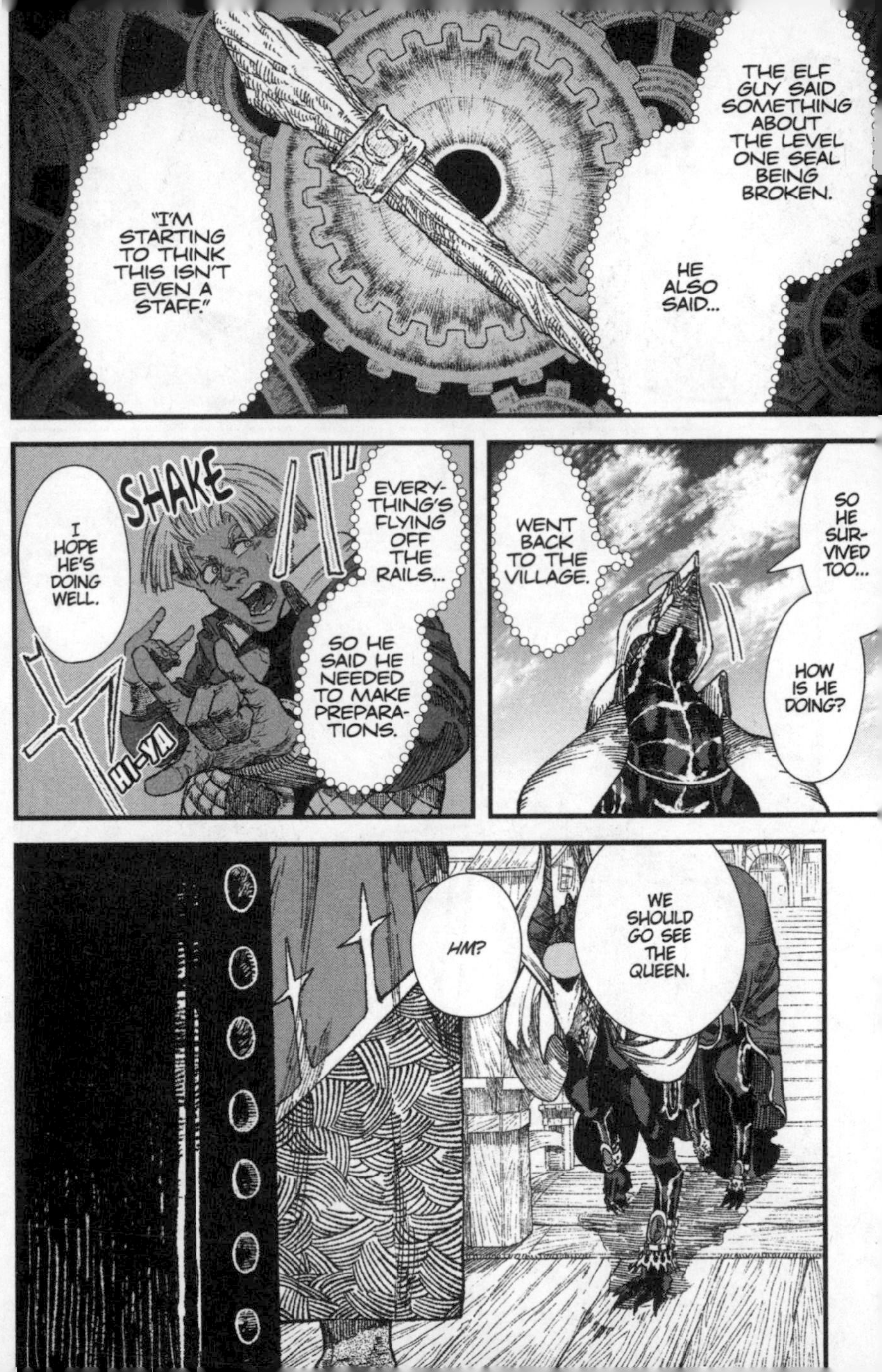
THE ELF GUY SAID SOMETHING ABOUT THE LEVEL ONE SEAL BEING BROKEN.
HE ALSO SAID...
"I'M STARTING TO THINK THIS ISN'T EVEN A STAFF."
SO HE SUR-VIVED TOO...
HOW IS HE DOING?
WENT BACK TO THE VILLAGE.
EVERY-THING'S FLYING OFF THE RAILS...
SO HE SAID HE NEEDED TO MAKE PREPARA-TIONS.
SHAKE
I HOPE HE'S DOING WELL.
HI-YA
WE SHOULD GO SEE THE QUEEN.
HM?

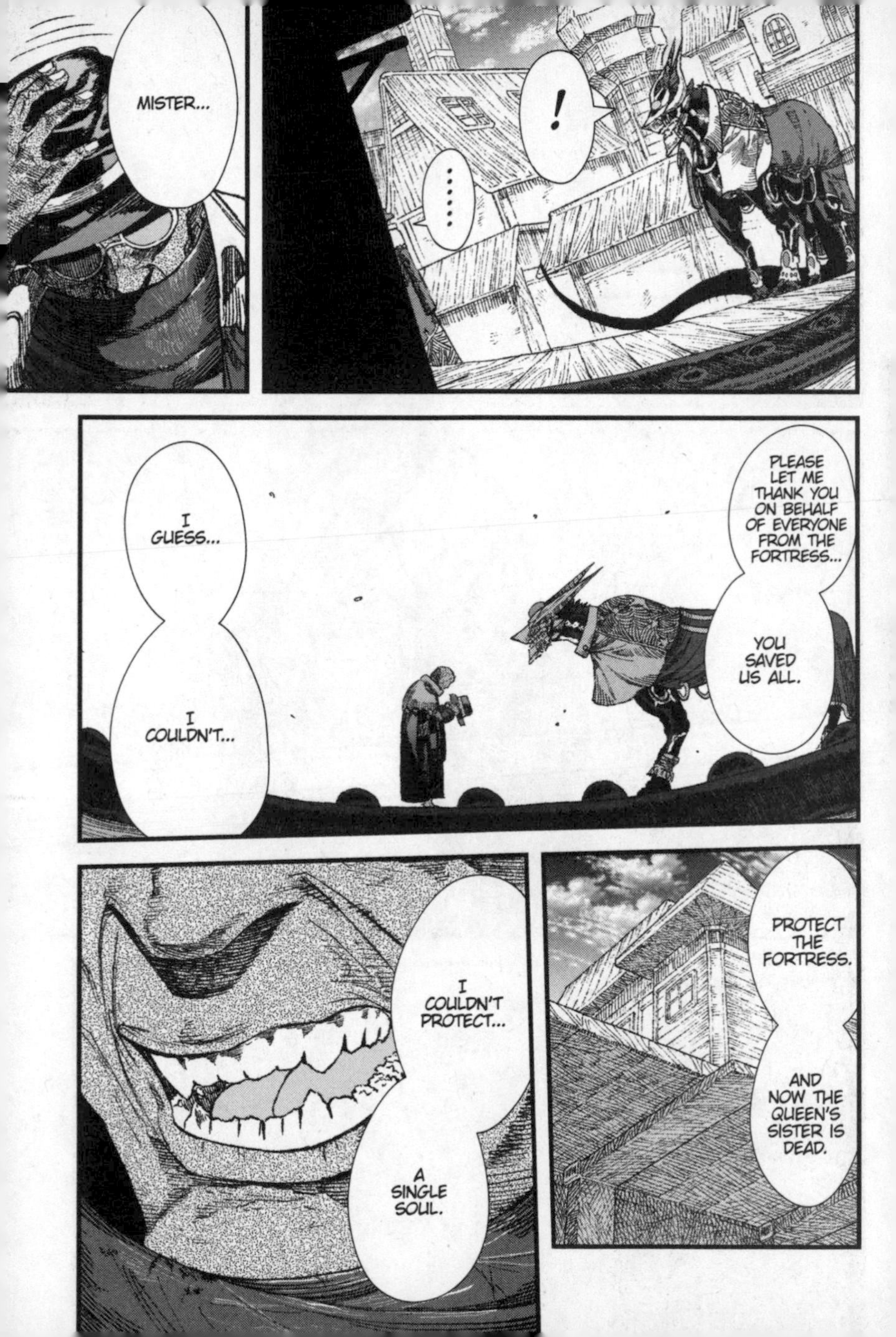

!
......
MISTER...
PLEASE LET ME THANK YOU ON BEHALF OF EVERYONE FROM THE FORTRESS...
YOU SAVED US ALL.
I GUESS...
I COULDN'T...
PROTECT THE FORTRESS.
AND NOW THE QUEEN'S SISTER IS DEAD.
I COULDN'T PROTECT...
A SINGLE SOUL.

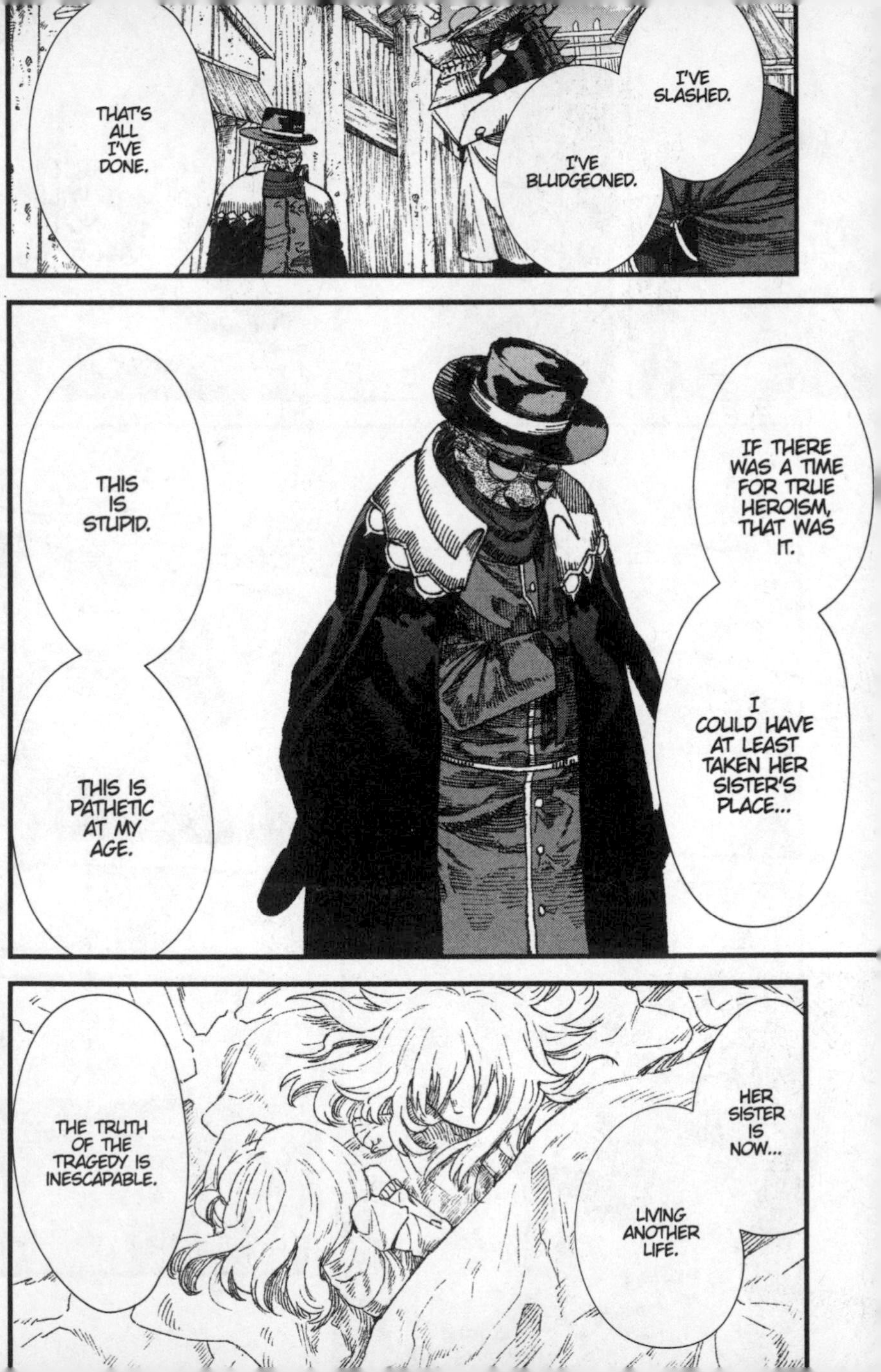

I'VE SLASHED.
I'VE BLUDGEONED.
THAT'S ALL I'VE DONE.
IF THERE WAS A TIME FOR TRUE HEROISM, THAT WAS IT.
I COULD HAVE AT LEAST TAKEN HER SISTER'S PLACE...
THIS IS STUPID.
THIS IS PATHETIC AT MY AGE.
HER SISTER IS NOW...
LIVING ANOTHER LIFE.
THE TRUTH OF THE TRAGEDY IS INESCAPABLE.

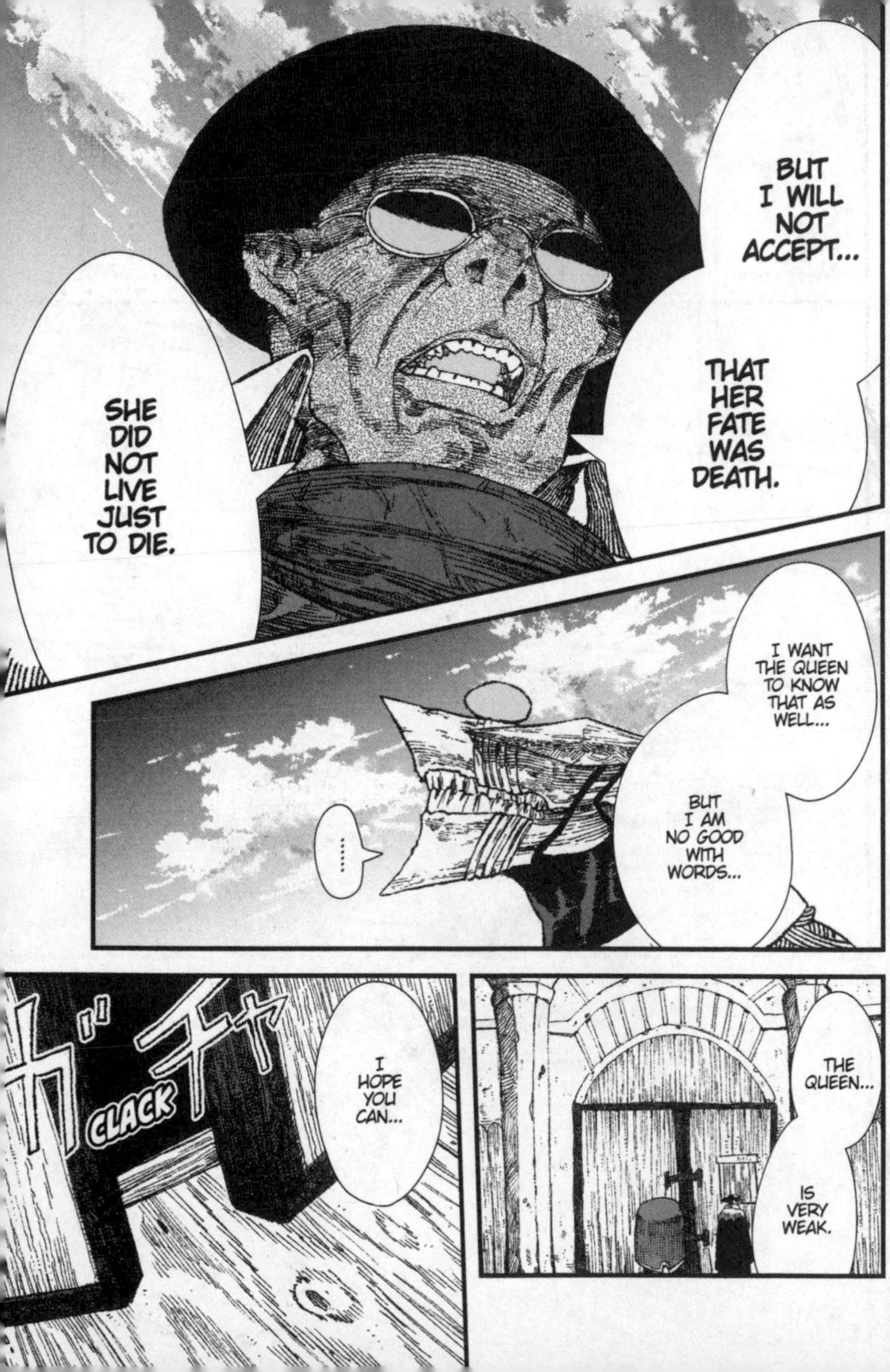
BUT I WILL NOT ACCEPT...
THAT HER FATE WAS DEATH.
SHE DID NOT LIVE JUST TO DIE.
I WANT THE QUEEN TO KNOW THAT AS WELL...
BUT I AM NO GOOD WITH WORDS...
......
THE QUEEN...
IS VERY WEAK.
I HOPE YOU CAN...
ガチャ
CLACK

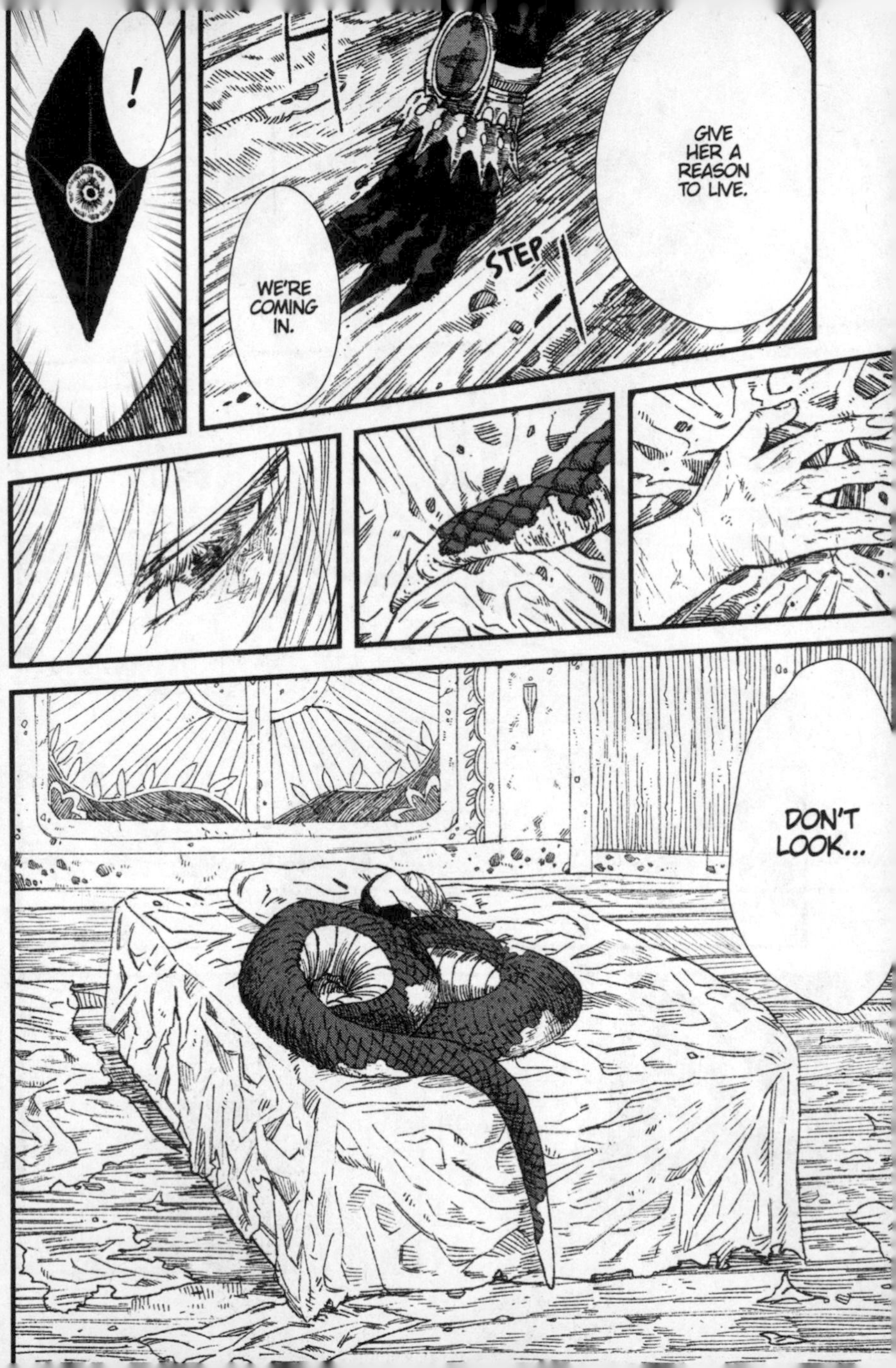
GIVE HER A REASON TO LIVE.
STEP
WE'RE COMING IN.
!
DON'T LOOK...

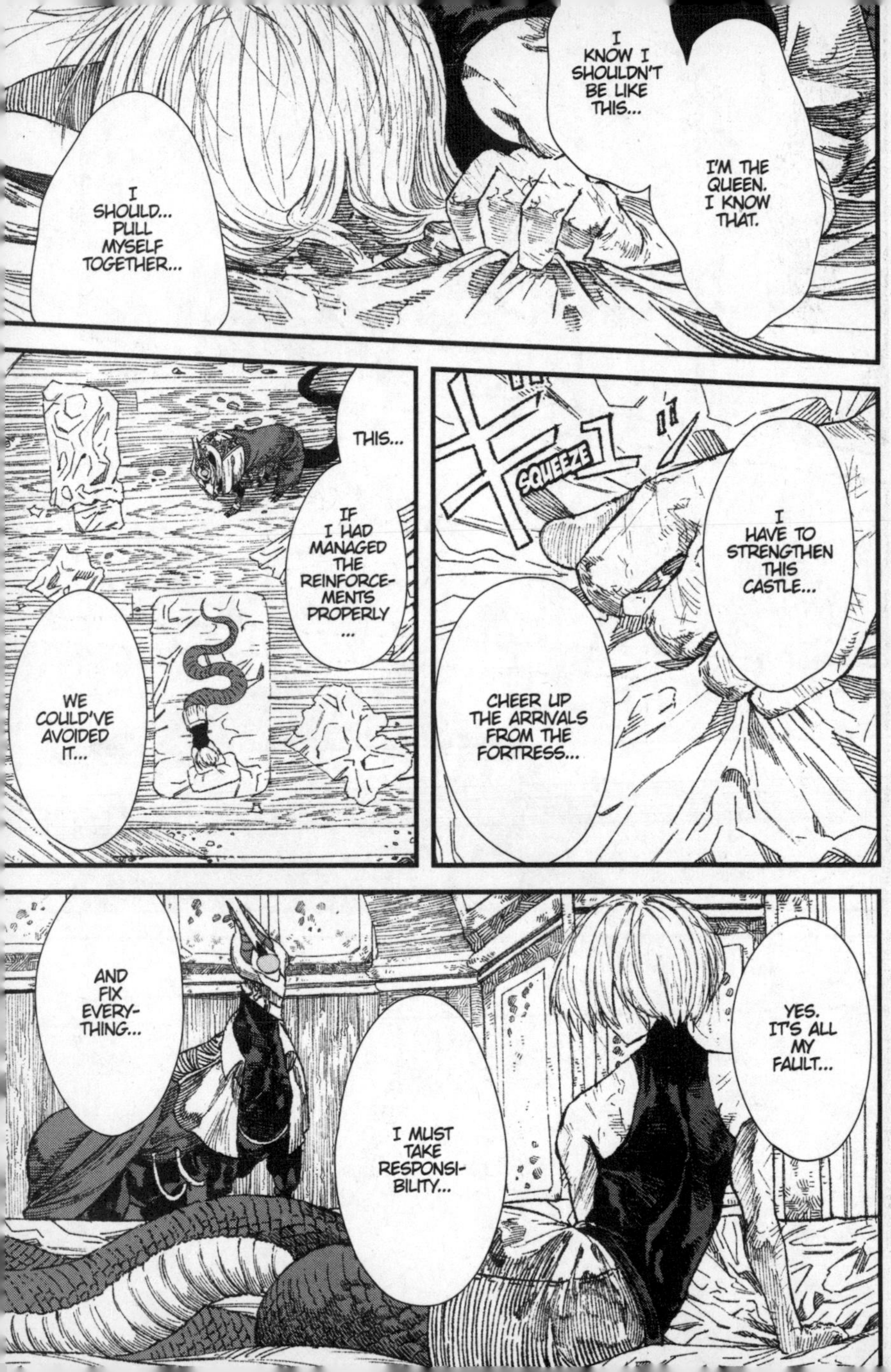
I KNOW I SHOULDN'T BE LIKE THIS...
I'M THE QUEEN. I KNOW THAT.
I SHOULD... PULL MYSELF TOGETHER...
SQUEEZE
I HAVE TO STRENGTHEN THIS CASTLE...
CHEER UP THE ARRIVALS FROM THE FORTRESS...
THIS...
IF I HAD MANAGED THE REINFORCEMENTS PROPERLY...
WE COULD'VE AVOIDED IT...
YES. IT'S ALL MY FAULT...
I MUST TAKE RESPONSIBILITY...
AND FIX EVERYTHING...

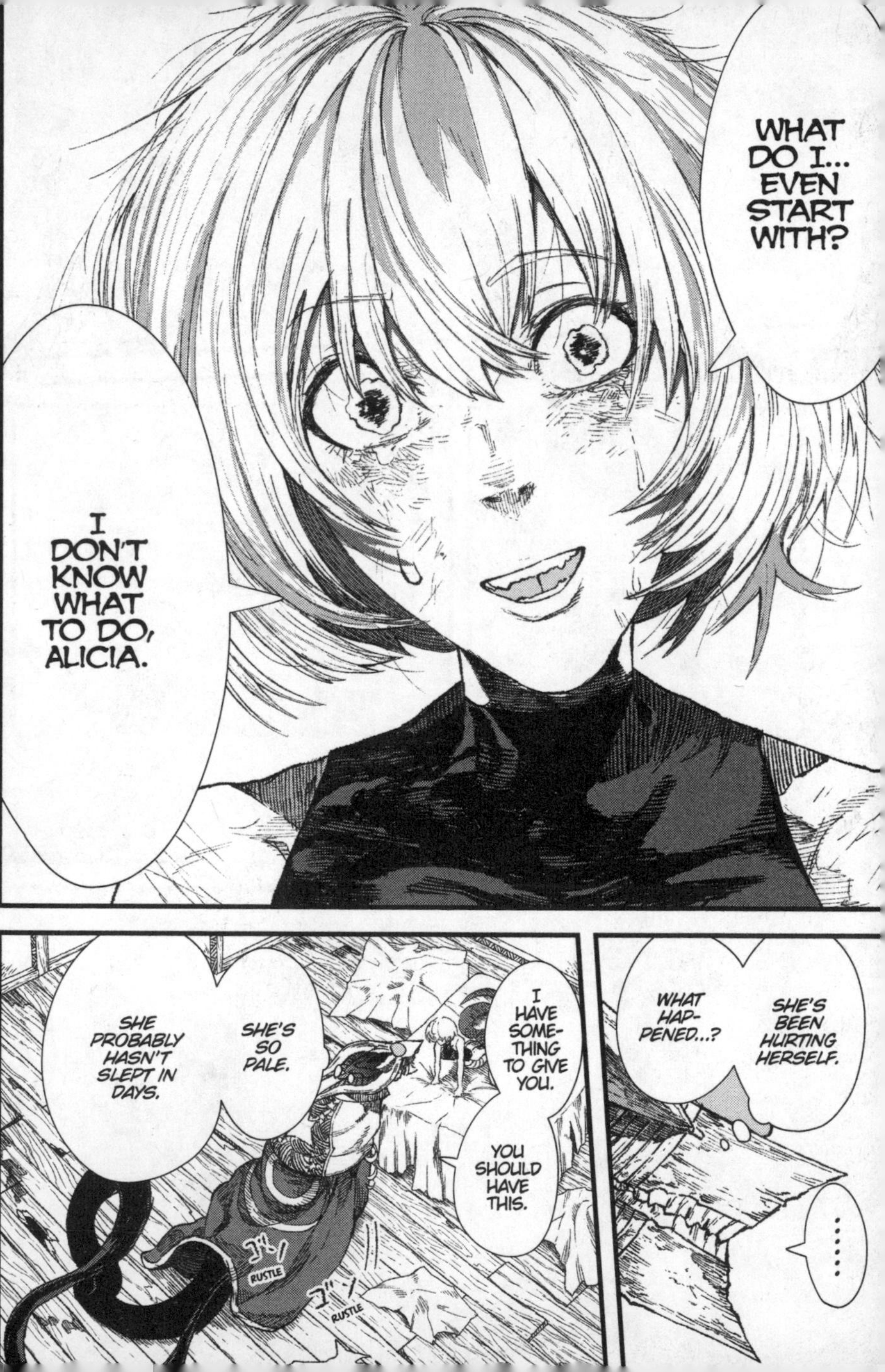
WHAT DO I... EVEN START WITH?
I DON'T KNOW WHAT TO DO, ALICIA.
SHE'S BEEN HURTING HERSELF.
WHAT HAPPENED...?
......
I HAVE SOMETHING TO GIVE YOU.
YOU SHOULD HAVE THIS.
SHE'S SO PALE.
SHE PROBABLY HASN'T SLEPT IN DAYS.
RUSTLE
RUSTLE

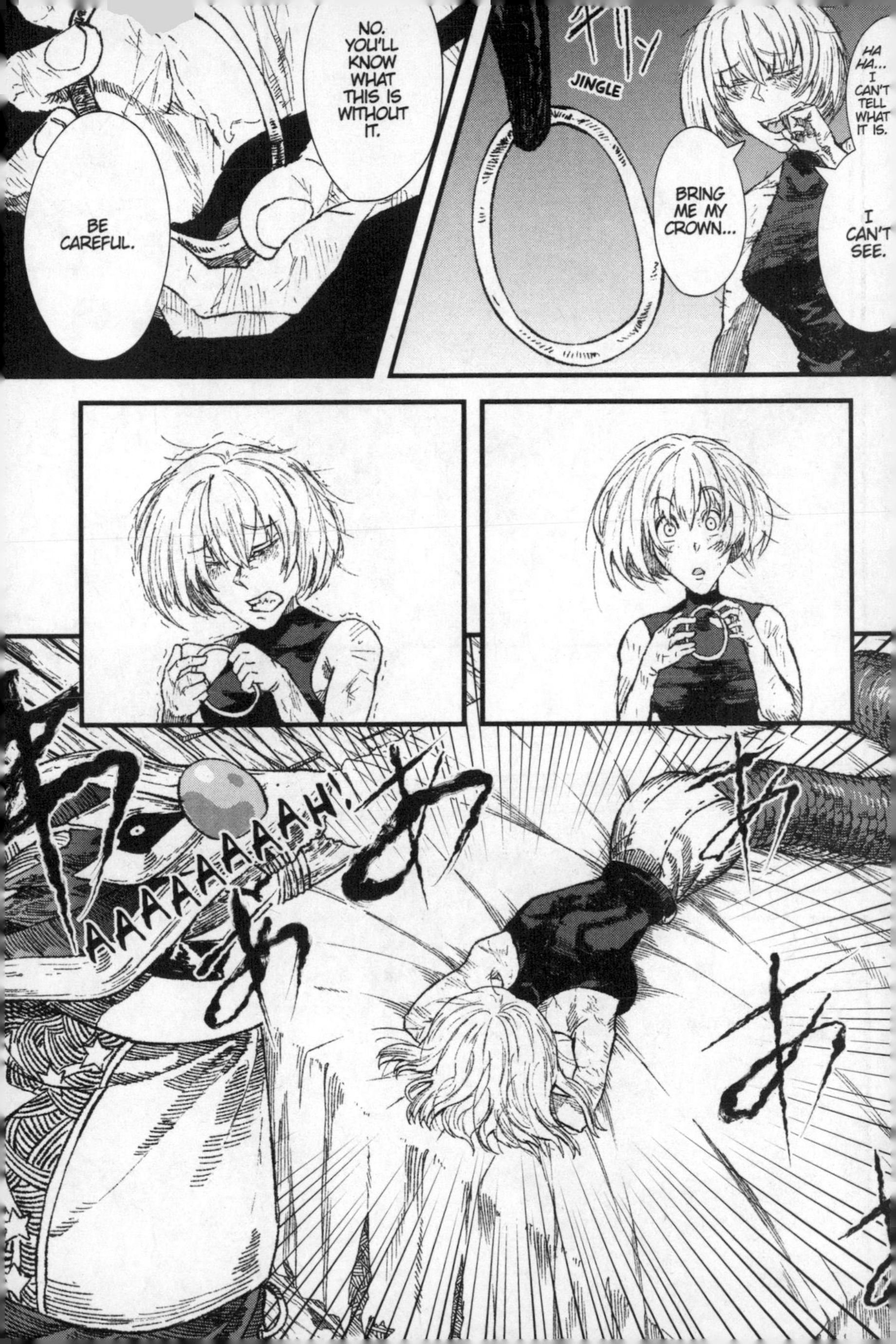
HA HA... I CAN'T TELL WHAT IT IS.
I CAN'T SEE.
BRING ME MY CROWN...
JINGLE
NO. YOU'LL KNOW WHAT THIS IS WITHOUT IT.
BE CAREFUL.
AAAAAAAAAH!

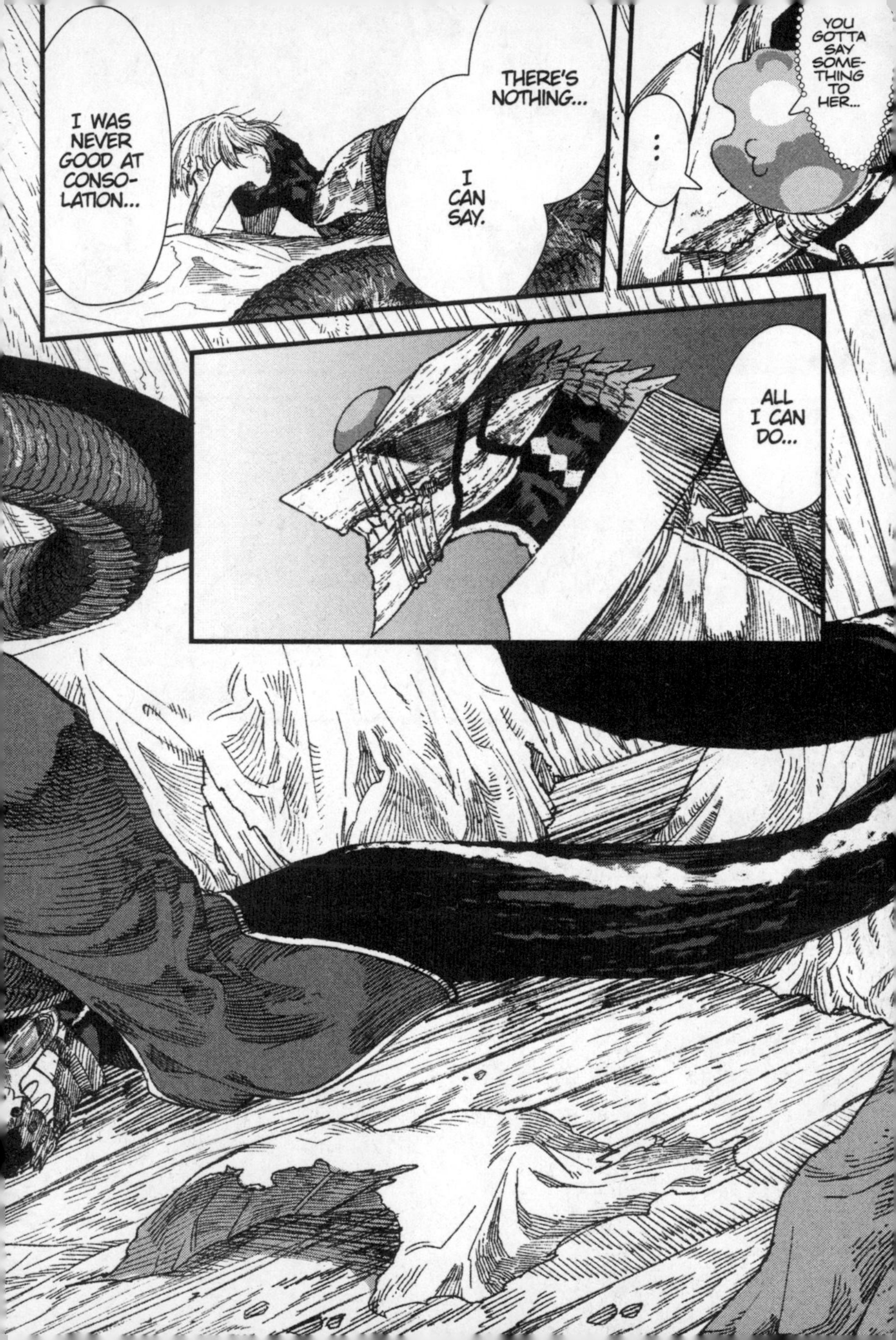
YOU GOTTA SAY SOME-THING TO HER...
...
THERE'S NOTHING...
I CAN SAY.
I WAS NEVER GOOD AT CONSO-LATION...
ALL I CAN DO...

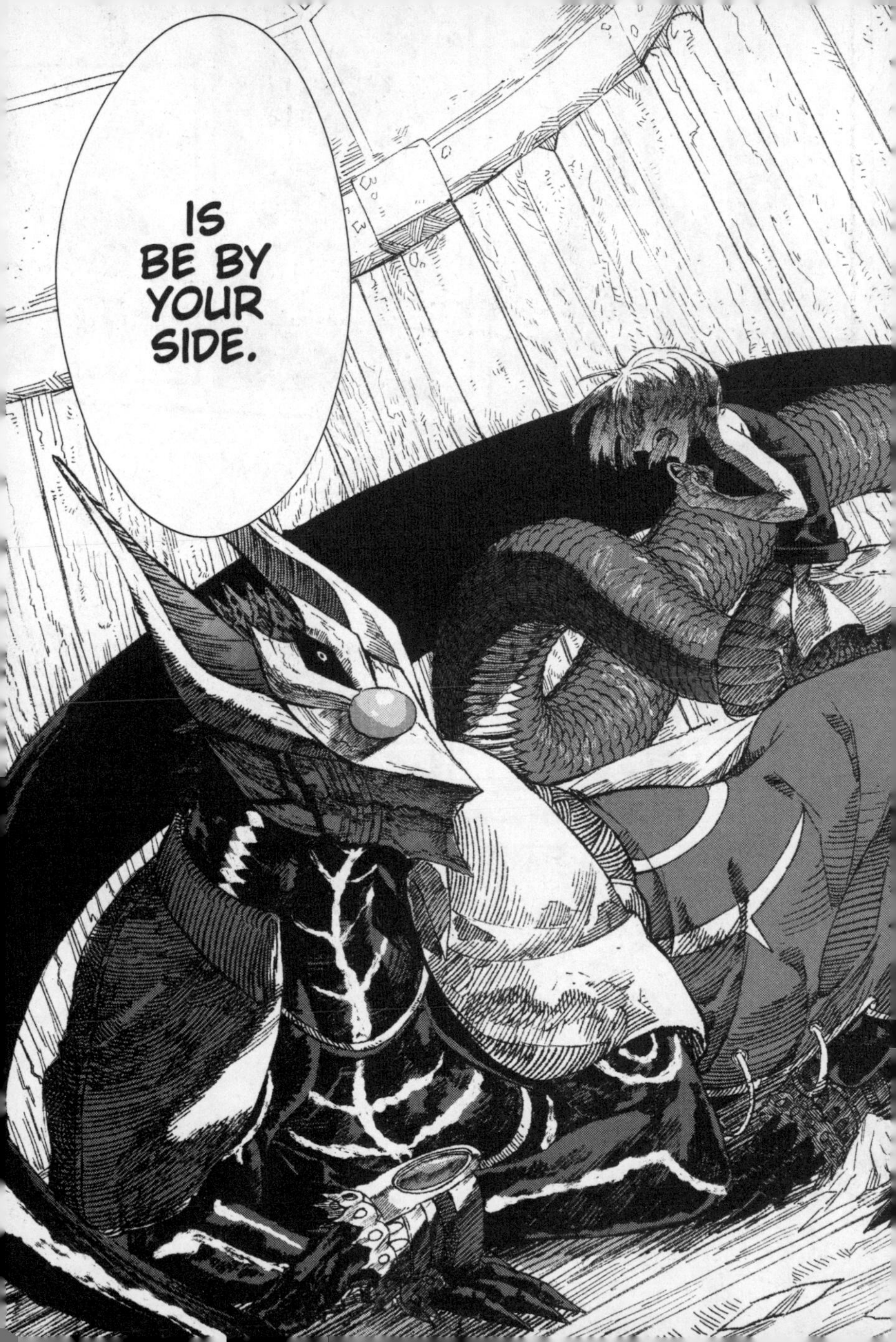
IS BE BY YOUR SIDE.

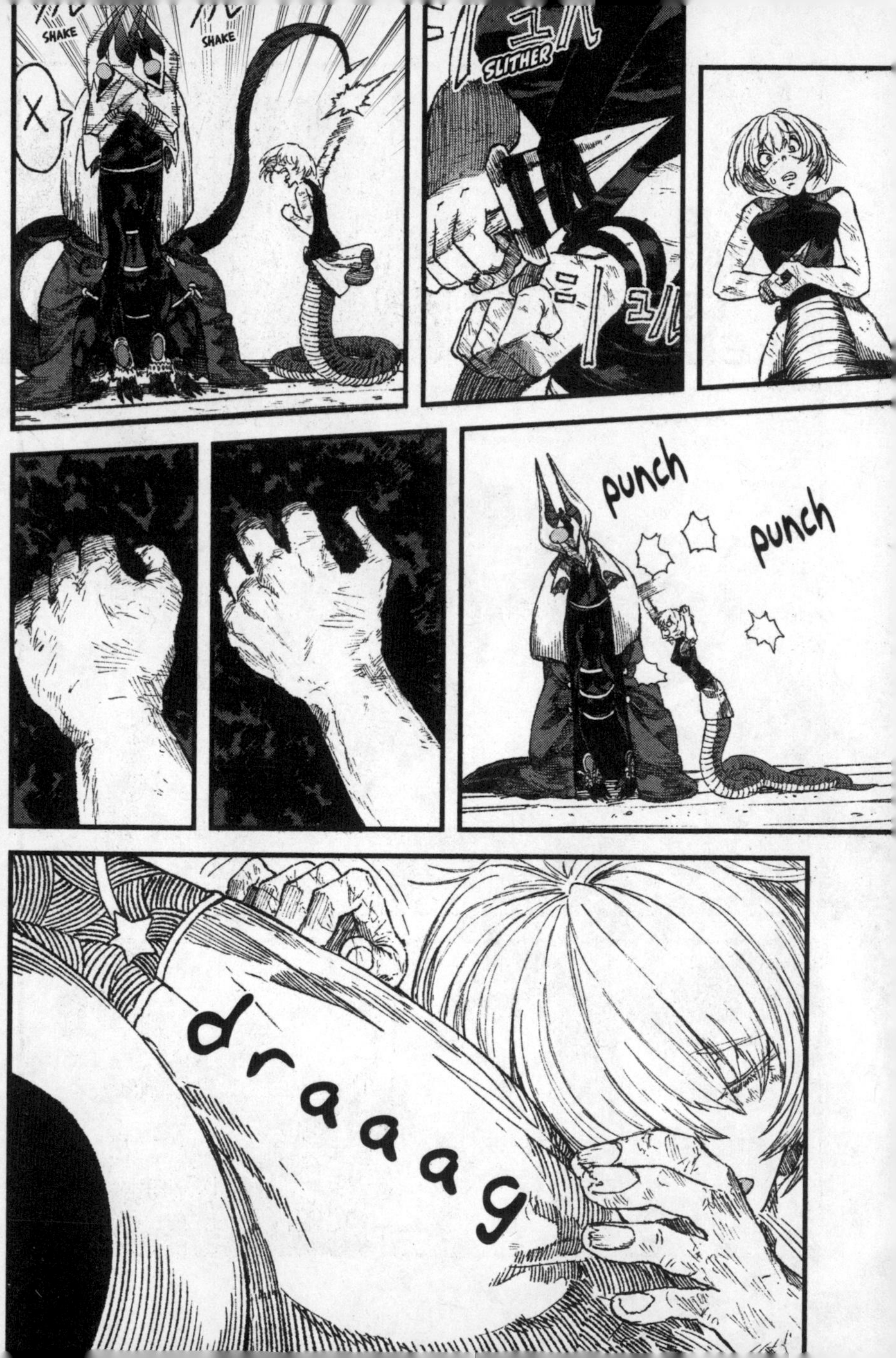
SLITHER
SHAKE
SHAKE
punch
punch
draaag

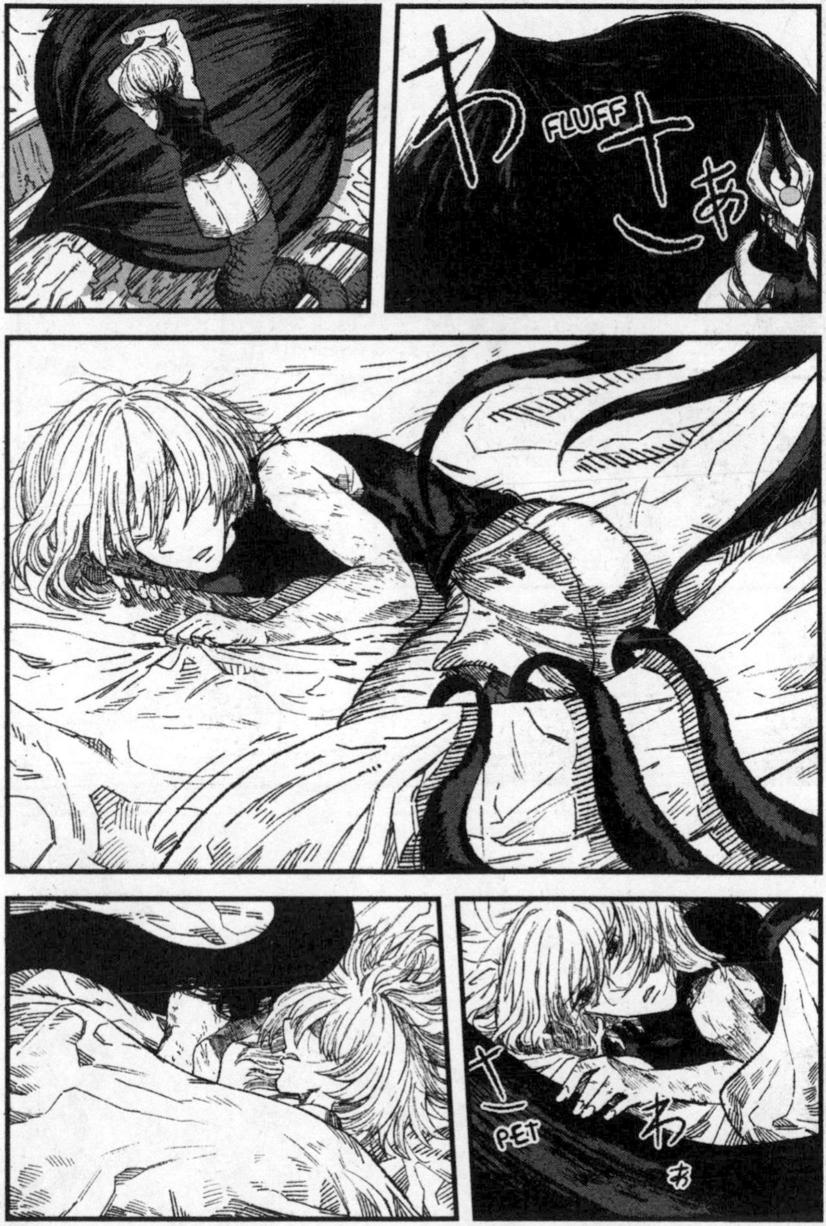
わさぁ
FLUFF
PET

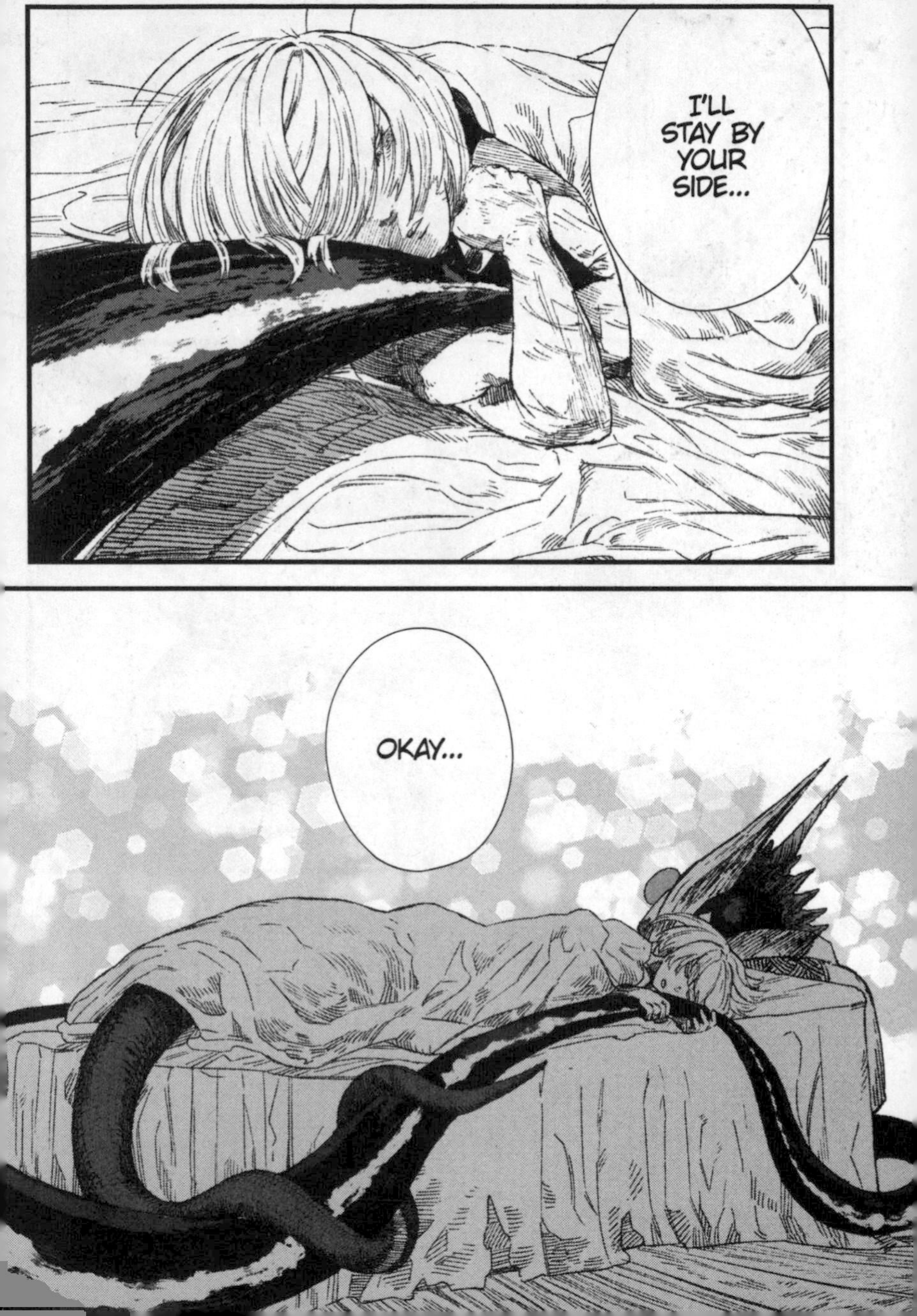
I'LL STAY BY YOUR SIDE...
OKAY...

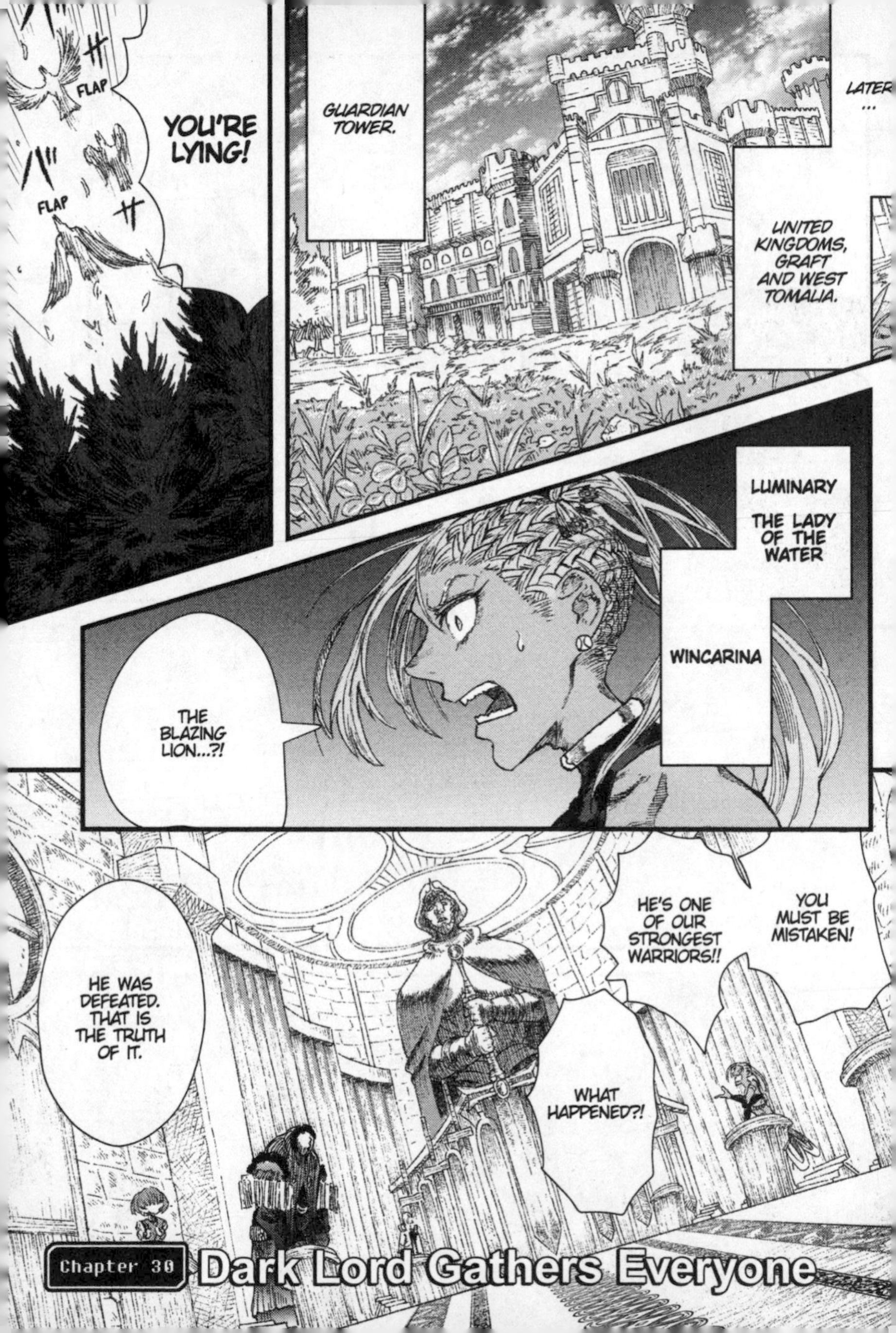
LATER...
UNITED KINGDOMS, GRAFT AND WEST TOMALIA.
GUARDIAN TOWER.
YOU'RE LYING!
FLAP
FLAP
LUMINARY
THE LADY OF THE WATER
WINCARINA
THE BLAZING LION...?!
YOU MUST BE MISTAKEN!
HE'S ONE OF OUR STRONGEST WARRIORS!!
WHAT HAPPENED?!
HE WAS DEFEATED. THAT IS THE TRUTH OF IT.
Chapter 30
Dark Lord Gathers Everyone

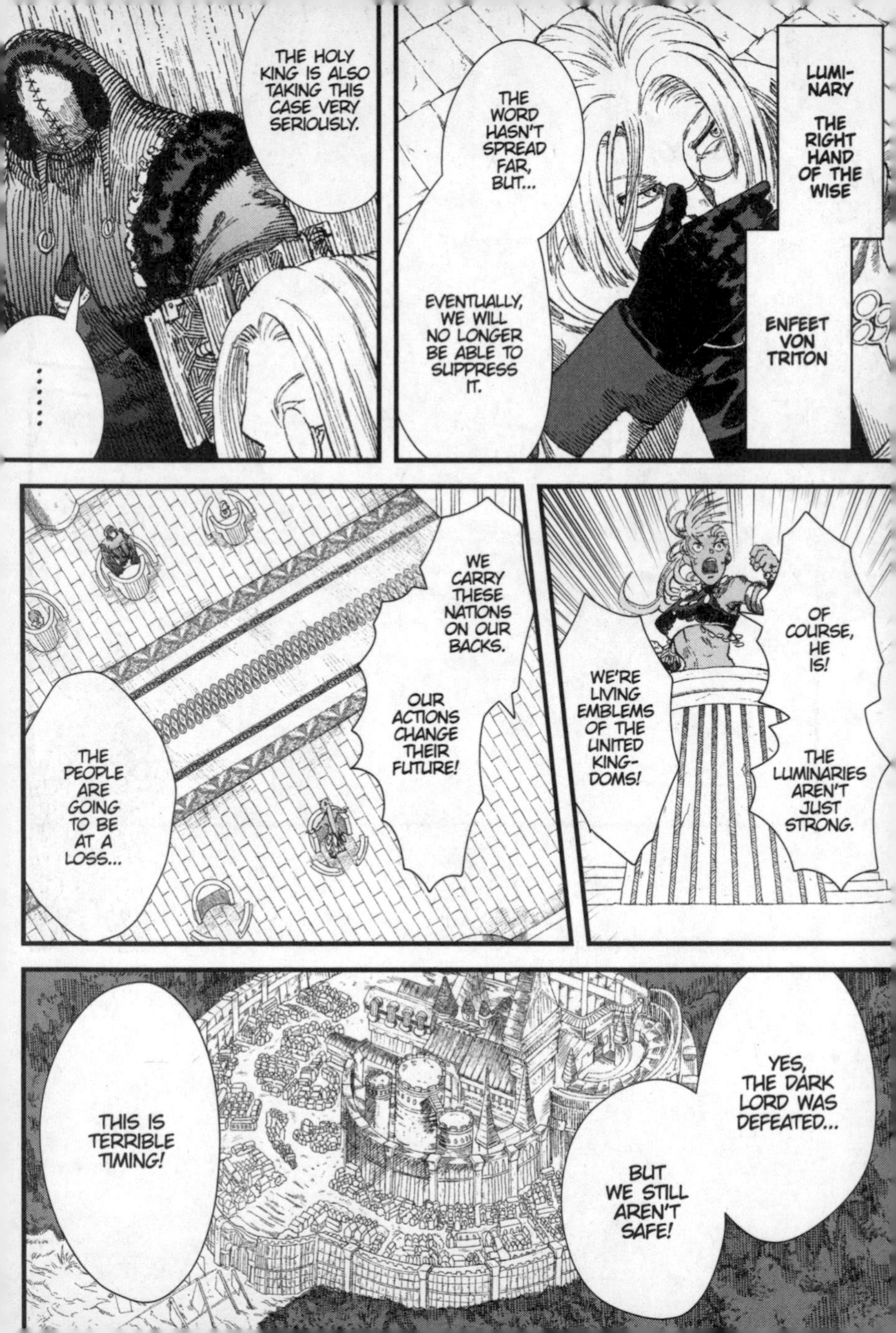
LUMINARY THE RIGHT HAND OF THE WISE
ENFEET VON TRITON
THE WORD HASN'T SPREAD FAR, BUT...
EVENTUALLY, WE WILL NO LONGER BE ABLE TO SUPPRESS IT.
THE HOLY KING IS ALSO TAKING THIS CASE VERY SERIOUSLY.
......
OF COURSE, HE IS!
THE LUMINARIES AREN'T JUST STRONG.
WE'RE LIVING EMBLEMS OF THE UNITED KINGDOMS!
WE CARRY THESE NATIONS ON OUR BACKS.
OUR ACTIONS CHANGE THEIR FUTURE!
THE PEOPLE ARE GOING TO BE AT A LOSS...
YES, THE DARK LORD WAS DEFEATED...
BUT WE STILL AREN'T SAFE!
THIS IS TERRIBLE TIMING!

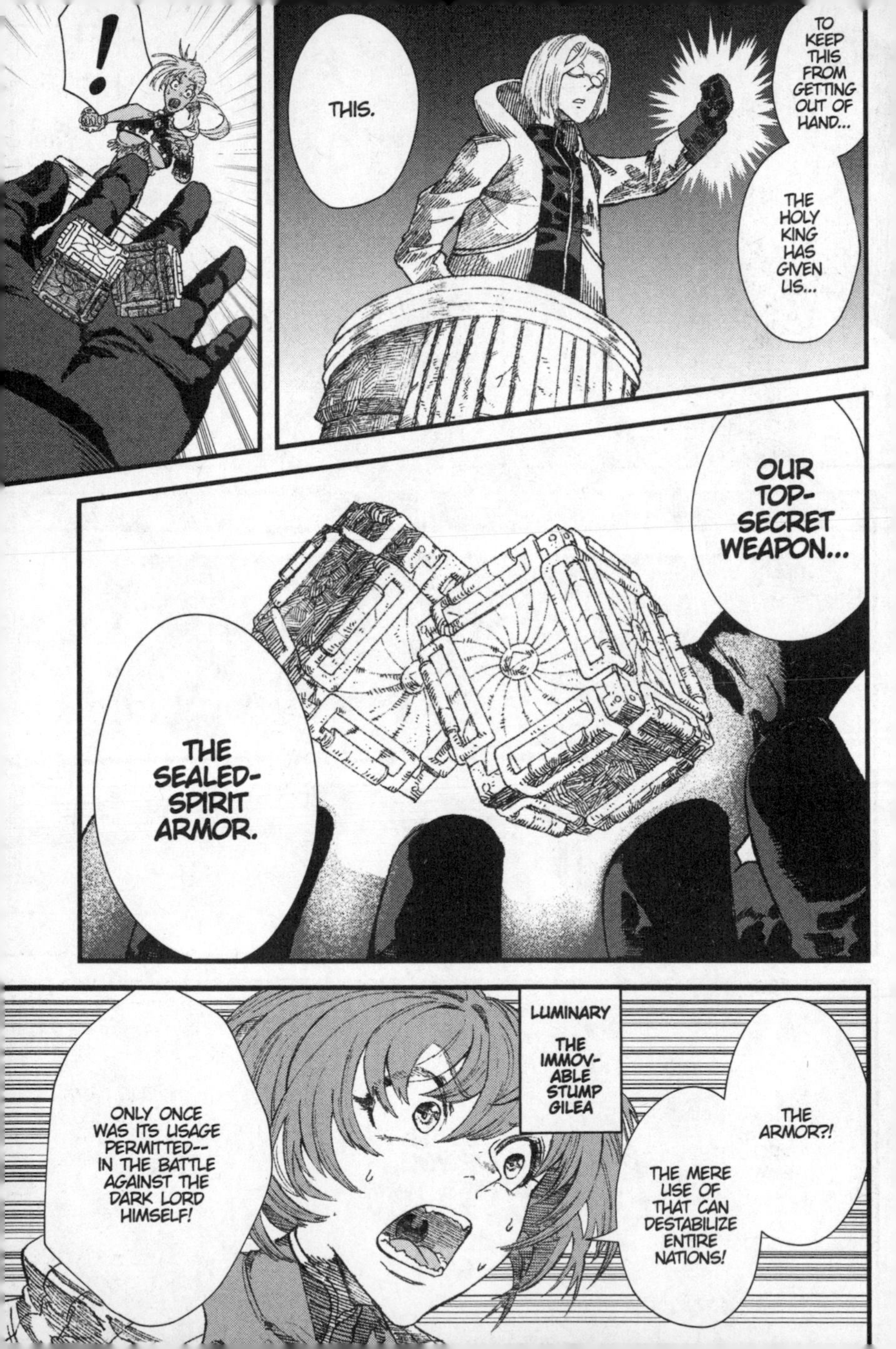
TO KEEP THIS FROM GETTING OUT OF HAND...
THE HOLY KING HAS GIVEN US...
THIS.
!
OUR TOP-SECRET WEAPON...
THE SEALED-SPIRIT ARMOR.
LUMINARY THE IMMOVABLE STUMP GILEA
THE ARMOR?!
THE MERE USE OF THAT CAN DESTABILIZE ENTIRE NATIONS!
ONLY ONCE WAS ITS USAGE PERMITTED-- IN THE BATTLE AGAINST THE DARK LORD HIMSELF!

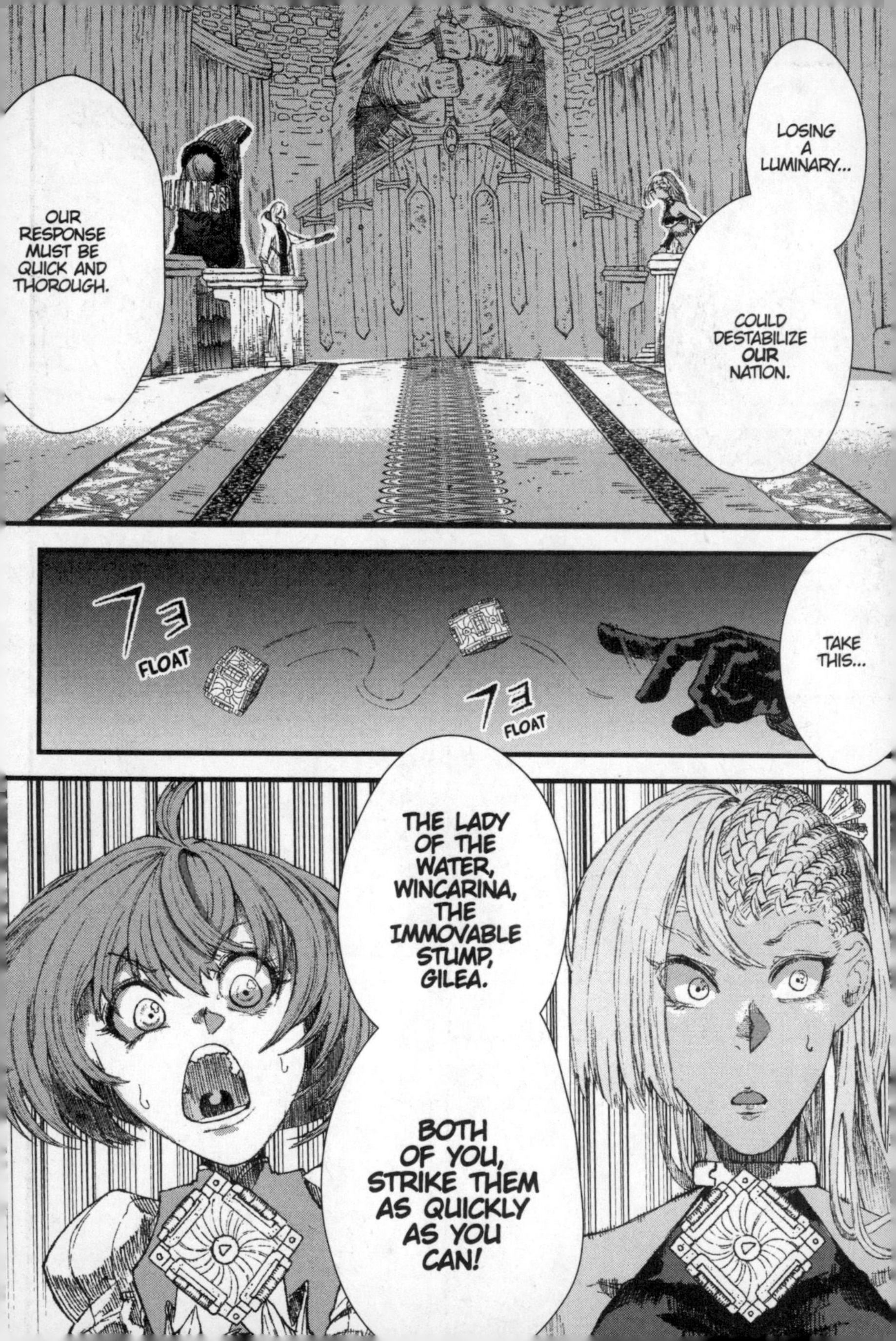
LOSING A LUMINARY... COULD DESTABILIZE OUR NATION.
OUR RESPONSE MUST BE QUICK AND THOROUGH.
TAKE THIS...
フヨ FLOAT
フヨ FLOAT
THE LADY OF THE WATER, WINCARINA, THE IMMOVABLE STUMP, GILEA.
BOTH OF YOU, STRIKE THEM AS QUICKLY AS YOU CAN!

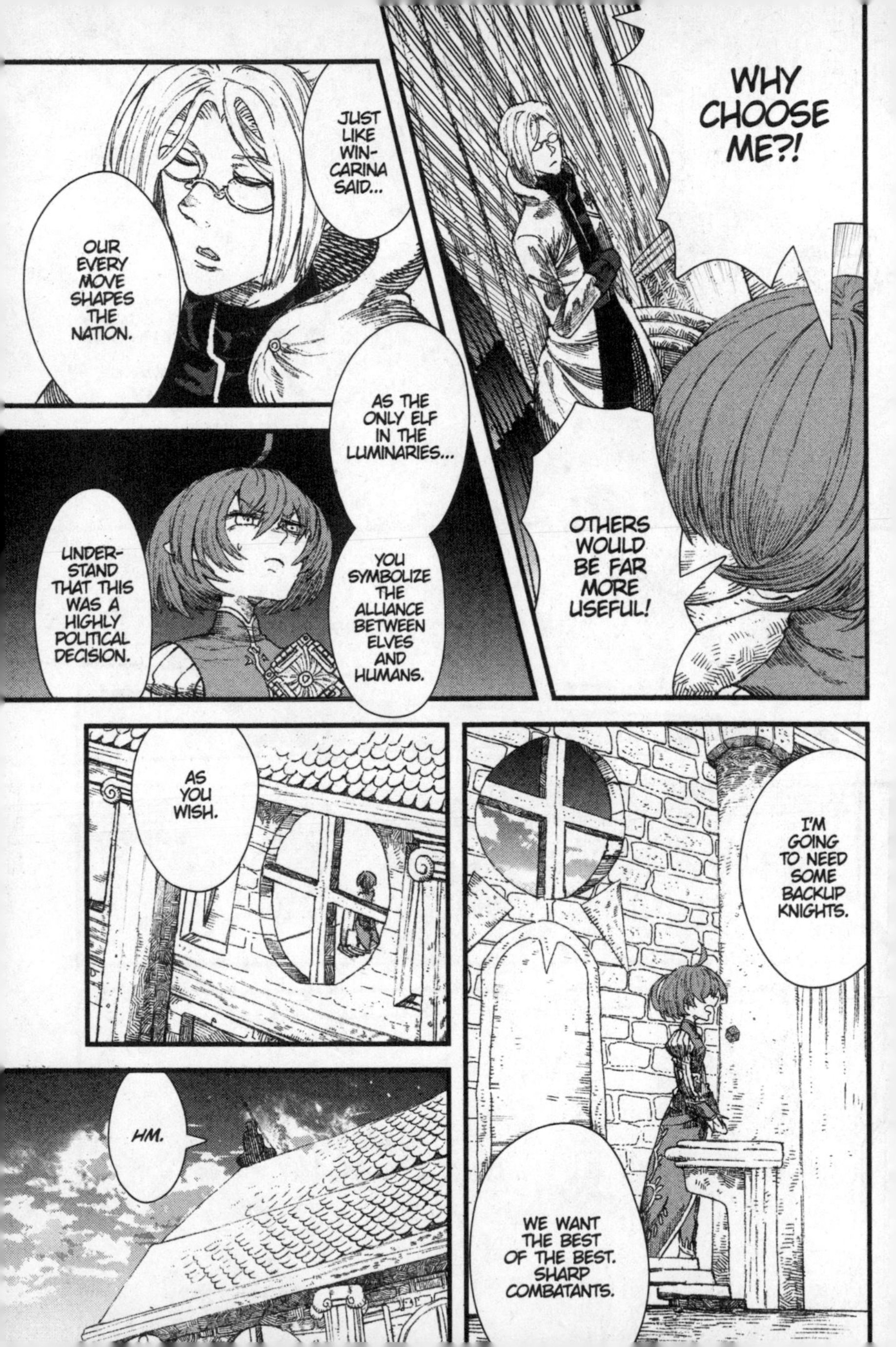
WHY CHOOSE ME?!
OTHERS WOULD BE FAR MORE USEFUL!
JUST LIKE WIN-CARINA SAID...
OUR EVERY MOVE SHAPES THE NATION.
AS THE ONLY ELF IN THE LUMINARIES...
YOU SYMBOLIZE THE ALLIANCE BETWEEN ELVES AND HUMANS.
UNDER-STAND THAT THIS WAS A HIGHLY POLITICAL DECISION.
I'M GOING TO NEED SOME BACKUP KNIGHTS.
WE WANT THE BEST OF THE BEST. SHARP COMBATANTS.
AS YOU WISH.
HM.

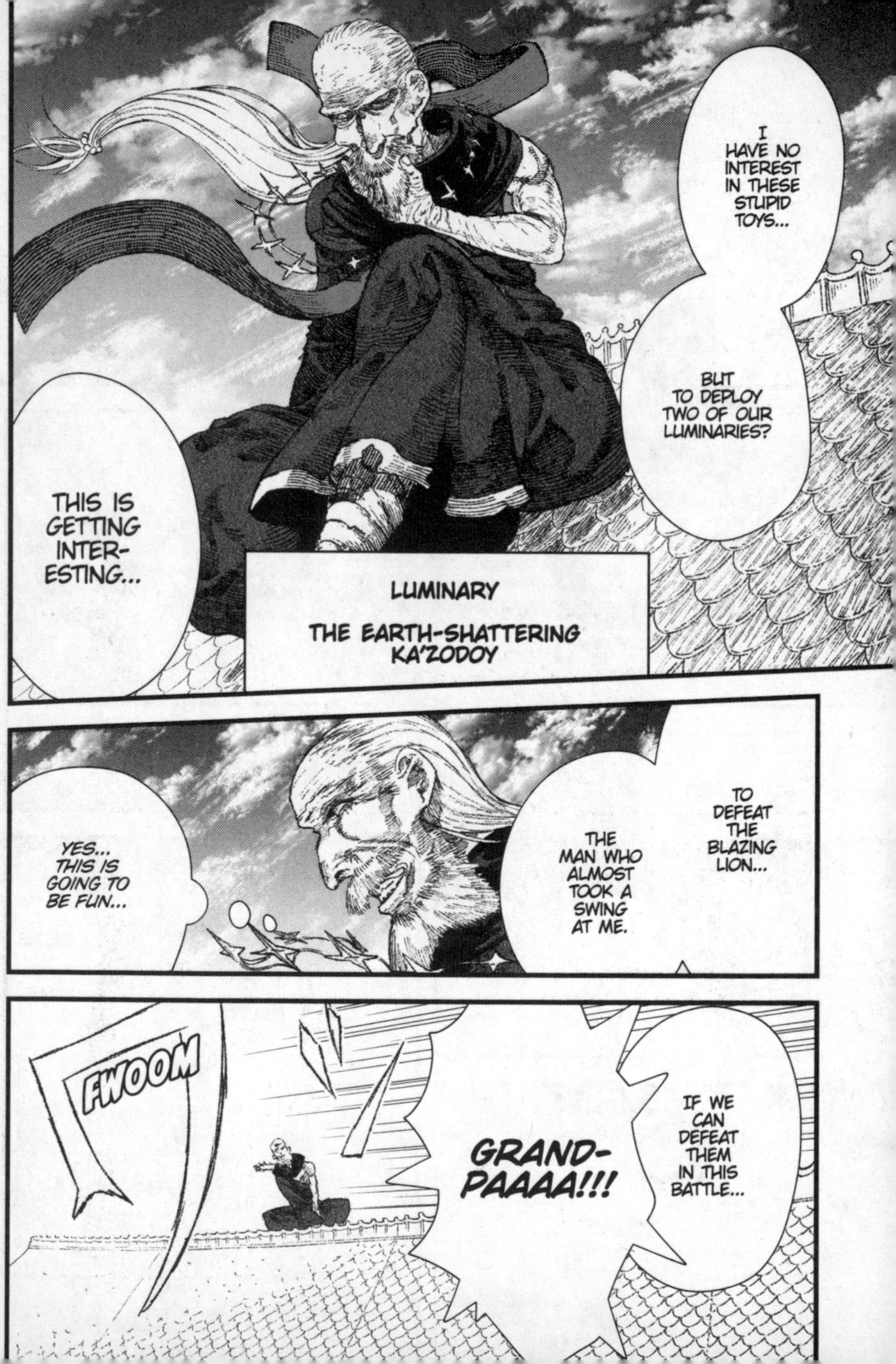

I HAVE NO INTEREST IN THESE STUPID TOYS...
BUT TO DEPLOY TWO OF OUR LUMINARIES?
THIS IS GETTING INTER-ESTING...
LUMINARY
THE EARTH-SHATTERING KA'ZODOY
TO DEFEAT THE BLAZING LION...
THE MAN WHO ALMOST TOOK A SWING AT ME.
YES... THIS IS GOING TO BE FUN...
IF WE CAN DEFEAT THEM IN THIS BATTLE...
GRAND-PAAAAA!!!
FWOOM

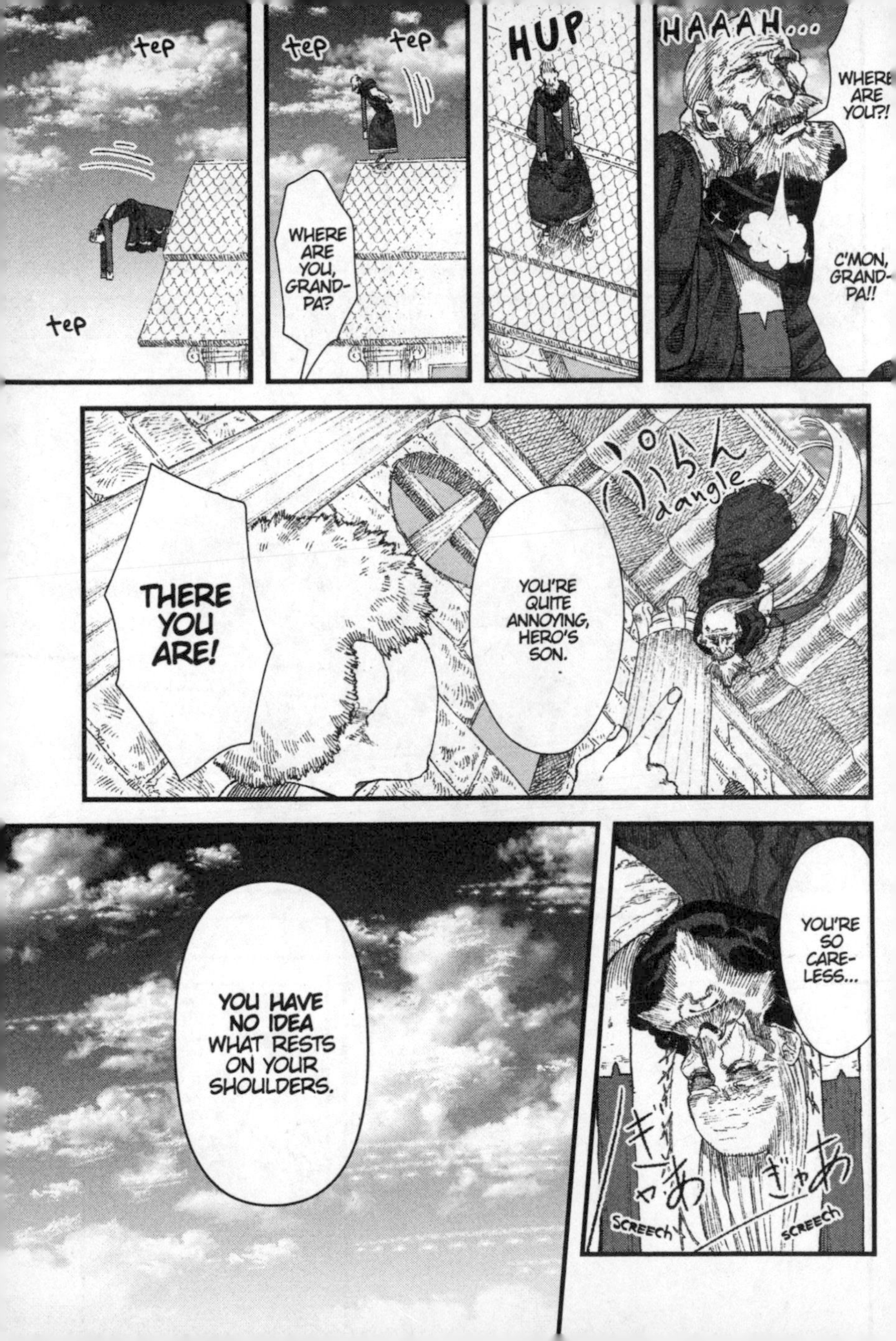
HAAAH...
WHERE ARE YOU?!
C'MON, GRANDPA!!
HUP
tep
tep
WHERE ARE YOU, GRANDPA?
tep
tep
ぷらん
dangle
YOU'RE QUITE ANNOYING, HERO'S SON.
THERE YOU ARE!
YOU'RE SO CARELESS...
ぎゃあ
ぎゃあ
SCREECH
SCREECH
YOU HAVE NO IDEA WHAT RESTS ON YOUR SHOULDERS.

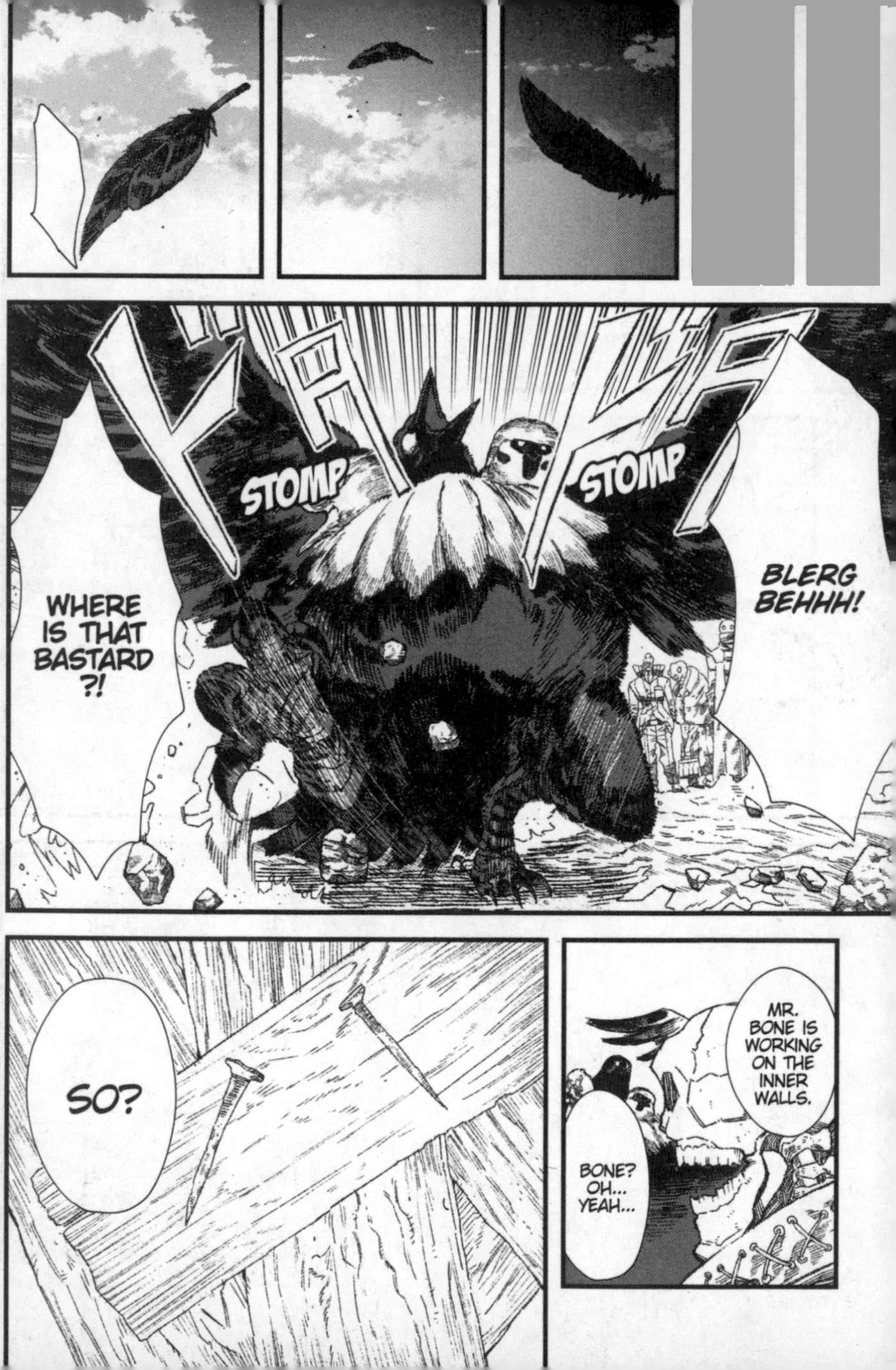
STOMP
STOMP
BLERG BEHHH!
WHERE IS THAT BASTARD ?!
MR. BONE IS WORKING ON THE INNER WALLS.
BONE? OH... YEAH...
SO?

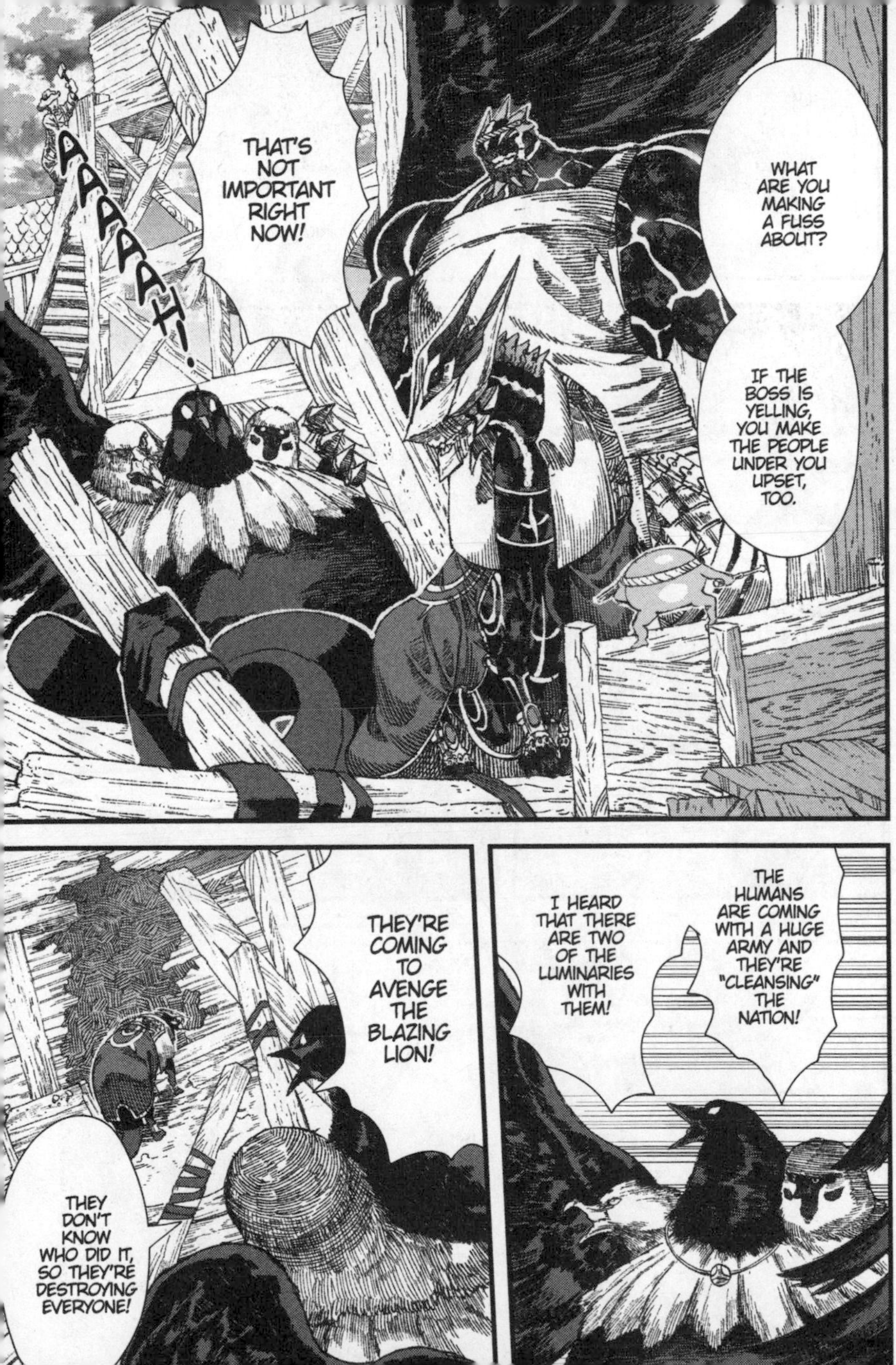
WHAT ARE YOU MAKING A FUSS ABOUT?
IF THE BOSS IS YELLING, YOU MAKE THE PEOPLE UNDER YOU UPSET, TOO.
THAT'S NOT IMPORTANT RIGHT NOW!
AAAAAH!
THE HUMANS ARE COMING WITH A HUGE ARMY AND THEY'RE "CLEANSING" THE NATION!
I HEARD THAT THERE ARE TWO OF THE LUMINARIES WITH THEM!
THEY'RE COMING TO AVENGE THE BLAZING LION!
THEY DON'T KNOW WHO DID IT, SO THEY'RE DESTROYING EVERYONE!

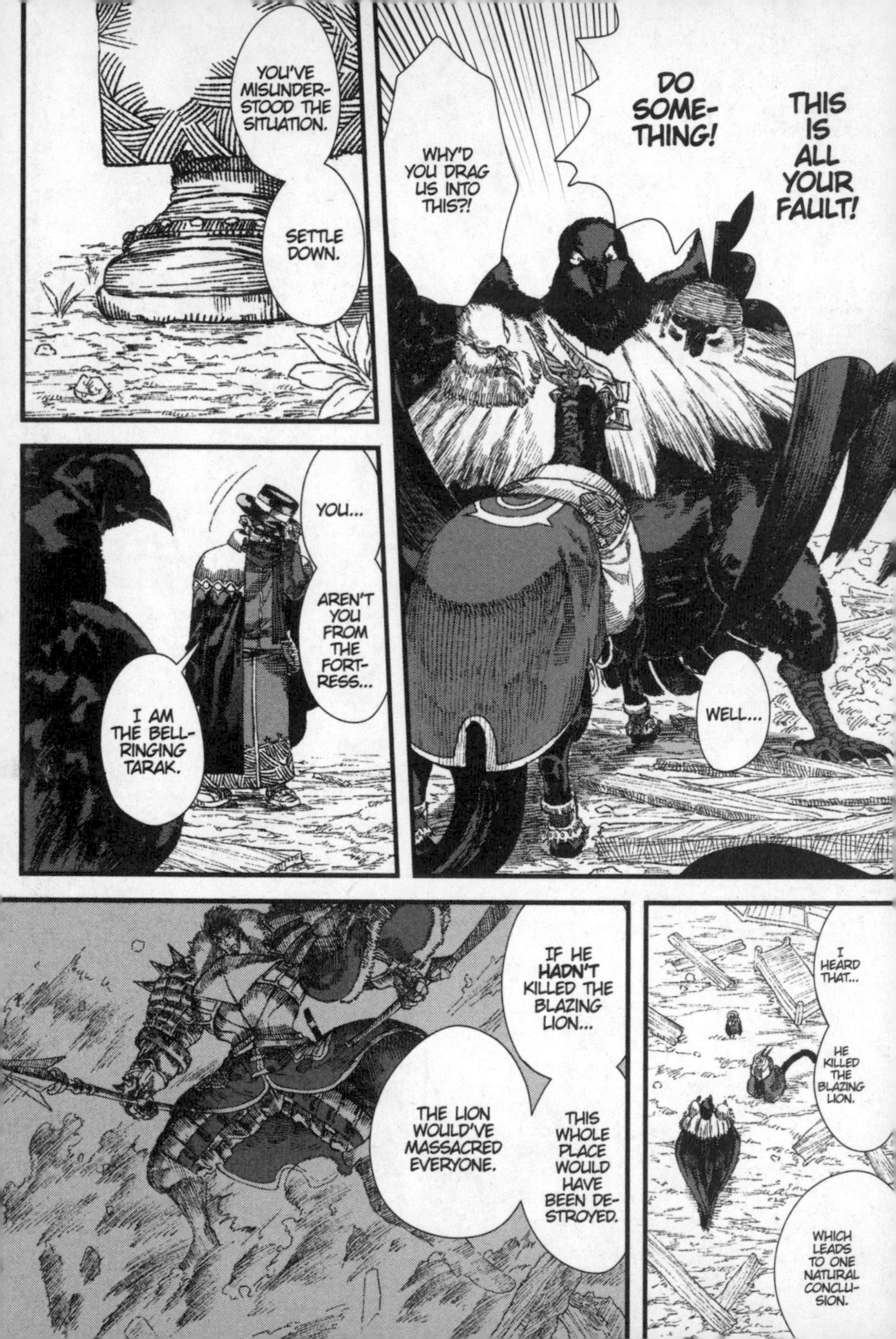
THIS IS ALL YOUR FAULT!
DO SOMETHING!
WHY'D YOU DRAG US INTO THIS?!
WELL...
YOU'VE MISUNDERSTOOD THE SITUATION.
SETTLE DOWN.
YOU...
AREN'T YOU FROM THE FORTRESS...
I AM THE BELL-RINGING TARAK.
I HEARD THAT...
HE KILLED THE BLAZING LION.
WHICH LEADS TO ONE NATURAL CONCLUSION.
IF HE **HADN'T** KILLED THE BLAZING LION...
THIS WHOLE PLACE WOULD HAVE BEEN DESTROYED.
THE LION WOULD'VE MASSACRED EVERYONE.

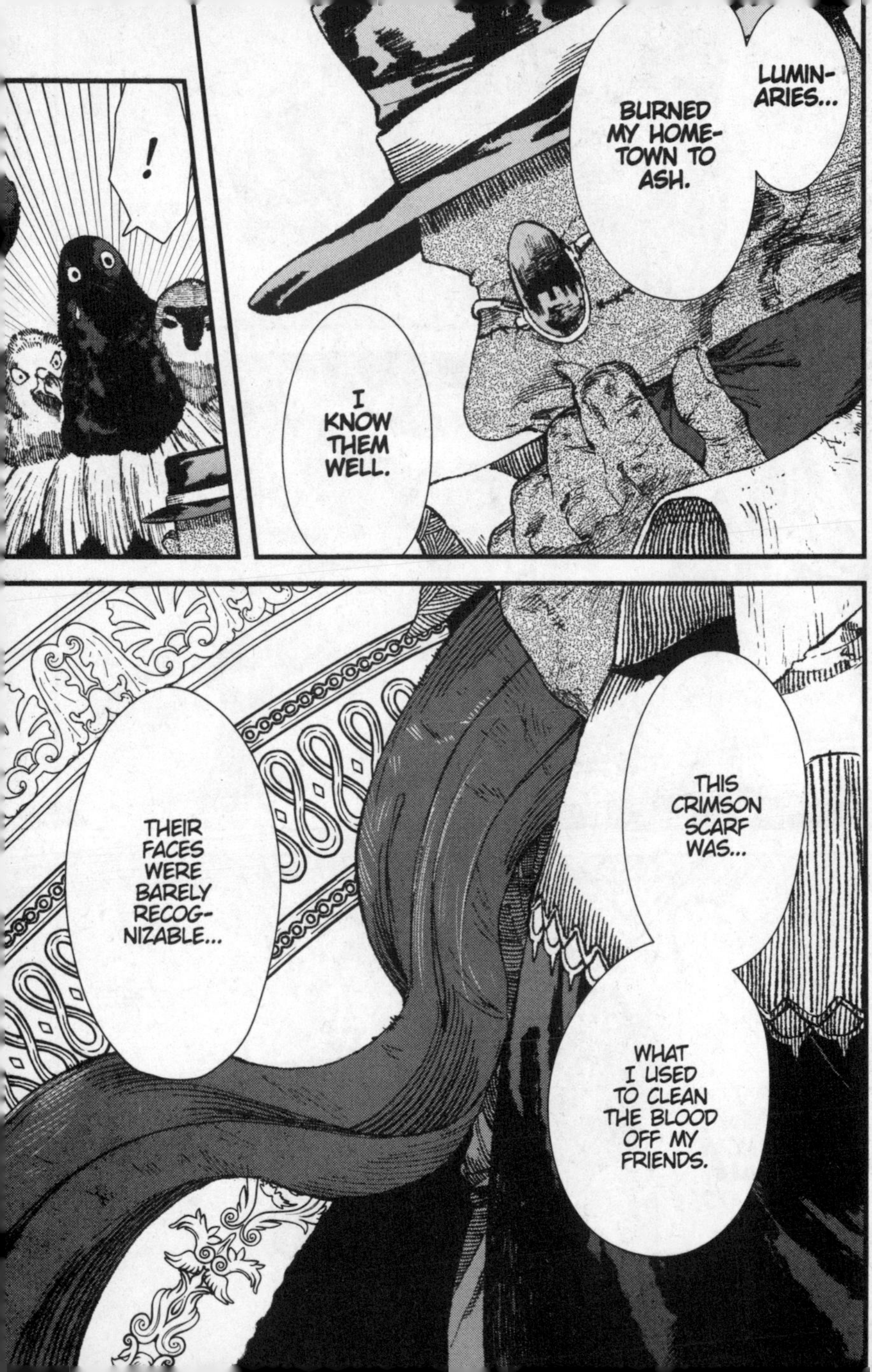
LUMINARIES...
BURNED MY HOME-TOWN TO ASH.
I KNOW THEM WELL.
!
THIS CRIMSON SCARF WAS...
WHAT I USED TO CLEAN THE BLOOD OFF MY FRIENDS.
THEIR FACES WERE BARELY RECOG-NIZABLE...

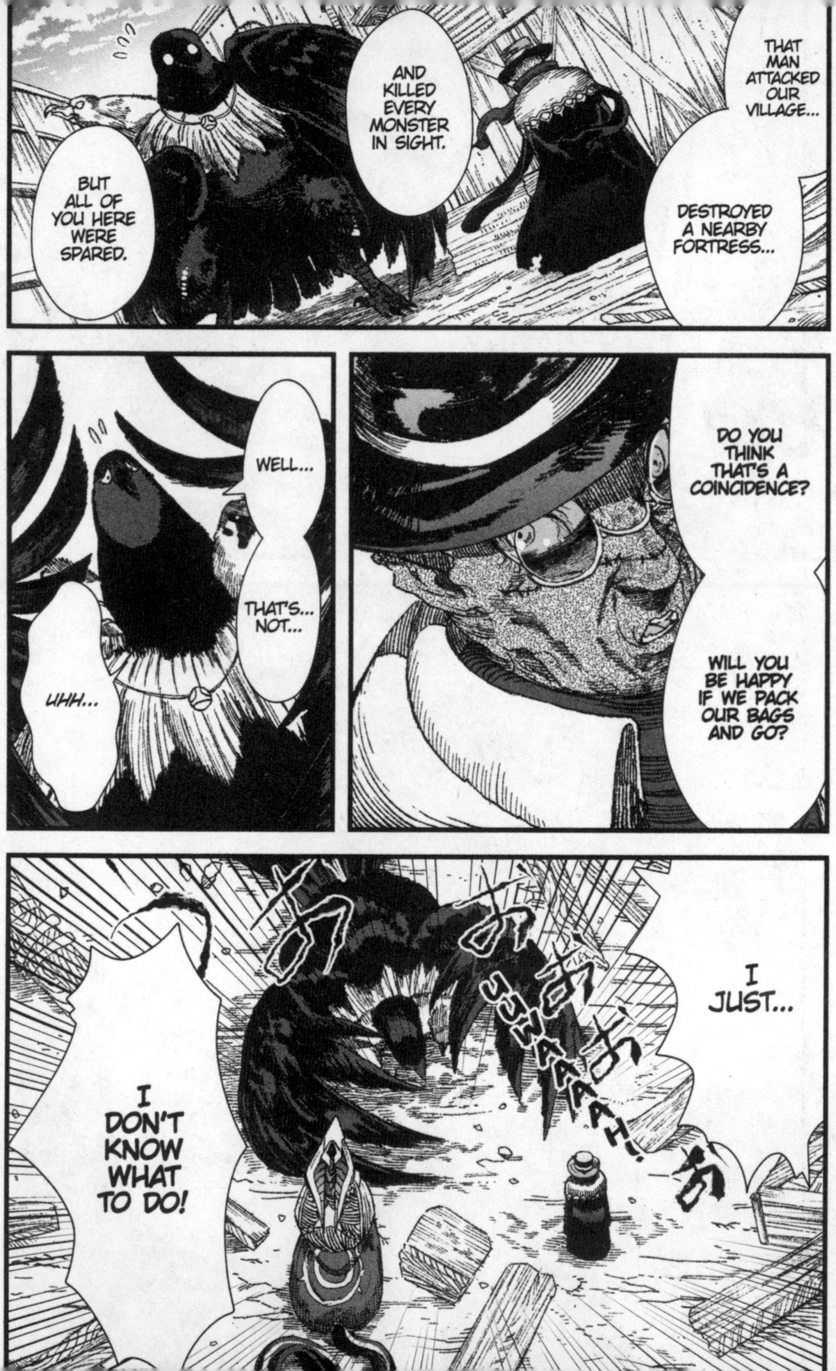
THAT MAN ATTACKED OUR VILLAGE...
DESTROYED A NEARBY FORTRESS...
AND KILLED EVERY MONSTER IN SIGHT.
BUT ALL OF YOU HERE WERE SPARED.
DO YOU THINK THAT'S A COINCIDENCE?
WILL YOU BE HAPPY IF WE PACK OUR BAGS AND GO?
WELL...
THAT'S... NOT...
UHH...
I JUST...
UWAAAAH!
I DON'T KNOW WHAT TO DO!

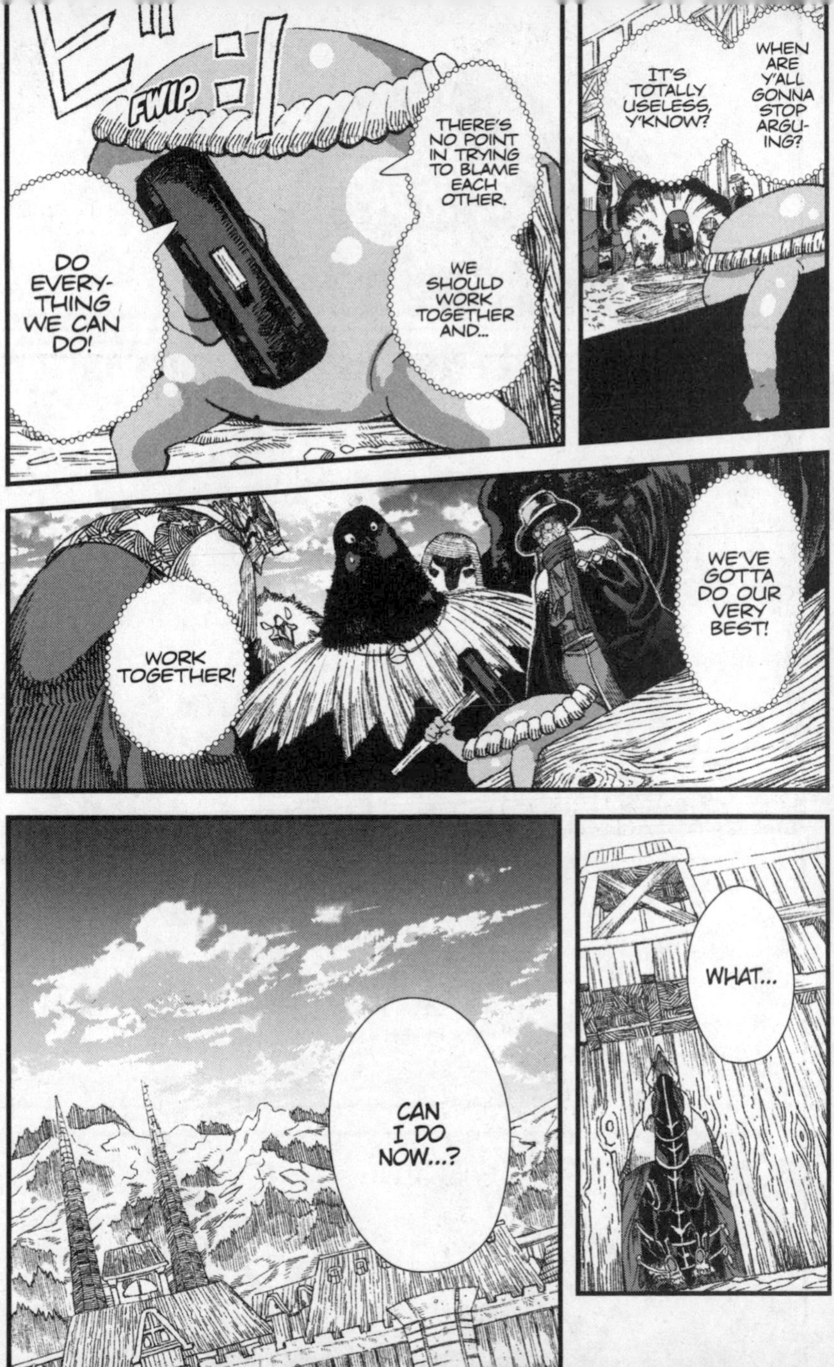
WHEN ARE Y'ALL GONNA STOP ARGU-ING?
IT'S TOTALLY USELESS, Y'KNOW?
FWIP
THERE'S NO POINT IN TRYING TO BLAME EACH OTHER.
WE SHOULD WORK TOGETHER AND...
DO EVERY-THING WE CAN DO!
WE'VE GOTTA DO OUR VERY BEST!
WORK TOGETHER!
WHAT...
CAN I DO NOW...?

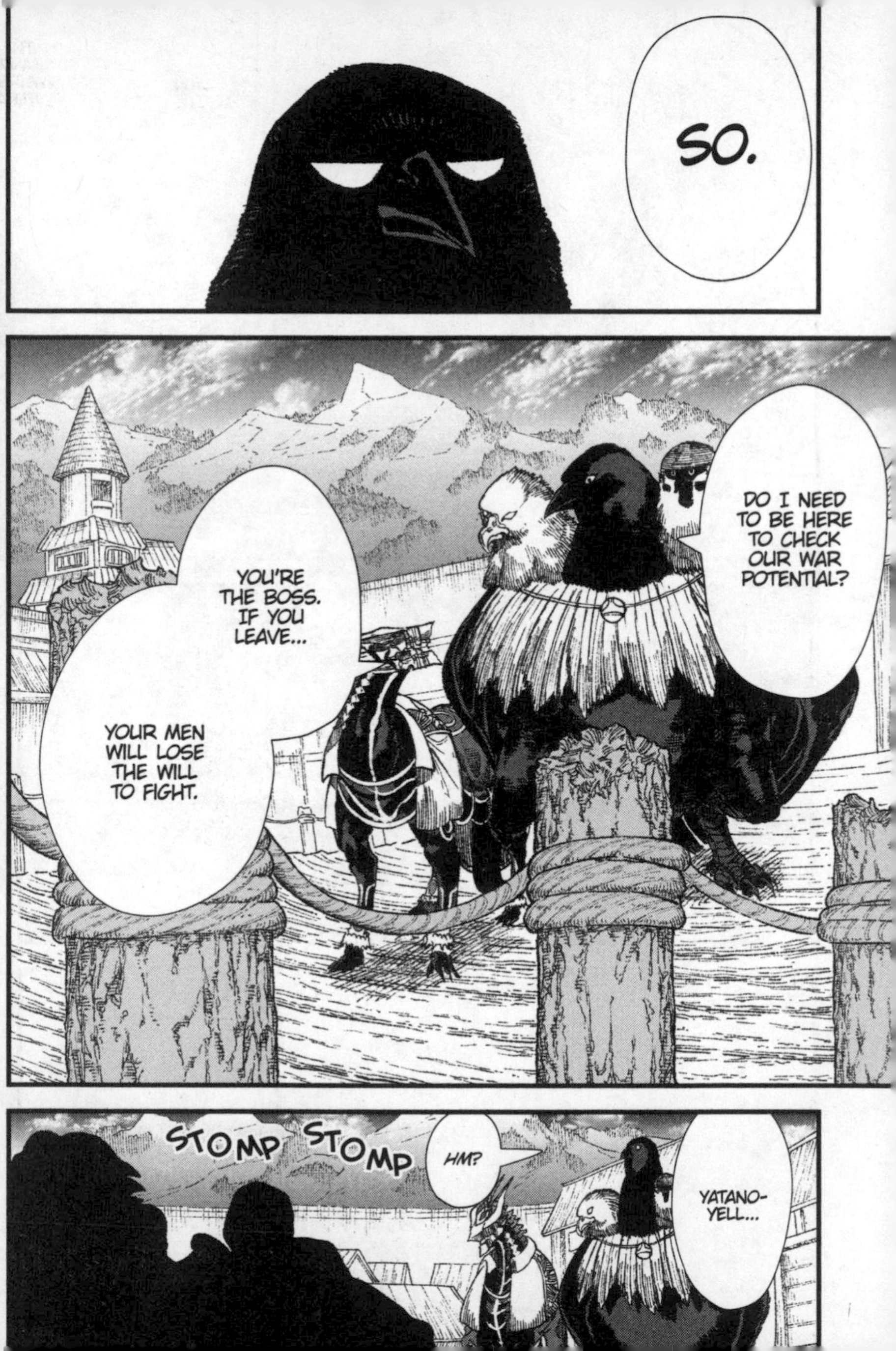
SO.
DO I NEED TO BE HERE TO CHECK OUR WAR POTENTIAL?
YOU'RE THE BOSS. IF YOU LEAVE...
YOUR MEN WILL LOSE THE WILL TO FIGHT.
YATANO-YELL...
HM?
STOMP STOMP

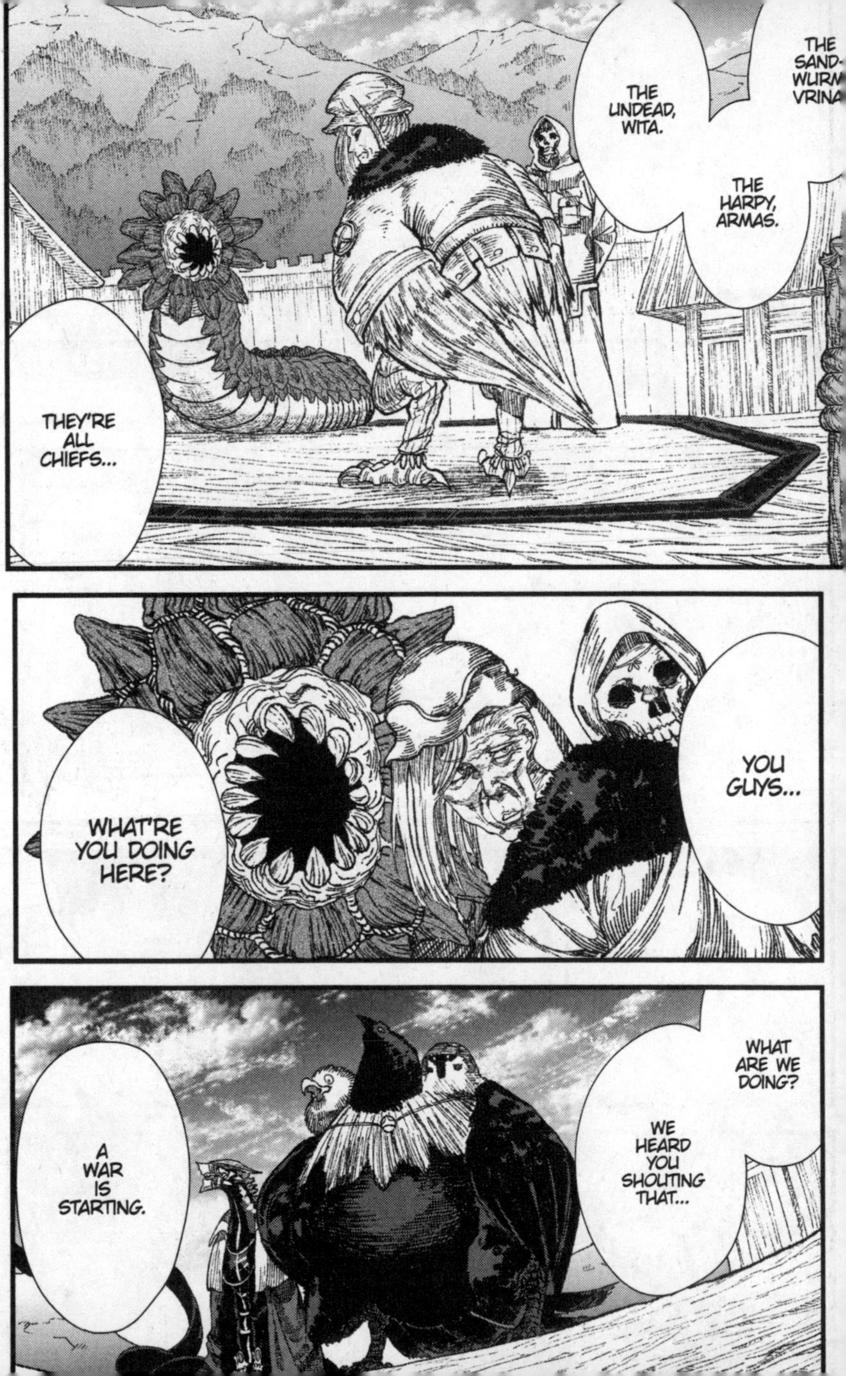
THE SAND-WURM VRINA
THE UNDEAD, WITA.
THE HARPY, ARMAS.
THEY'RE ALL CHIEFS...
YOU GUYS...
WHAT'RE YOU DOING HERE?
WHAT ARE WE DOING?
WE HEARD YOU SHOUTING THAT...
A WAR IS STARTING.

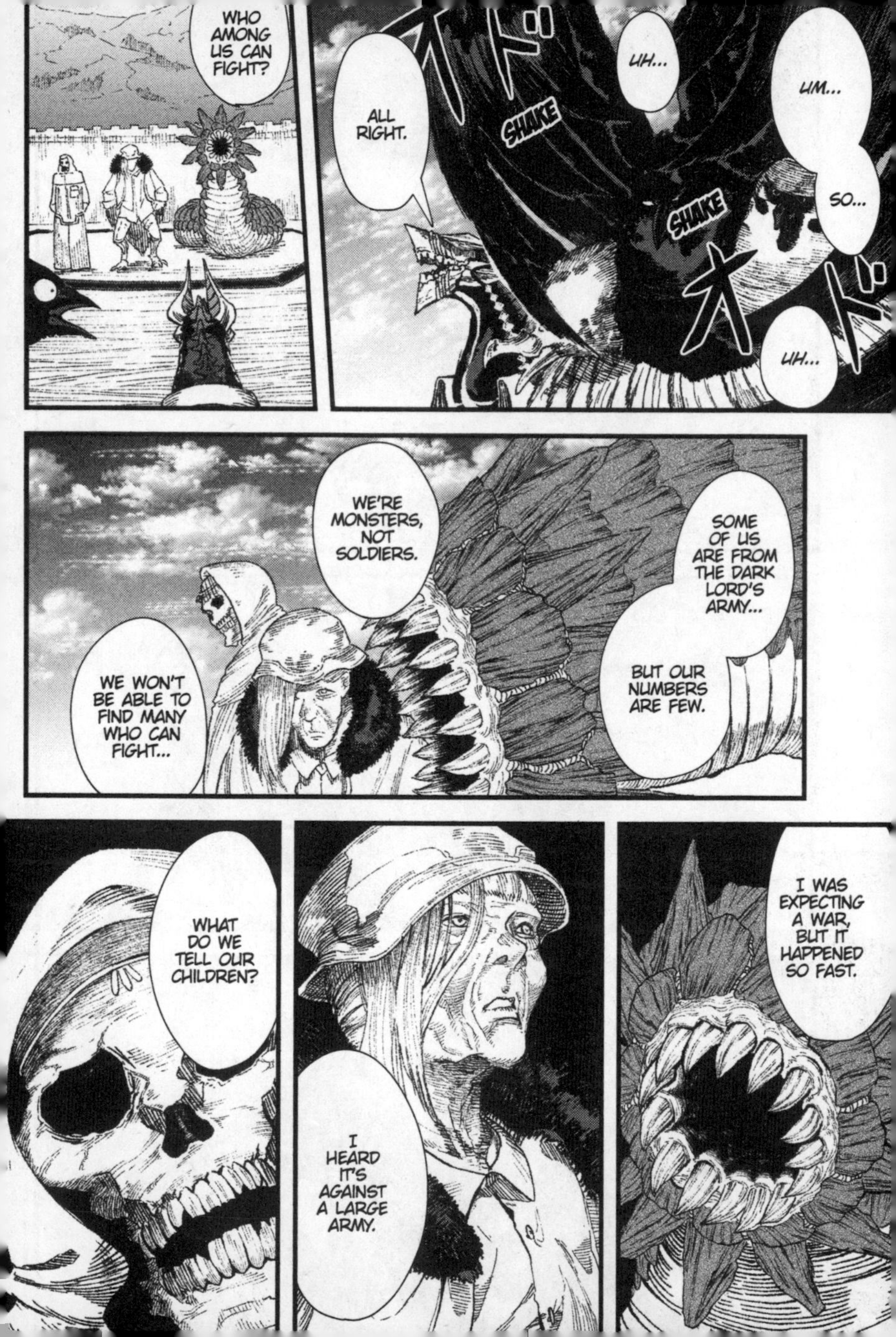
UM...
SO...
UH...
UH...
SHAKE
SHAKE
ALL RIGHT.
WHO AMONG US CAN FIGHT?
SOME OF US ARE FROM THE DARK LORD'S ARMY...
BUT OUR NUMBERS ARE FEW.
WE'RE MONSTERS, NOT SOLDIERS.
WE WON'T BE ABLE TO FIND MANY WHO CAN FIGHT...
I WAS EXPECTING A WAR, BUT IT HAPPENED SO FAST.
I HEARD IT'S AGAINST A LARGE ARMY.
WHAT DO WE TELL OUR CHILDREN?

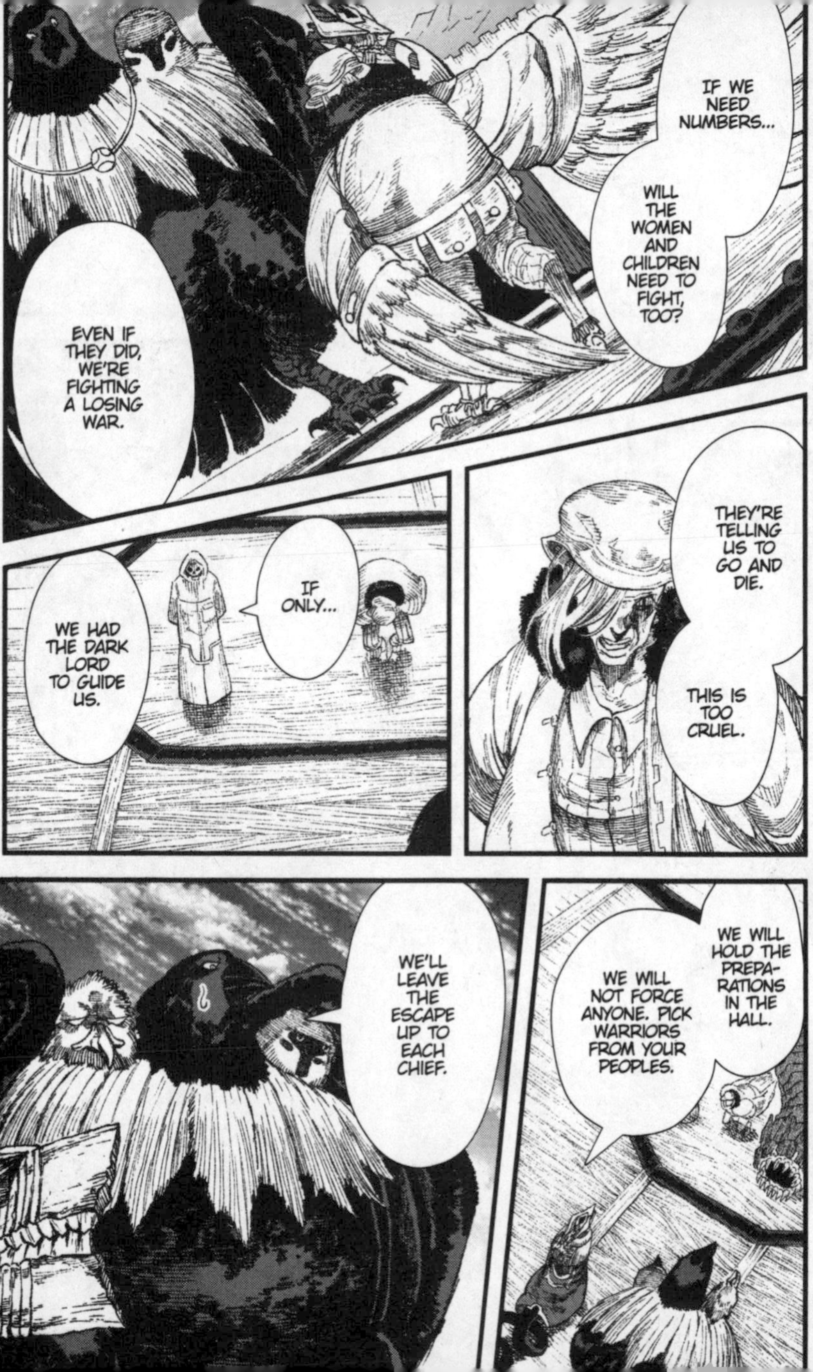
IF WE NEED NUMBERS...
WILL THE WOMEN AND CHILDREN NEED TO FIGHT, TOO?
EVEN IF THEY DID, WE'RE FIGHTING A LOSING WAR.
THEY'RE TELLING US TO GO AND DIE.
THIS IS TOO CRUEL.
IF ONLY...
WE HAD THE DARK LORD TO GUIDE US.
WE WILL HOLD THE PREPARATIONS IN THE HALL.
WE WILL NOT FORCE ANYONE. PICK WARRIORS FROM YOUR PEOPLES.
WE'LL LEAVE THE ESCAPE UP TO EACH CHIEF.

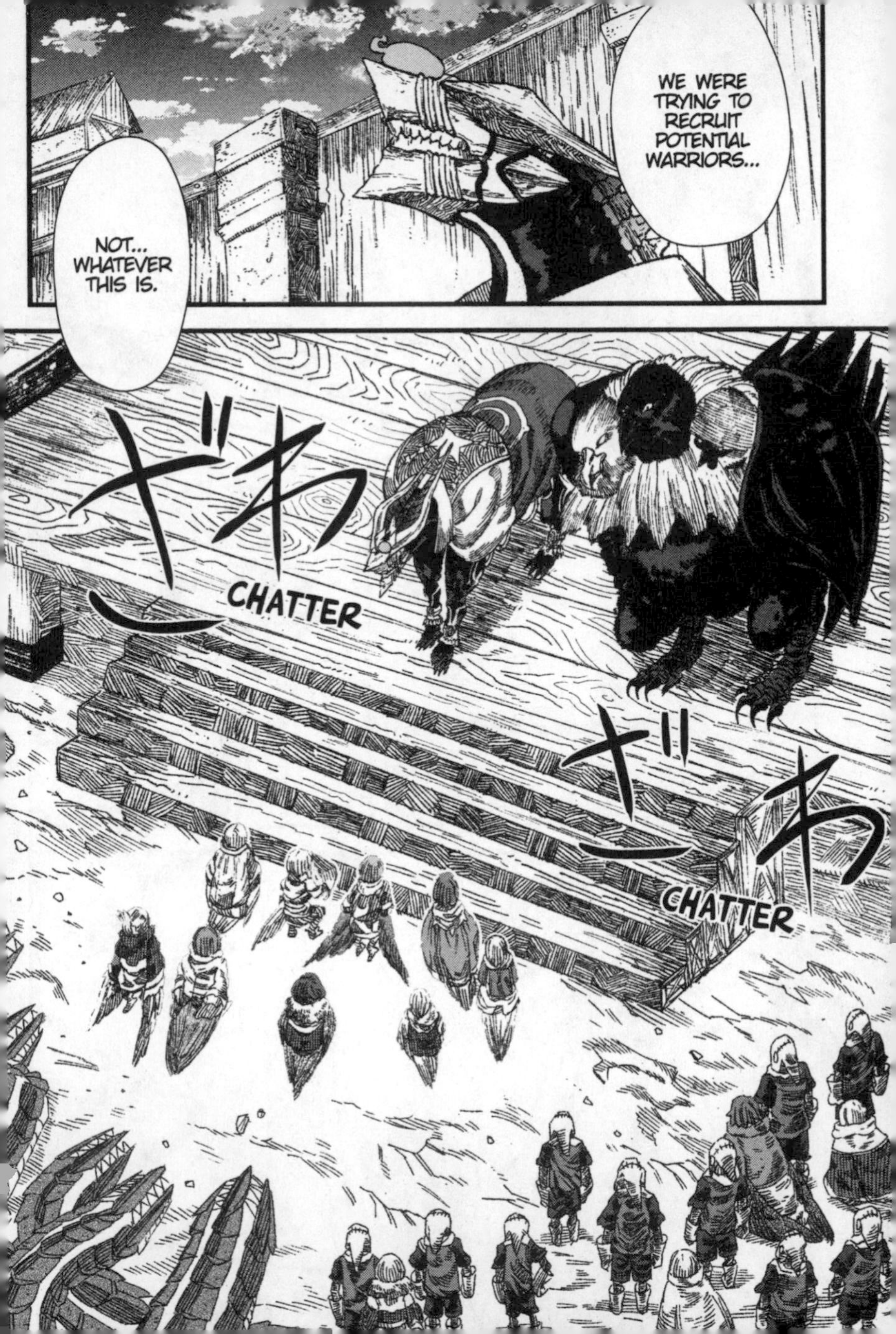
WE WERE TRYING TO RECRUIT POTENTIAL WARRIORS...
NOT... WHATEVER THIS IS.
ざわっ
CHATTER
ざわっ
CHATTER

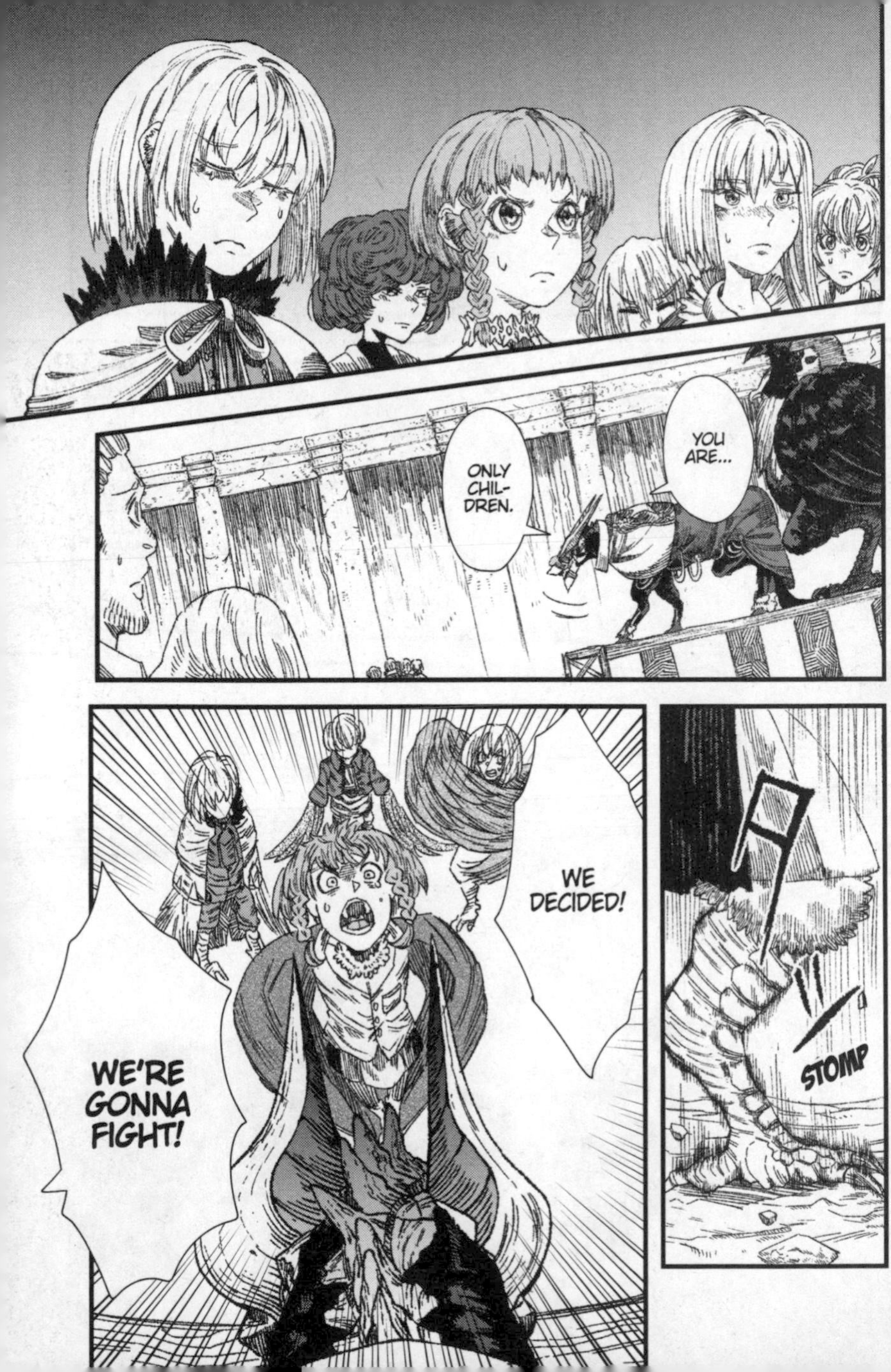
YOU ARE...
ONLY CHIL-DREN.
STOMP
WE DECIDED!
WE'RE GONNA FIGHT!

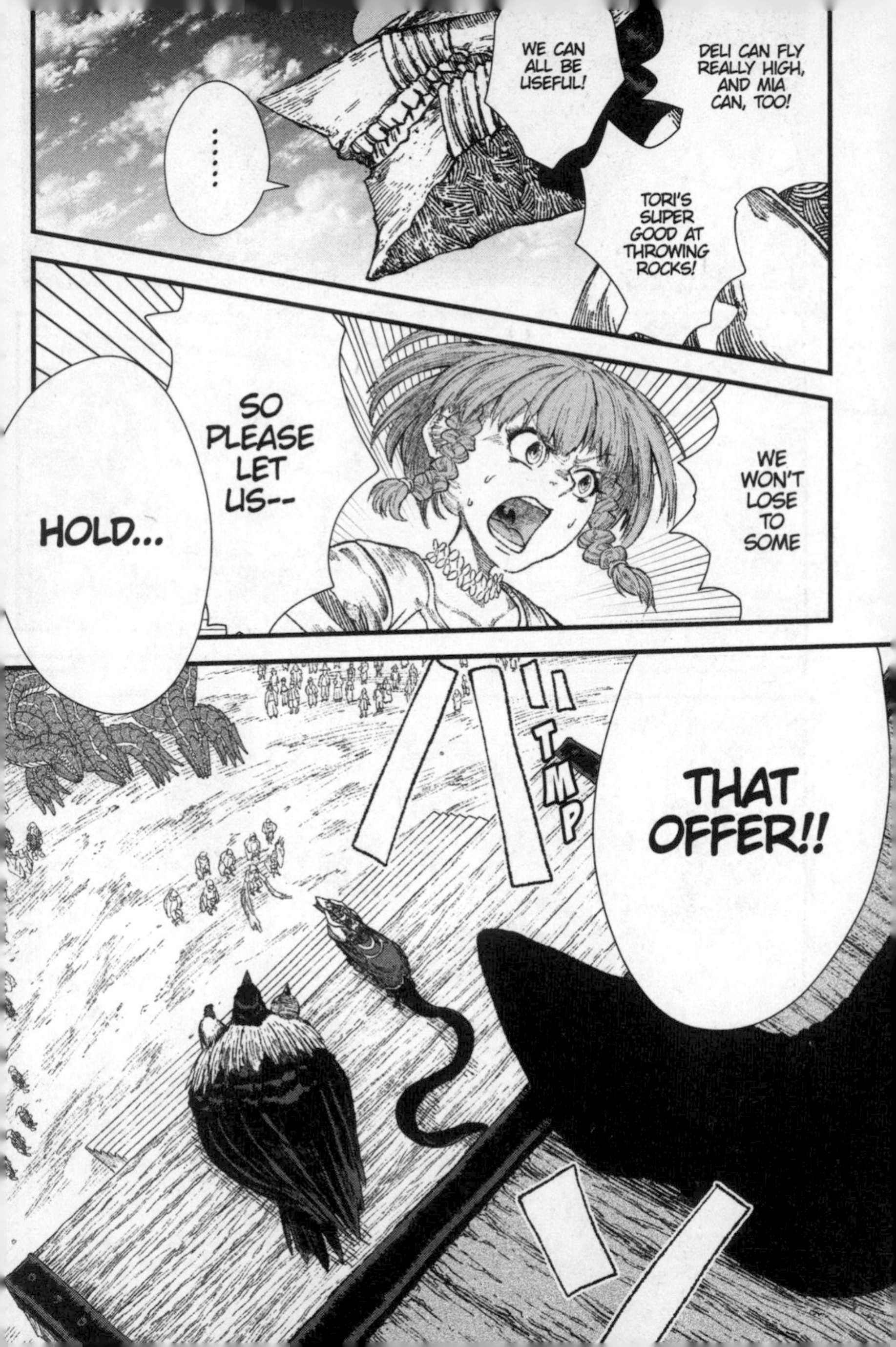
DELI CAN FLY REALLY HIGH, AND MIA CAN, TOO!
TORI'S SUPER GOOD AT THROWING ROCKS!
WE CAN ALL BE USEFUL!
......
WE WON'T LOSE TO SOME
SO PLEASE LET US--
HOLD...
TMP
THAT OFFER!!

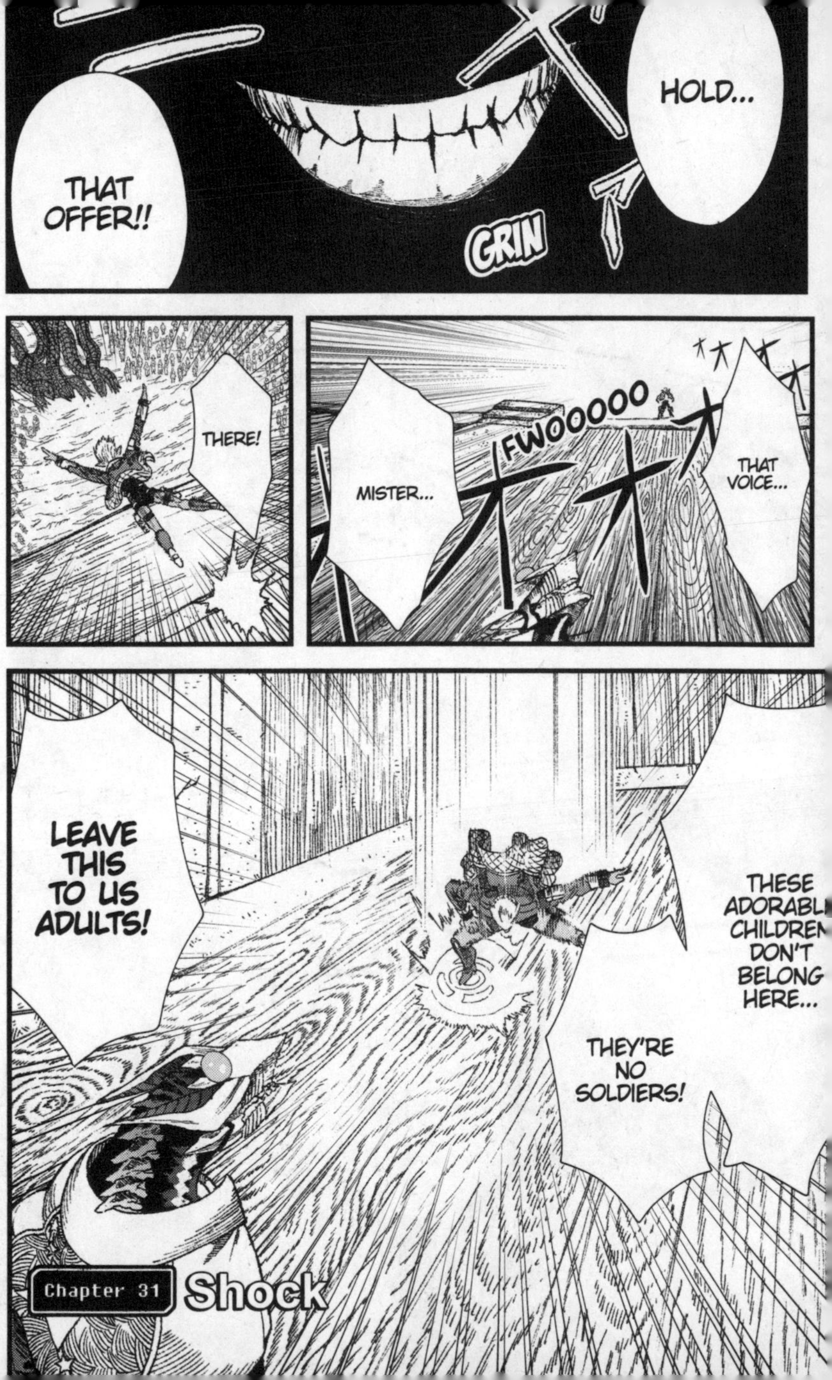
HOLD...
GRIN
THAT OFFER!!
THAT VOICE...
FWOOOOO
MISTER...
THERE!
THESE ADORABL CHILDREN DON'T BELONG HERE...
THEY'RE NO SOLDIERS!
LEAVE THIS TO US ADULTS!
Chapter 31 Shock

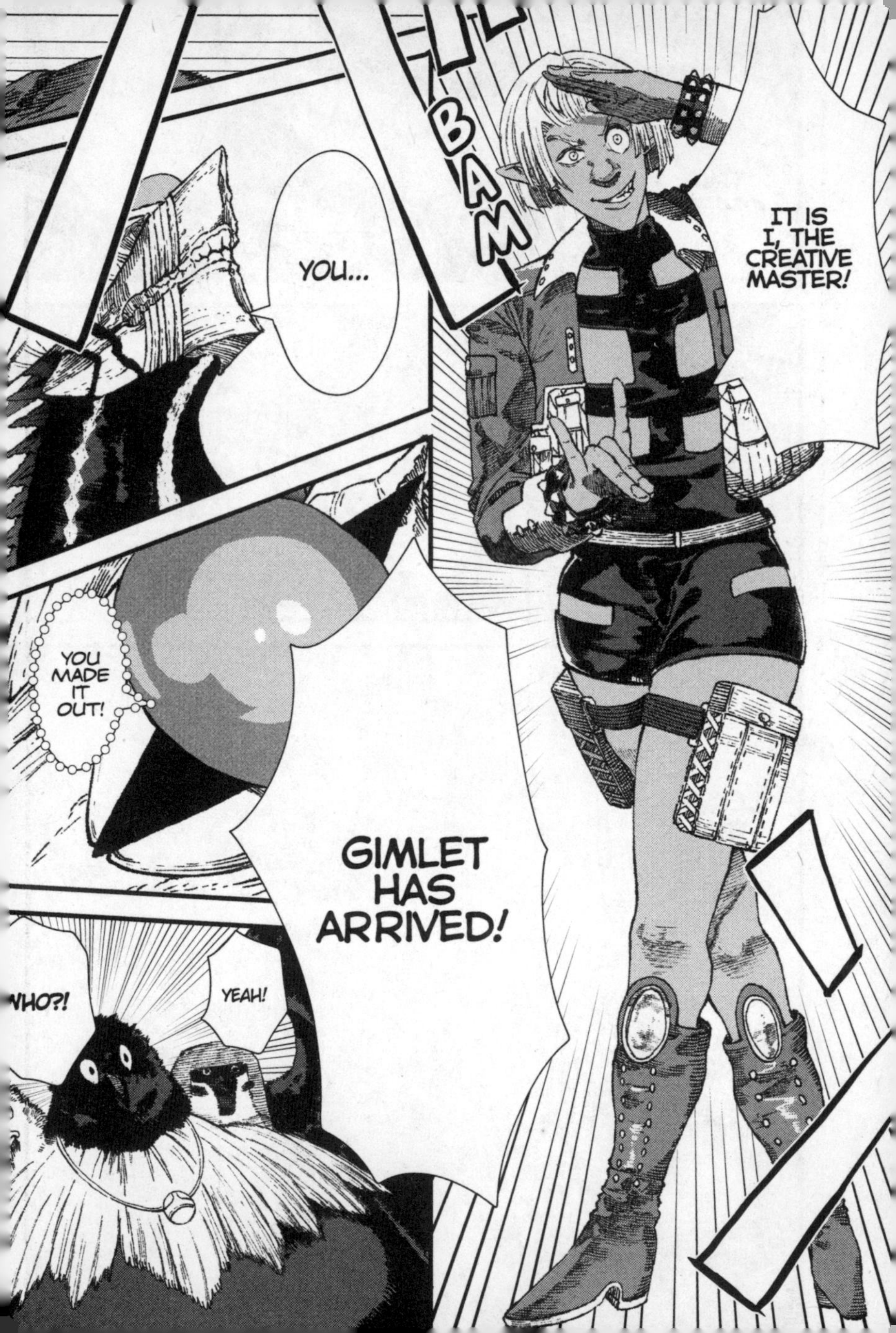
BAM
IT IS I, THE CREATIVE MASTER!
GIMLET HAS ARRIVED!
YOU...
YOU MADE IT OUT!
YEAH!
WHO?!

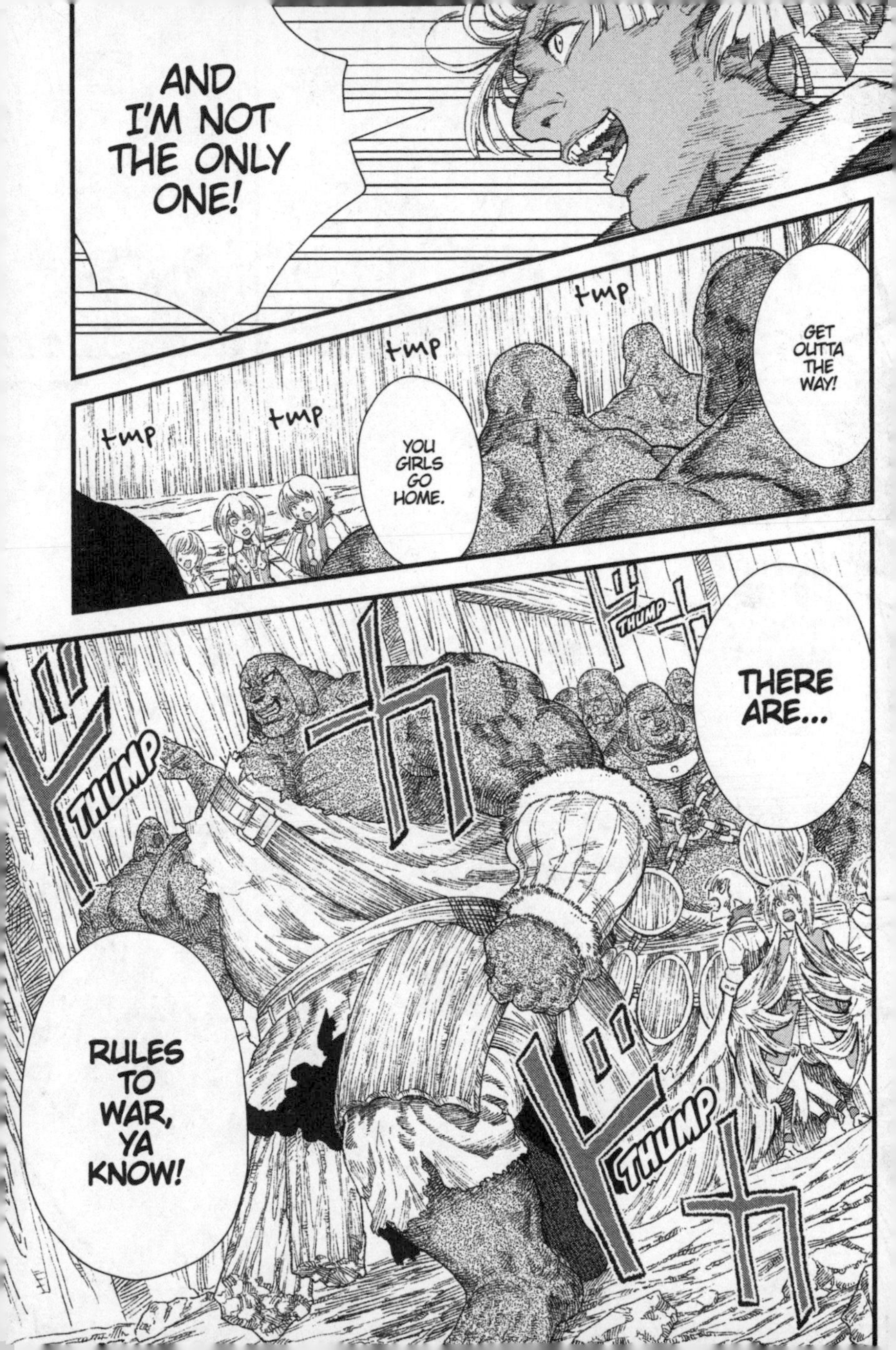
AND I'M NOT THE ONLY ONE!
tmp
GET OUTTA THE WAY!
tmp
tmp
tmp
YOU GIRLS GO HOME.
THUMP
THERE ARE...
THUMP
THUMP
RULES TO WAR, YA KNOW!

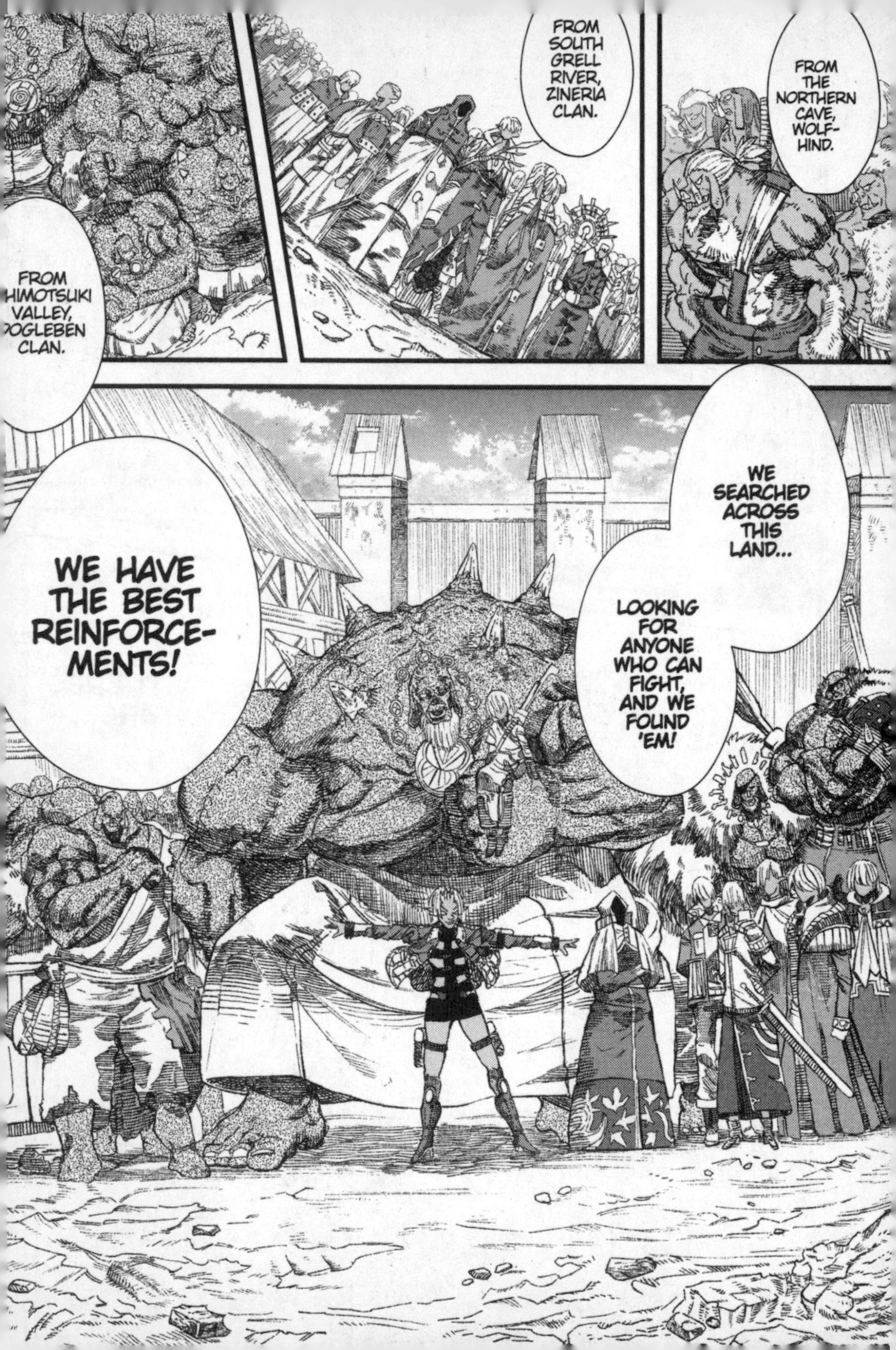
FROM THE NORTHERN CAVE, WOLF-HIND.
FROM SOUTH GRELL RIVER, ZINERIA CLAN.
FROM HIMOTSUKI VALLEY, OGLEBEN CLAN.
WE SEARCHED ACROSS THIS LAND...
LOOKING FOR ANYONE WHO CAN FIGHT, AND WE FOUND 'EM!
WE HAVE THE BEST REINFORCE-MENTS!

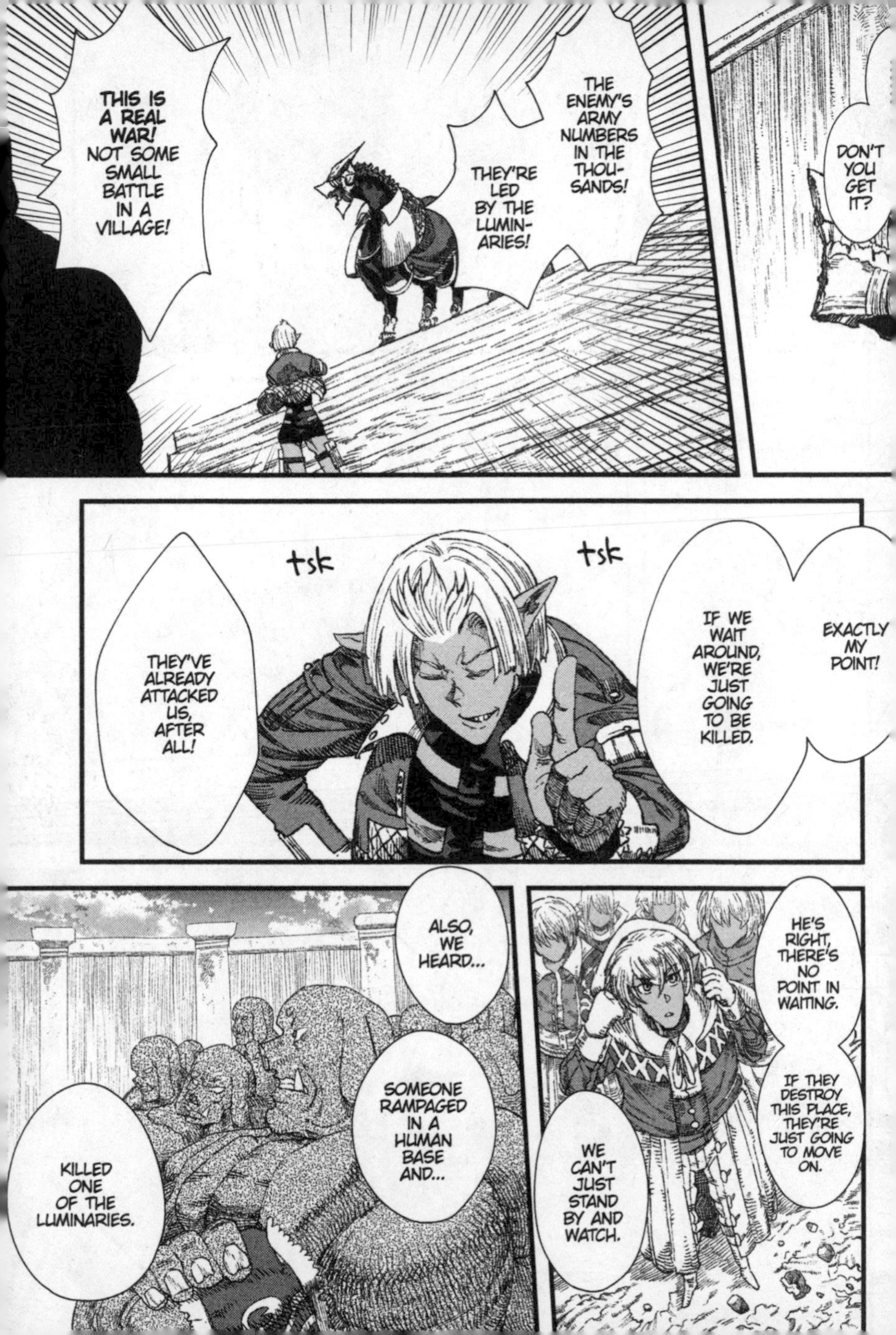
DON'T YOU GET IT?
THE ENEMY'S ARMY NUMBERS IN THE THOUSANDS!
THEY'RE LED BY THE LUMINARIES!
THIS IS A REAL WAR! NOT SOME SMALL BATTLE IN A VILLAGE!
EXACTLY MY POINT!
tsk
IF WE WAIT AROUND, WE'RE JUST GOING TO BE KILLED.
tsk
THEY'VE ALREADY ATTACKED US, AFTER ALL!
HE'S RIGHT, THERE'S NO POINT IN WAITING.
IF THEY DESTROY THIS PLACE, THEY'RE JUST GOING TO MOVE ON.
WE CAN'T JUST STAND BY AND WATCH.
ALSO, WE HEARD...
SOMEONE RAMPAGED IN A HUMAN BASE AND...
KILLED ONE OF THE LUMINARIES.

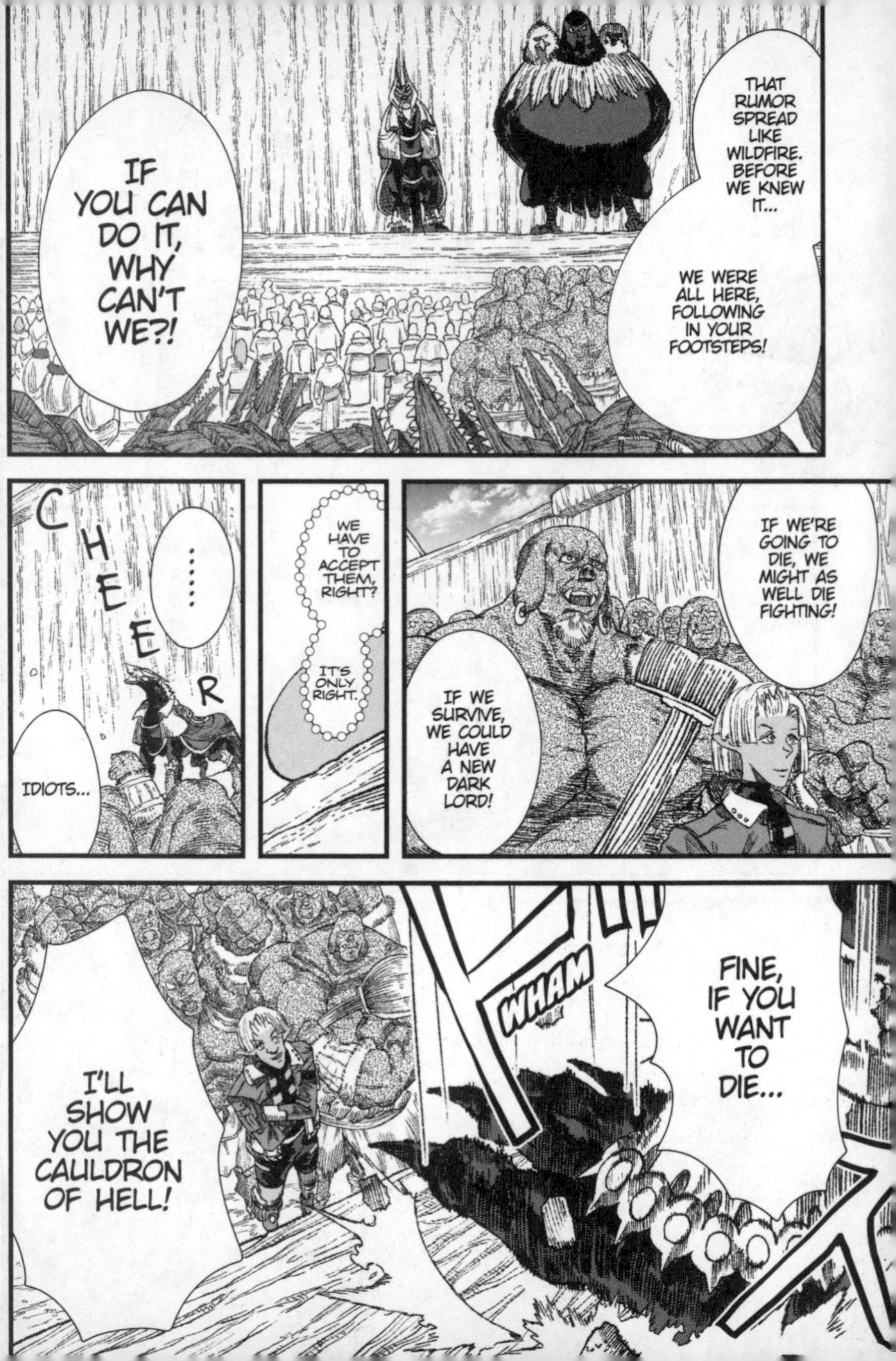
THAT RUMOR SPREAD LIKE WILDFIRE. BEFORE WE KNEW IT...
WE WERE ALL HERE, FOLLOWING IN YOUR FOOTSTEPS!
IF YOU CAN DO IT, WHY CAN'T WE?!
IF WE'RE GOING TO DIE, WE MIGHT AS WELL DIE FIGHTING!
IF WE SURVIVE, WE COULD HAVE A NEW DARK LORD!
WE HAVE TO ACCEPT THEM, RIGHT?
IT'S ONLY RIGHT.
CHEER
......
IDIOTS...
FINE, IF YOU WANT TO DIE...
WHAM
I'LL SHOW YOU THE CAULDRON OF HELL!

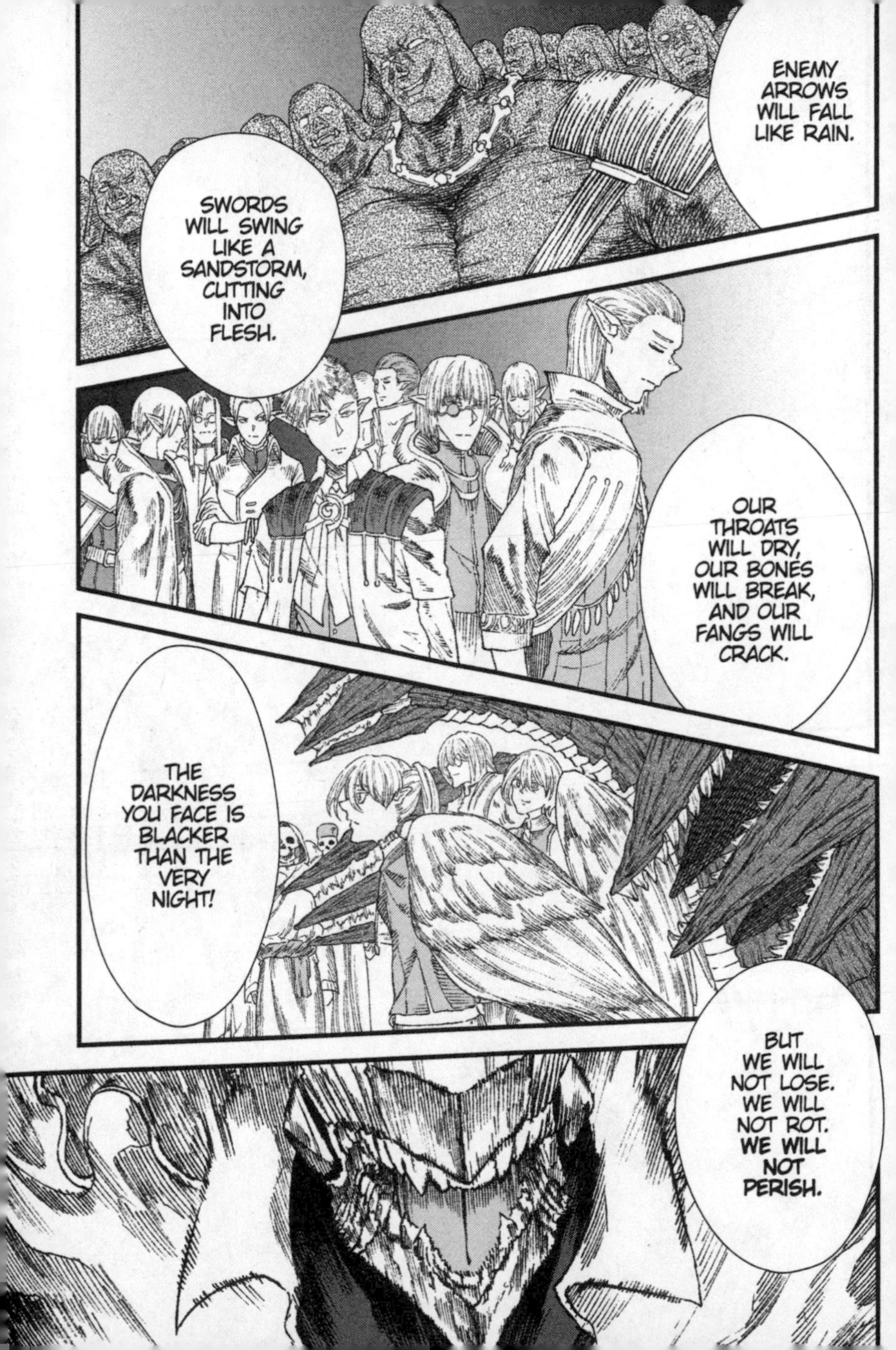
ENEMY ARROWS WILL FALL LIKE RAIN.
SWORDS WILL SWING LIKE A SANDSTORM, CUTTING INTO FLESH.
OUR THROATS WILL DRY, OUR BONES WILL BREAK, AND OUR FANGS WILL CRACK.
THE DARKNESS YOU FACE IS BLACKER THAN THE VERY NIGHT!
BUT WE WILL NOT LOSE. WE WILL NOT ROT. WE WILL NOT PERISH.

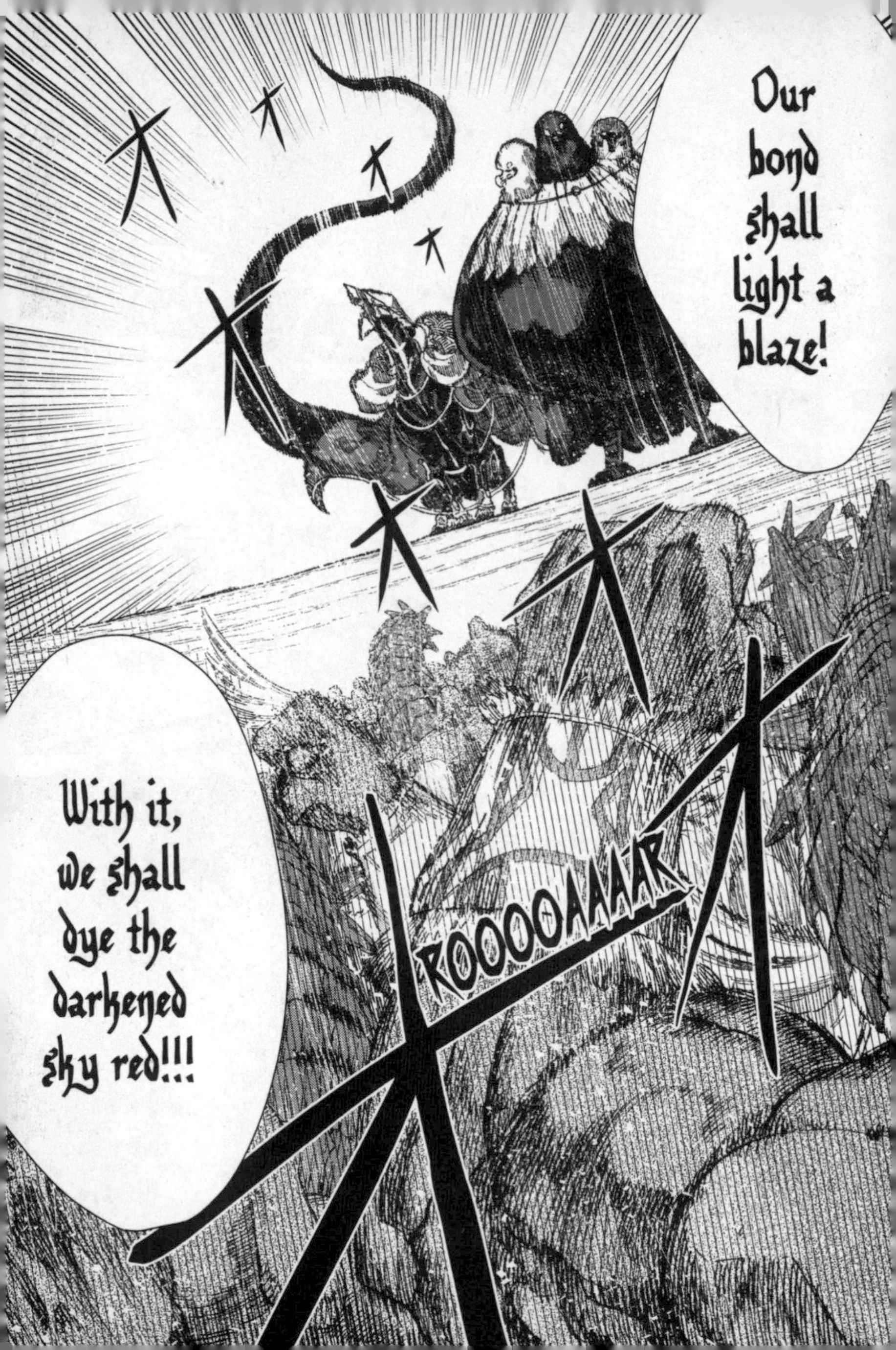
Our bond shall light a blaze!
With it, we shall dye the darkened sky red!!!
ROOOOAAAAR

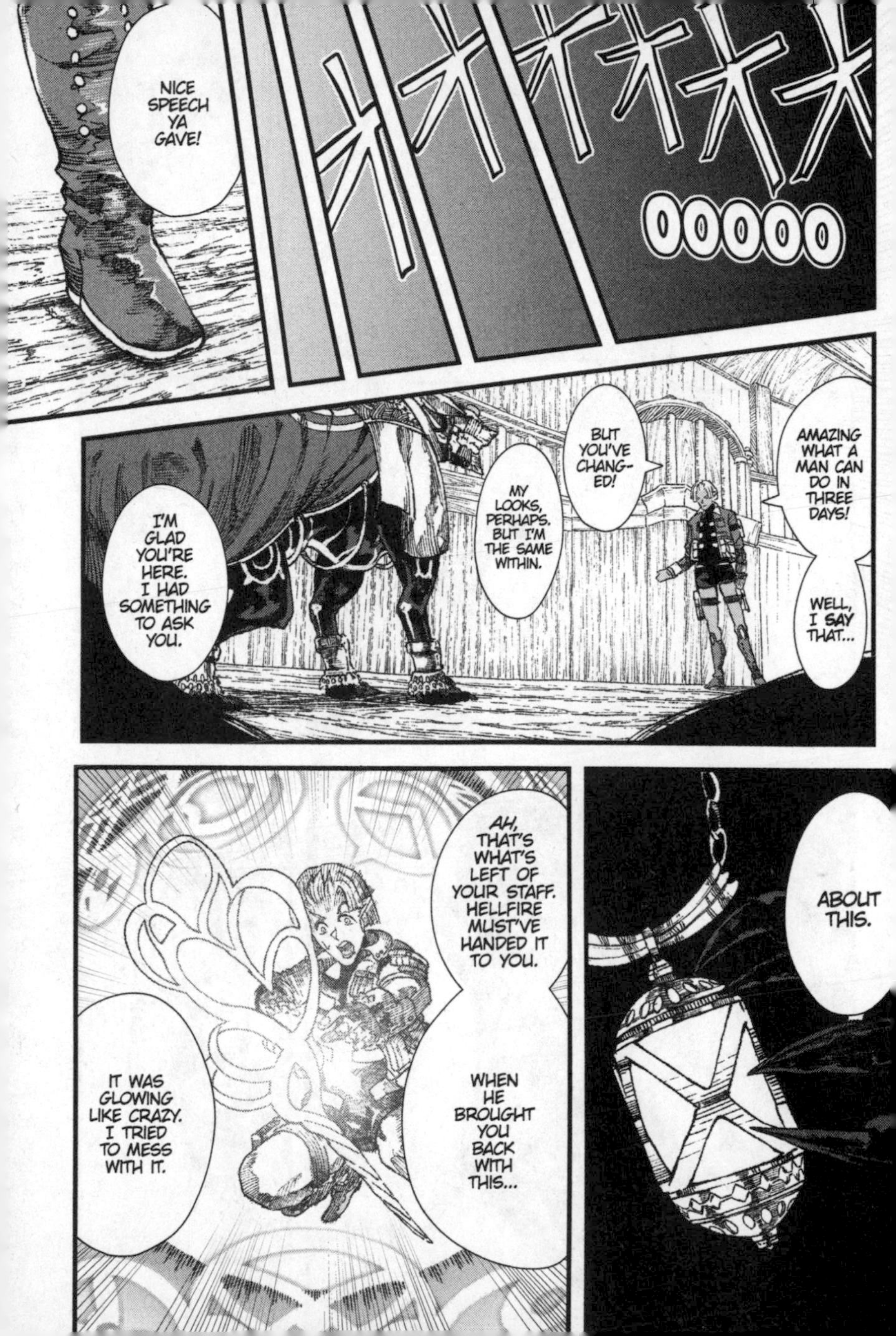
OOOOO
NICE SPEECH YA GAVE!
AMAZING WHAT A MAN CAN DO IN THREE DAYS!
WELL, I SAY THAT...
BUT YOU'VE CHANG-ED!
MY LOOKS, PERHAPS. BUT I'M THE SAME WITHIN.
I'M GLAD YOU'RE HERE. I HAD SOMETHING TO ASK YOU.
ABOUT THIS.
AH, THAT'S WHAT'S LEFT OF YOUR STAFF. HELLFIRE MUST'VE HANDED IT TO YOU.
WHEN HE BROUGHT YOU BACK WITH THIS...
IT WAS GLOWING LIKE CRAZY. I TRIED TO MESS WITH IT.

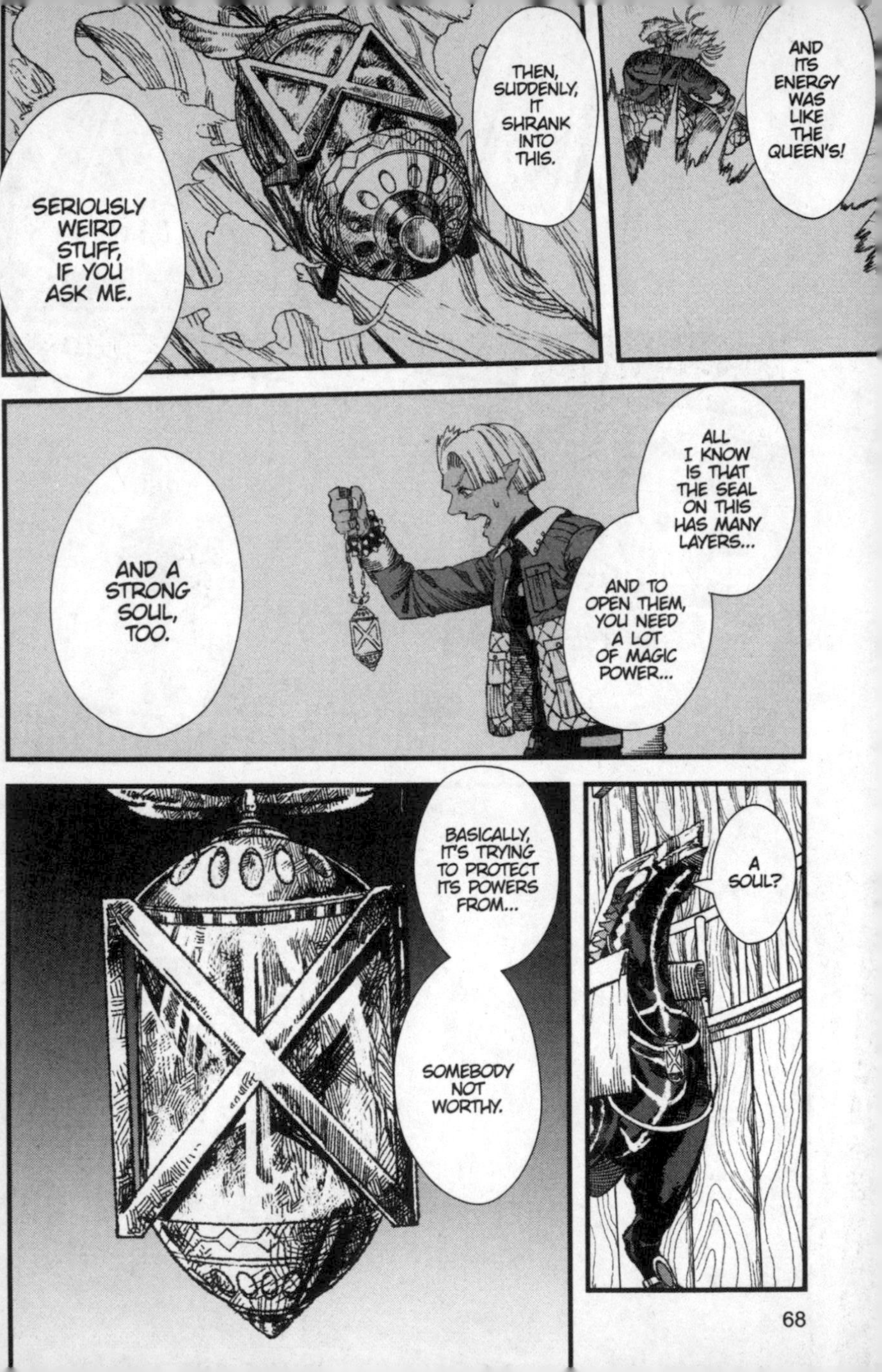
AND ITS ENERGY WAS LIKE THE QUEEN'S!
THEN, SUDDENLY, IT SHRANK INTO THIS.
SERIOUSLY WEIRD STUFF, IF YOU ASK ME.
ALL I KNOW IS THAT THE SEAL ON THIS HAS MANY LAYERS...
AND TO OPEN THEM, YOU NEED A LOT OF MAGIC POWER...
AND A STRONG SOUL, TOO.
A SOUL?
BASICALLY, IT'S TRYING TO PROTECT ITS POWERS FROM...
SOMEBODY NOT WORTHY.

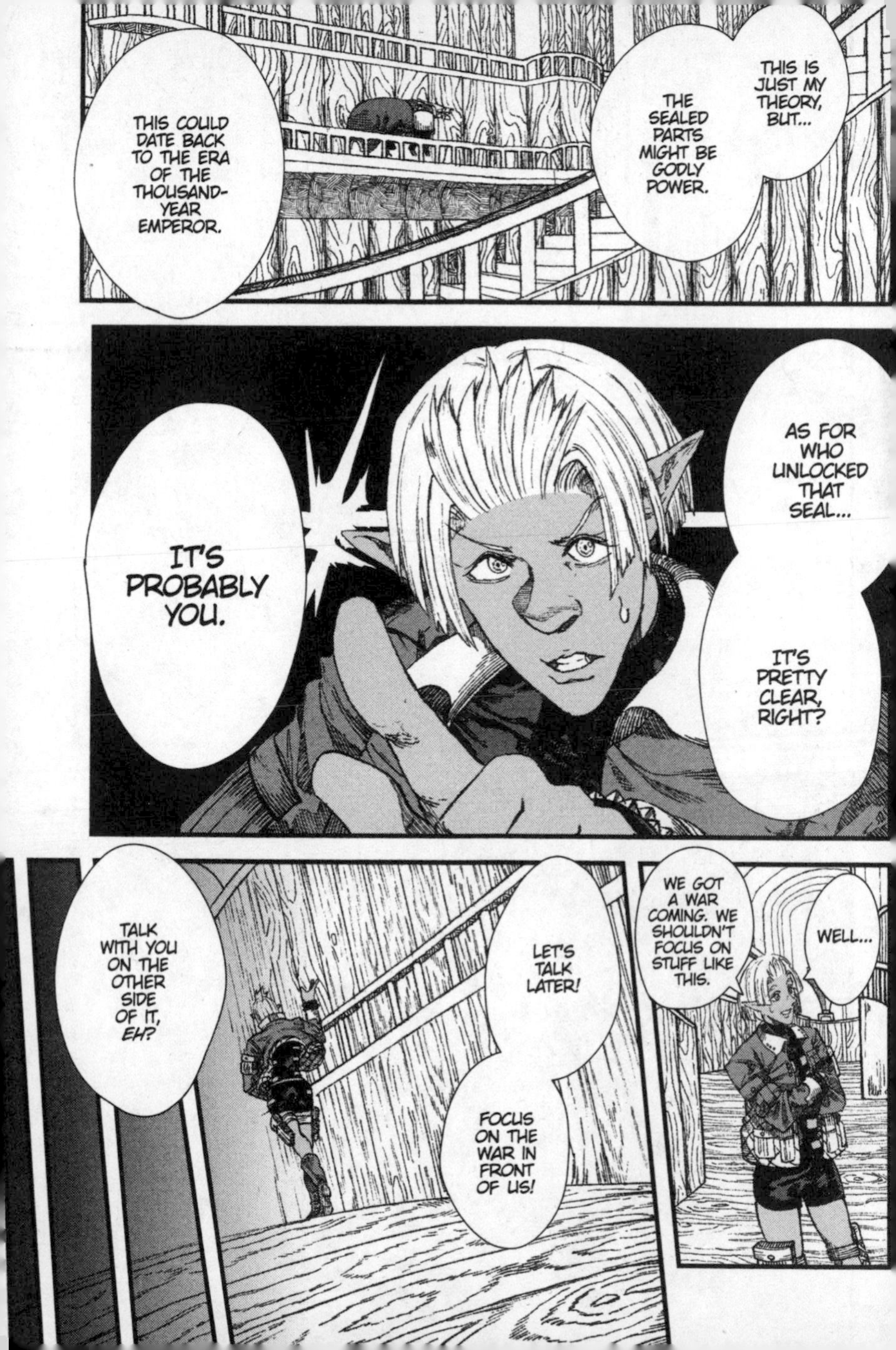
THIS IS JUST MY THEORY, BUT...
THE SEALED PARTS MIGHT BE GODLY POWER.
THIS COULD DATE BACK TO THE ERA OF THE THOUSAND-YEAR EMPEROR.
AS FOR WHO UNLOCKED THAT SEAL...
IT'S PRETTY CLEAR, RIGHT?
IT'S PROBABLY YOU.
WELL...
WE GOT A WAR COMING. WE SHOULDN'T FOCUS ON STUFF LIKE THIS.
LET'S TALK LATER!
FOCUS ON THE WAR IN FRONT OF US!
TALK WITH YOU ON THE OTHER SIDE OF IT, EH?

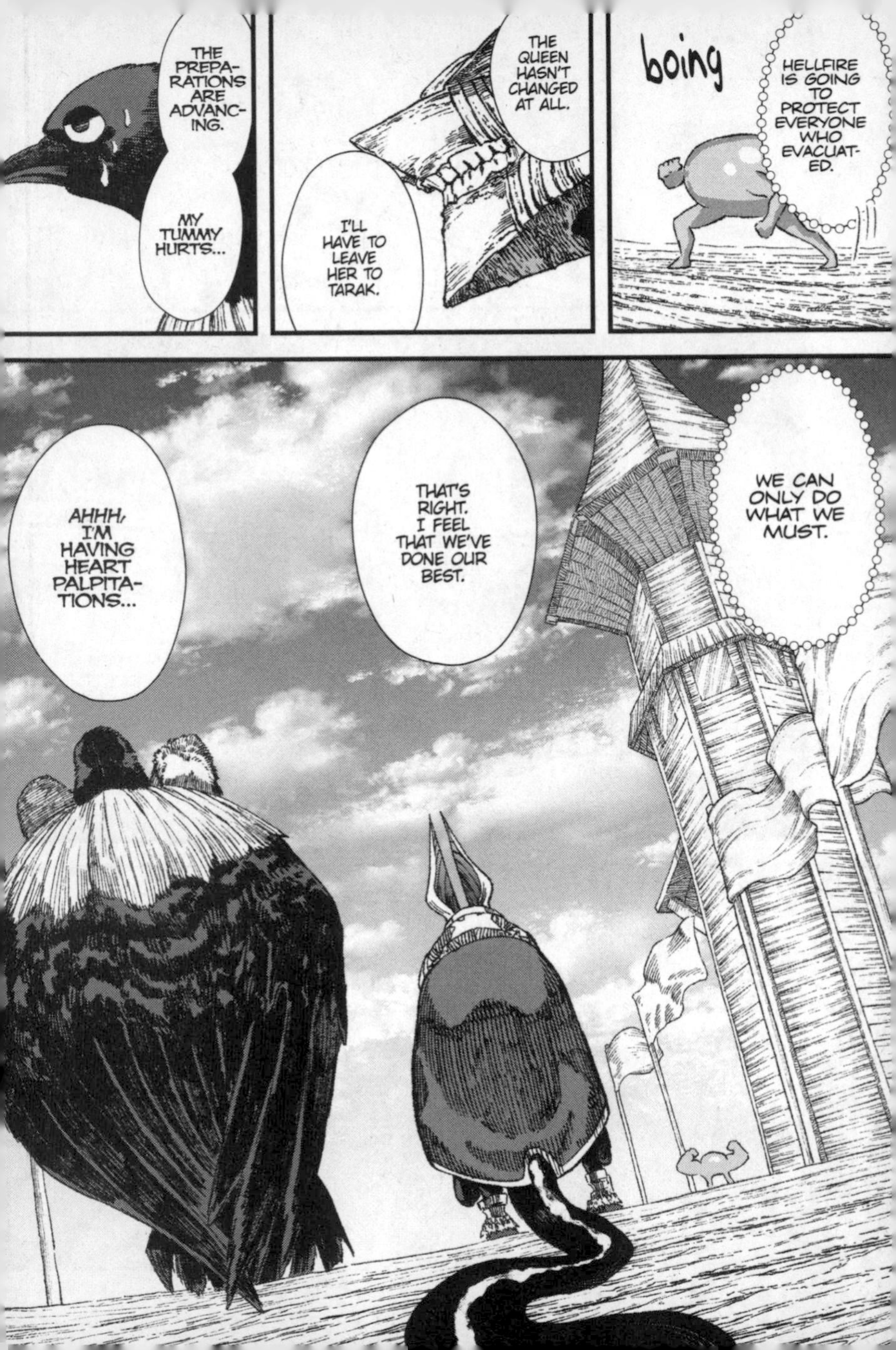
boing
HELLFIRE IS GOING TO PROTECT EVERYONE WHO EVACUAT-ED.
THE QUEEN HASN'T CHANGED AT ALL.
I'LL HAVE TO LEAVE HER TO TARAK.
THE PREPA-RATIONS ARE ADVANC-ING.
MY TUMMY HURTS...
WE CAN ONLY DO WHAT WE MUST.
THAT'S RIGHT. I FEEL THAT WE'VE DONE OUR BEST.
AHHH, I'M HAVING HEART PALPITA-TIONS...

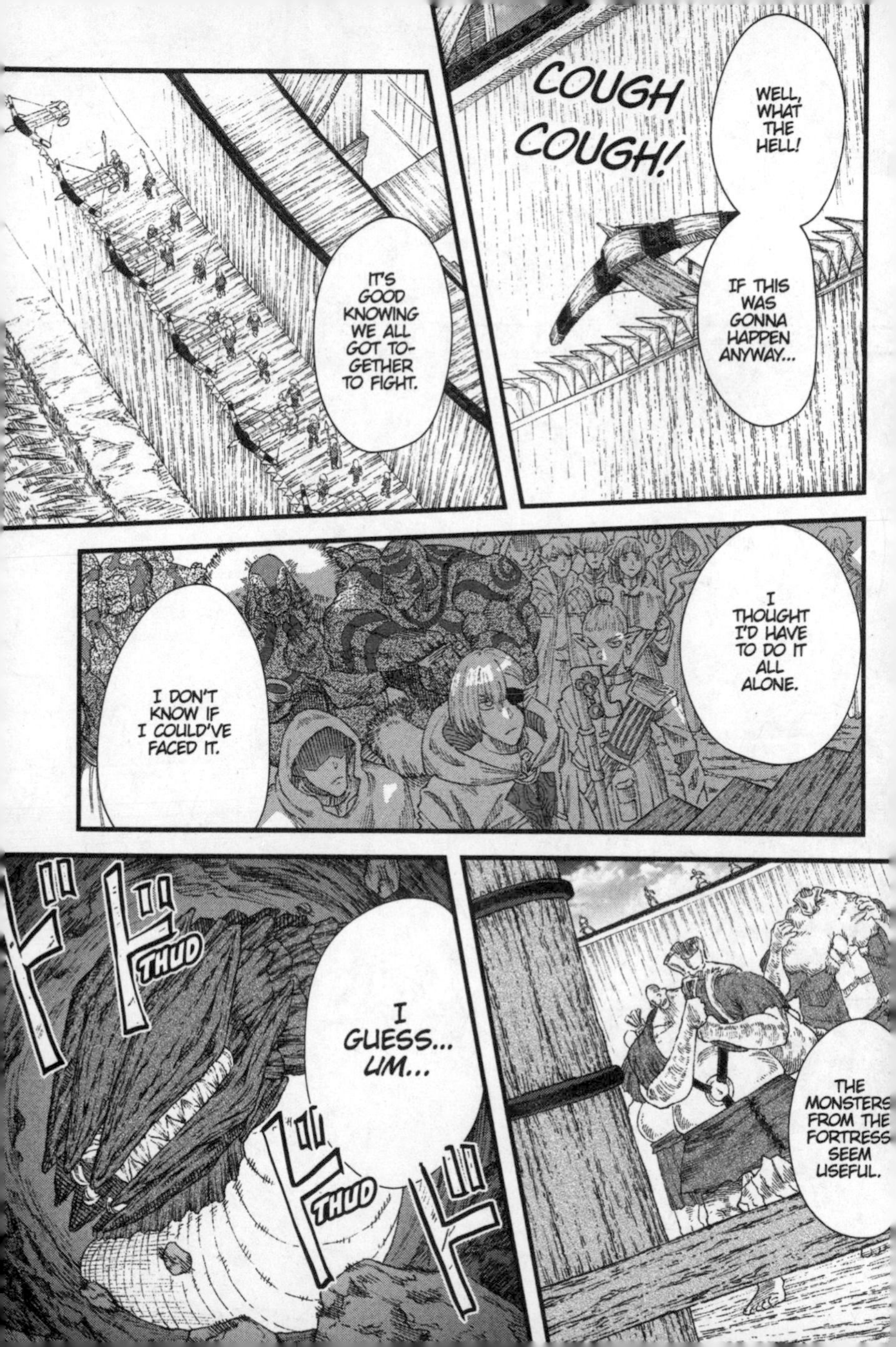
COUGH COUGH!
WELL, WHAT THE HELL!
IF THIS WAS GONNA HAPPEN ANYWAY...
IT'S GOOD KNOWING WE ALL GOT TO-GETHER TO FIGHT.
I THOUGHT I'D HAVE TO DO IT ALL ALONE.
I DON'T KNOW IF I COULD'VE FACED IT.
THE MONSTERS FROM THE FORTRESS SEEM USEFUL.
I GUESS... UM...
THUD
THUD

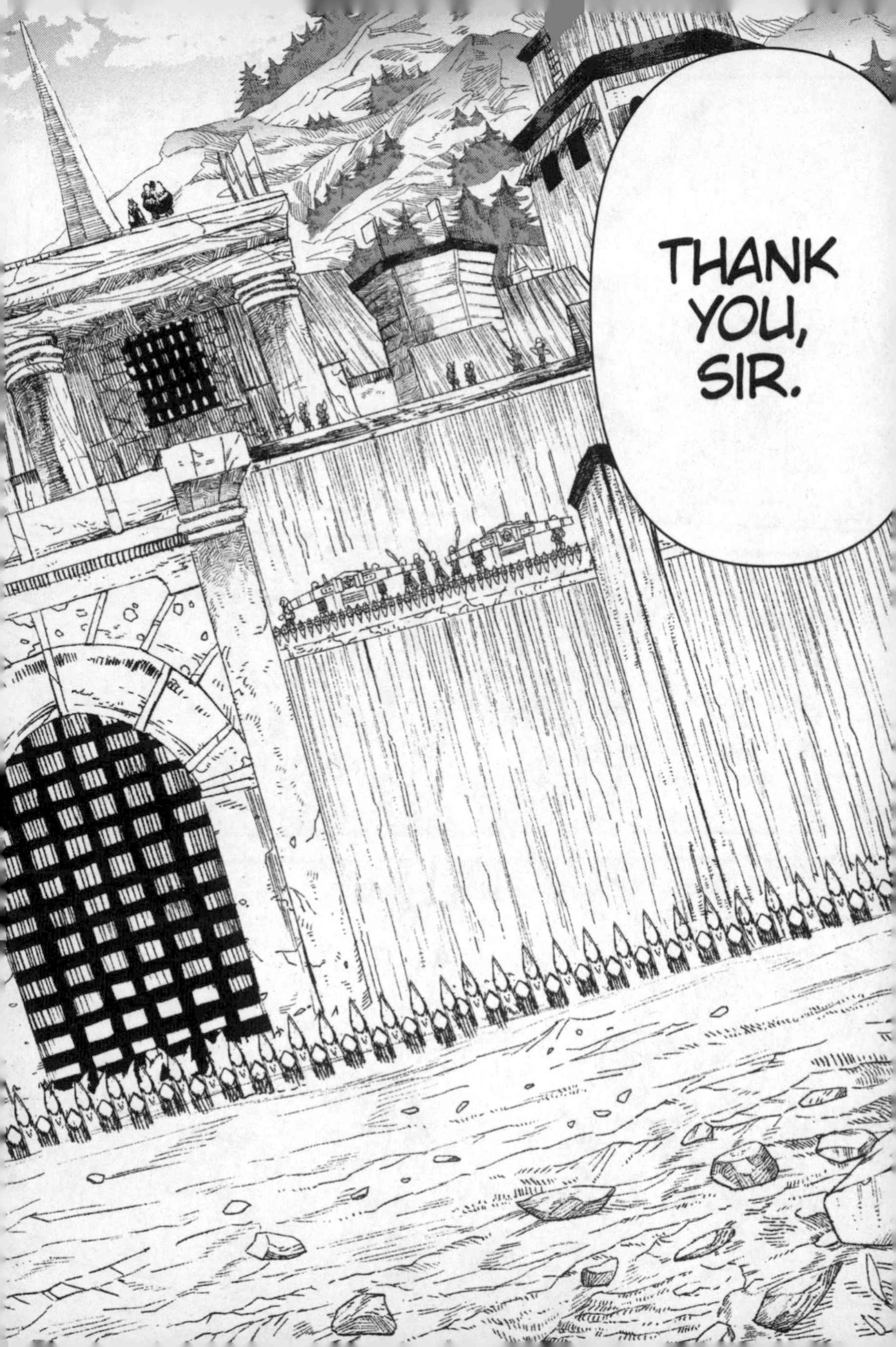
THANK YOU, SIR.

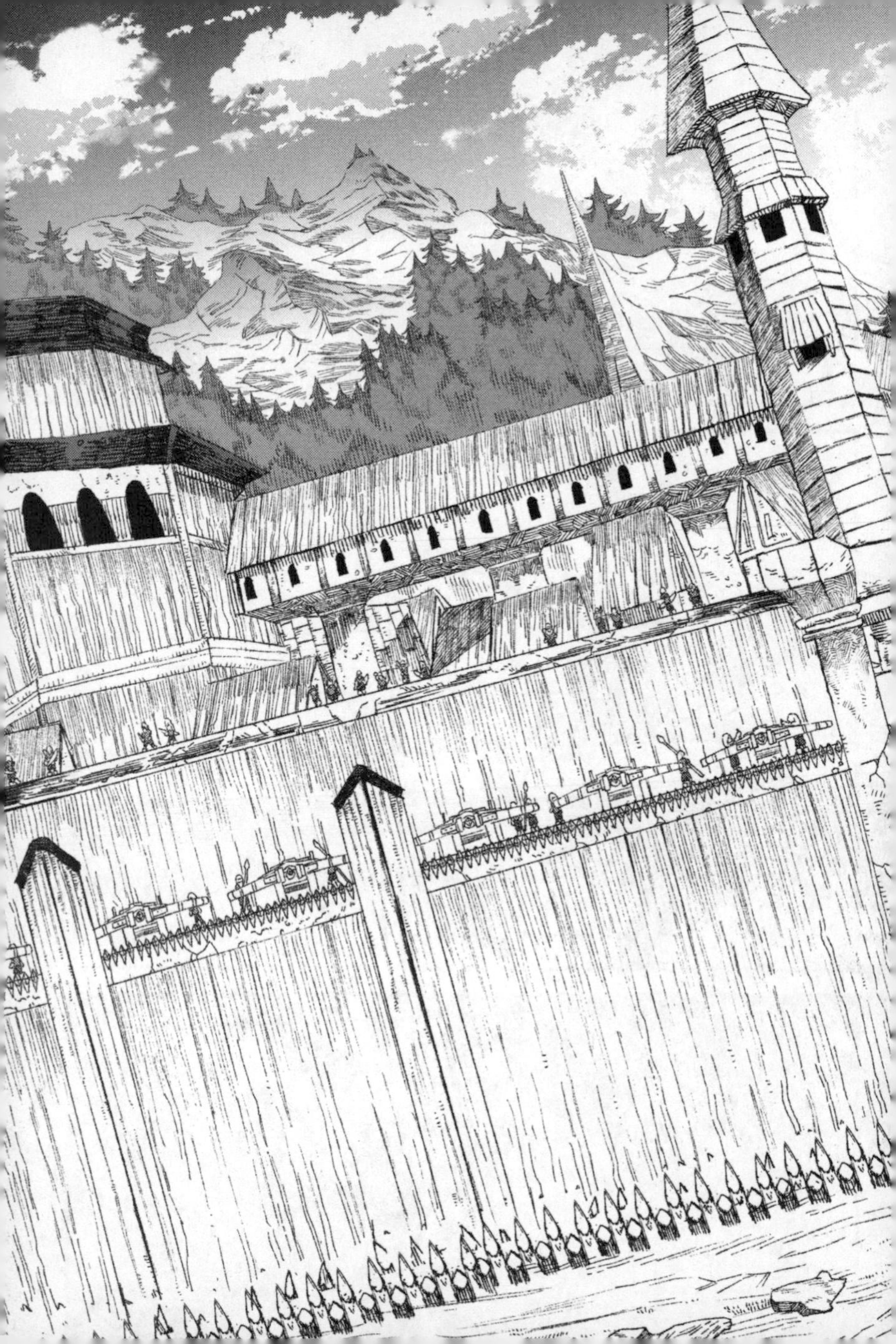

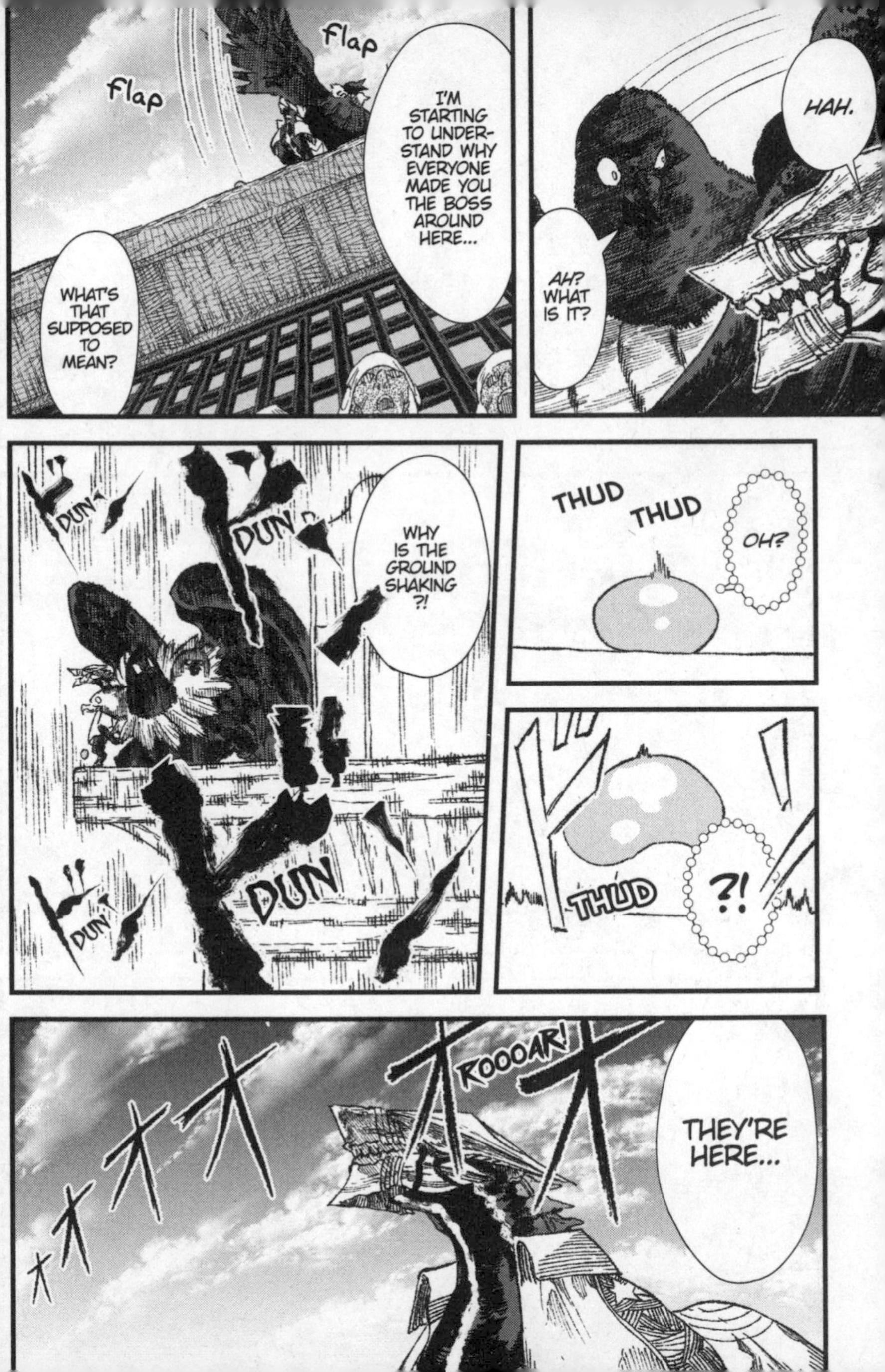
HAH.
AH? WHAT IS IT?
Flap
Flap
I'M STARTING TO UNDER-STAND WHY EVERYONE MADE YOU THE BOSS AROUND HERE...
WHAT'S THAT SUPPOSED TO MEAN?
THUD
THUD
OH?
THUD
?!
DUN
DUN
WHY IS THE GROUND SHAKING ?!
DUN
DUN
ROOOAR!
THEY'RE HERE...

thud

thud

CRAAAAACK

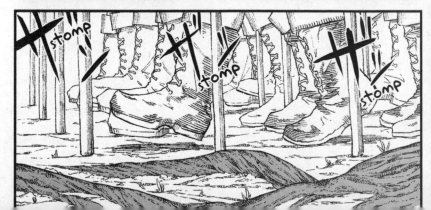

stomp

stomp

stomp

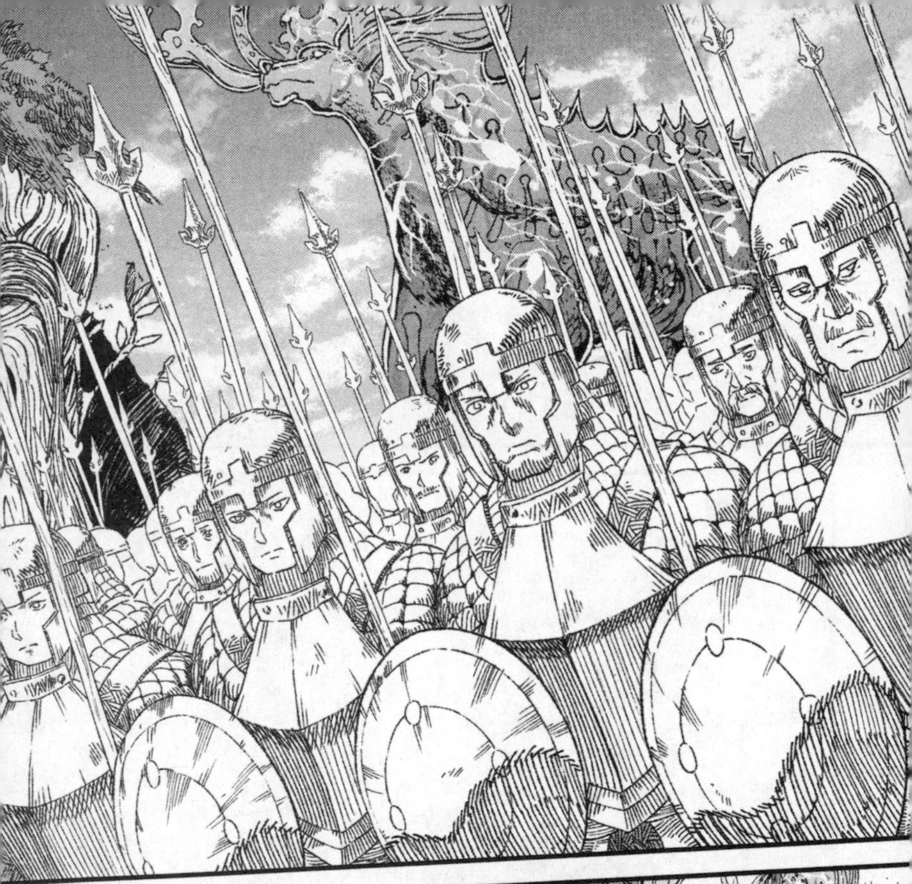
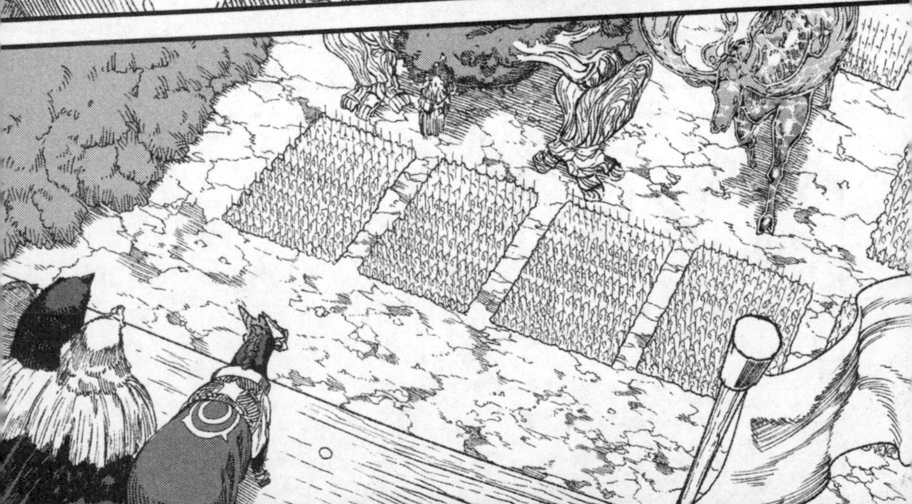

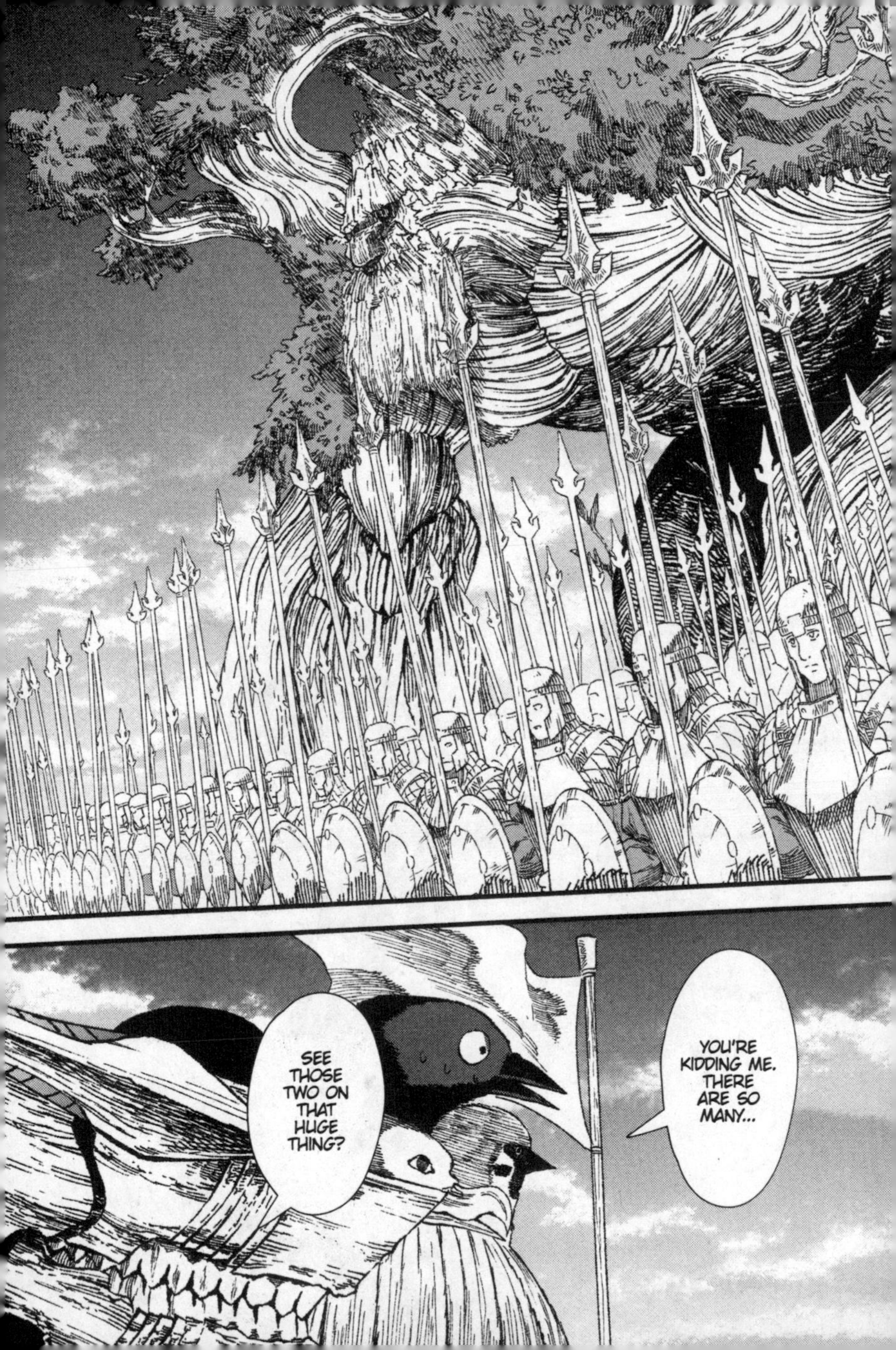
YOU'RE KIDDING ME. THERE ARE SO MANY...
SEE THOSE TWO ON THAT HUGE THING?

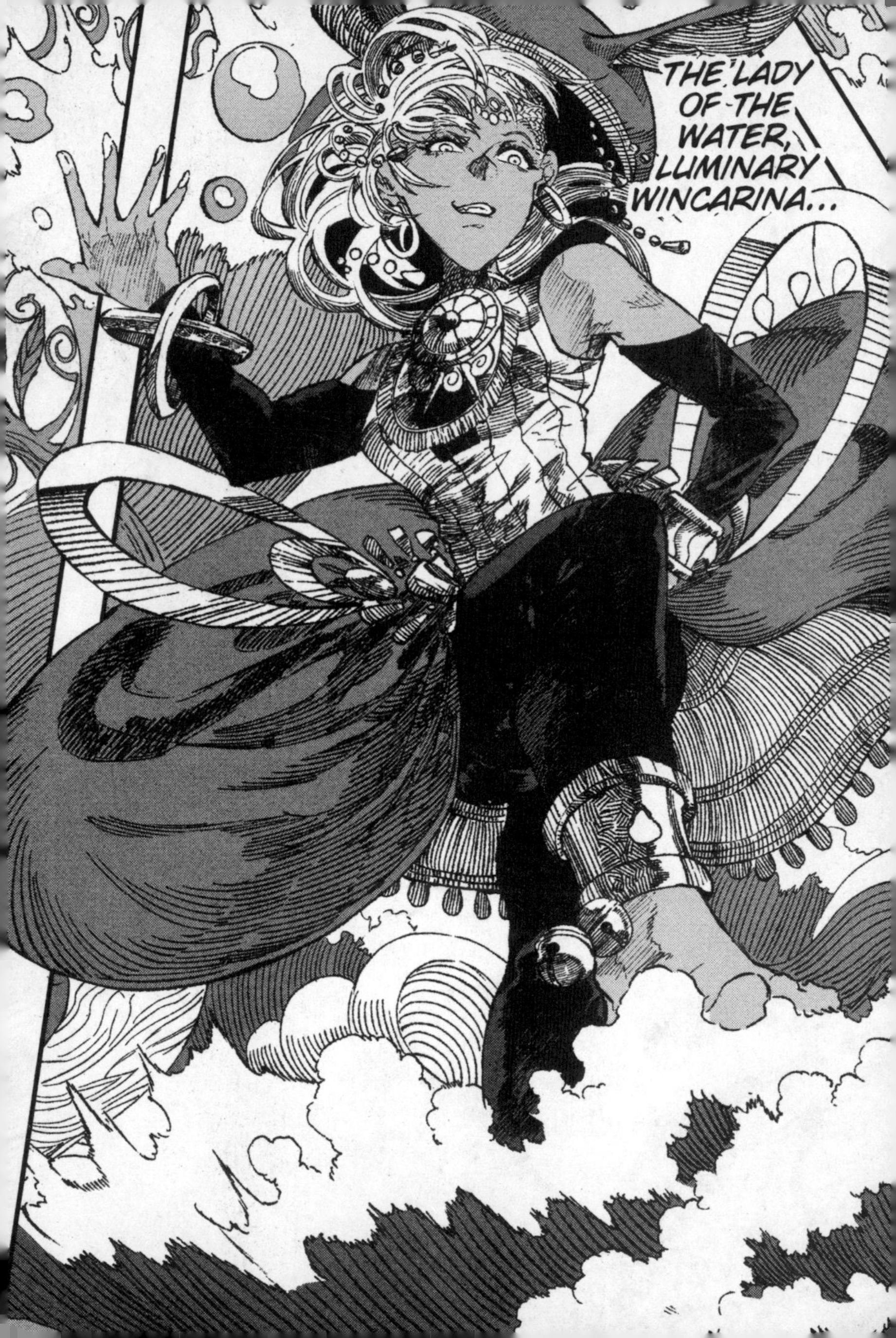
THE LADY OF THE WATER, LUMINARY WINCARINA...

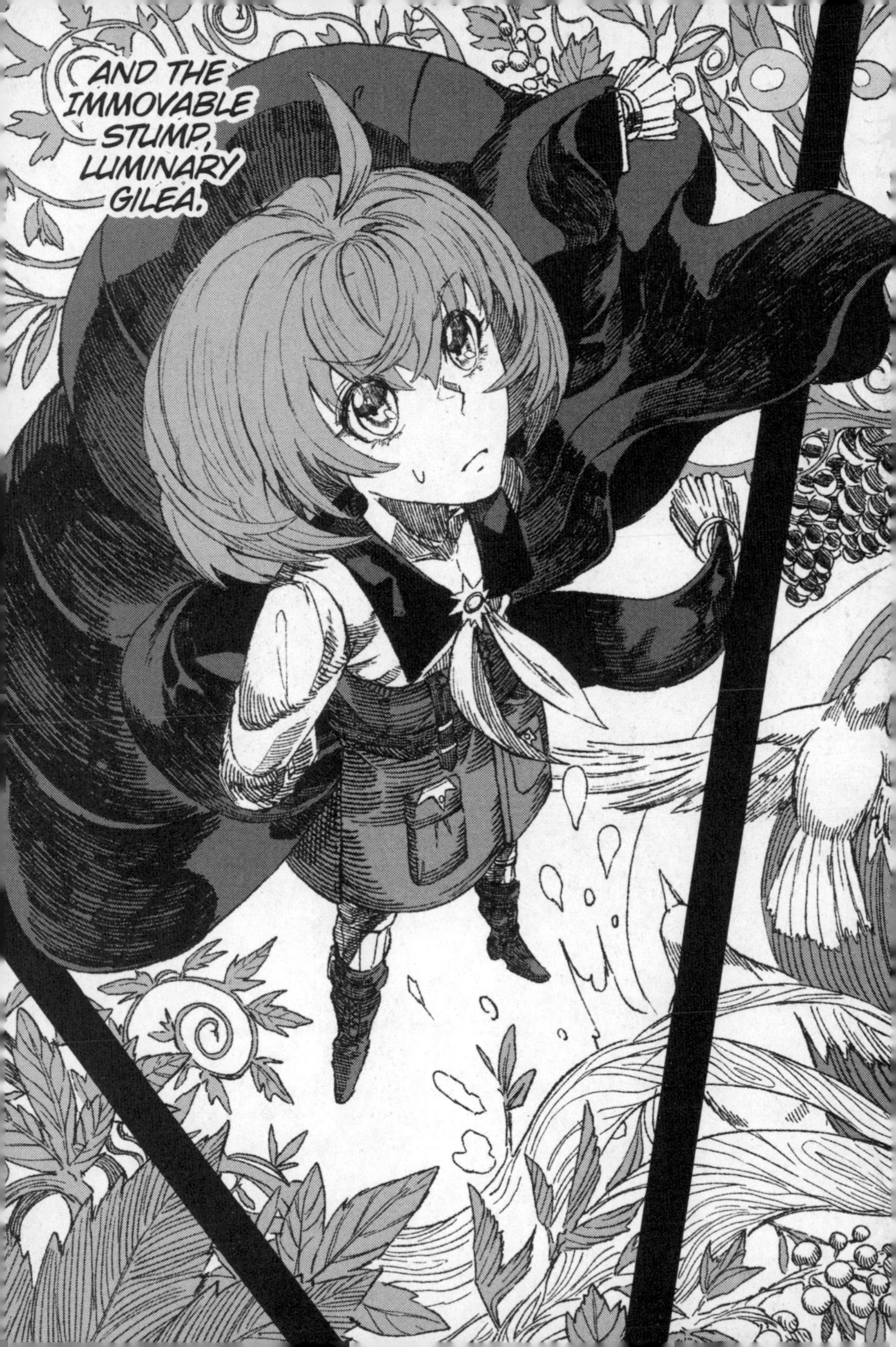
AND THE IMMOVABLE STUMP, LUMINARY GILEA.

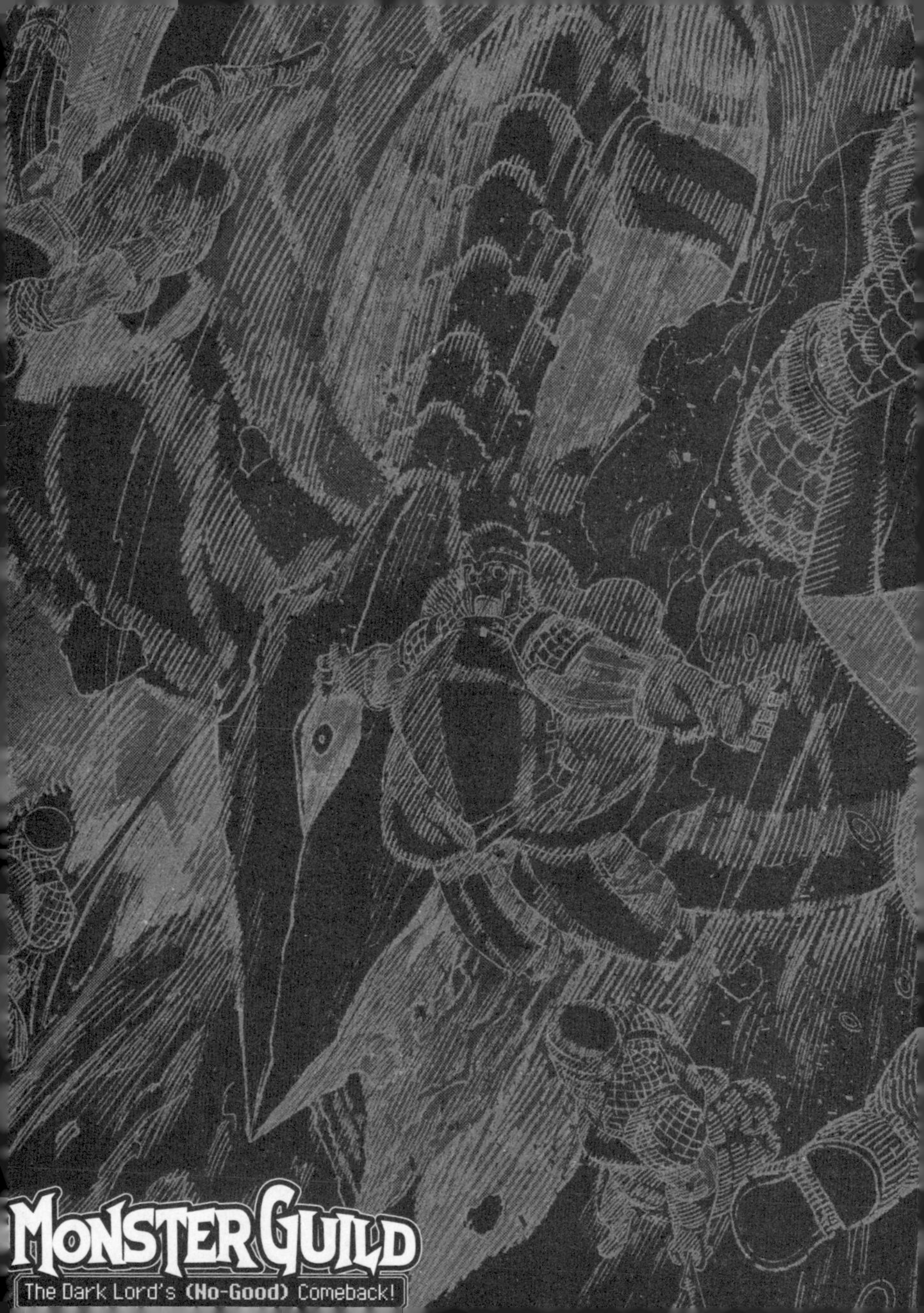
MONSTER GUILD
The Dark Lord's (No-Good) Comeback!

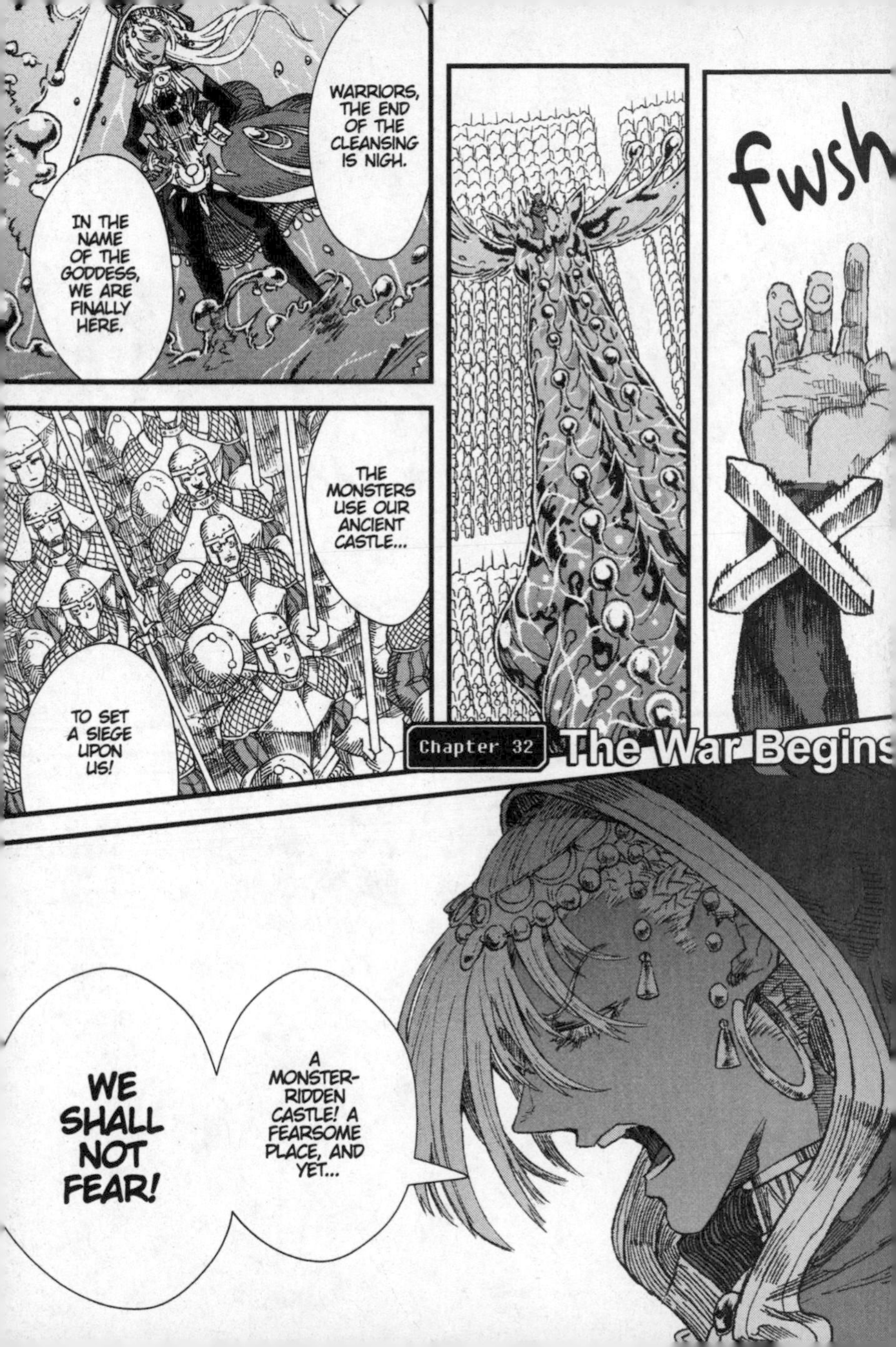
fwsh
WARRIORS, THE END OF THE CLEANSING IS NIGH.
IN THE NAME OF THE GODDESS, WE ARE FINALLY HERE.
THE MONSTERS USE OUR ANCIENT CASTLE...
TO SET A SIEGE UPON US!
Chapter 32 The War Begins
A MONSTER-RIDDEN CASTLE! A FEARSOME PLACE, AND YET...
WE SHALL NOT FEAR!

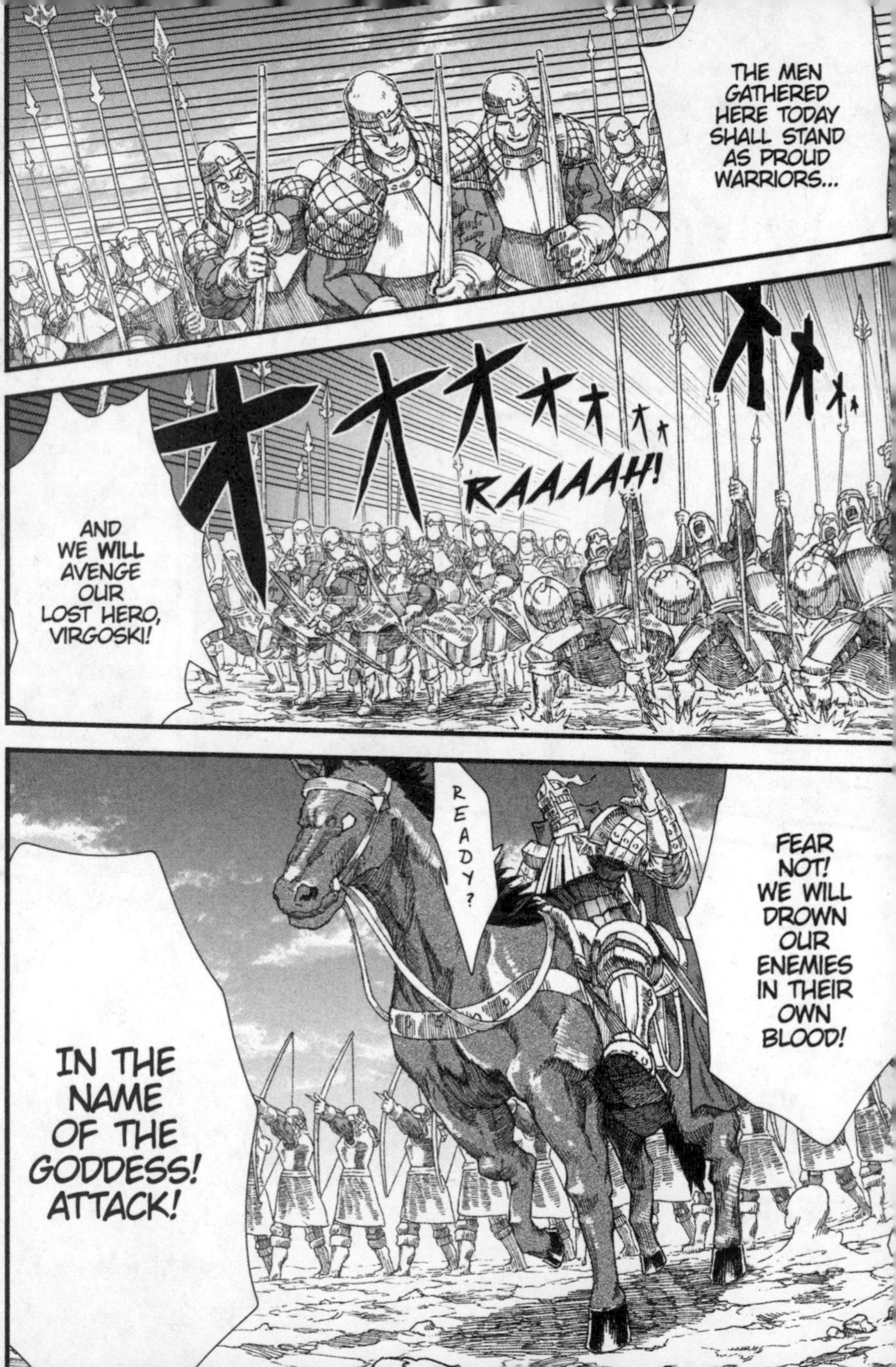
THE MEN GATHERED HERE TODAY SHALL STAND AS PROUD WARRIORS...
AND WE WILL AVENGE OUR LOST HERO, VIRGOSKI!
RAAAAH!
FEAR NOT! WE WILL DROWN OUR ENEMIES IN THEIR OWN BLOOD!
READY?
IN THE NAME OF THE GODDESS! ATTACK!

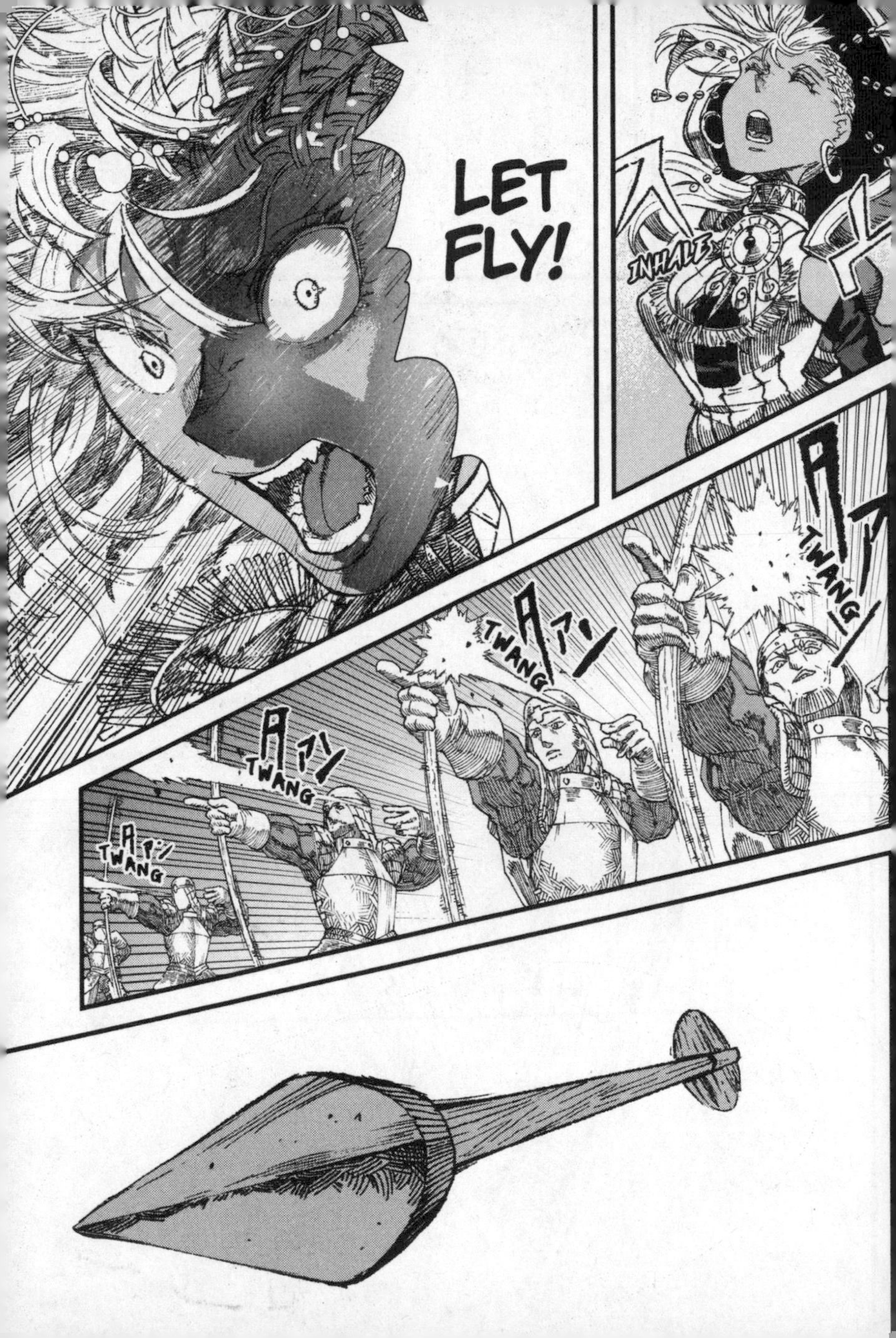

INHALE
LET FLY!
TWANG
TWANG
TWANG
TWANG

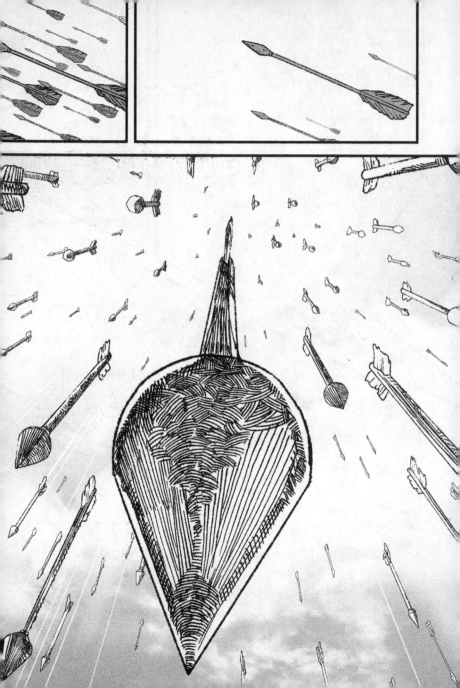

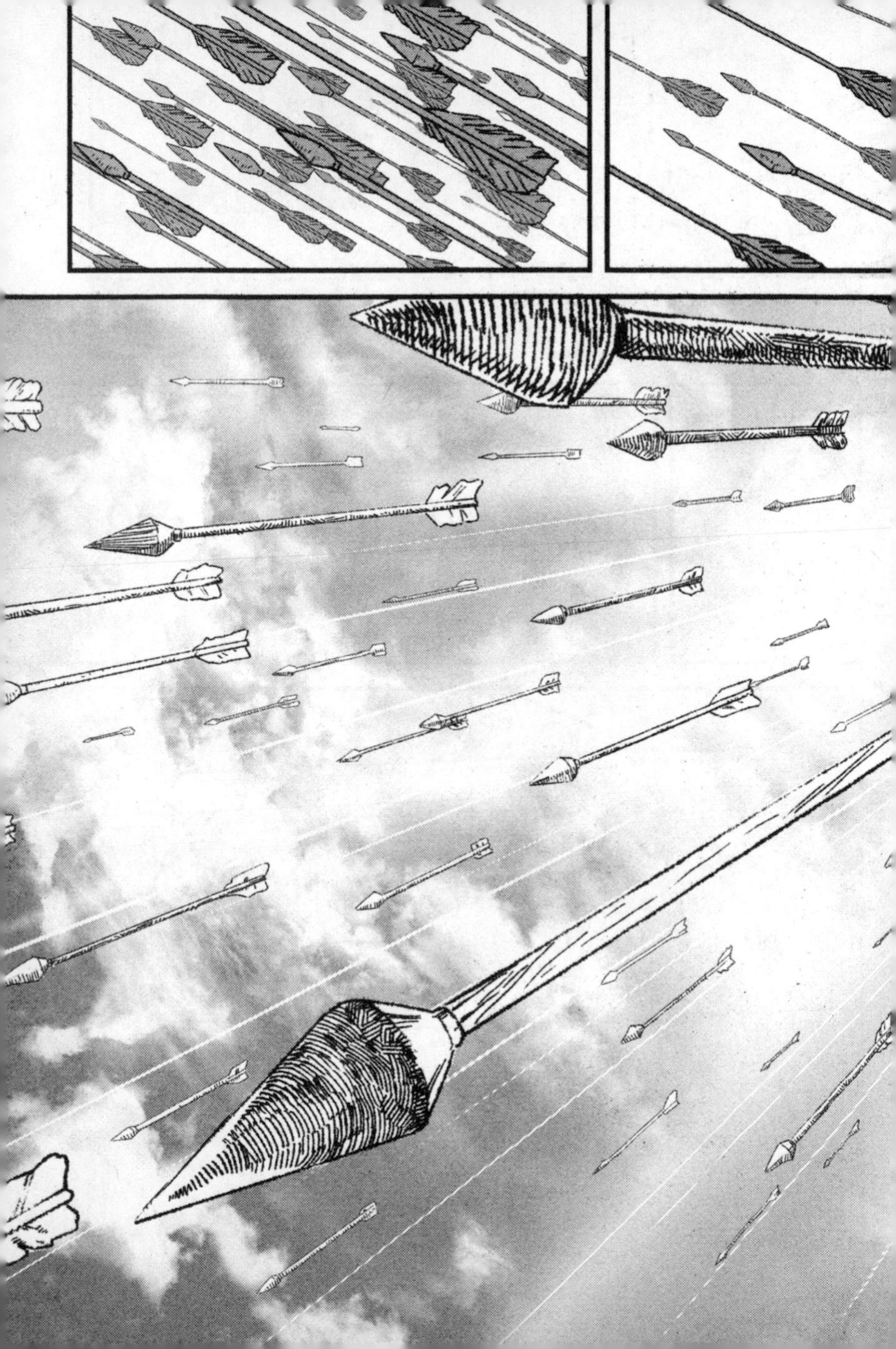

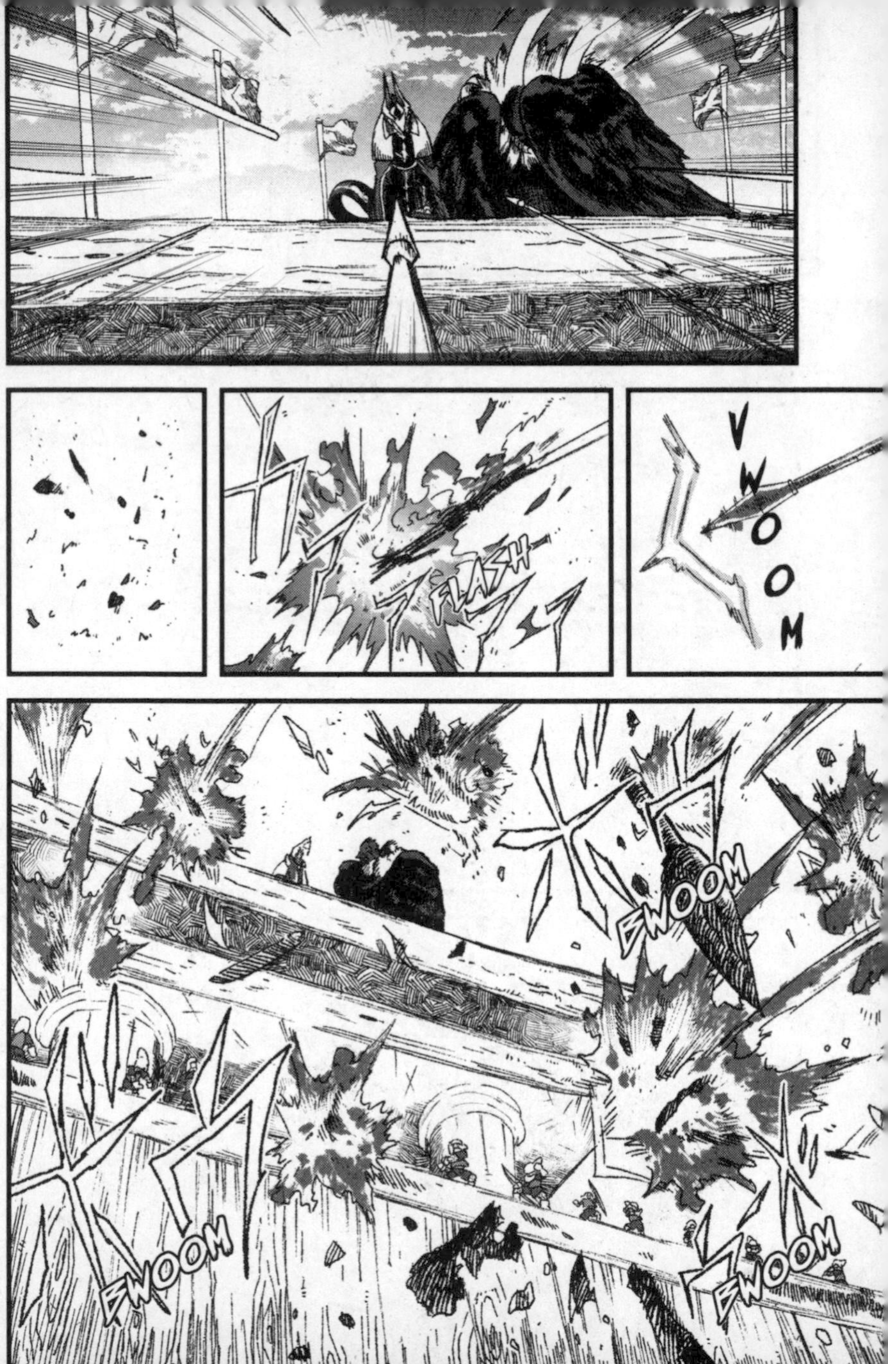
VWOOM
FLASH
EWOOM
EWOOM
EWOOM

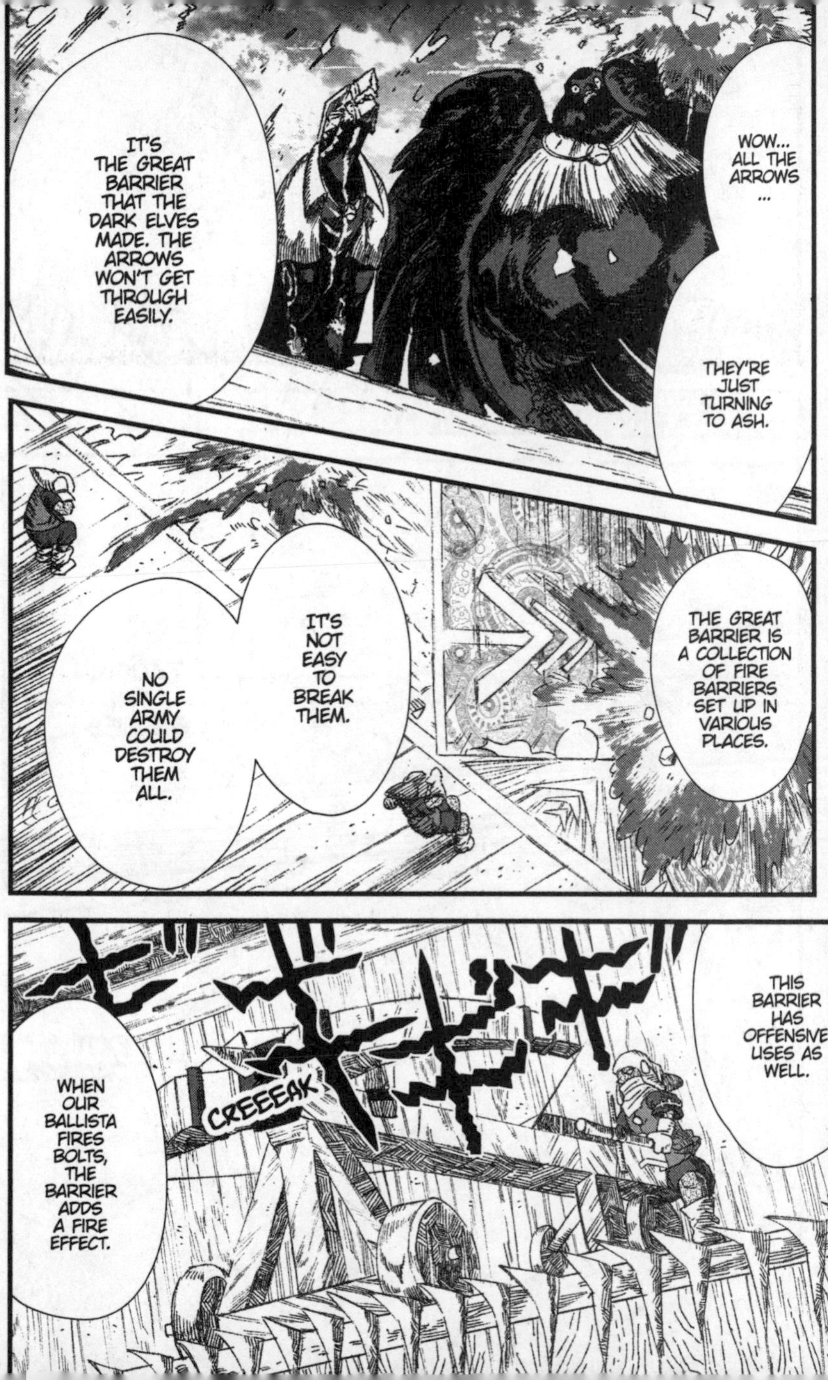
WOW... ALL THE ARROWS ...
THEY'RE JUST TURNING TO ASH.
IT'S THE GREAT BARRIER THAT THE DARK ELVES MADE. THE ARROWS WON'T GET THROUGH EASILY.
THE GREAT BARRIER IS A COLLECTION OF FIRE BARRIERS SET UP IN VARIOUS PLACES.
IT'S NOT EASY TO BREAK THEM.
NO SINGLE ARMY COULD DESTROY THEM ALL.
THIS BARRIER HAS OFFENSIVE USES AS WELL.
CREEEAK
WHEN OUR BALLISTA FIRES BOLTS, THE BARRIER ADDS A FIRE EFFECT.

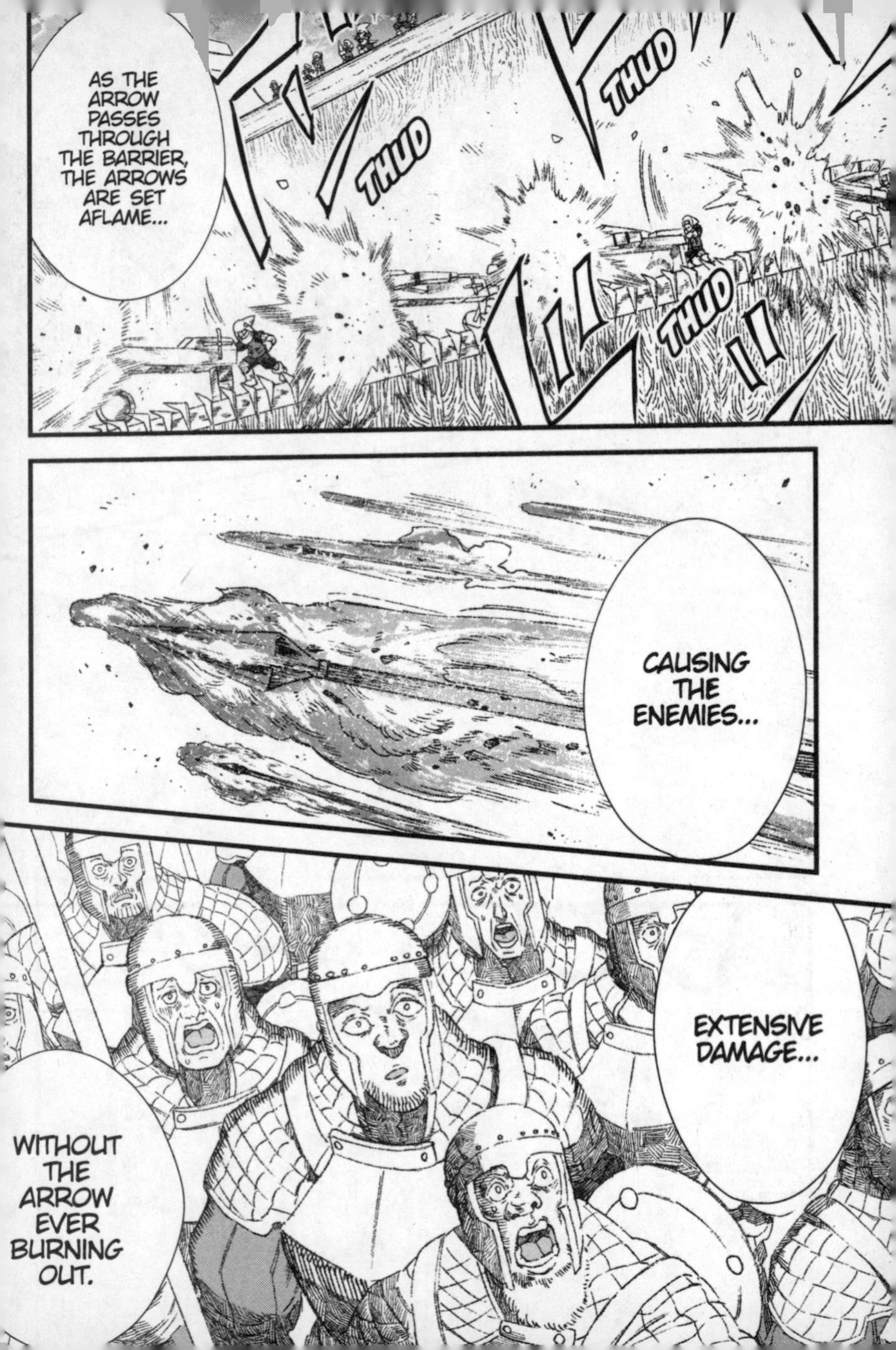
THUD
AS THE ARROW PASSES THROUGH THE BARRIER, THE ARROWS ARE SET AFLAME...
THUD
THUD
CAUSING THE ENEMIES...
EXTENSIVE DAMAGE...
WITHOUT THE ARROW EVER BURNING OUT.

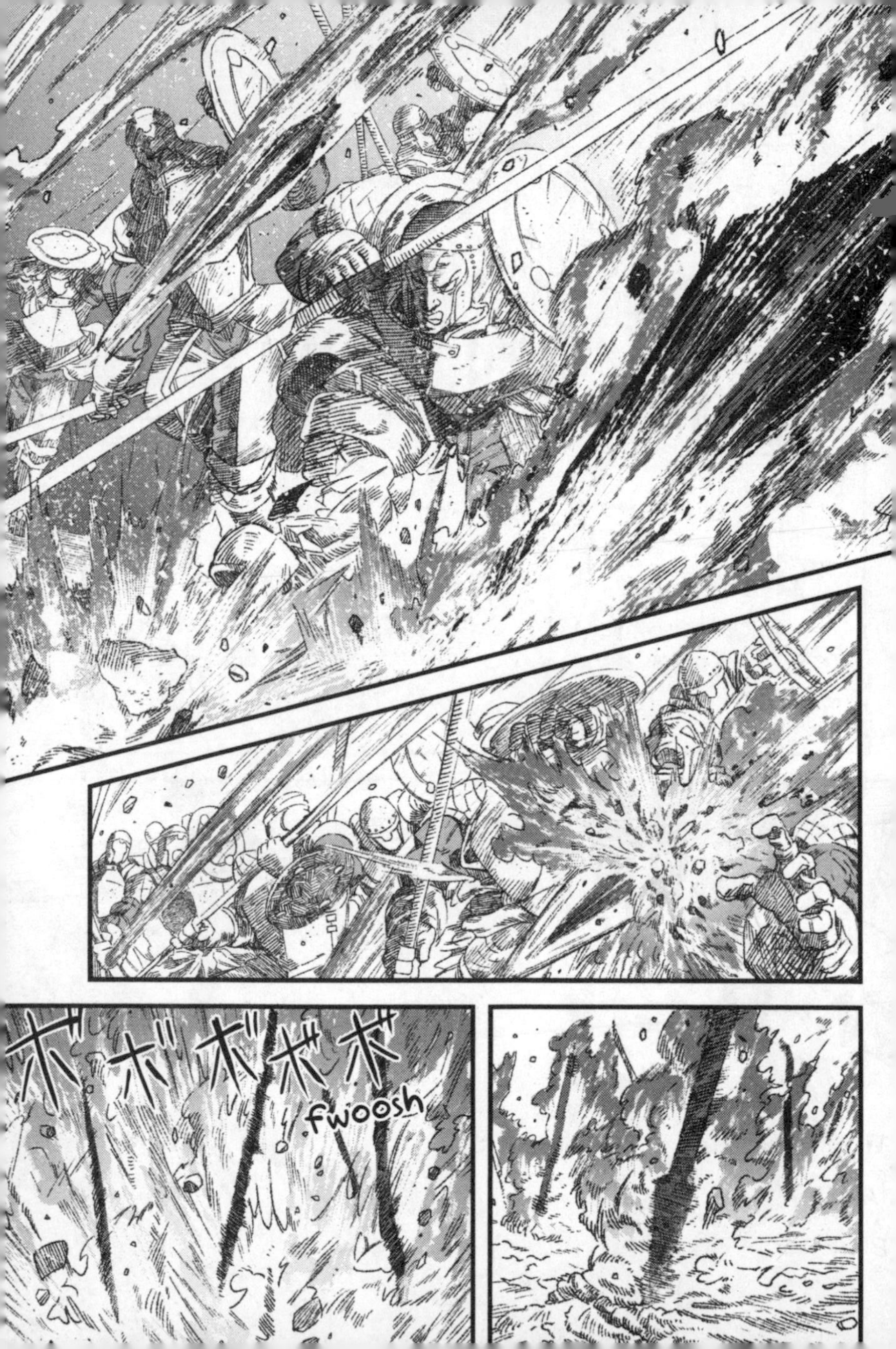
ボボボボボ
fwoosh

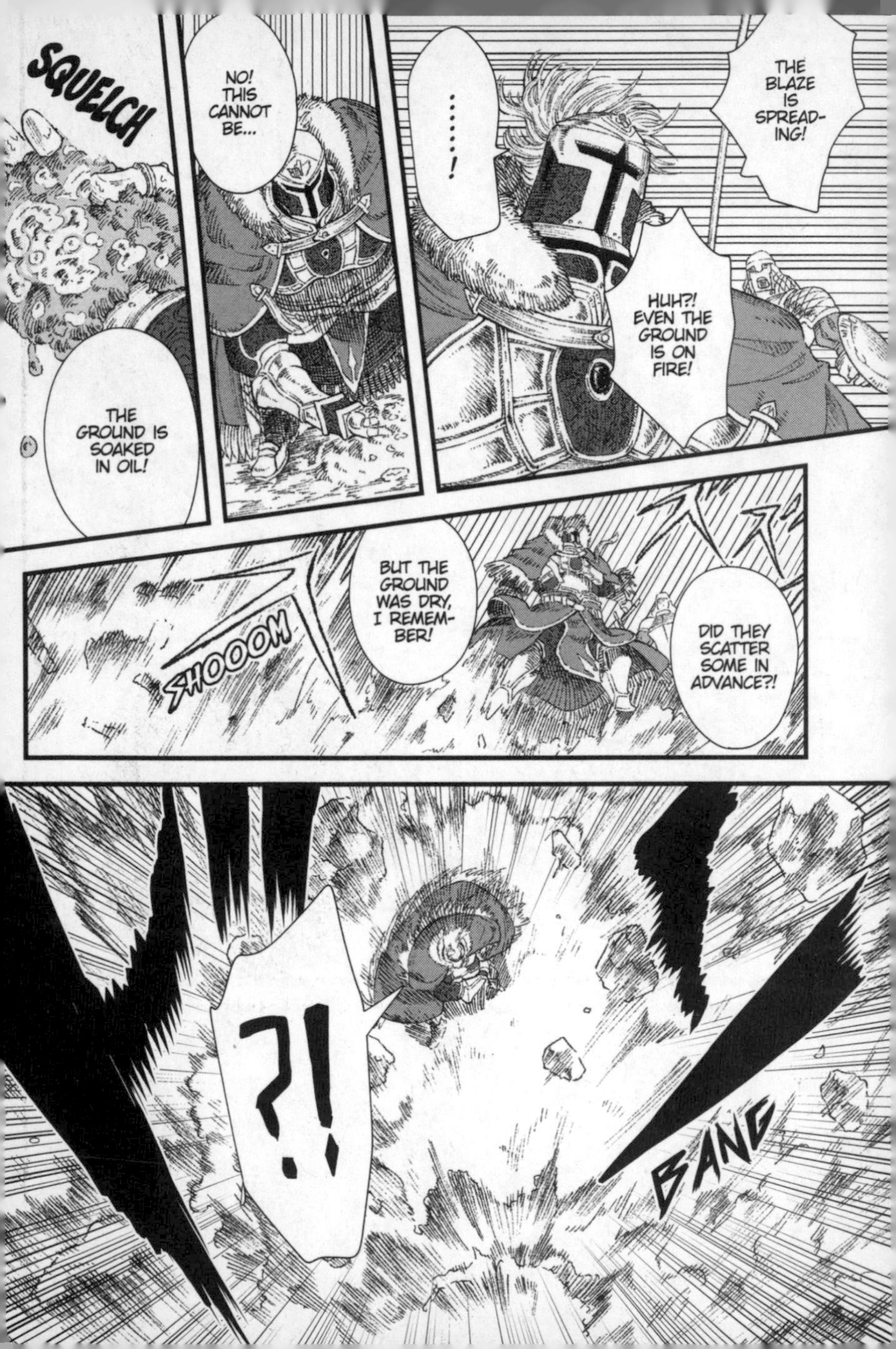
THE BLAZE IS SPREAD-ING!
HUH?! EVEN THE GROUND IS ON FIRE!
......!
NO! THIS CANNOT BE...
SQUELCH
THE GROUND IS SOAKED IN OIL!
DID THEY SCATTER SOME IN ADVANCE?!
BUT THE GROUND WAS DRY, I REMEM-BER!
SHOOOM
BANG
?!

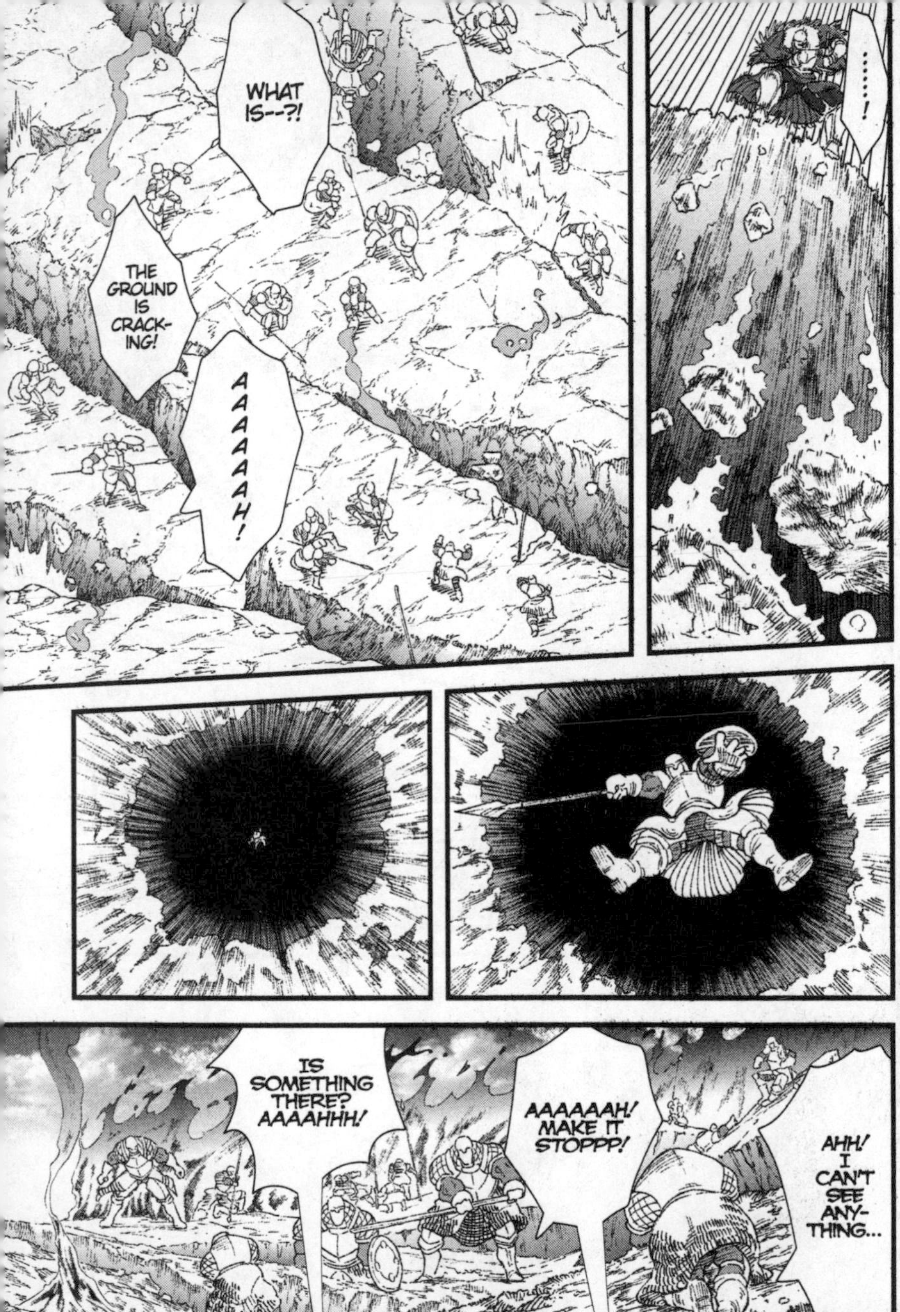
......!
WHAT IS--?!
THE GROUND IS CRACKING!
AAAAAAAH!
?
AHH! I CAN'T SEE ANYTHING...
AAAAAAH! MAKE IT STOPPP!
IS SOMETHING THERE? AAAAHHH!

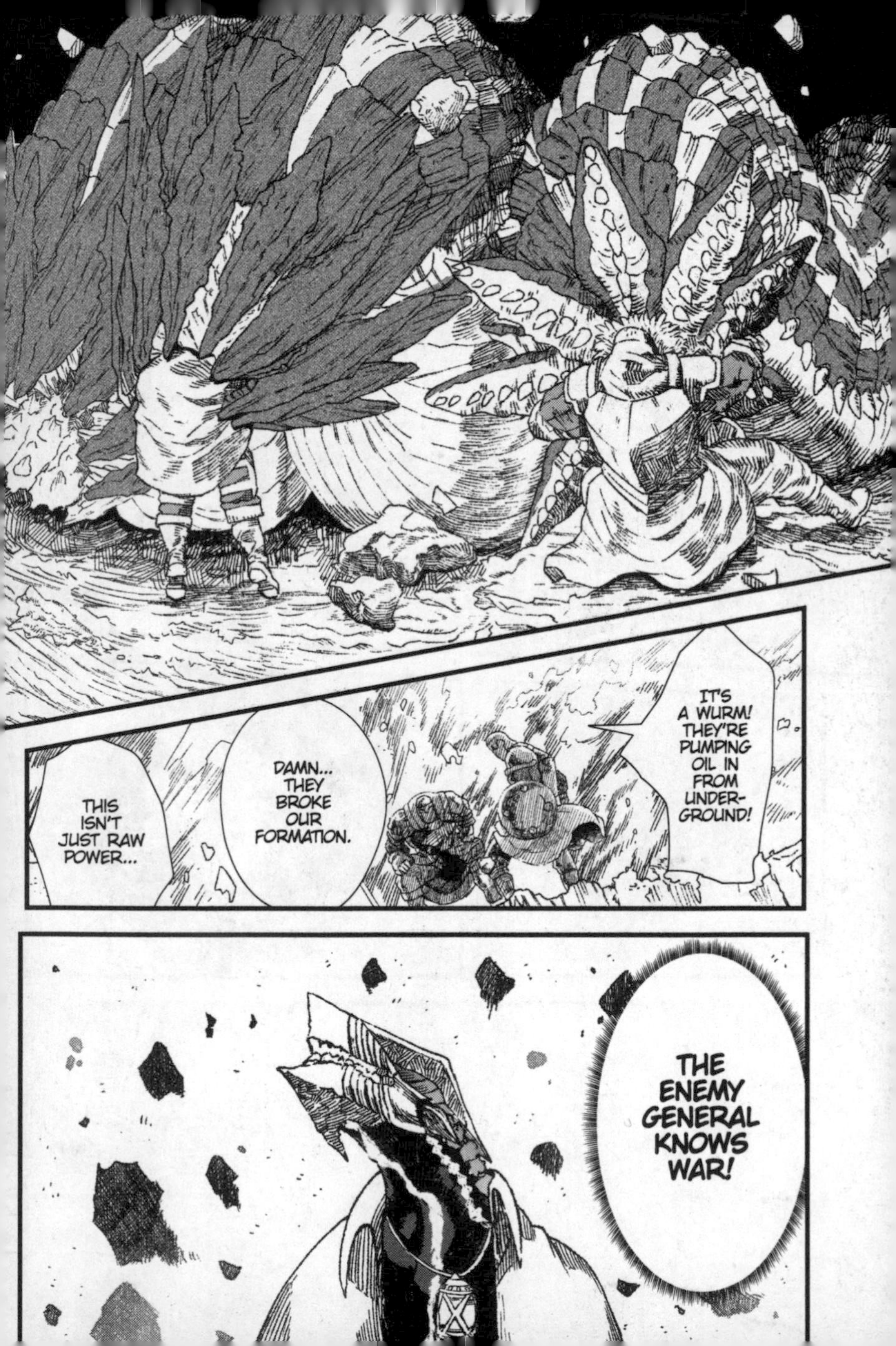
IT'S A WURM! THEY'RE PUMPING OIL IN FROM UNDER-GROUND!
DAMN... THEY BROKE OUR FORMATION.
THIS ISN'T JUST RAW POWER...
THE ENEMY GENERAL KNOWS WAR!

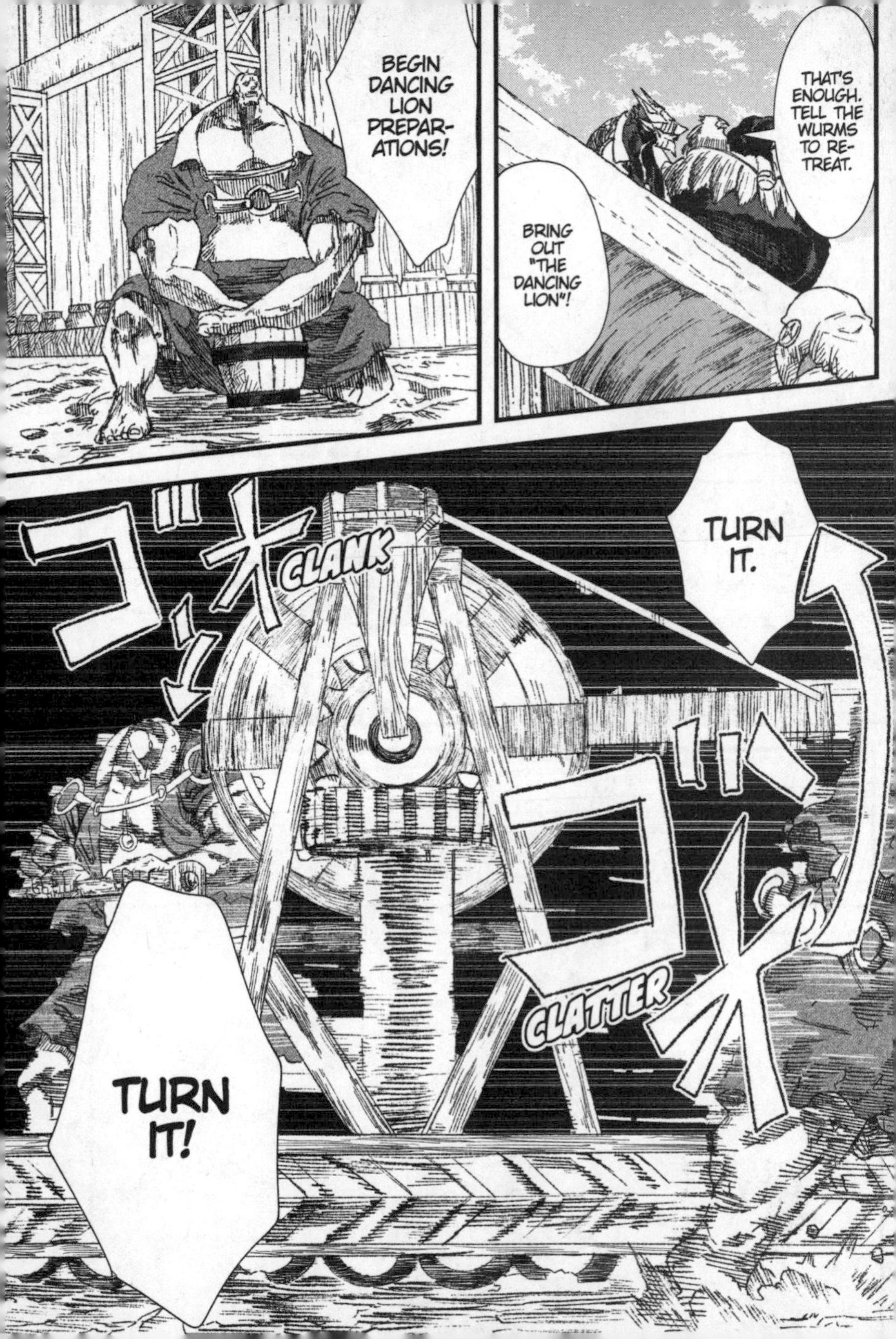
THAT'S ENOUGH. TELL THE WURMS TO RE-TREAT.
BRING OUT "THE DANCING LION"!
BEGIN DANCING LION PREPAR-ATIONS!
TURN IT.
CLANK
CLATTER
TURN IT!

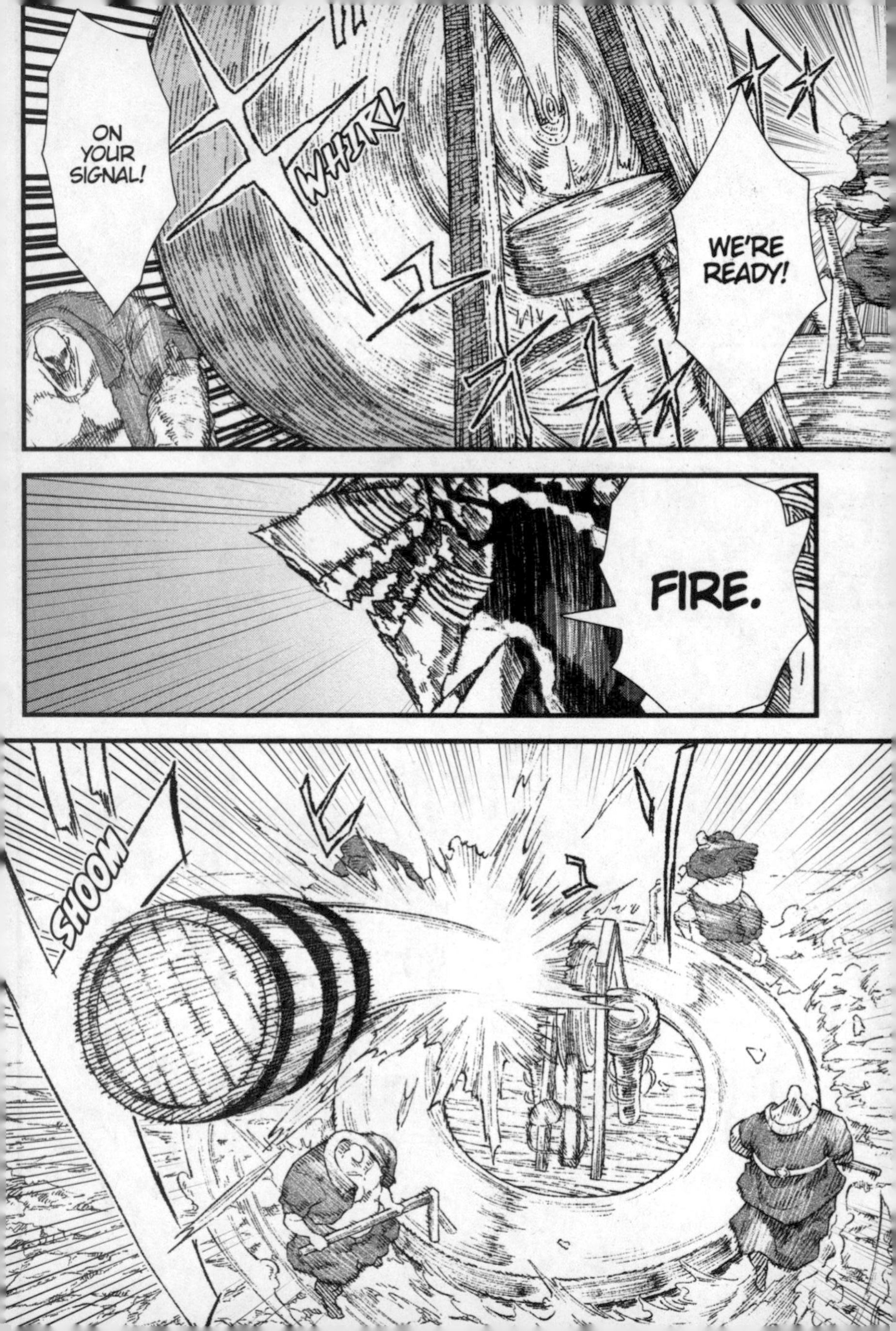
WE'RE READY!
WHIRL
ON YOUR SIGNAL!
FIRE.
SHOOM

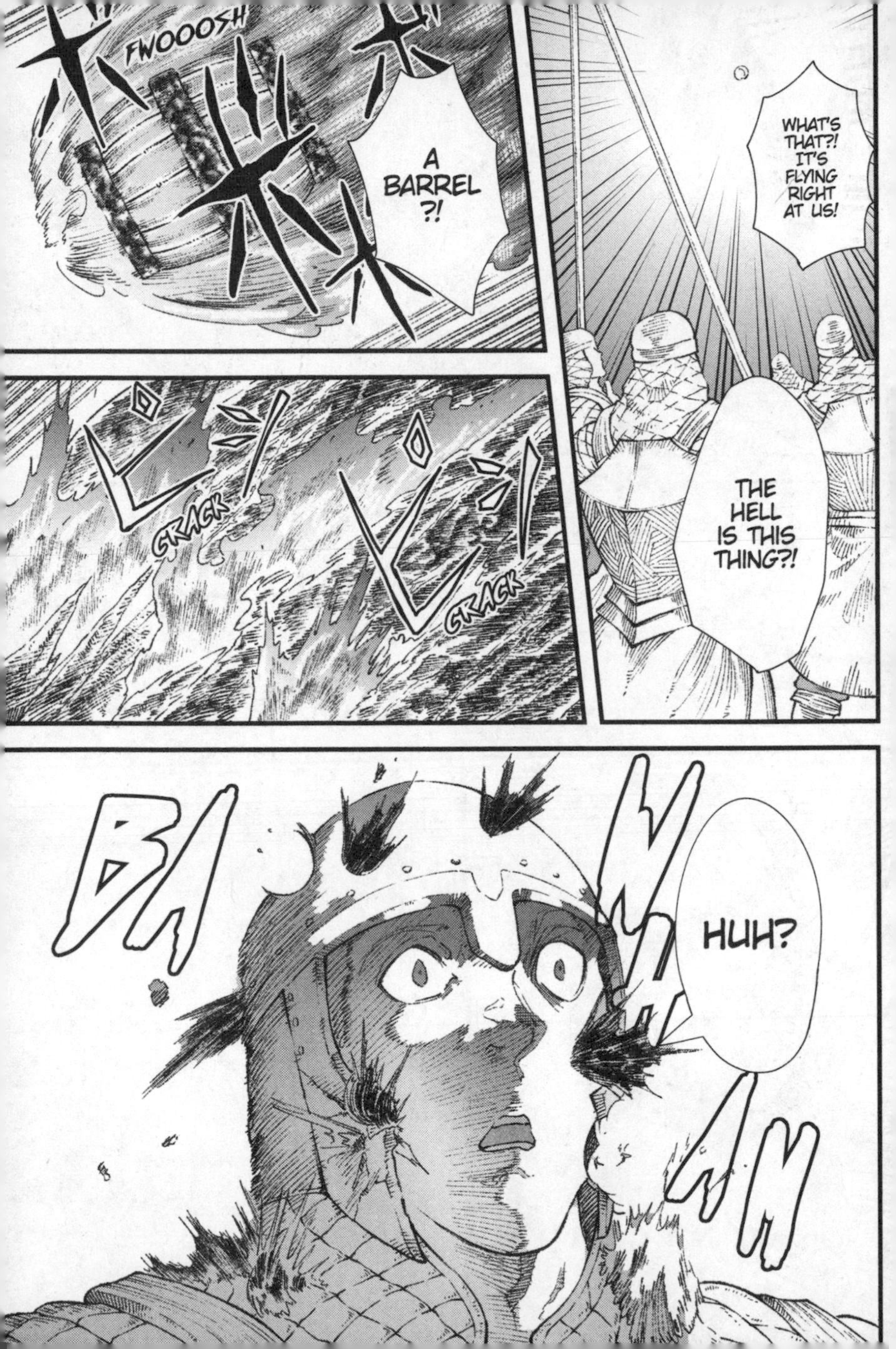
WHAT'S THAT?! IT'S FLYING RIGHT AT US!
THE HELL IS THIS THING?!
FWOOOSH
A BARREL ?!
CRACK
CRACK
HUH?

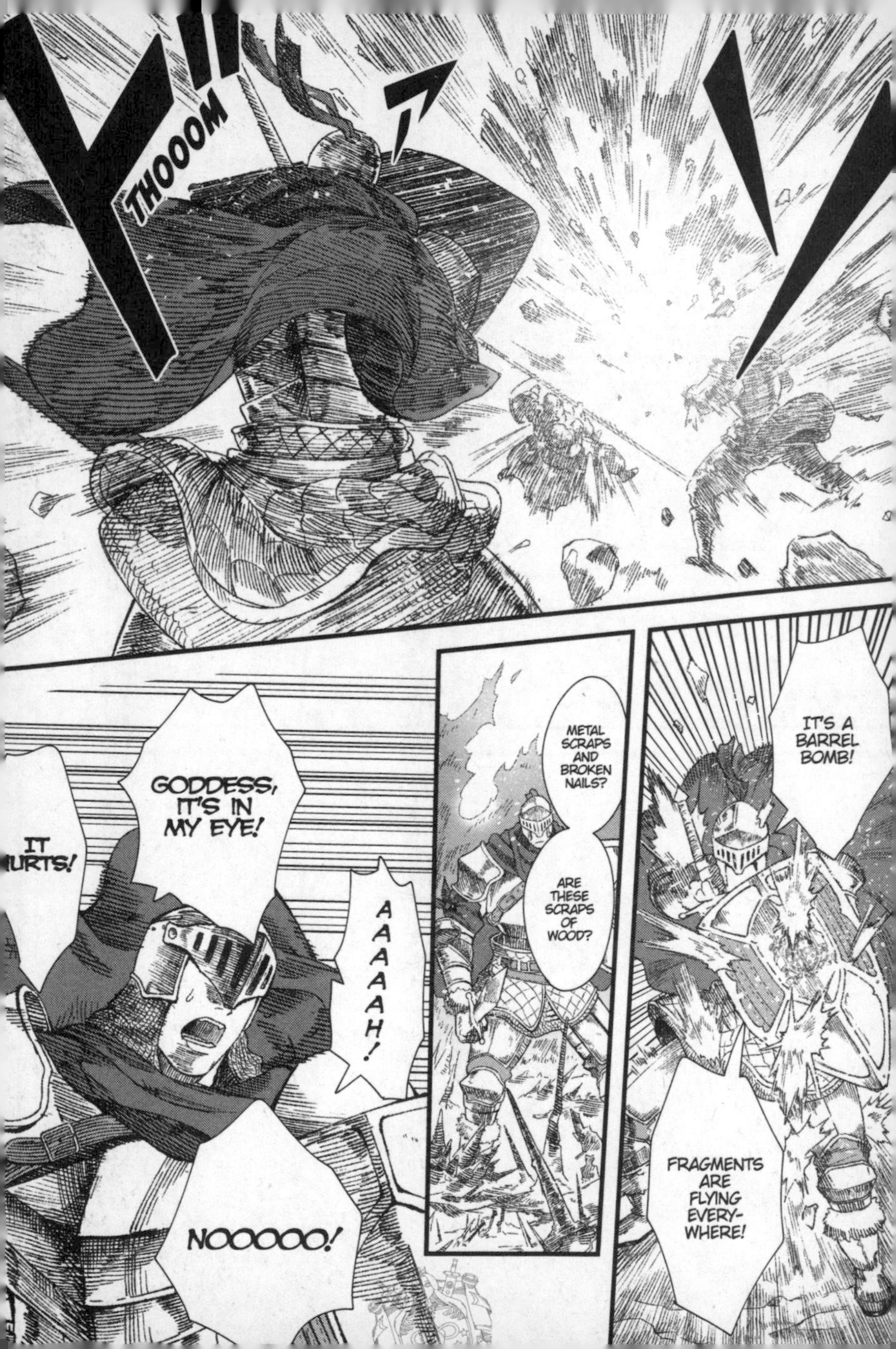
THOOOM
IT'S A BARREL BOMB!
FRAGMENTS ARE FLYING EVERY-WHERE!
METAL SCRAPS AND BROKEN NAILS?
ARE THESE SCRAPS OF WOOD?
AAAAAH!
GODDESS, IT'S IN MY EYE!
IT URTS!
NOOOOO!

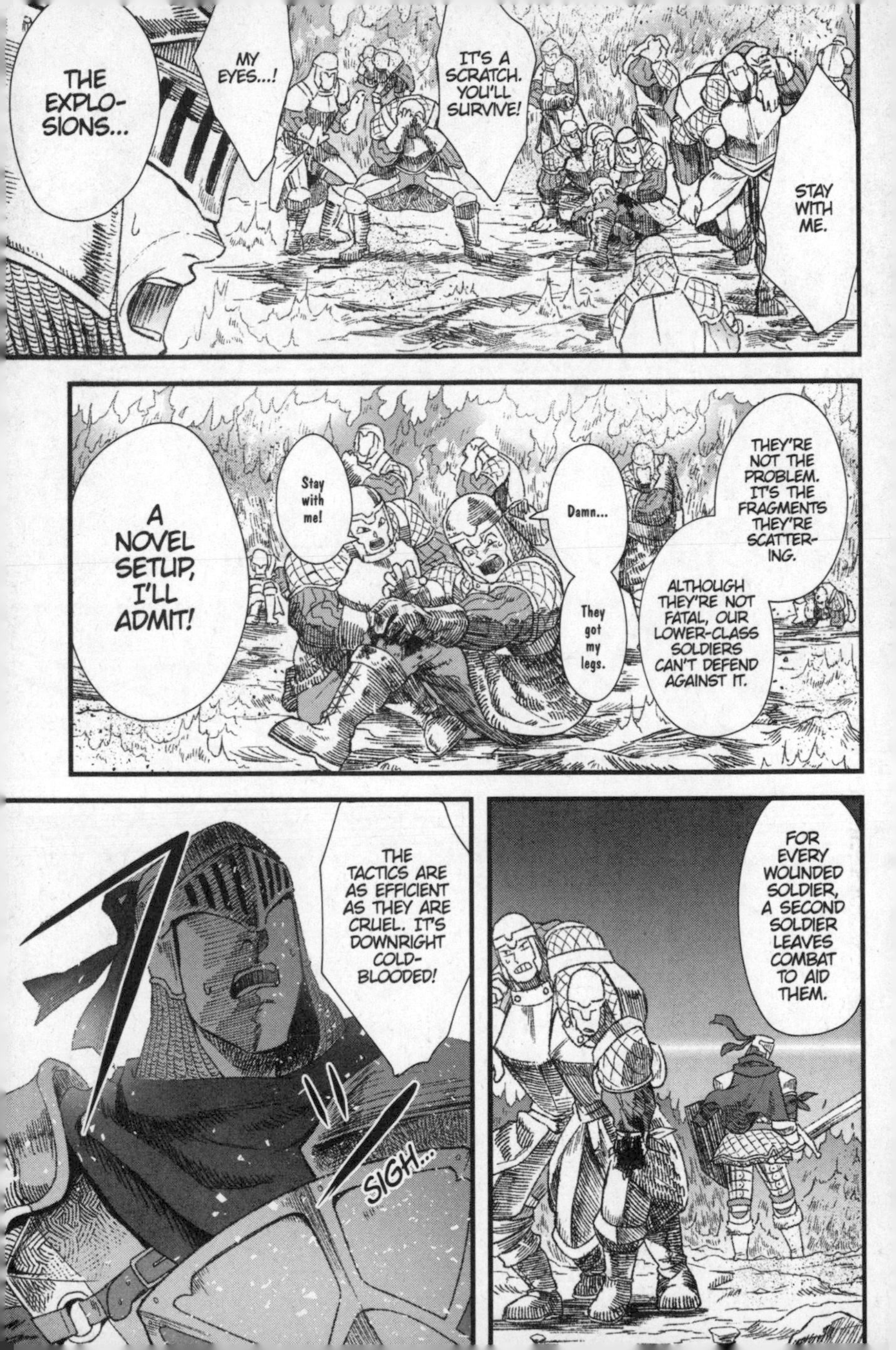
STAY WITH ME.
IT'S A SCRATCH. YOU'LL SURVIVE!
MY EYES...!
THE EXPLO-SIONS...
THEY'RE NOT THE PROBLEM. IT'S THE FRAGMENTS THEY'RE SCATTER-ING.
ALTHOUGH THEY'RE NOT FATAL, OUR LOWER-CLASS SOLDIERS CAN'T DEFEND AGAINST IT.
Damn...
They got my legs.
Stay with me!
A NOVEL SETUP, I'LL ADMIT!
FOR EVERY WOUNDED SOLDIER, A SECOND SOLDIER LEAVES COMBAT TO AID THEM.
THE TACTICS ARE AS EFFICIENT AS THEY ARE CRUEL. IT'S DOWNRIGHT COLD-BLOODED!
SIGH...

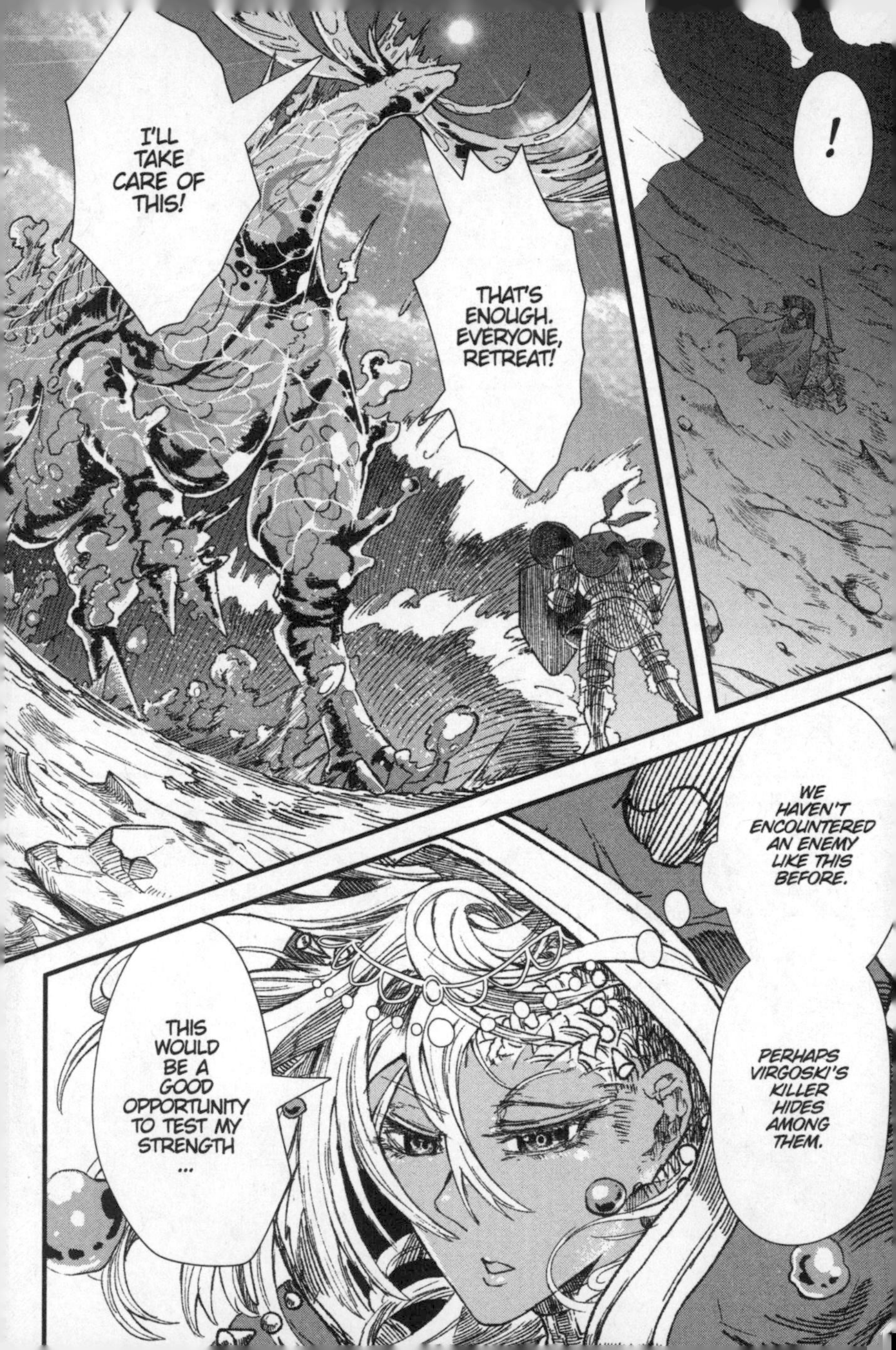
!
THAT'S ENOUGH. EVERYONE, RETREAT!
I'LL TAKE CARE OF THIS!
WE HAVEN'T ENCOUNTERED AN ENEMY LIKE THIS BEFORE.
PERHAPS VIRGOSKI'S KILLER HIDES AMONG THEM.
THIS WOULD BE A GOOD OPPORTUNITY TO TEST MY STRENGTH ...

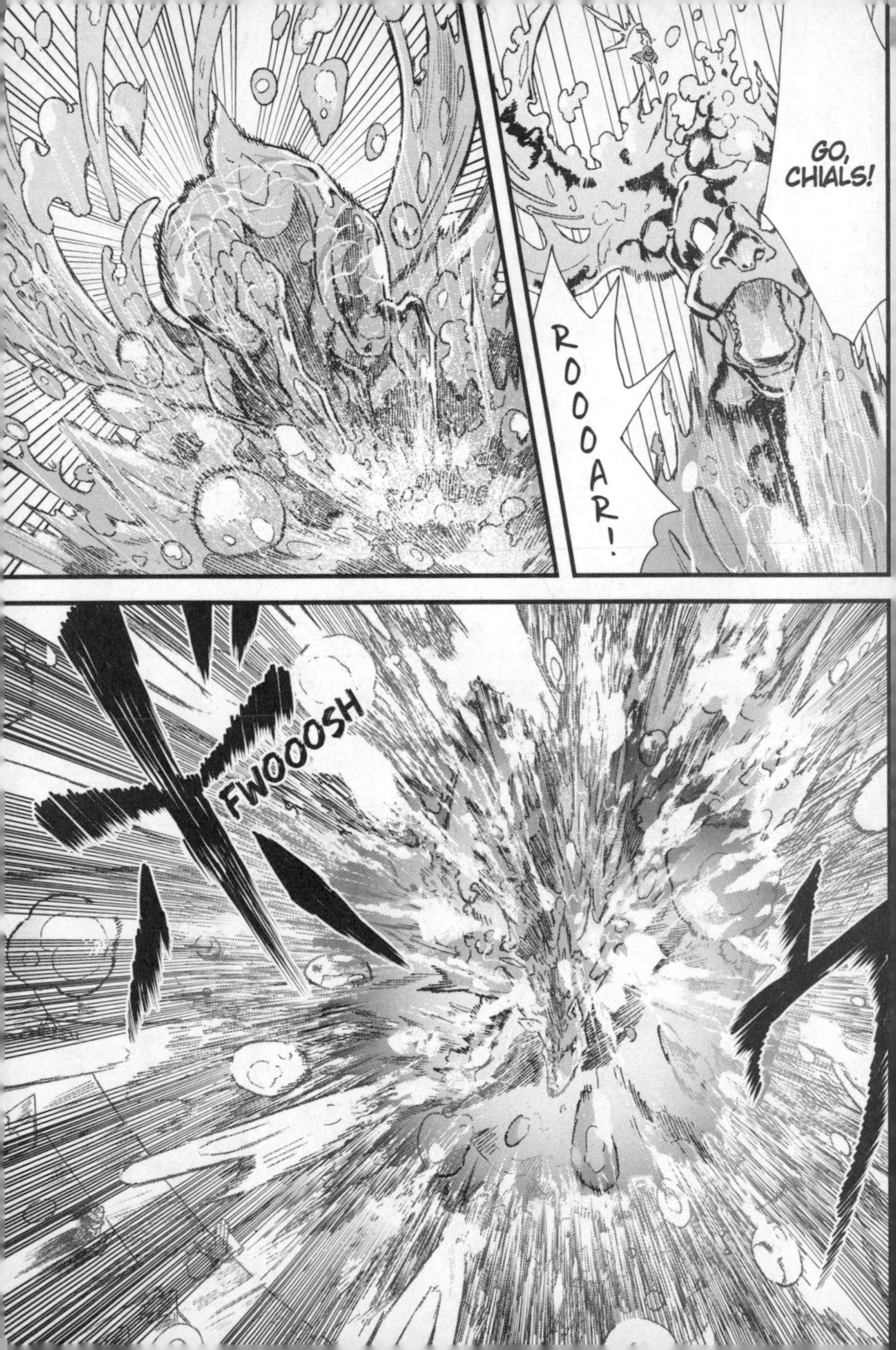
GO, CHIALS!
ROOOOAR!
FWOOOSH

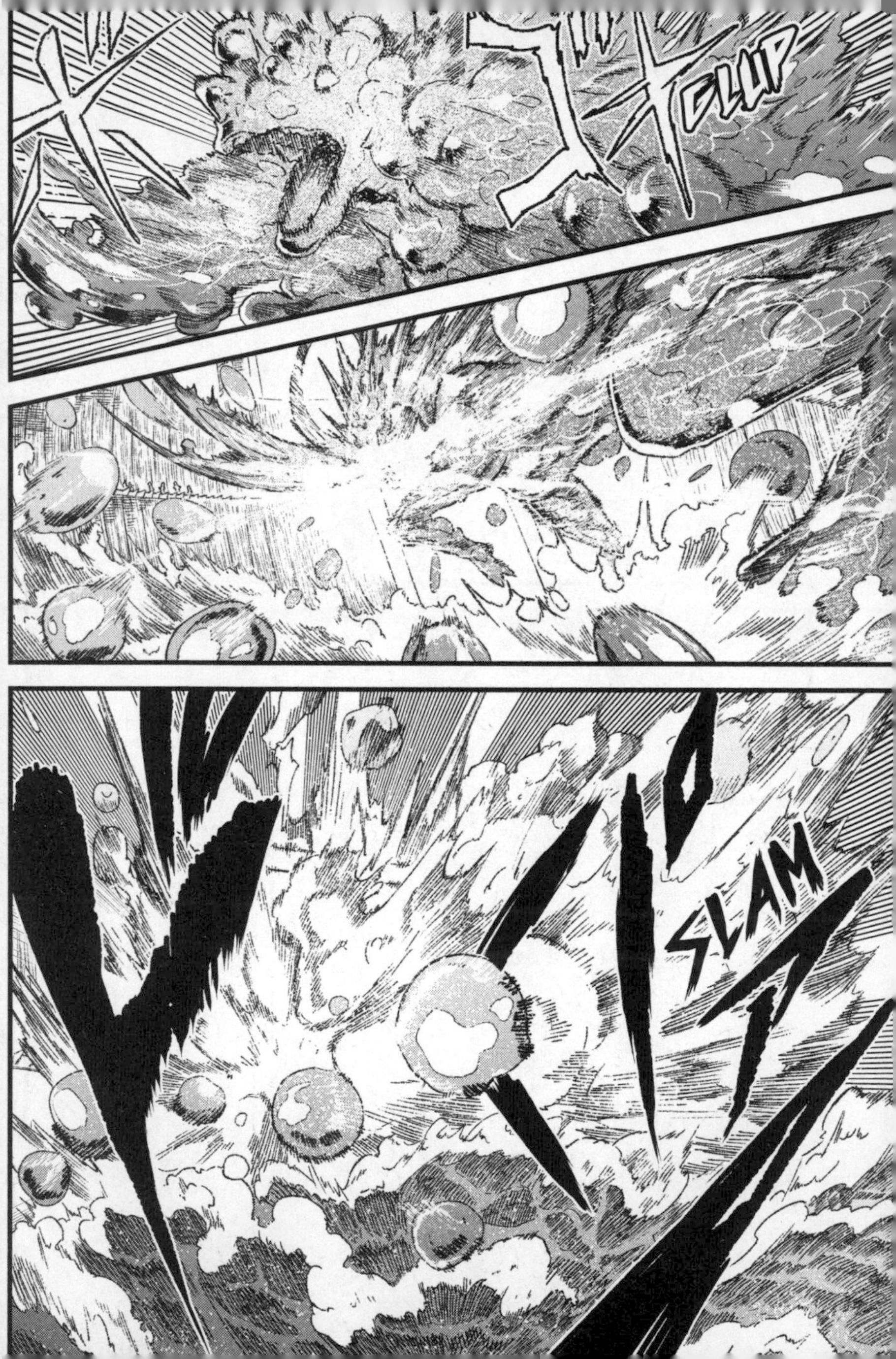
GLUP
SLAM

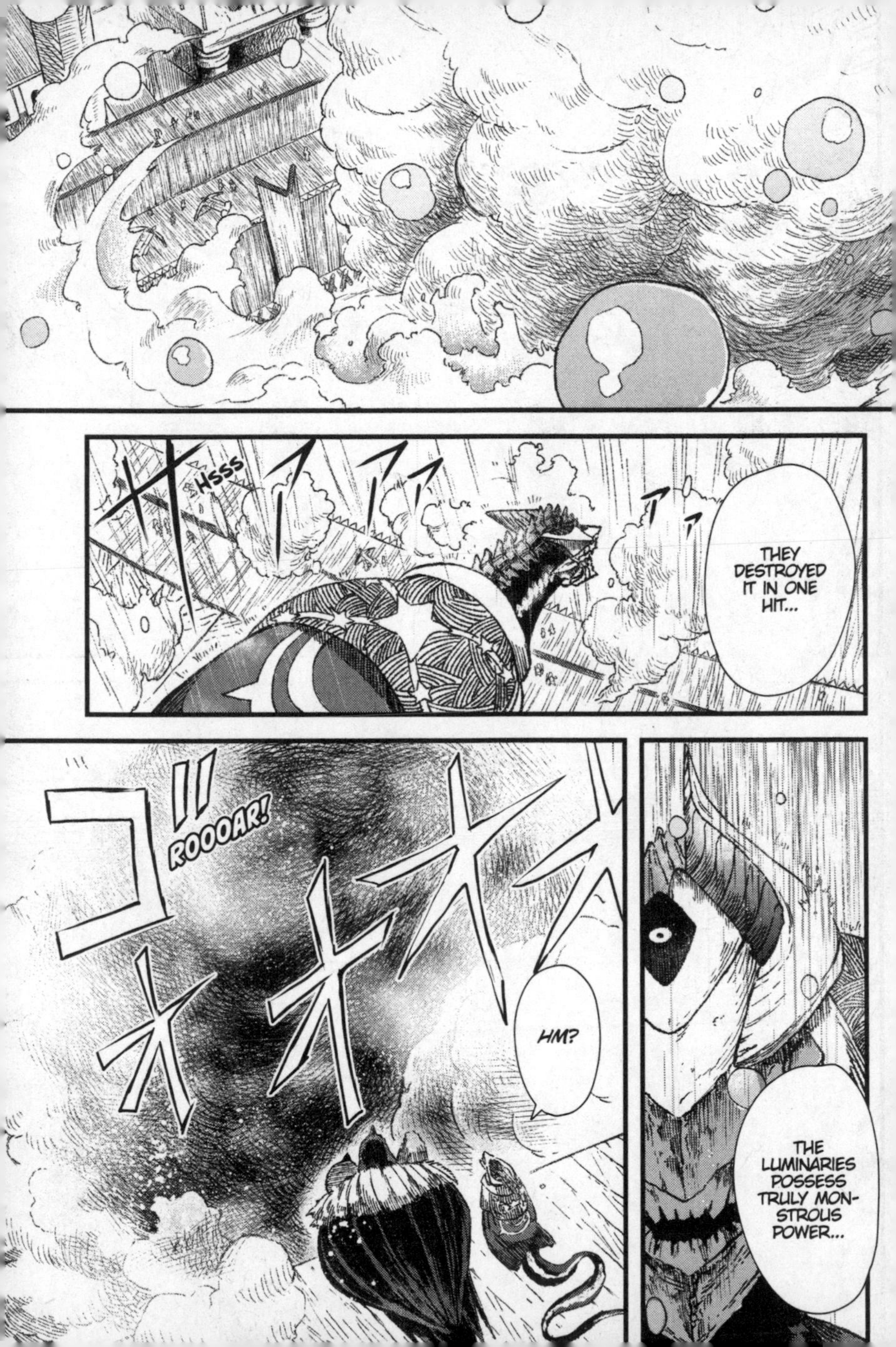
THEY DESTROYED IT IN ONE HIT...
HSSS
THE LUMINARIES POSSESS TRULY MON-STROUS POWER...
ROOOAR!
HM?

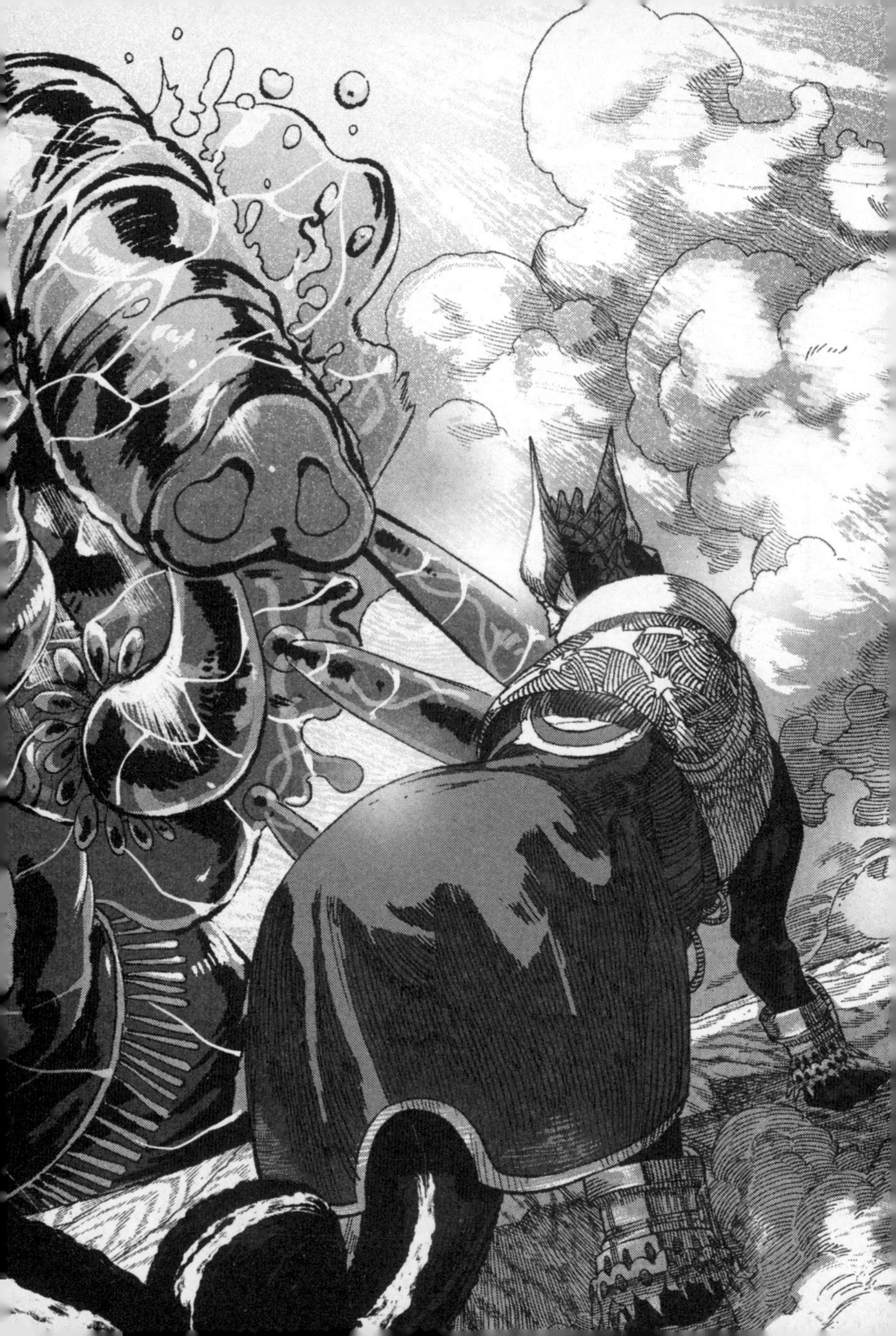

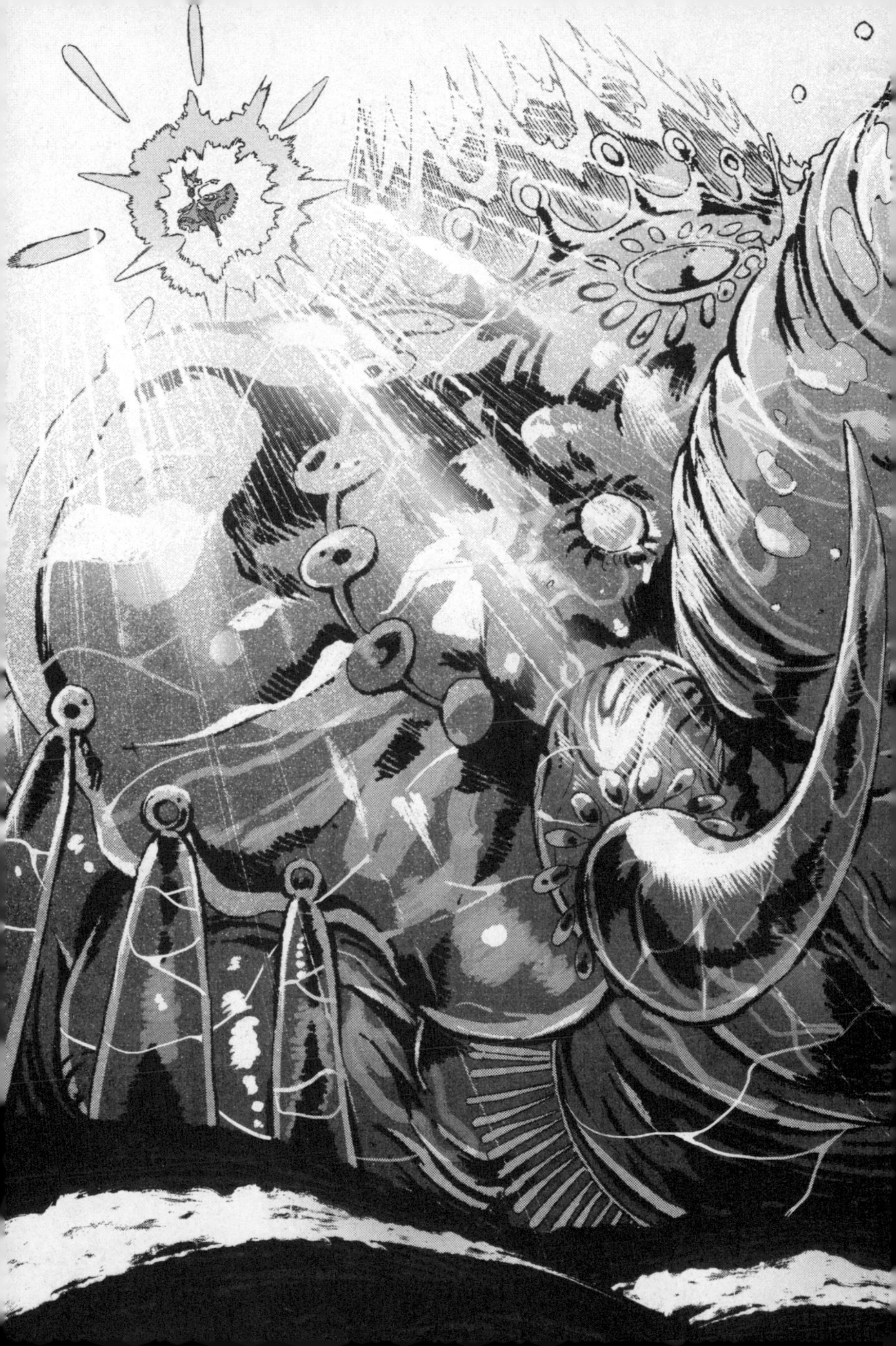

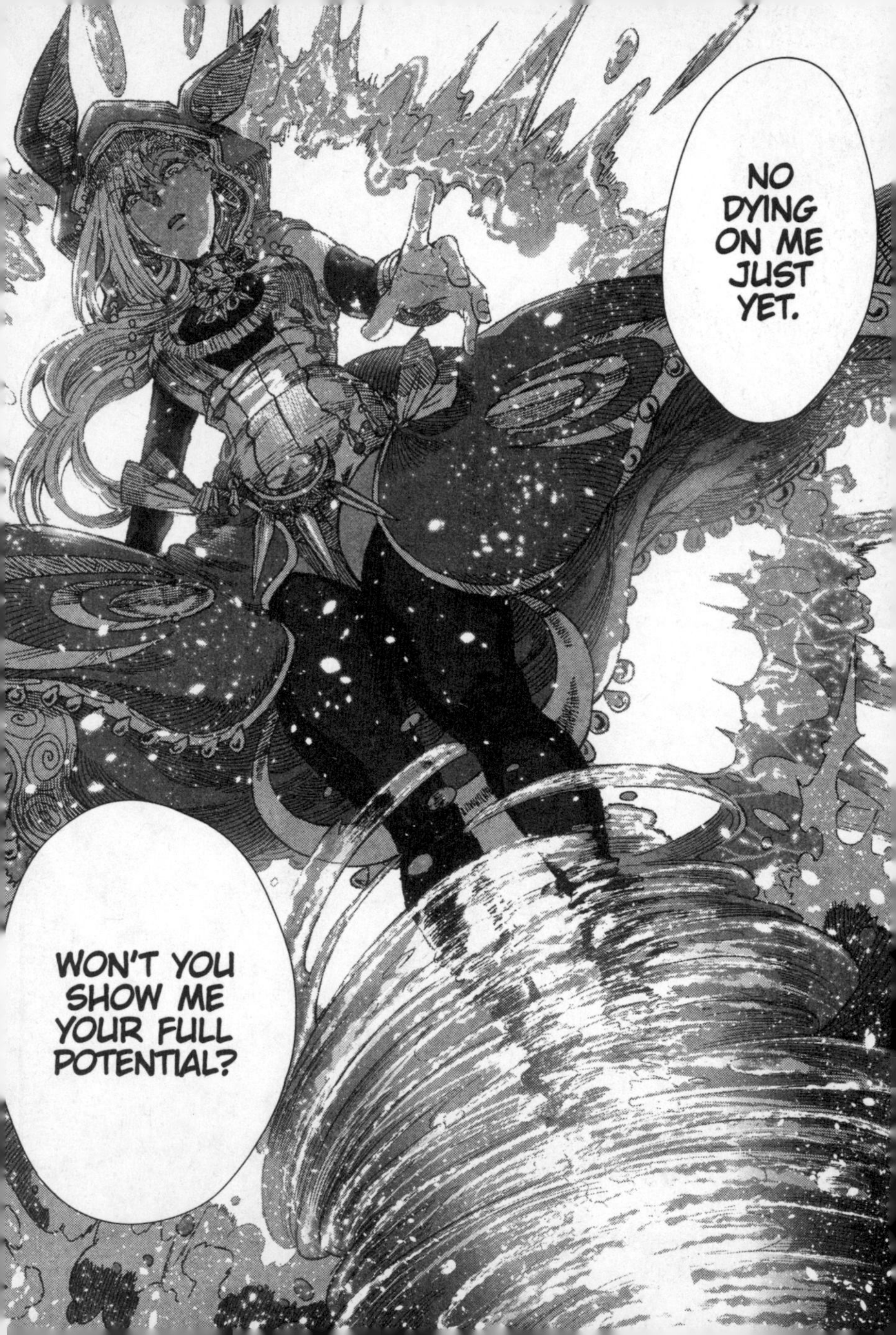
NO DYING ON ME JUST YET.
WON'T YOU SHOW ME YOUR FULL POTENTIAL?

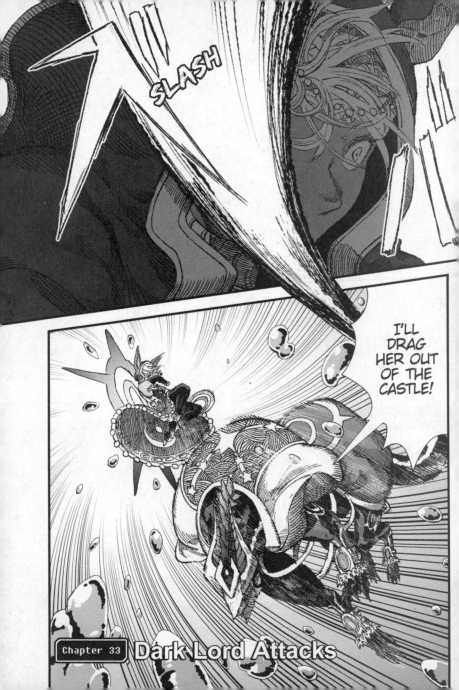

SLASH

I'LL DRAG HER OUT OF THE CASTLE!

Chapter 33 Dark Lord Attacks

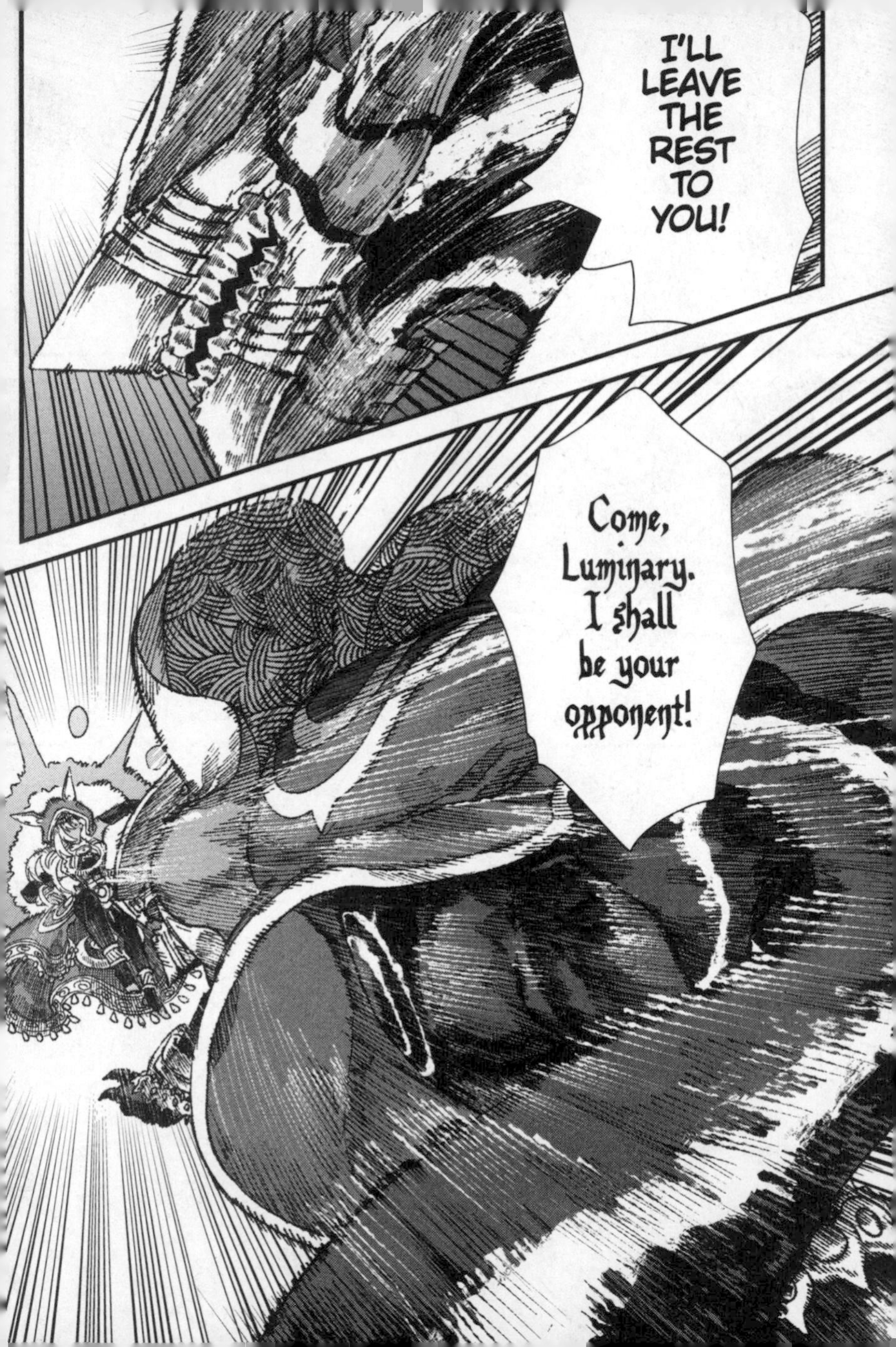
I'LL LEAVE THE REST TO YOU!
Come, Luminary. I shall be your opponent!

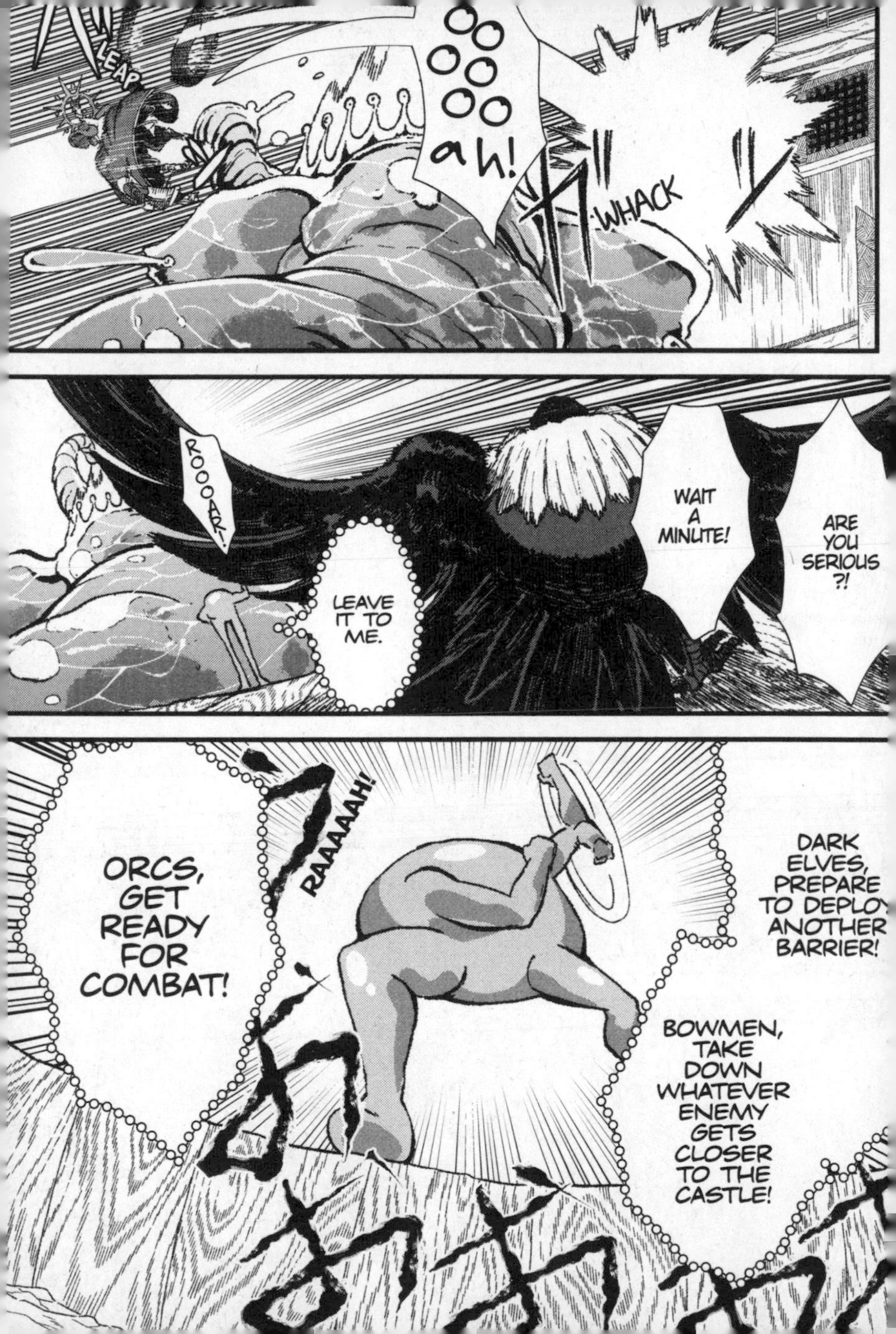

WHACK
OOOOOOOO ah!
LEAP
ARE YOU SERIOUS?!
WAIT A MINUTE!
LEAVE IT TO ME.
ROOOAR!
DARK ELVES, PREPARE TO DEPLOY ANOTHER BARRIER!
BOWMEN, TAKE DOWN WHATEVER ENEMY GETS CLOSER TO THE CASTLE!
RAAAAAAH!
ORCS, GET READY FOR COMBAT!

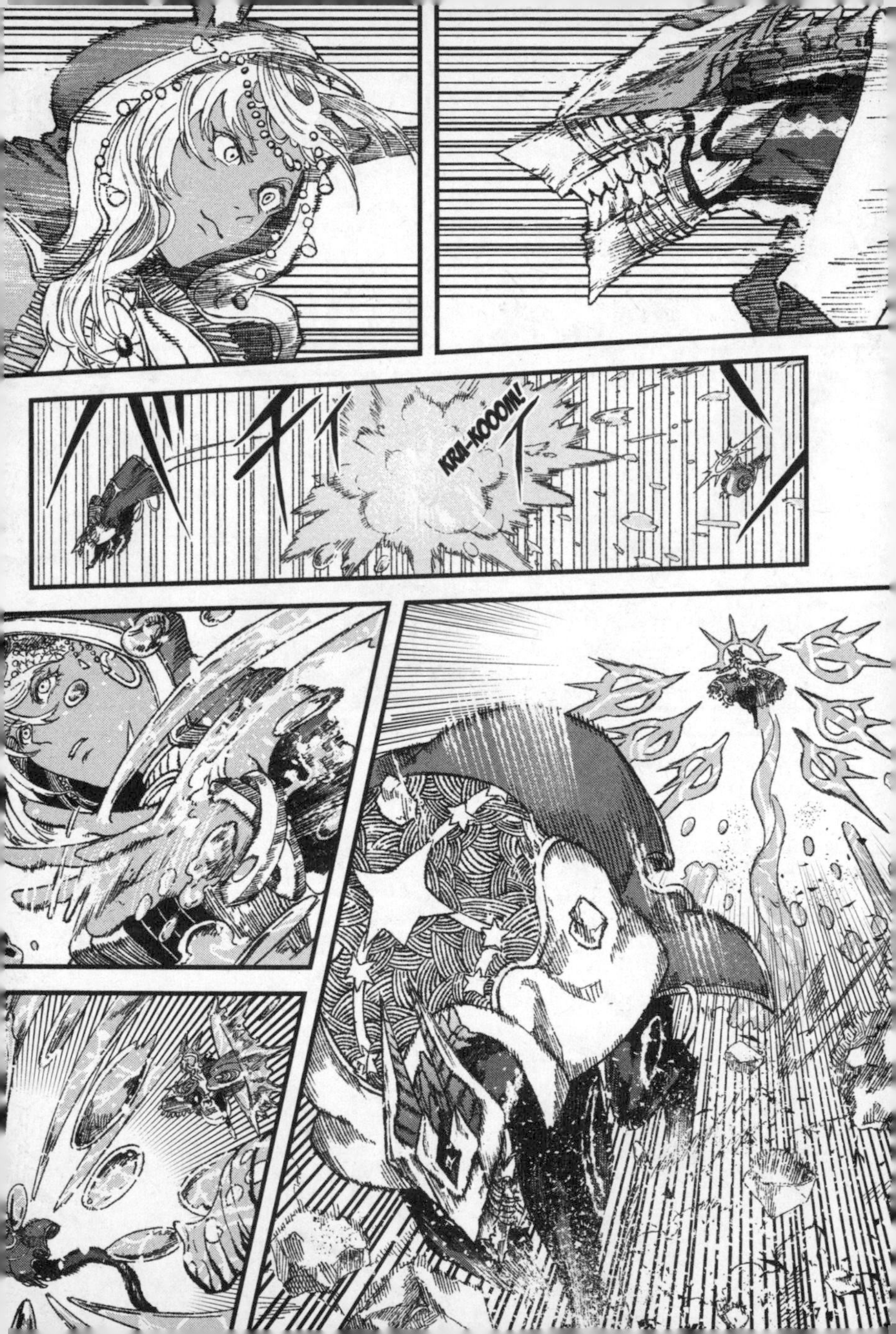
KRA-KOOOM!

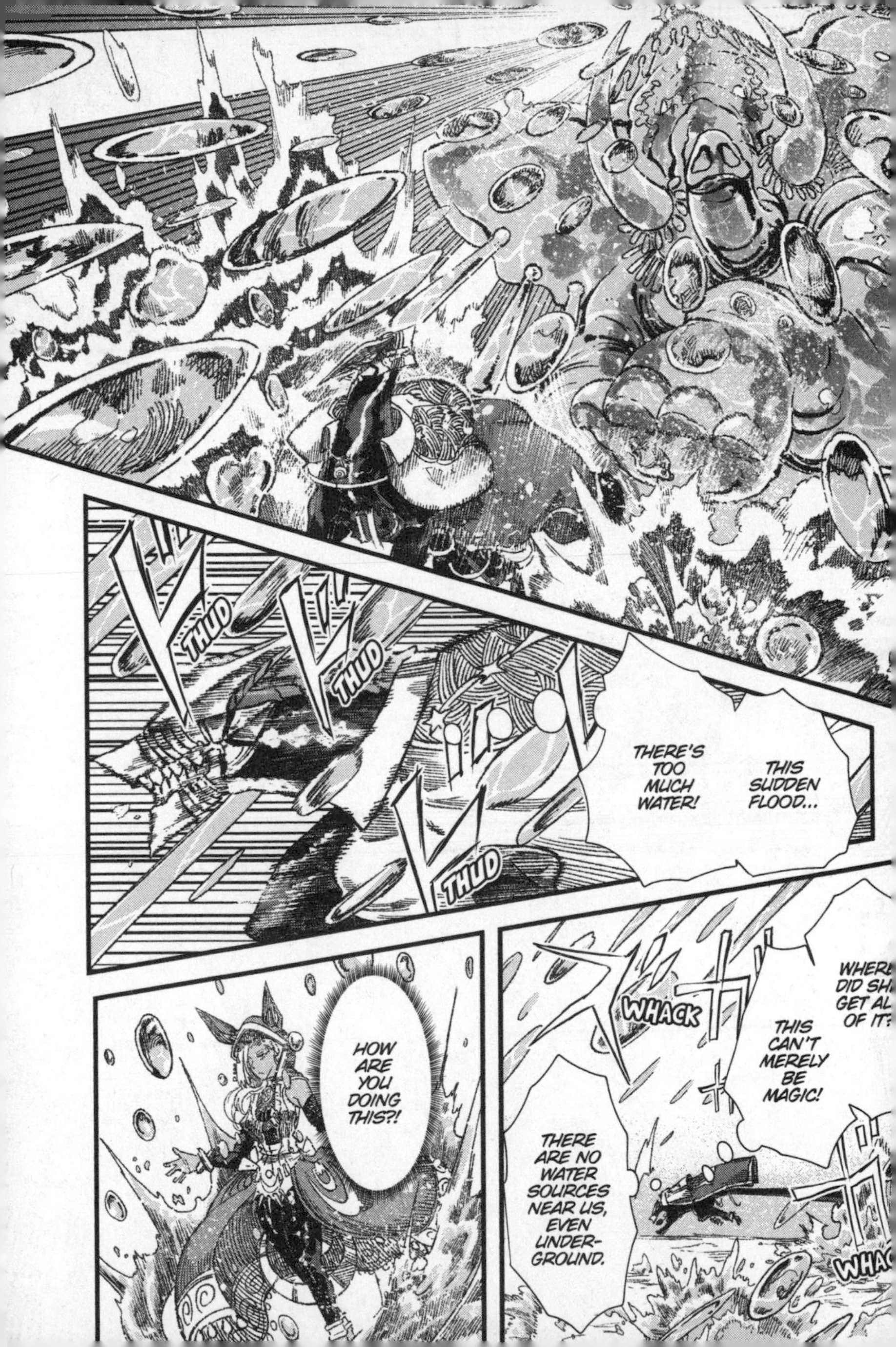
THUD
THUD
THUD
THIS SUDDEN FLOOD...
THERE'S TOO MUCH WATER!
WHACK
WHERE DID SH GET AL OF IT?
THIS CAN'T MERELY BE MAGIC!
THERE ARE NO WATER SOURCES NEAR US, EVEN UNDER-GROUND.
WHAC
HOW ARE YOU DOING THIS?!

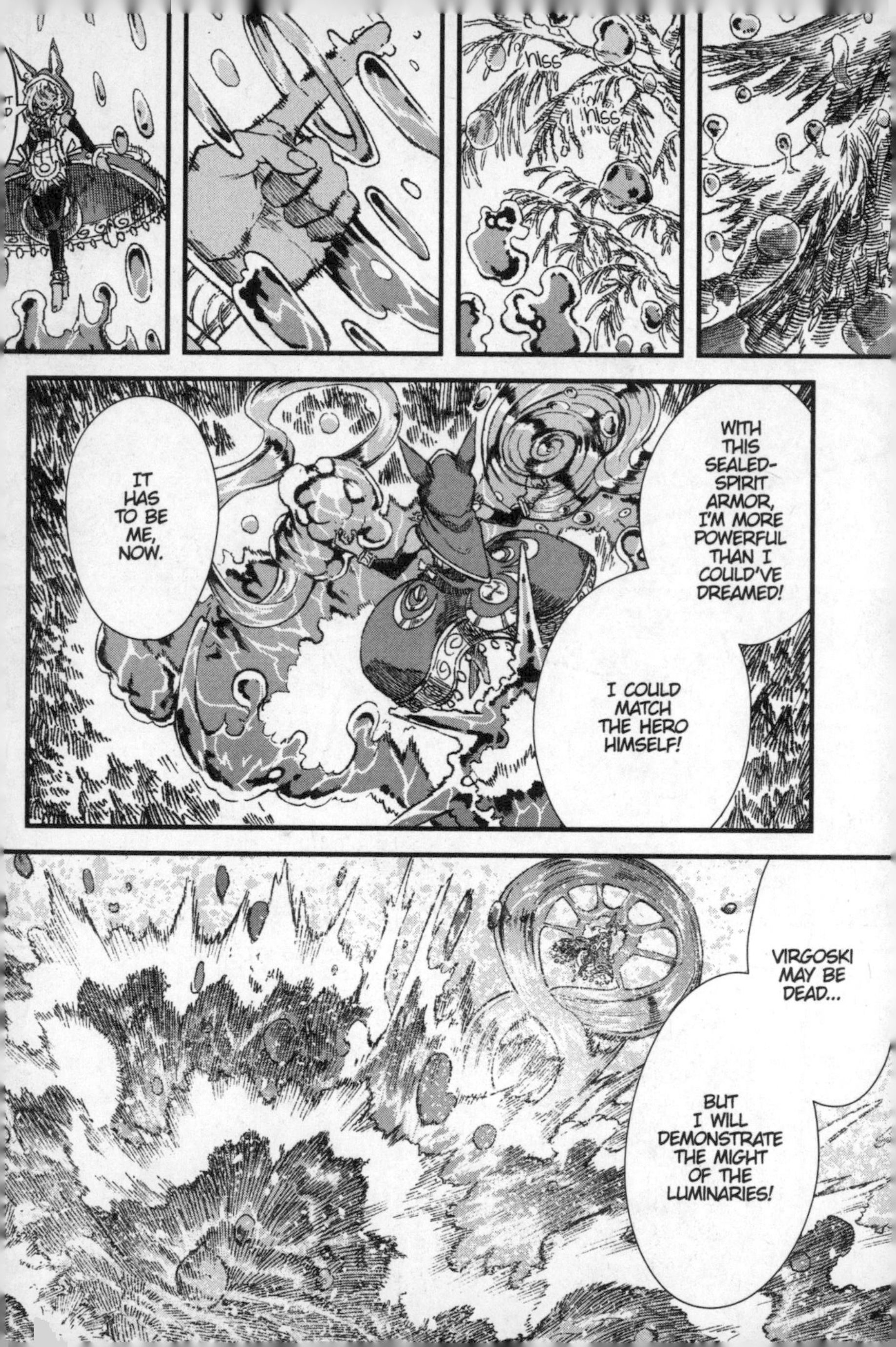

hiss
hiss
WITH THIS SEALED-SPIRIT ARMOR, I'M MORE POWERFUL THAN I COULD'VE DREAMED!
I COULD MATCH THE HERO HIMSELF!
IT HAS TO BE ME, NOW.
VIRGOSKI MAY BE DEAD...
BUT I WILL DEMONSTRATE THE MIGHT OF THE LUMINARIES!

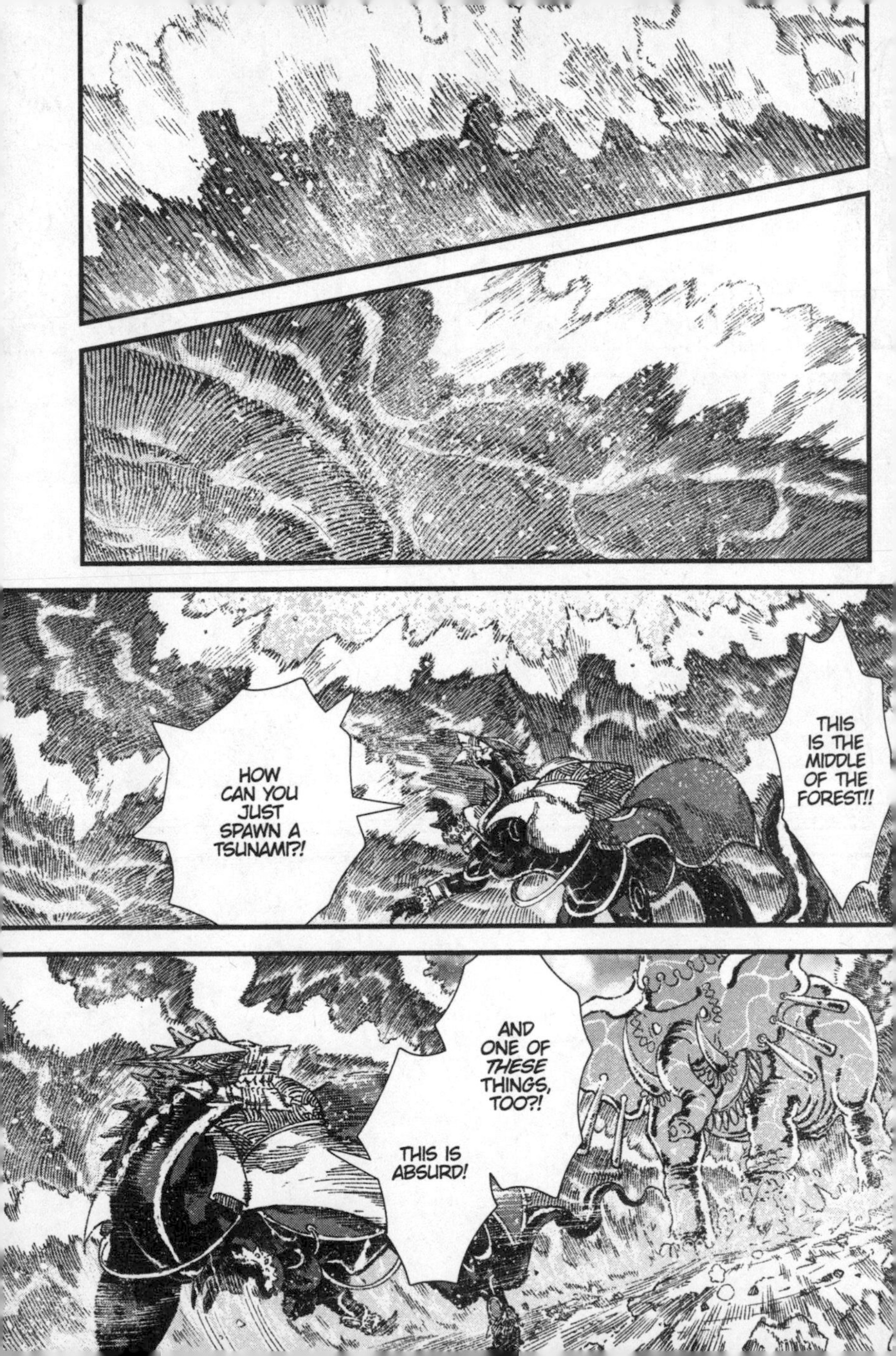
THIS IS THE MIDDLE OF THE FOREST!!
HOW CAN YOU JUST SPAWN A TSUNAMI?!
AND ONE OF *THESE* THINGS, TOO?!
THIS IS ABSURD!

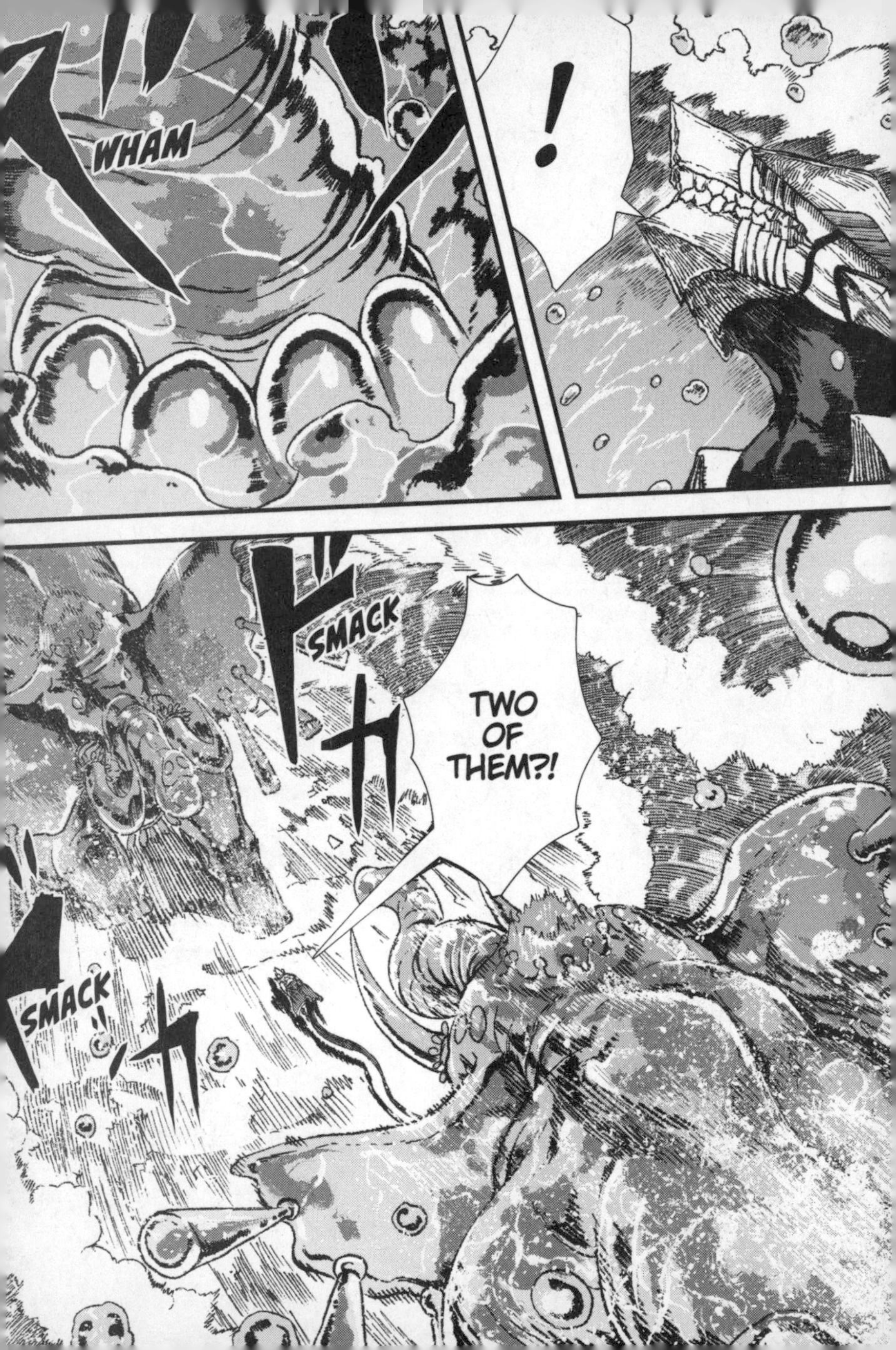
!
WHAM
TWO OF THEM?!
SMACK
SMACK

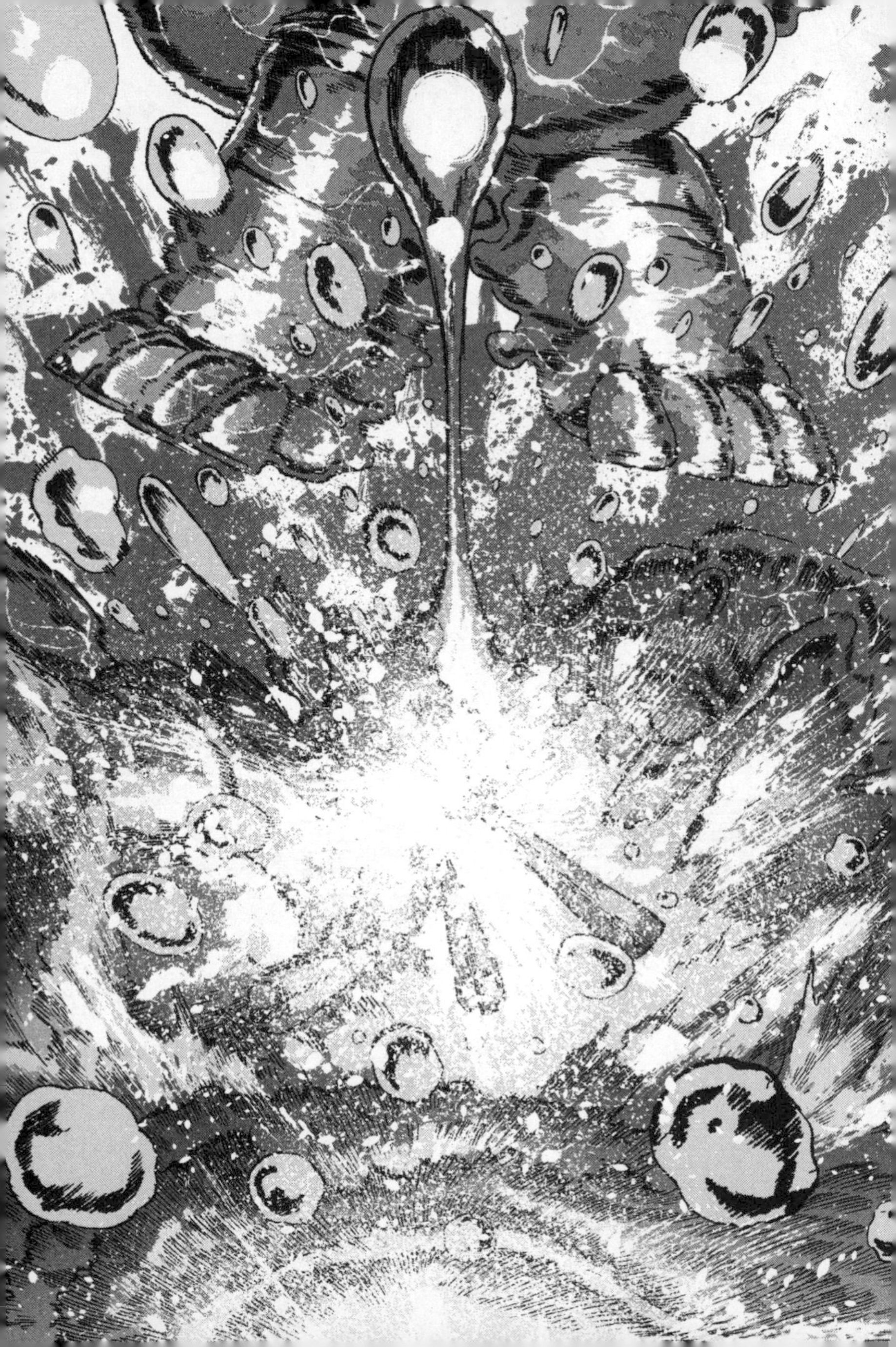

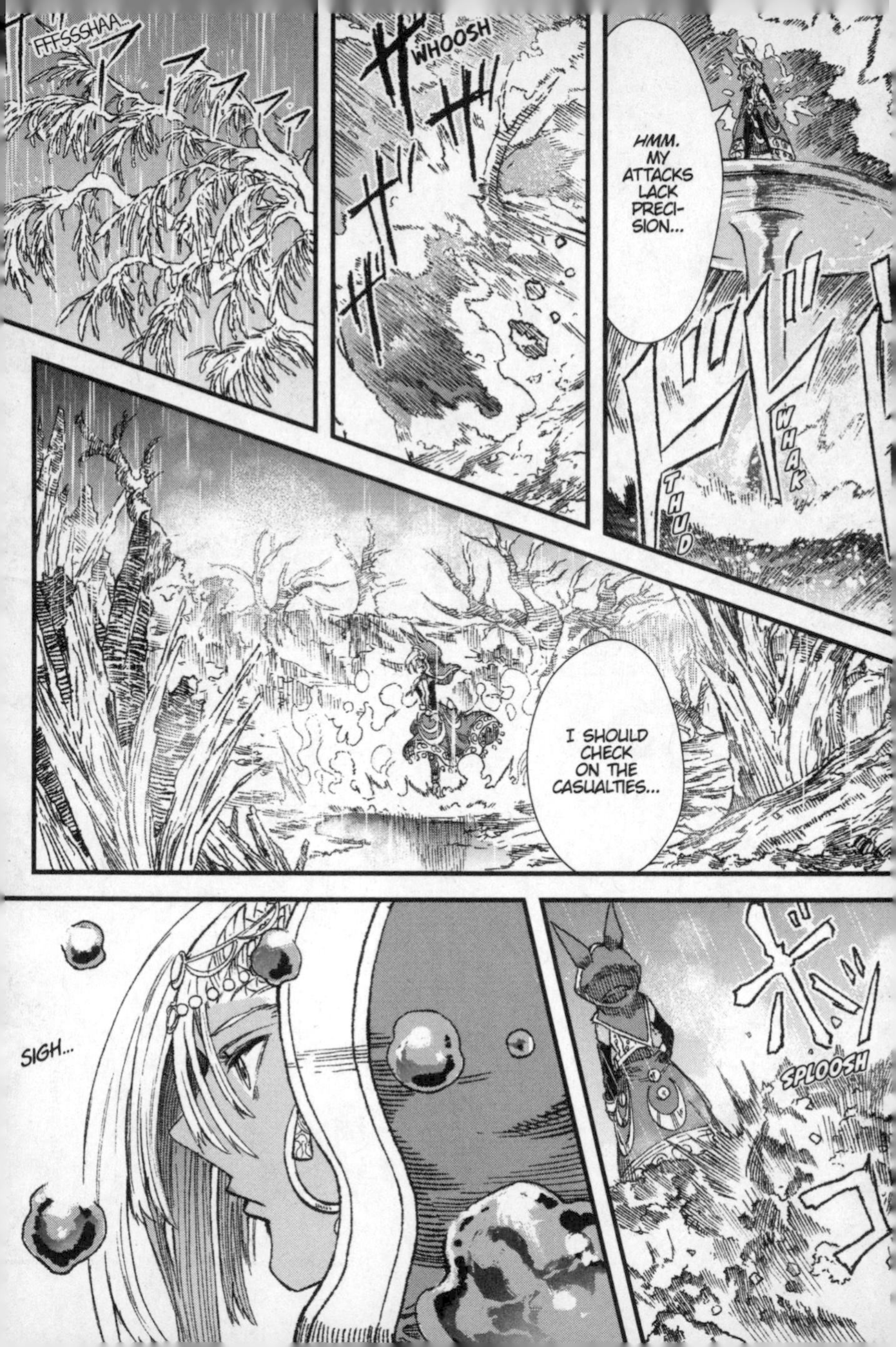
HMM. MY ATTACKS LACK PRECISION...
WHAK
THUD
WHOOSH
FFFSSSHAA...
I SHOULD CHECK ON THE CASUALTIES...
SPLOOSH
SIGH...

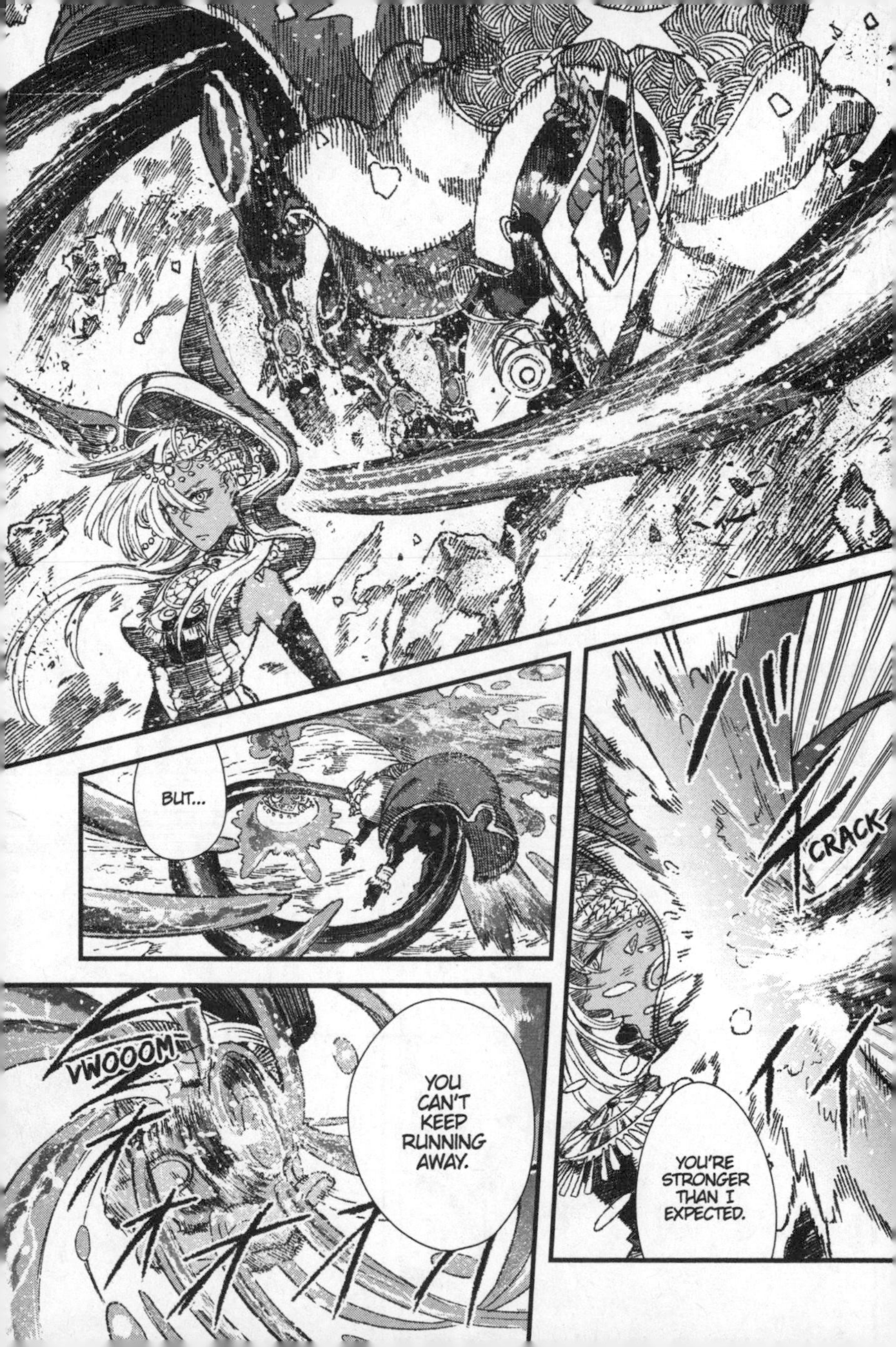
CRACK
YOU'RE STRONGER THAN I EXPECTED.
BUT...
VWOOOM
YOU CAN'T KEEP RUNNING AWAY.

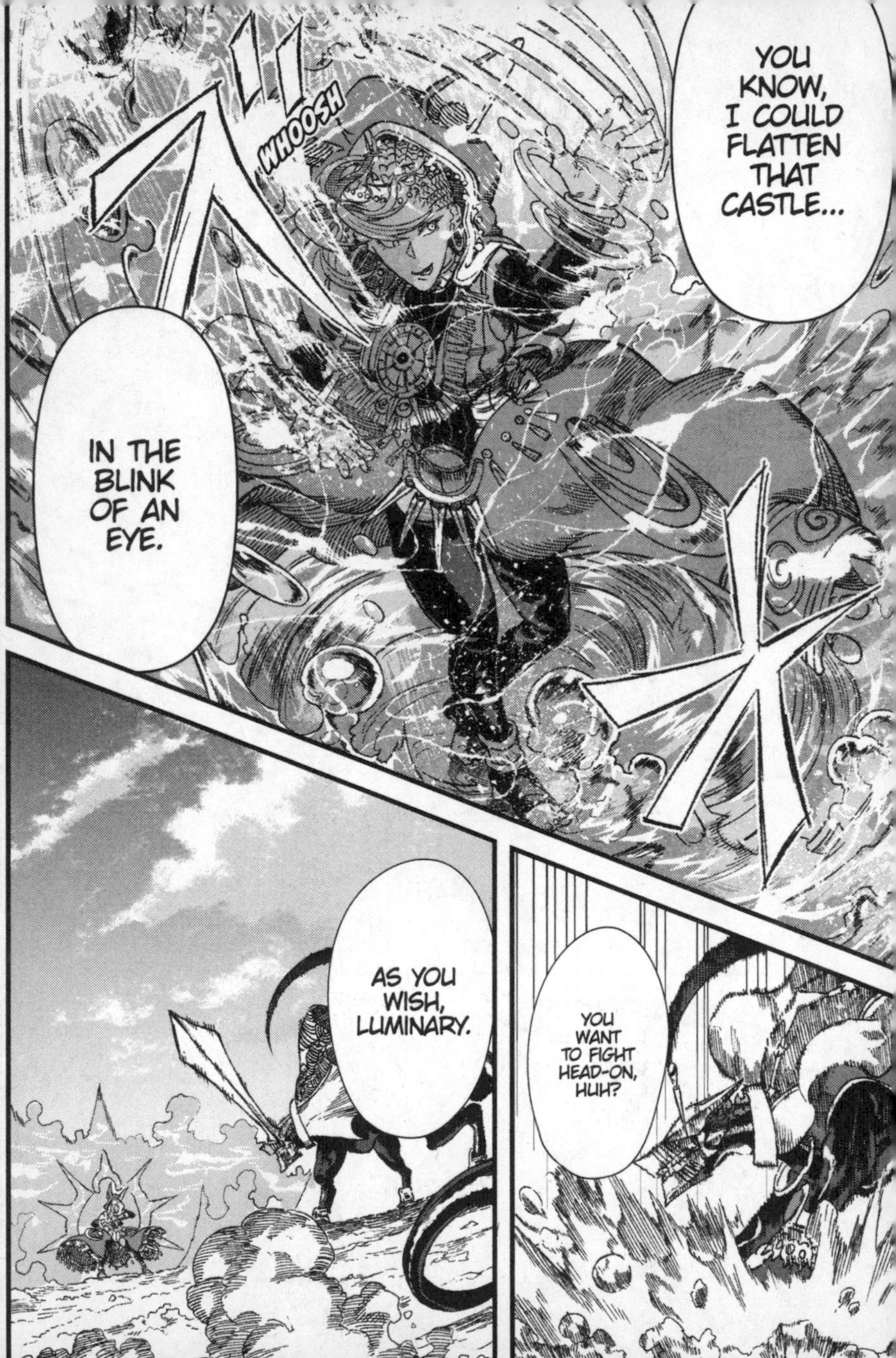
YOU KNOW, I COULD FLATTEN THAT CASTLE...
WHOOSH
IN THE BLINK OF AN EYE.
YOU WANT TO FIGHT HEAD-ON, HUH?
AS YOU WISH, LUMINARY.

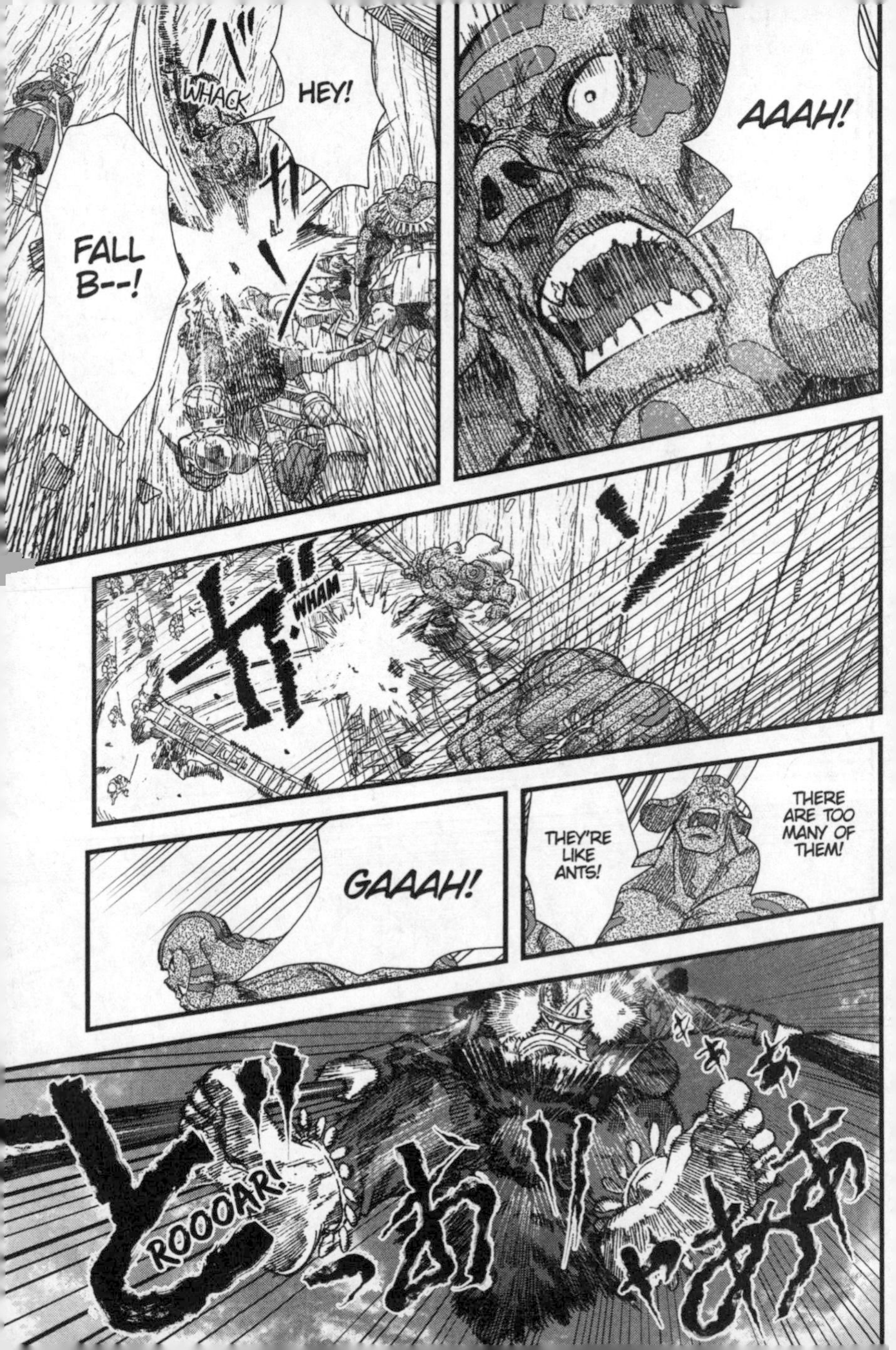
AAAH!
HEY!
WHACK
FALL B--!
WHAM
THERE ARE TOO MANY OF THEM!
THEY'RE LIKE ANTS!
GAAAH!
ROOOAR!

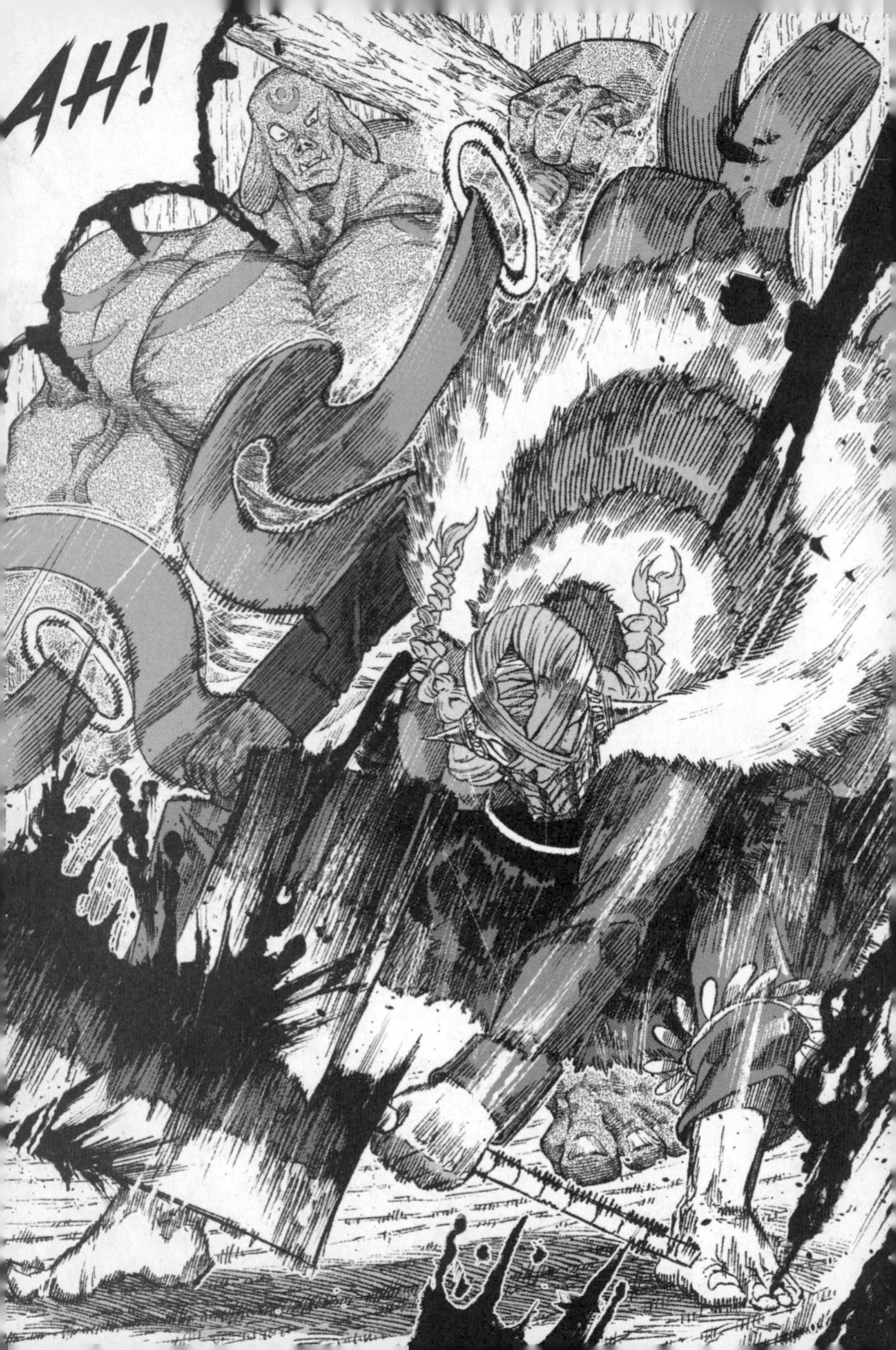
AH!

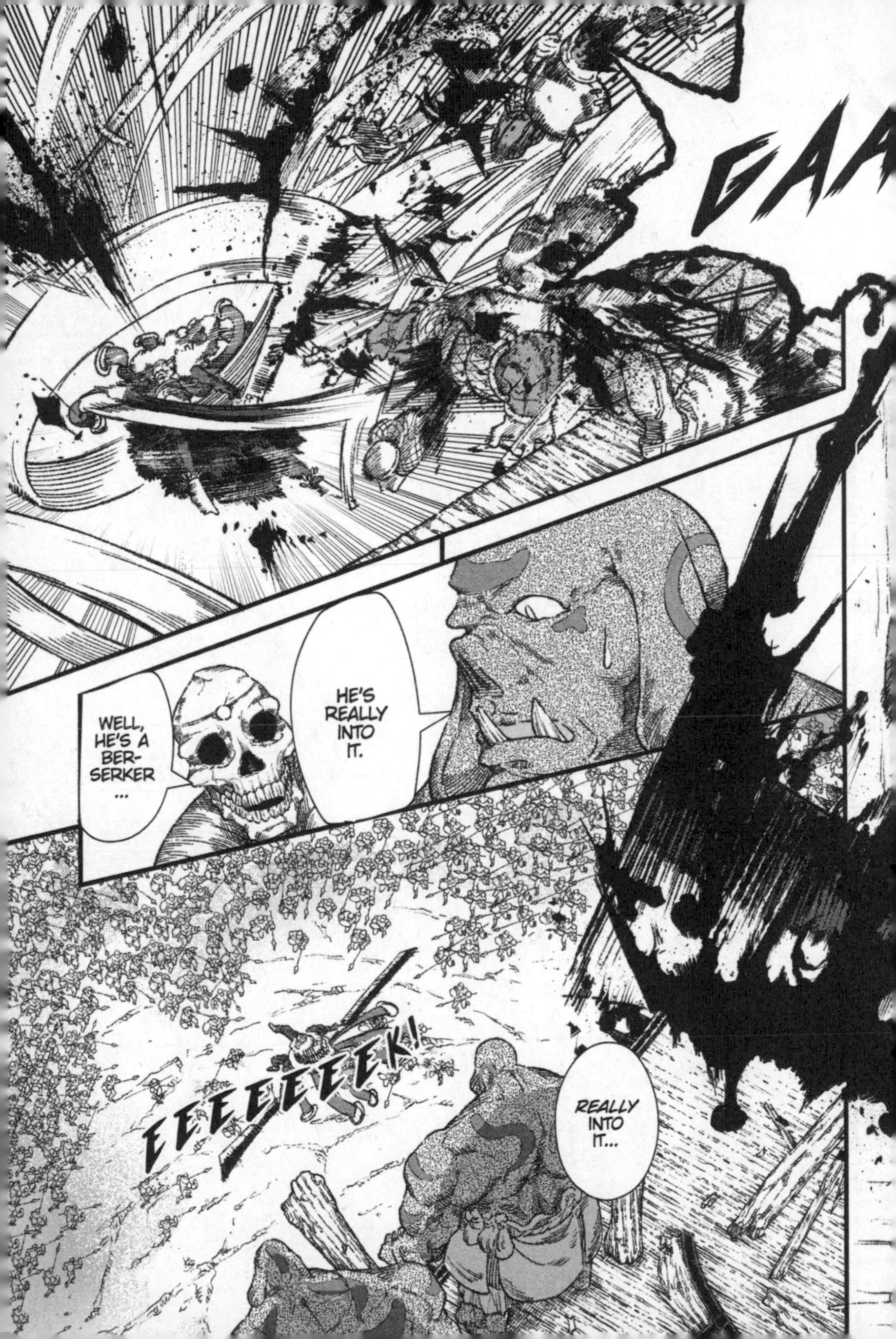
GAA
HE'S REALLY INTO IT.
WELL, HE'S A BER-SERKER ...
EEEEEEEEK!
REALLY INTO IT...

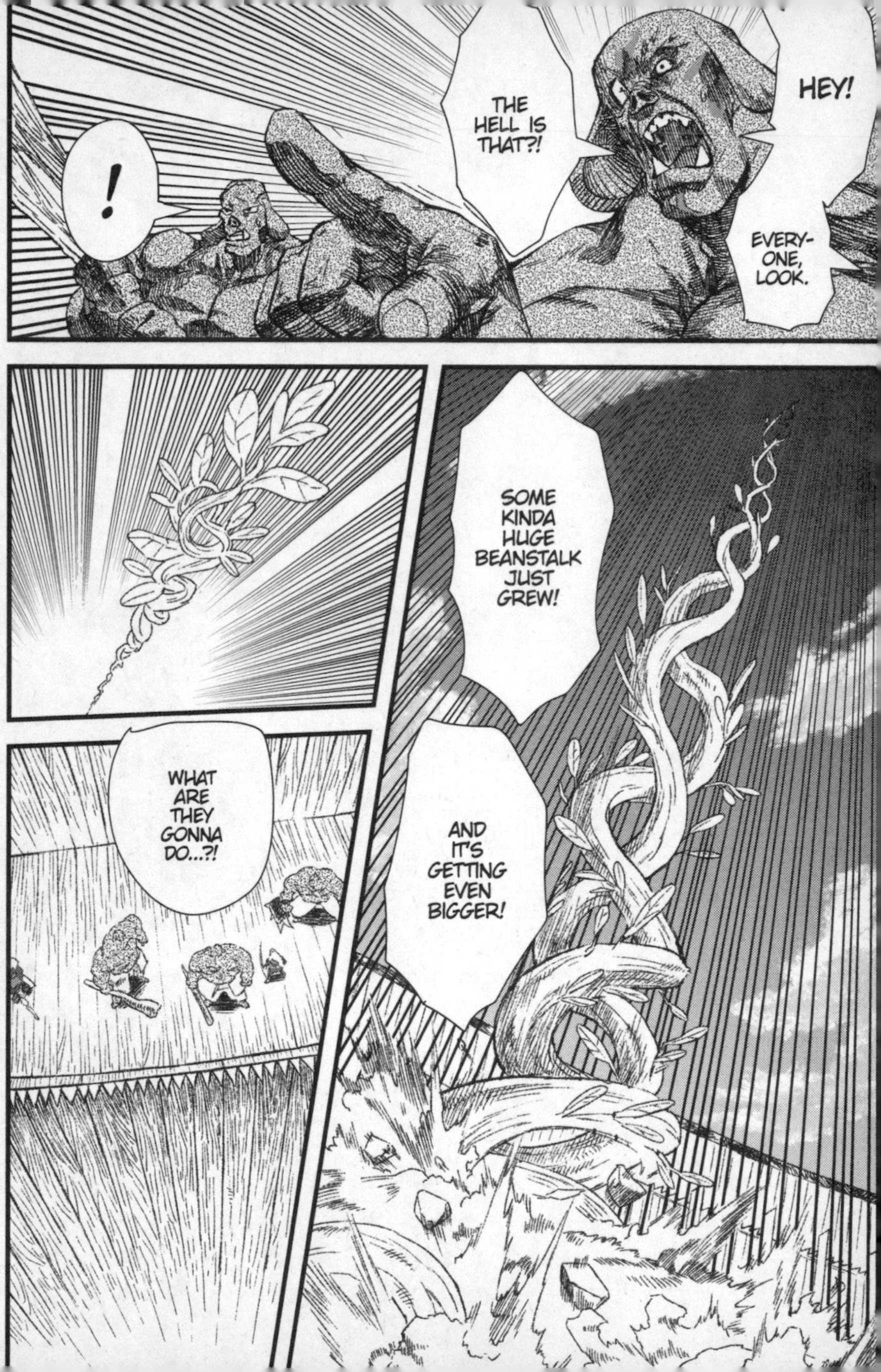
HEY!
EVERY-ONE, LOOK.
THE HELL IS THAT?!
!
SOME KINDA HUGE BEANSTALK JUST GREW!
AND IT'S GETTING EVEN BIGGER!
WHAT ARE THEY GONNA DO...?!

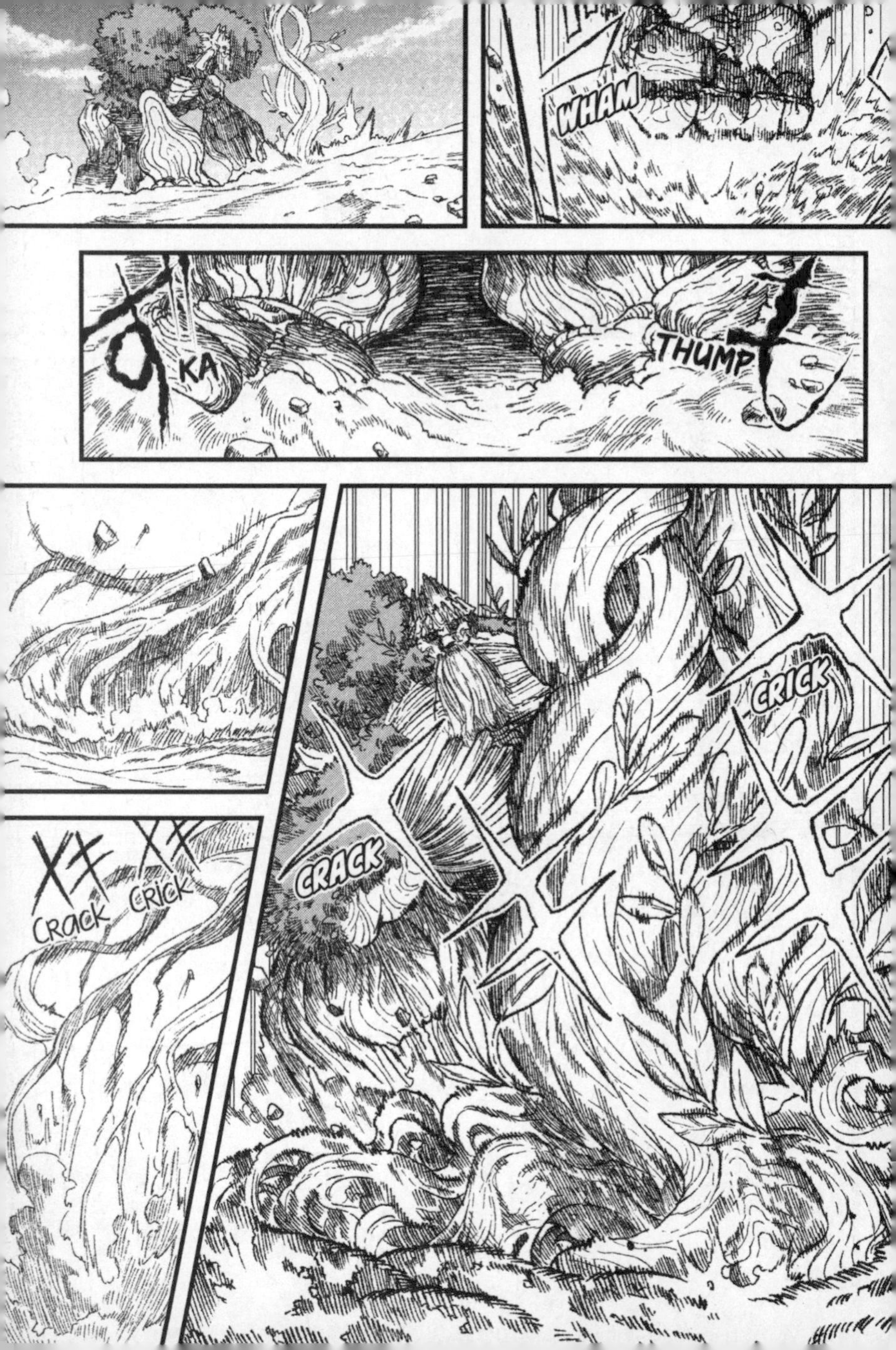
WHAM
THUMP
KA
CRICK
CRACK
CRICK
CRACK

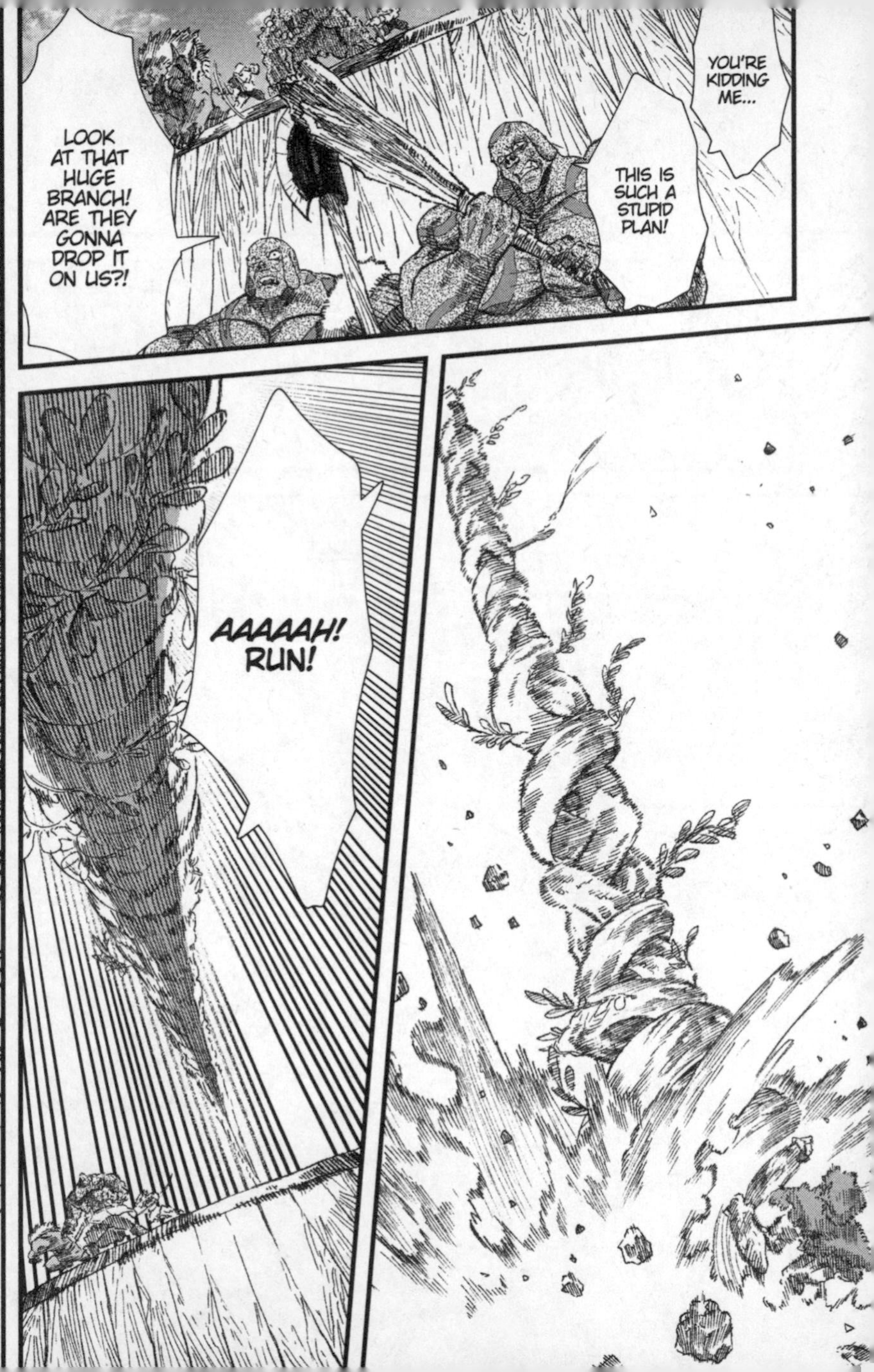
YOU'RE KIDDING ME...
THIS IS SUCH A STUPID PLAN!
LOOK AT THAT HUGE BRANCH! ARE THEY GONNA DROP IT ON US?!
AAAAAH! RUN!

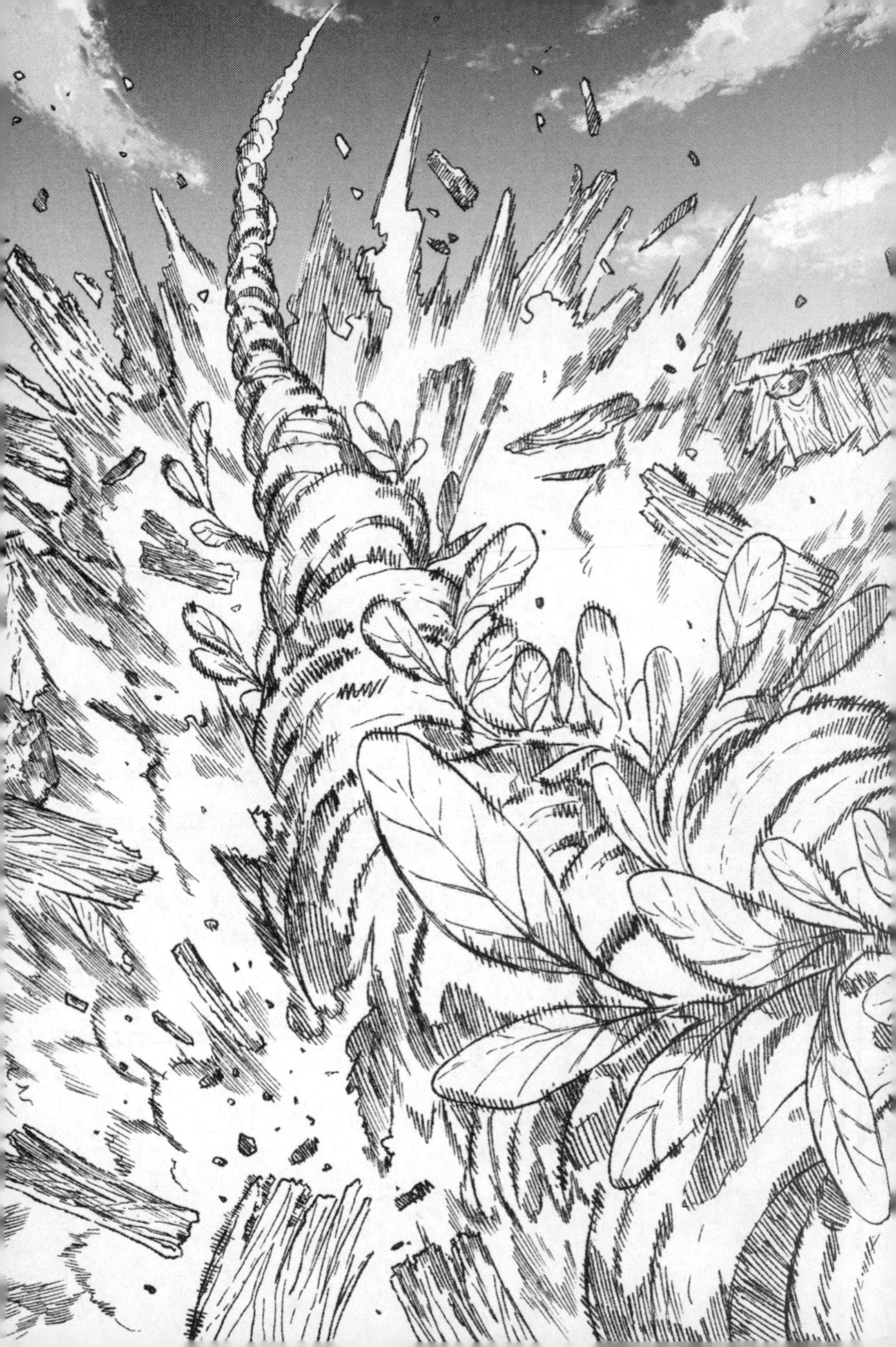

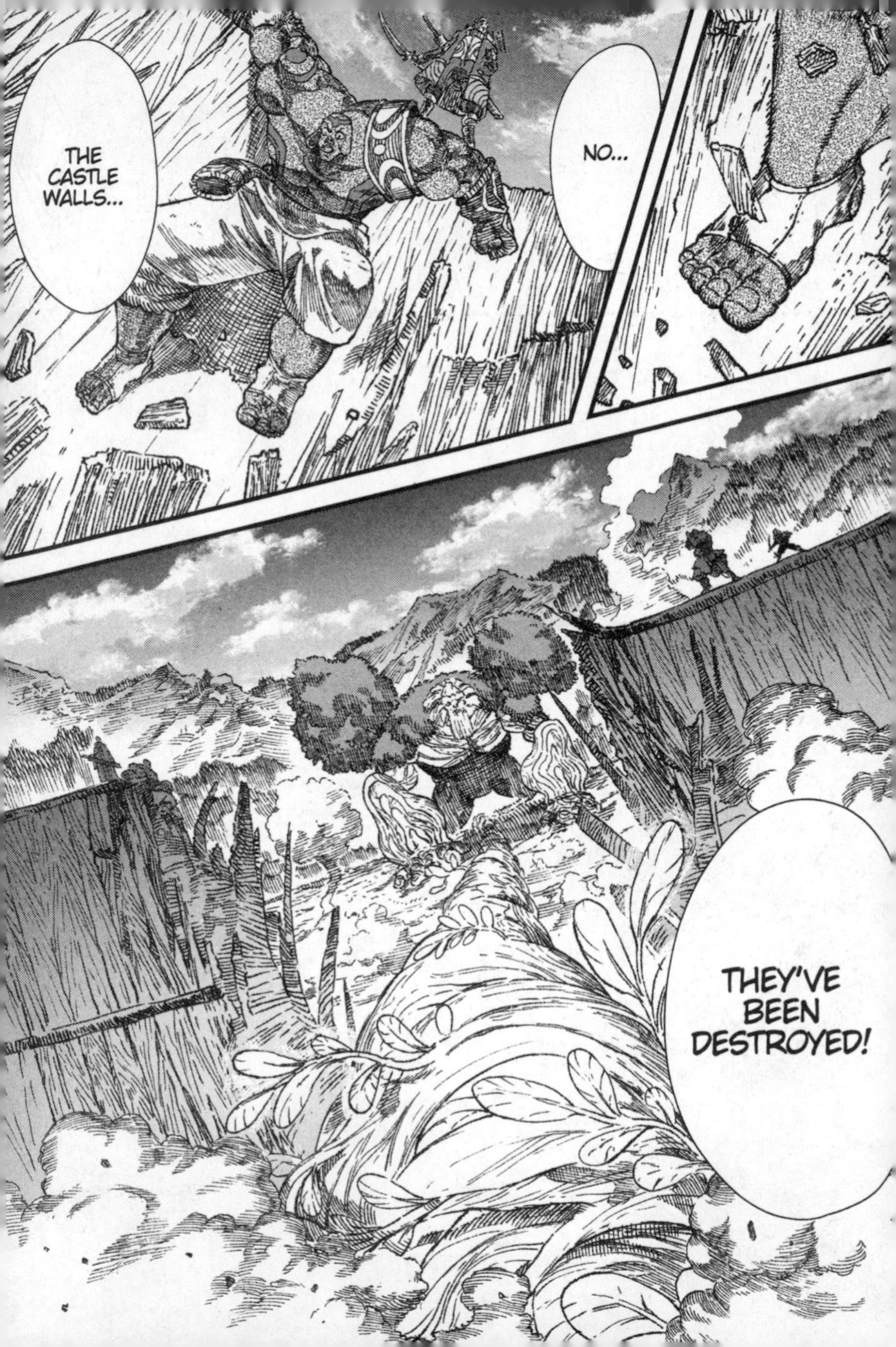
NO...
THE CASTLE WALLS...
THEY'VE BEEN DESTROYED!

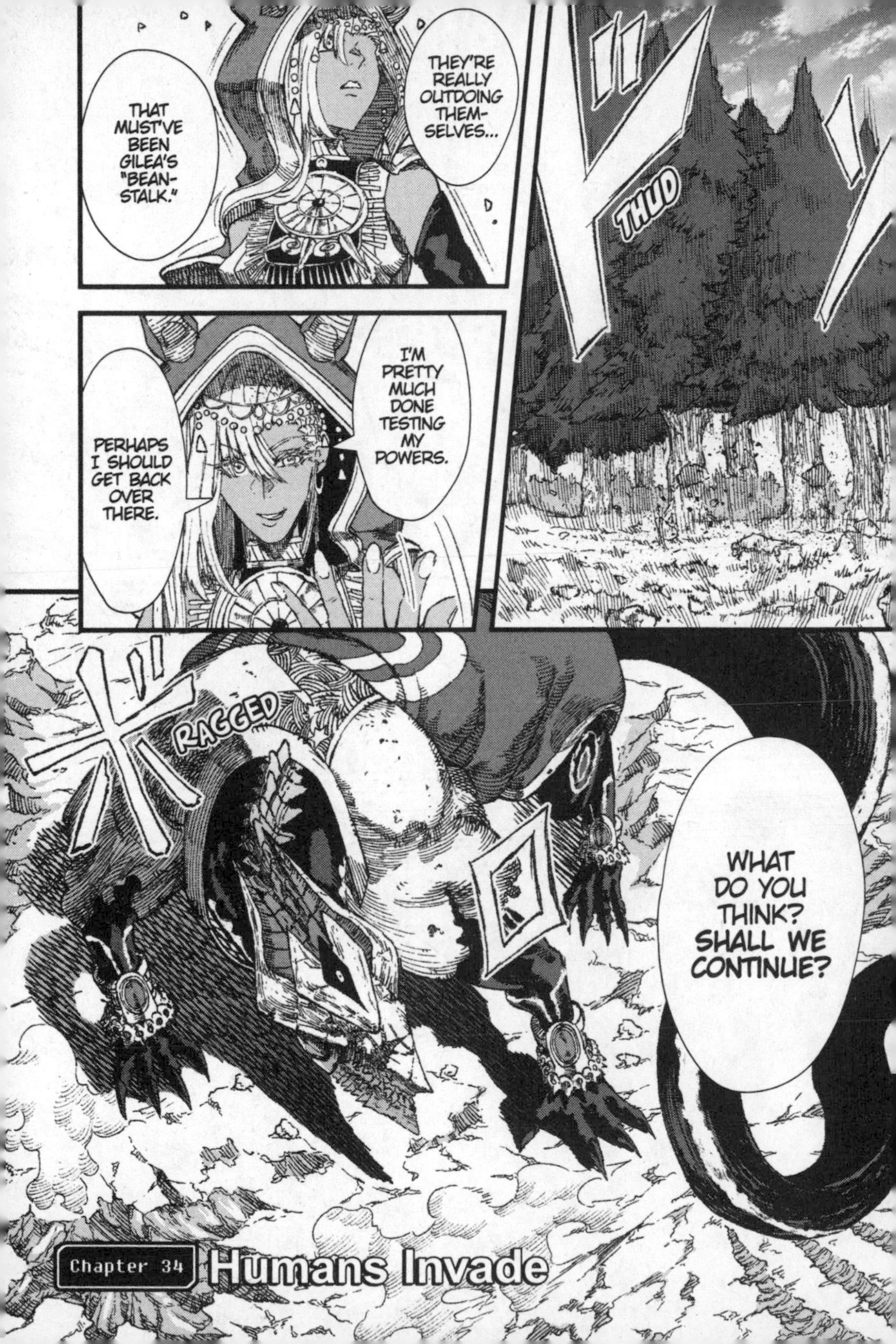
THUD
THEY'RE REALLY OUTDOING THEM-SELVES...
THAT MUST'VE BEEN GILEA'S "BEAN-STALK."
I'M PRETTY MUCH DONE TESTING MY POWERS.
PERHAPS I SHOULD GET BACK OVER THERE.
RAGGED
WHAT DO YOU THINK? SHALL WE CONTINUE?

Chapter 34 Humans Invade

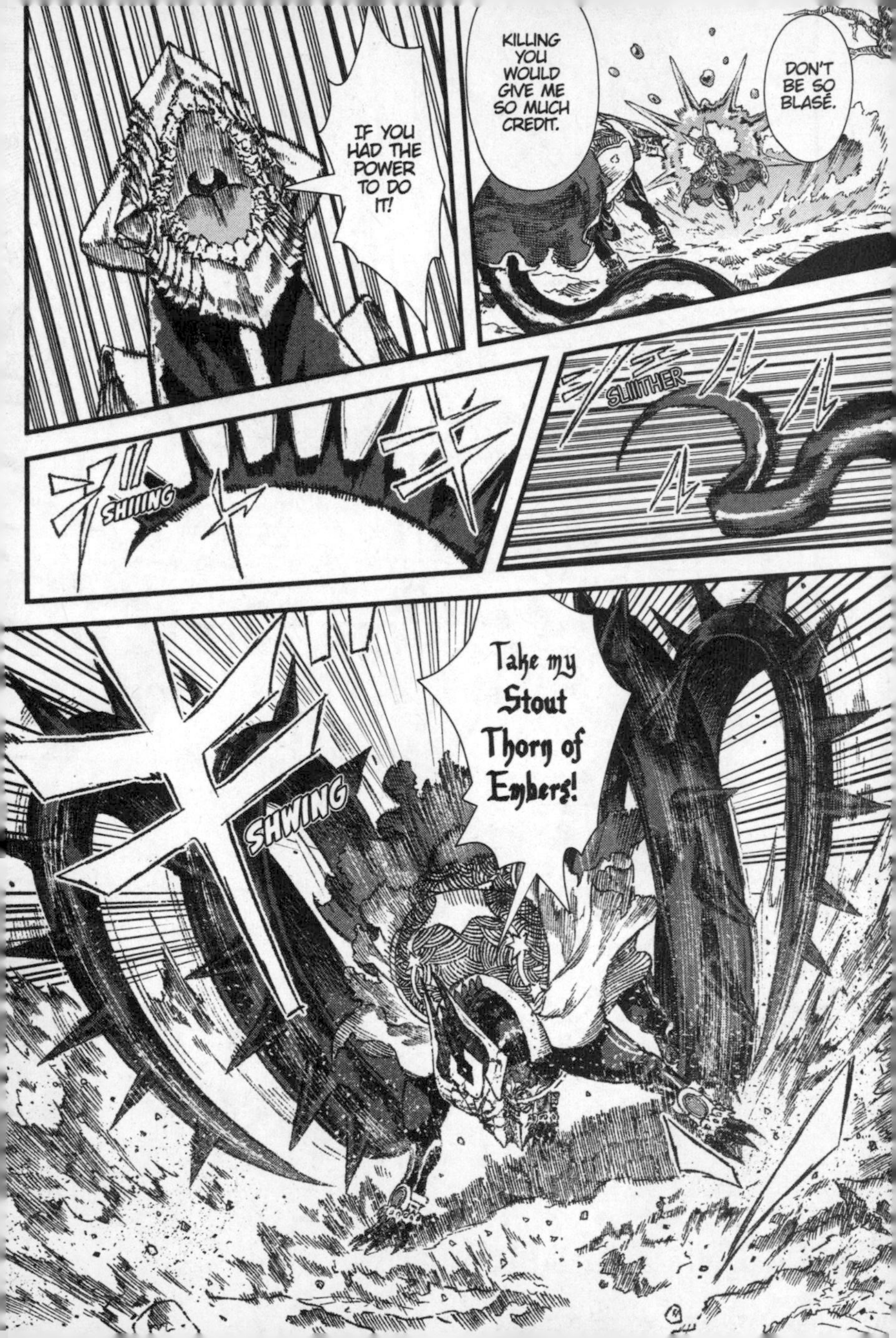
DON'T BE SO BLASÉ.
KILLING YOU WOULD GIVE ME SO MUCH CREDIT.
IF YOU HAD THE POWER TO DO IT!
SLIIITHER
SHIIING
Take my Stout Thorn of Embers!
SHWING

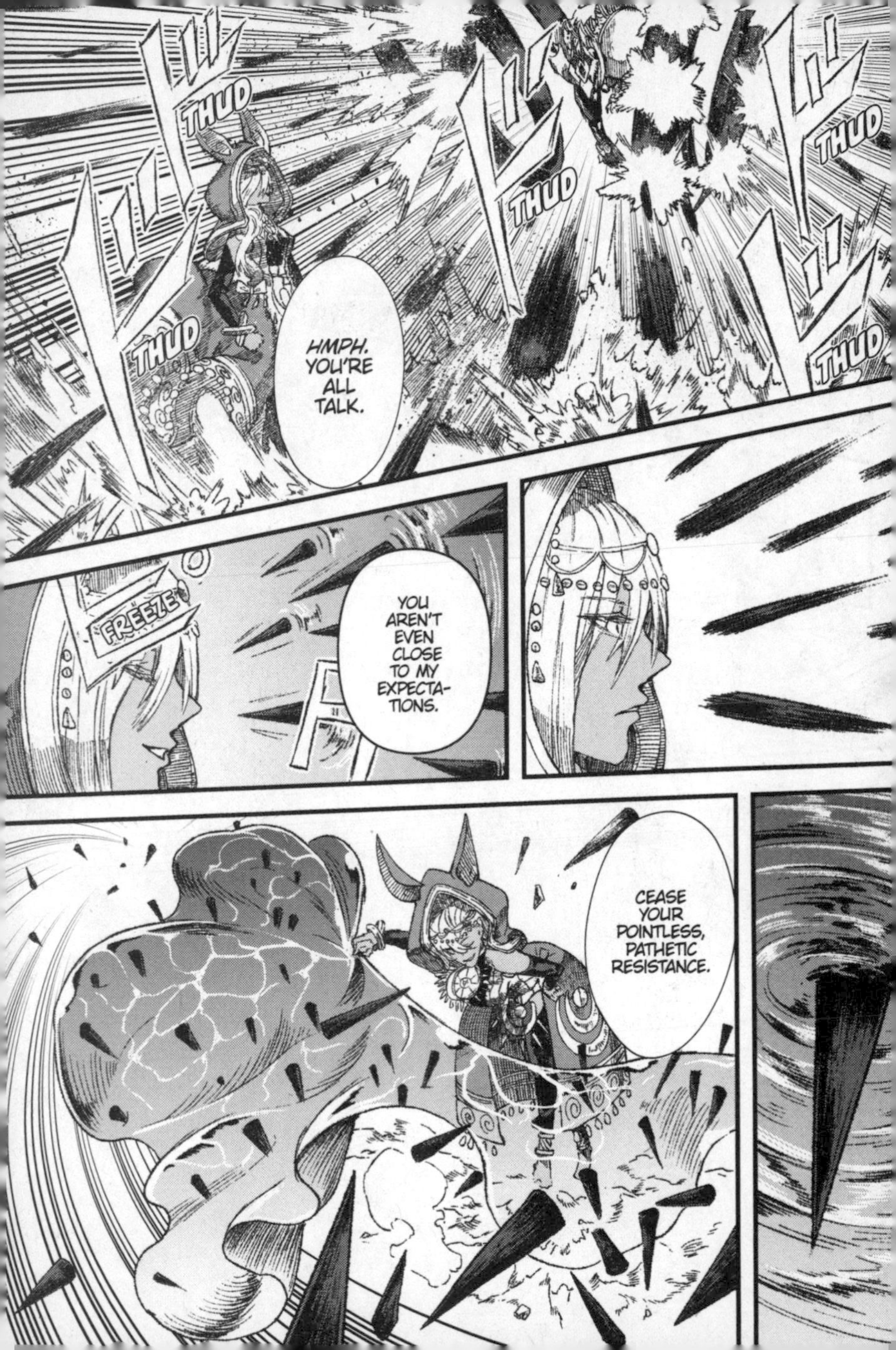
THUD
THUD
THUD
THUD
HMPH. YOU'RE ALL TALK.
THUD
YOU AREN'T EVEN CLOSE TO MY EXPECTATIONS.
FREEZE
CEASE YOUR POINTLESS, PATHETIC RESISTANCE.

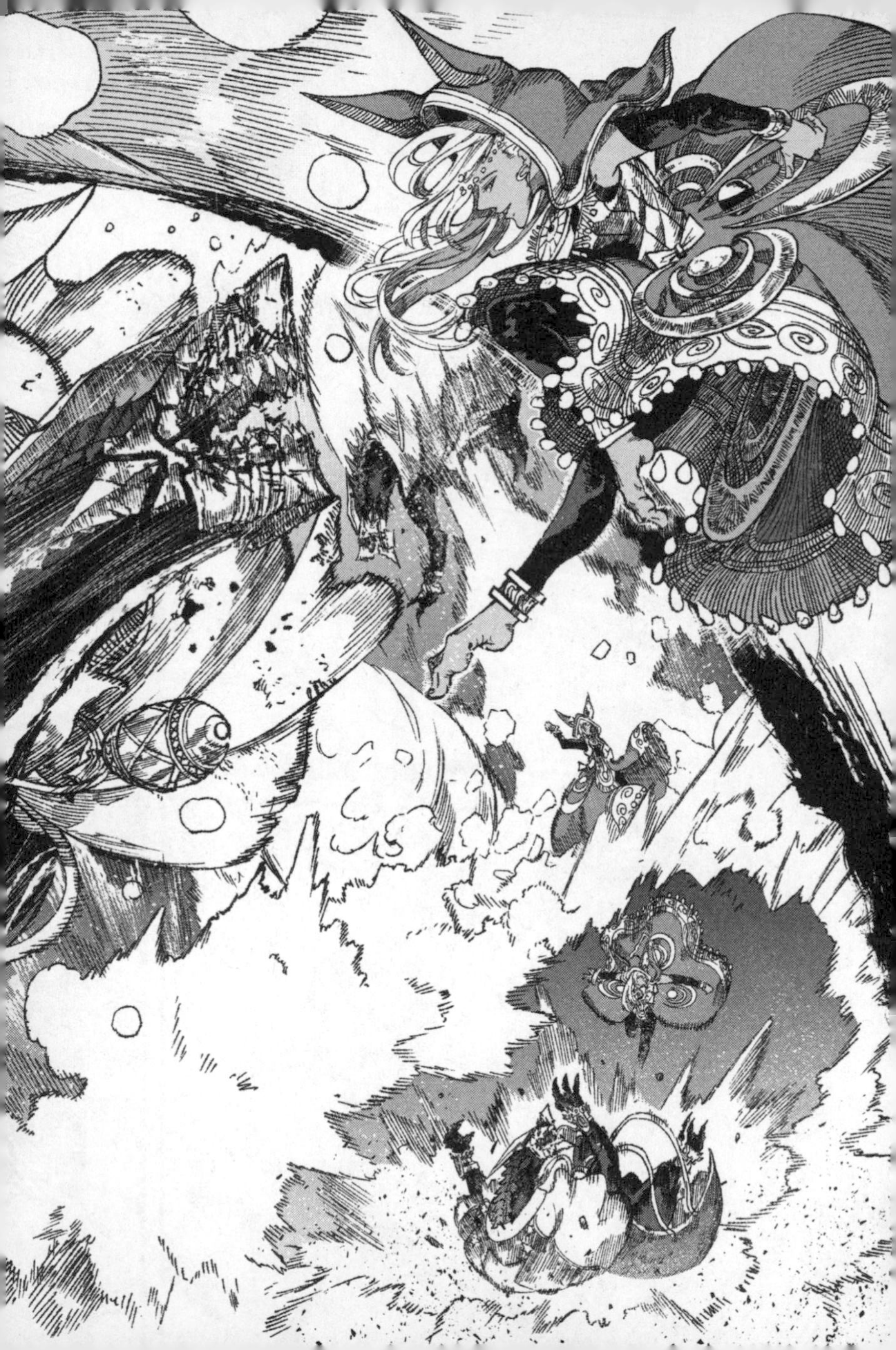

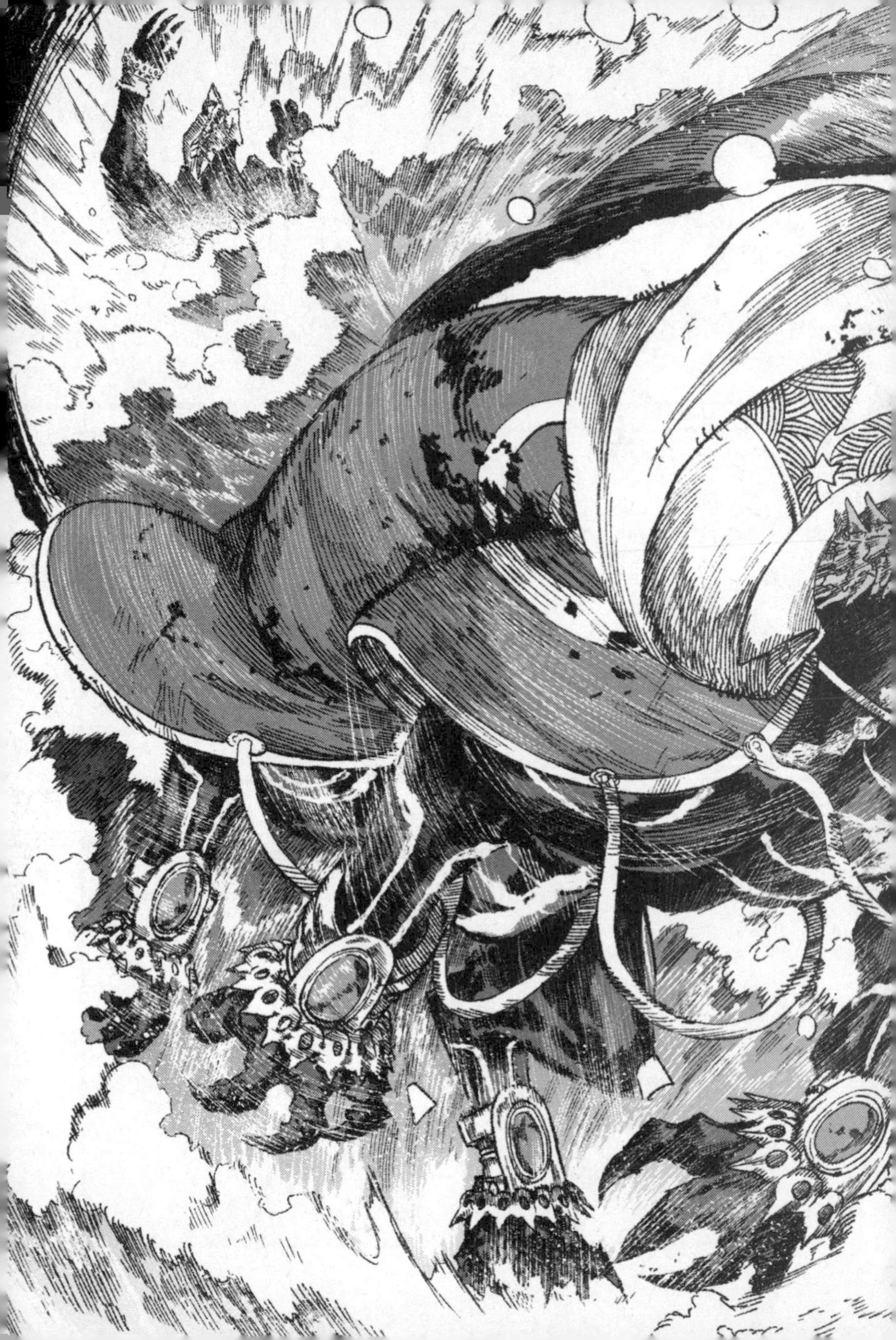

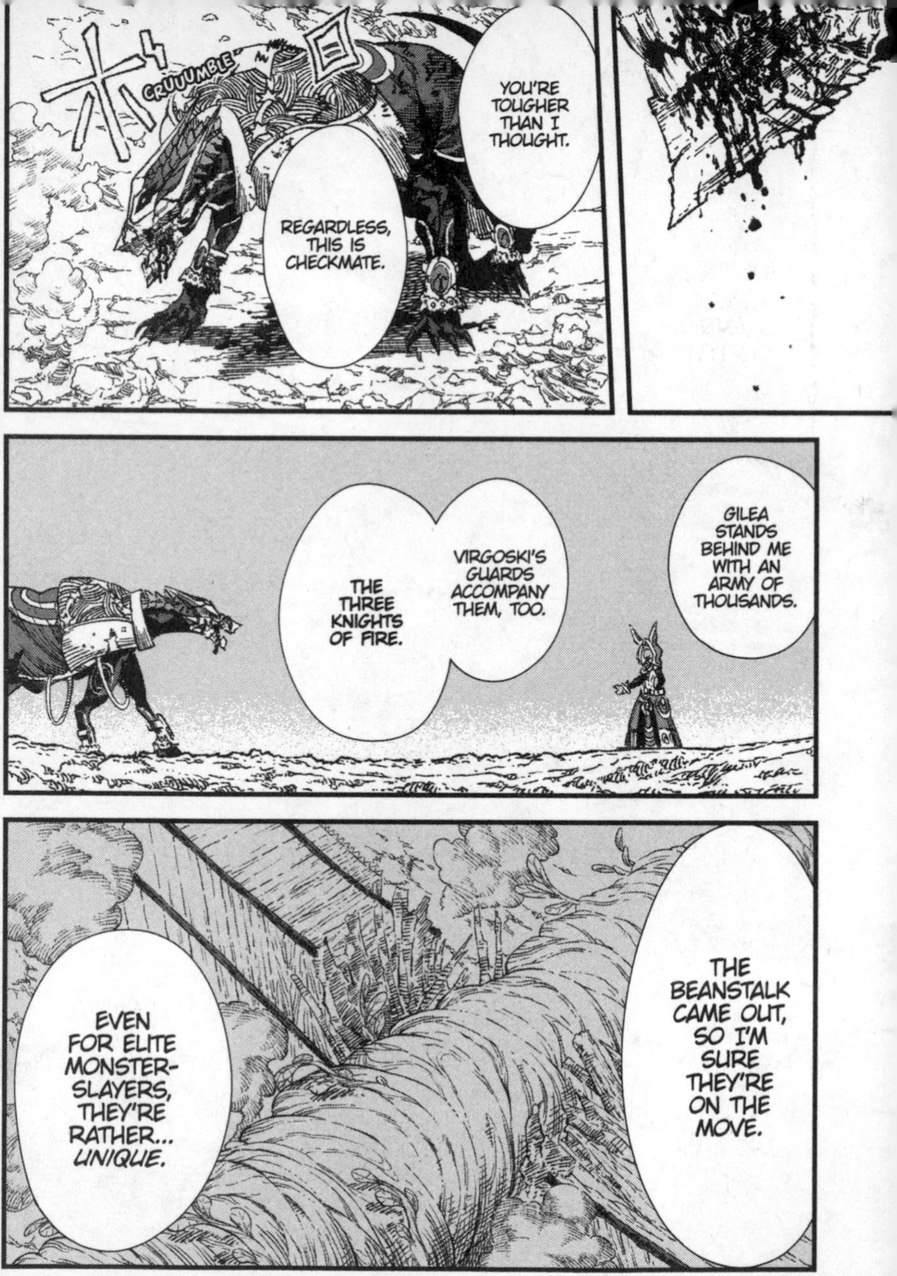
YOU'RE TOUGHER THAN I THOUGHT.
REGARDLESS, THIS IS CHECKMATE.
CRUUUMBLE
GILEA STANDS BEHIND ME WITH AN ARMY OF THOUSANDS.
VIRGOSKI'S GUARDS ACCOMPANY THEM, TOO.
THE THREE KNIGHTS OF FIRE.
THE BEANSTALK CAME OUT, SO I'M SURE THEY'RE ON THE MOVE.
EVEN FOR ELITE MONSTER-SLAYERS, THEY'RE RATHER... *UNIQUE.*

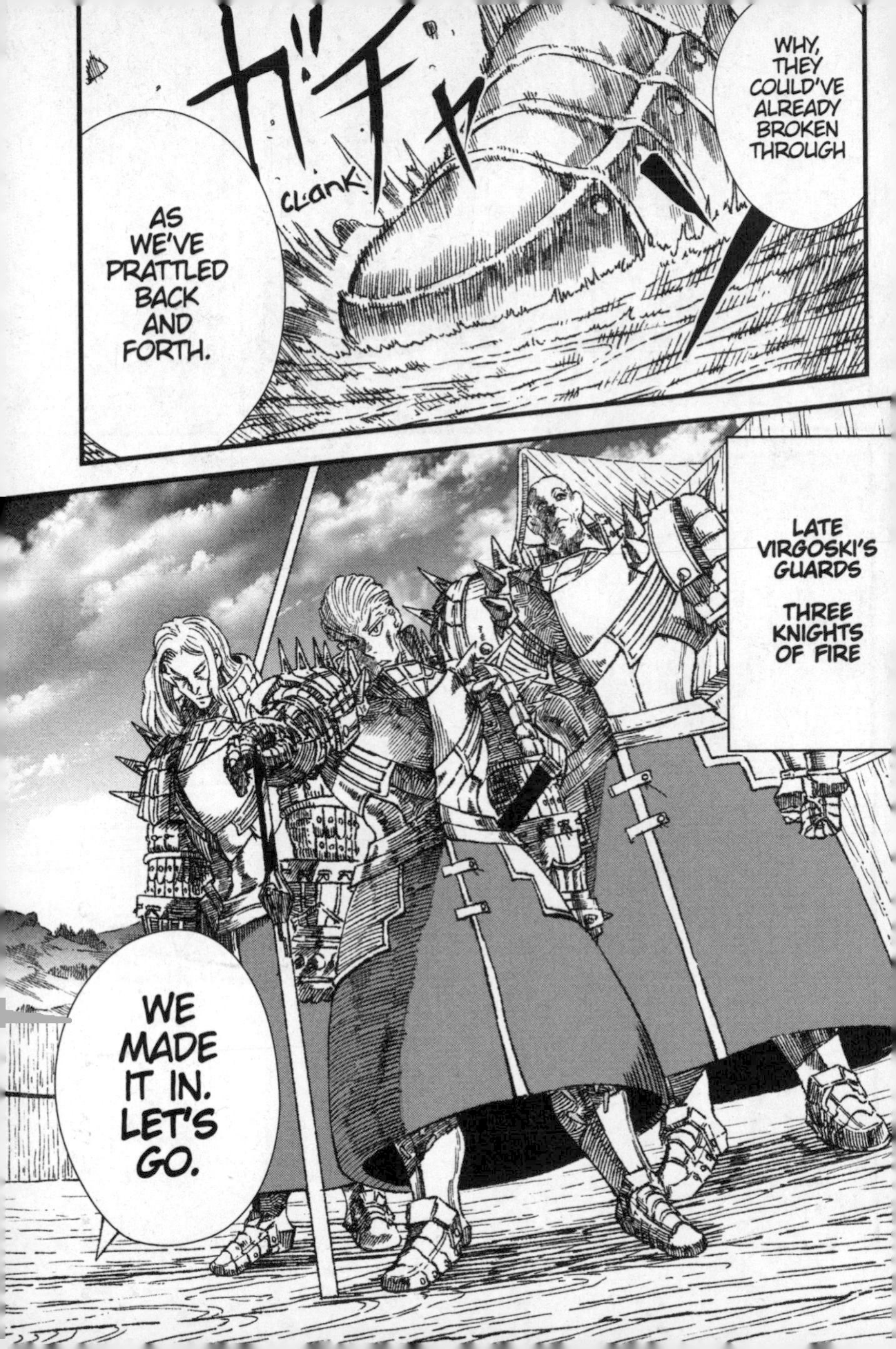
WHY, THEY COULD'VE ALREADY BROKEN THROUGH
ガチャ
CLANK!
AS WE'VE PRATTLED BACK AND FORTH.
LATE VIRGOSKI'S GUARDS
THREE KNIGHTS OF FIRE
WE MADE IT IN. LET'S GO.

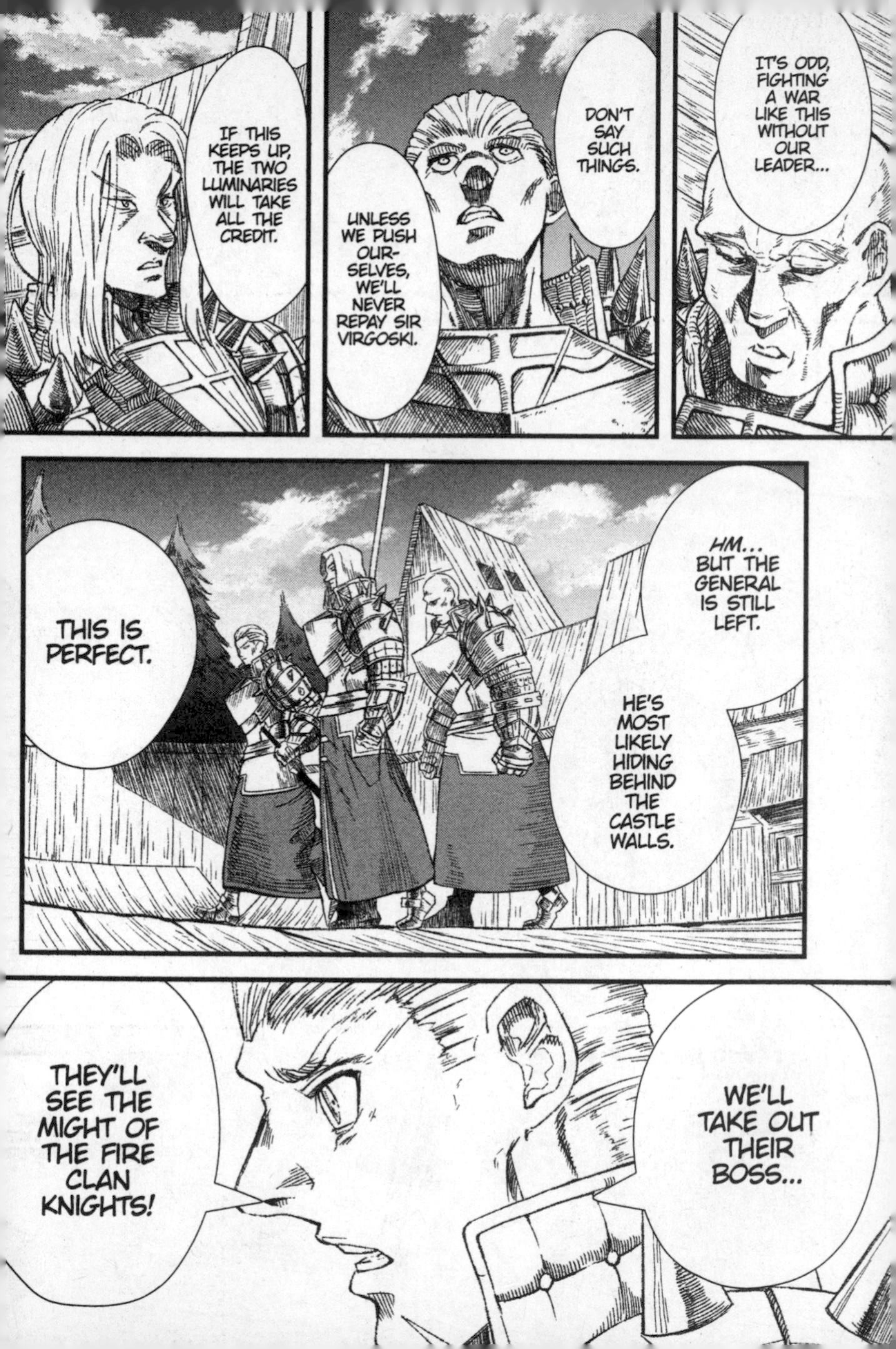
IT'S ODD, FIGHTING A WAR LIKE THIS WITHOUT OUR LEADER...
DON'T SAY SUCH THINGS.
UNLESS WE PUSH OURSELVES, WE'LL NEVER REPAY SIR VIRGOSKI.
IF THIS KEEPS UP, THE TWO LUMINARIES WILL TAKE ALL THE CREDIT.
HM... BUT THE GENERAL IS STILL LEFT.
HE'S MOST LIKELY HIDING BEHIND THE CASTLE WALLS.
THIS IS PERFECT.
WE'LL TAKE OUT THEIR BOSS...
THEY'LL SEE THE MIGHT OF THE FIRE CLAN KNIGHTS!

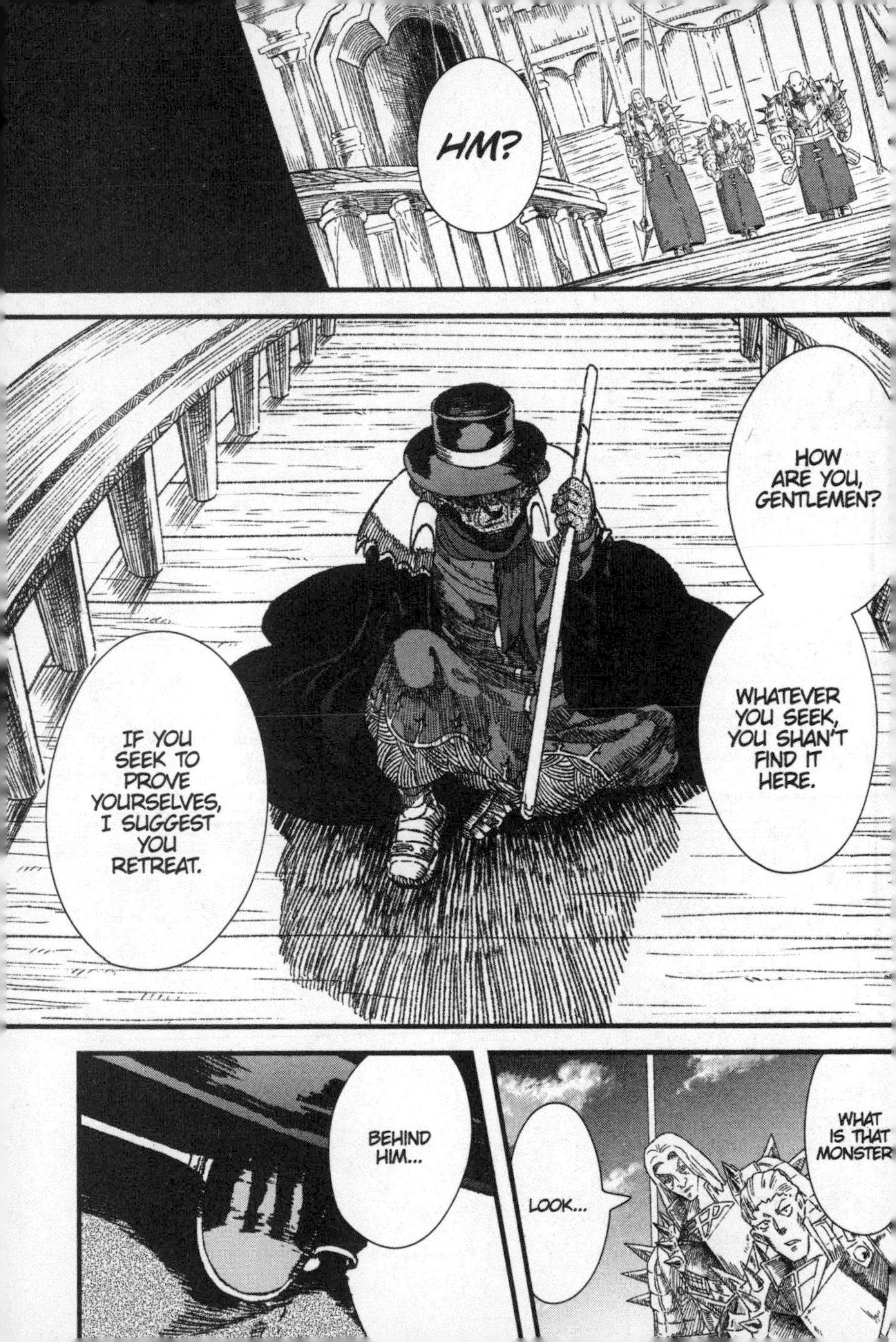
HM?
HOW ARE YOU, GENTLEMEN?
WHATEVER YOU SEEK, YOU SHAN'T FIND IT HERE.
IF YOU SEEK TO PROVE YOURSELVES, I SUGGEST YOU RETREAT.
WHAT IS THAT MONSTER
LOOK...
BEHIND HIM...

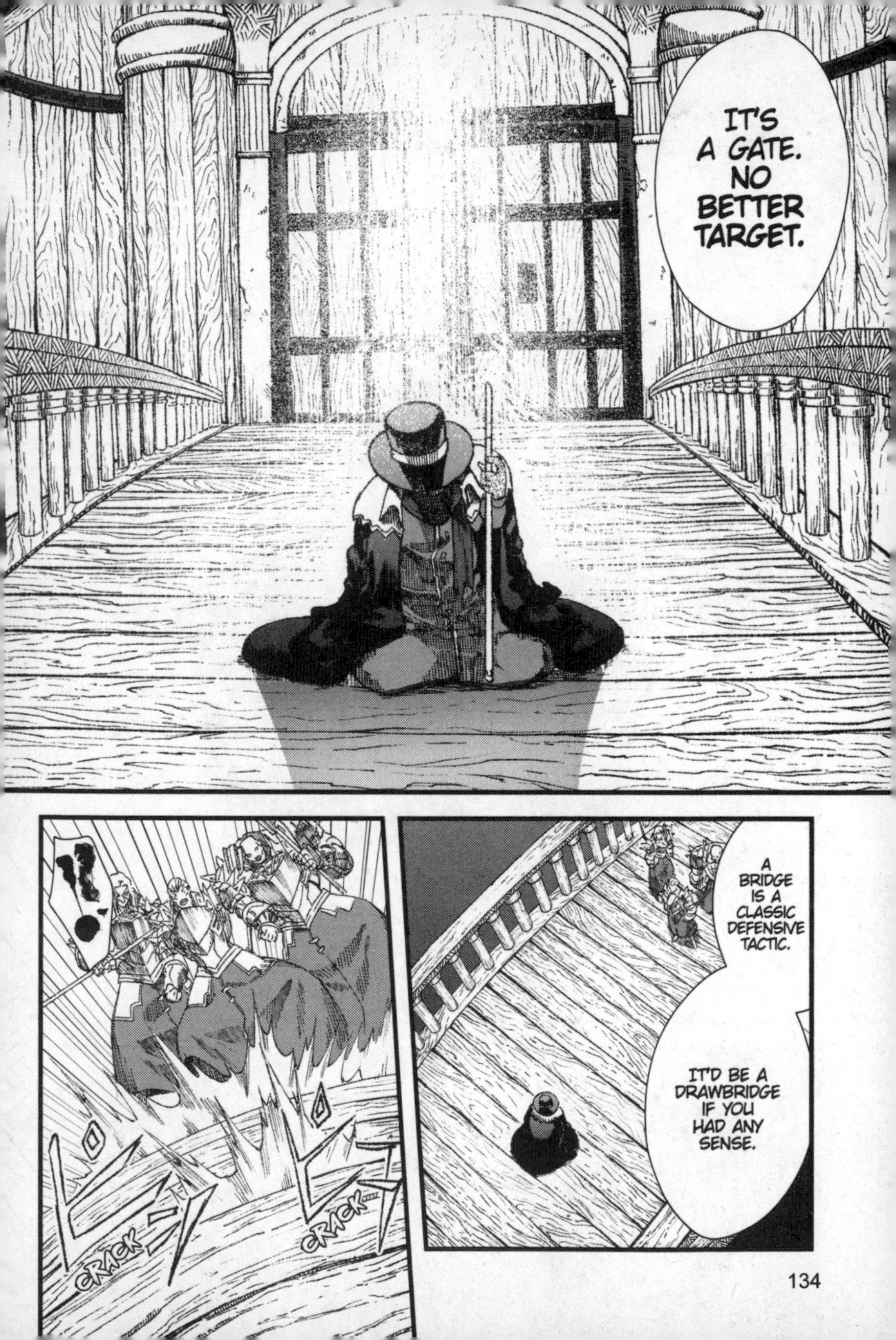
IT'S A GATE. NO BETTER TARGET.
A BRIDGE IS A CLASSIC DEFENSIVE TACTIC.
IT'D BE A DRAWBRIDGE IF YOU HAD ANY SENSE.
!
CRACK
CRACK

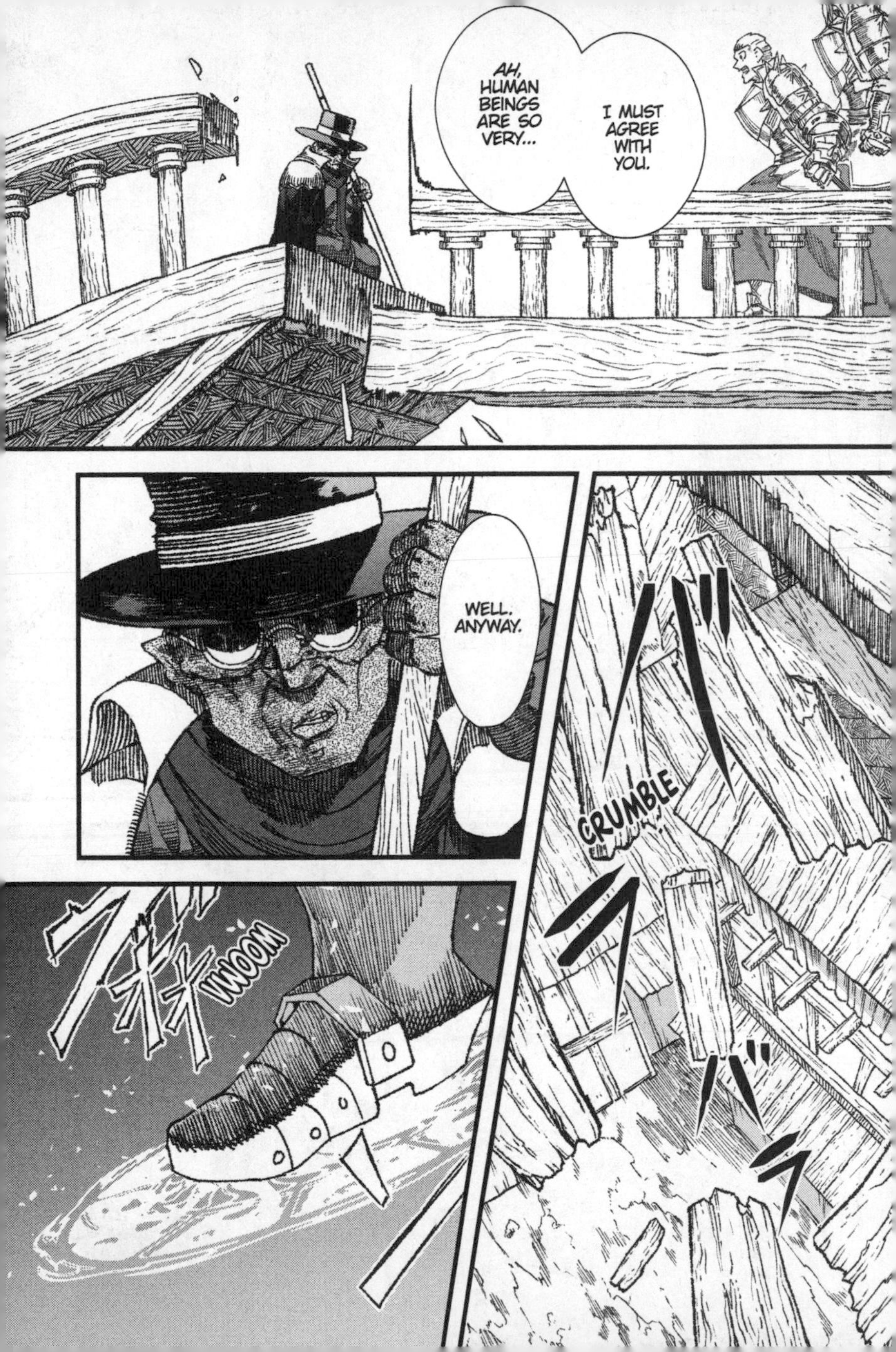
I MUST AGREE WITH YOU.
AH, HUMAN BEINGS ARE SO VERY...
CRUMBLE
WELL. ANYWAY.
VWOOM

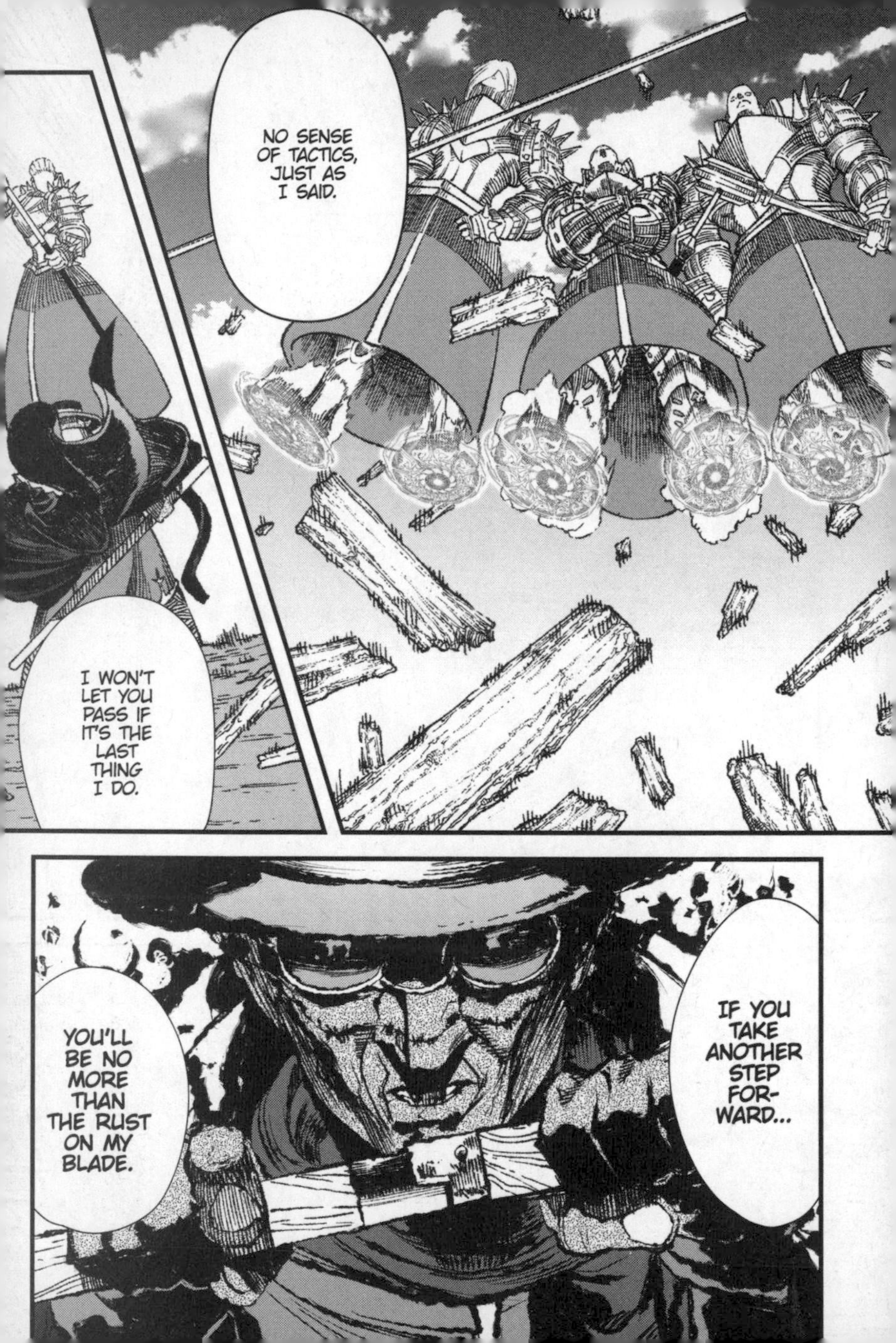
NO SENSE OF TACTICS, JUST AS I SAID.
I WON'T LET YOU PASS IF IT'S THE LAST THING I DO.
IF YOU TAKE ANOTHER STEP FOR-WARD...
YOU'LL BE NO MORE THAN THE RUST ON MY BLADE.

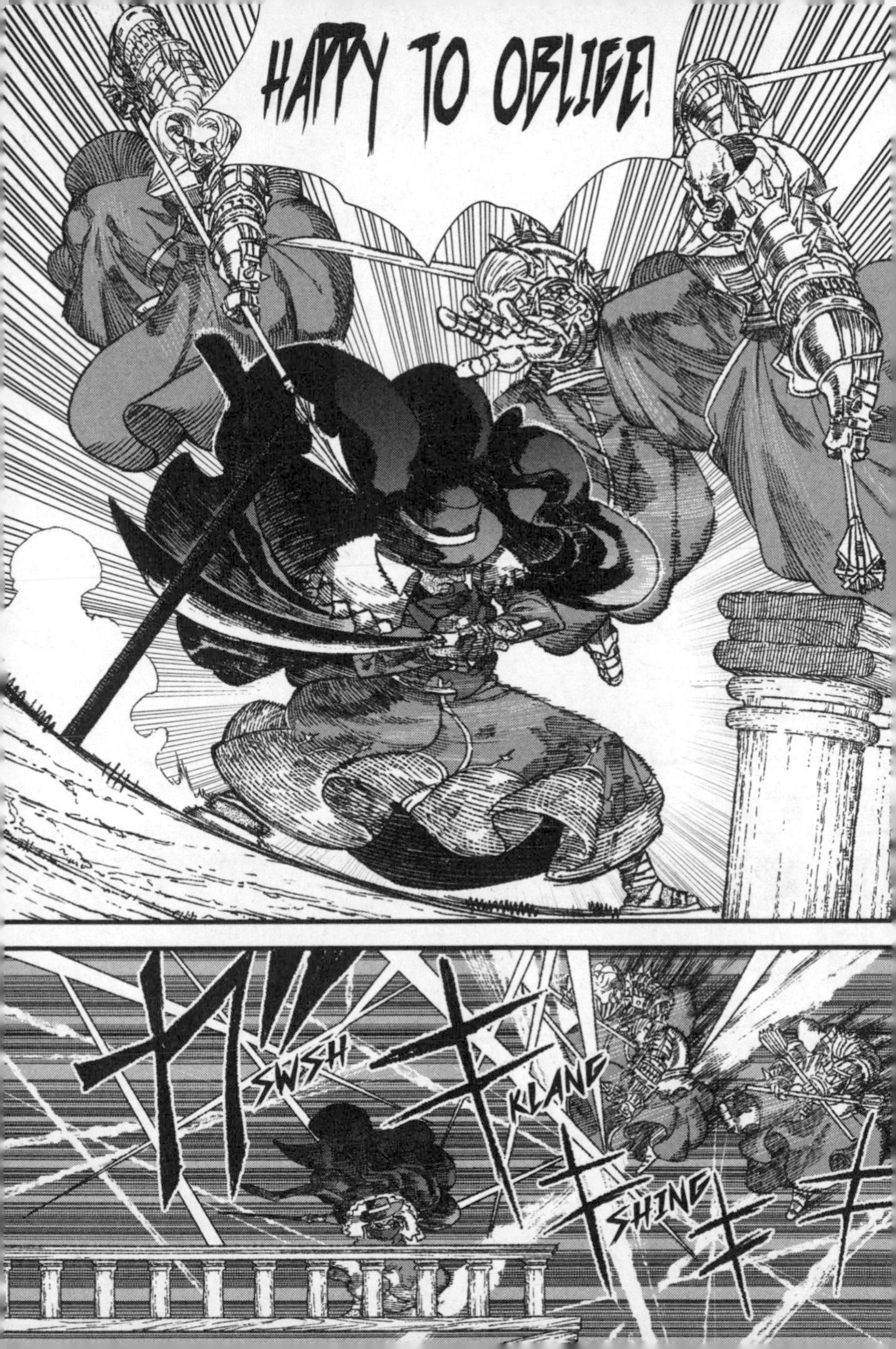
HAPPY TO OBLIGE!
KLANG
SHING
SWSH

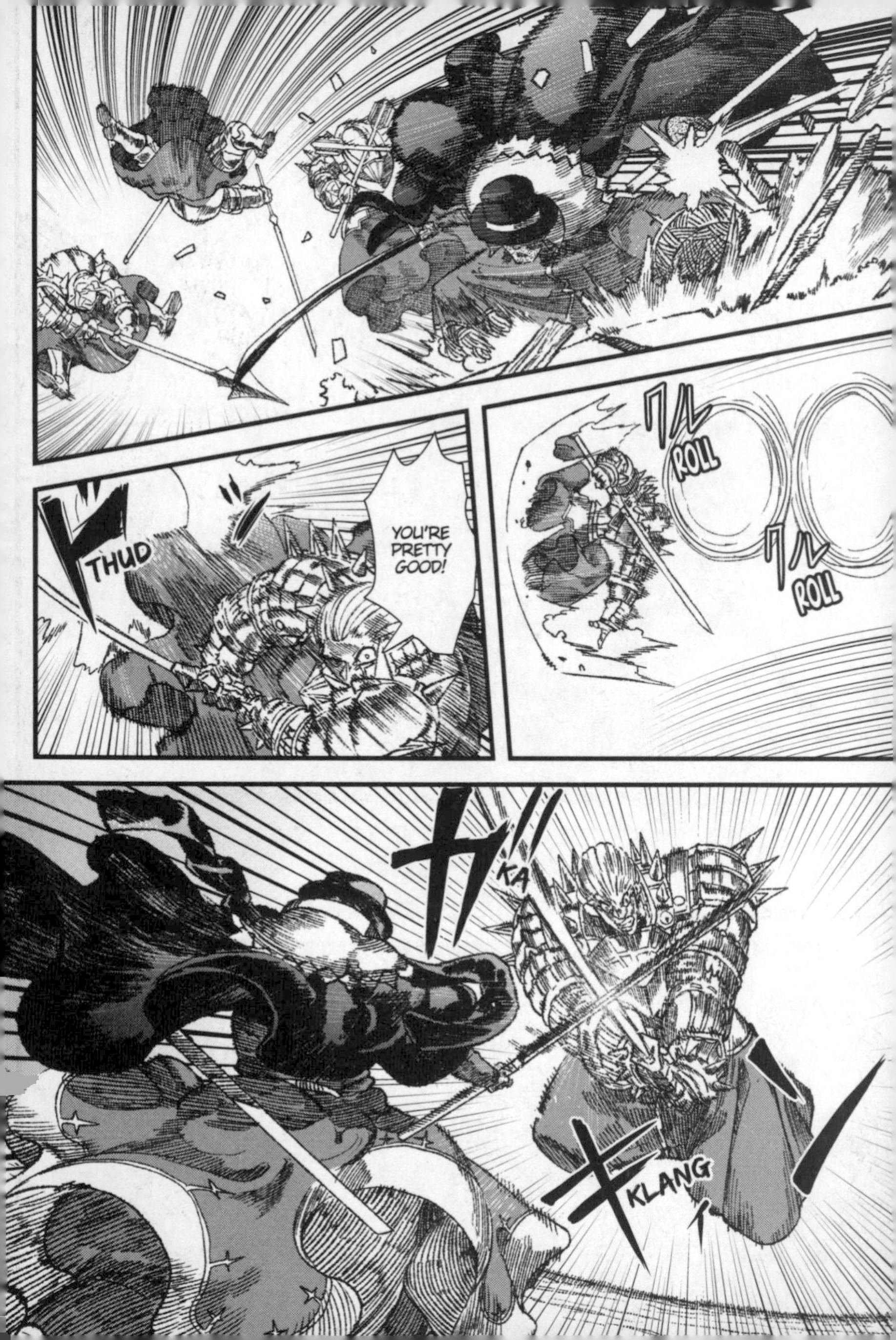
ROLL
ROLL
THUD
YOU'RE PRETTY GOOD!
KA
KLANG

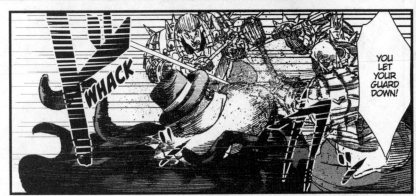

WHACK

YOU LET YOUR GUARD DOWN!

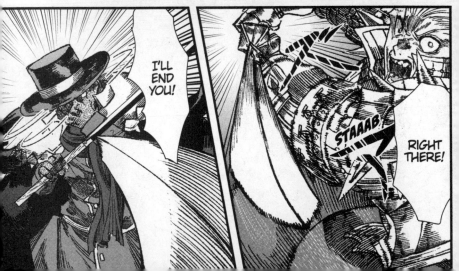

I'LL END YOU!

STAAAB

RIGHT THERE!

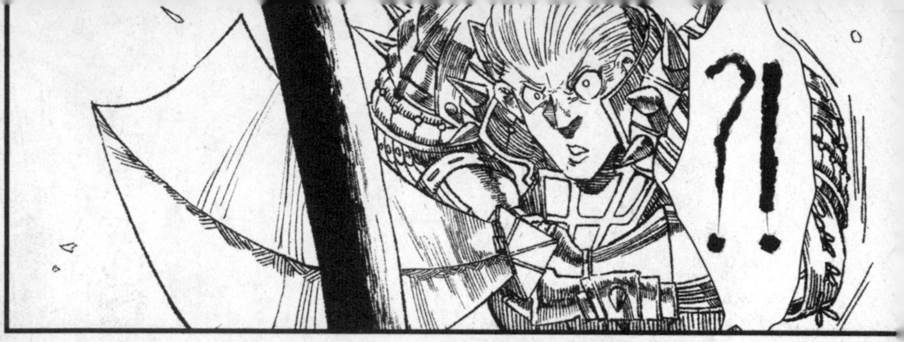
?!
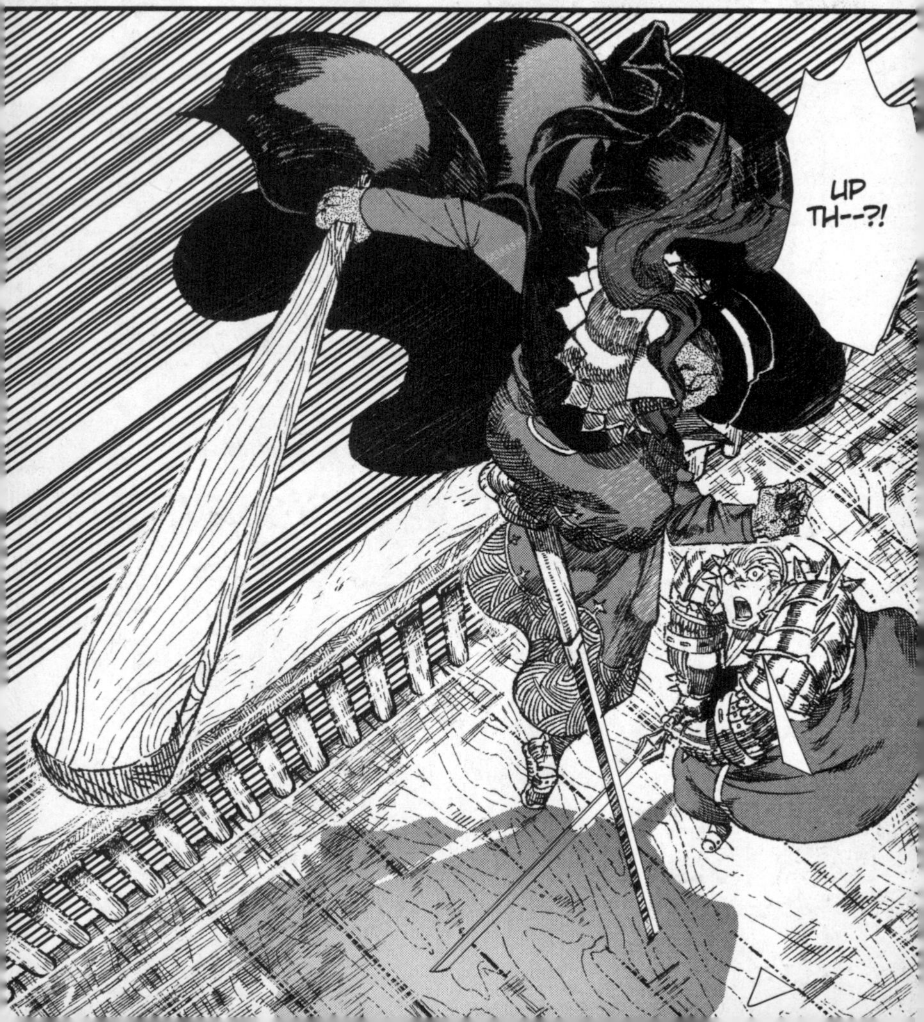
UP TH--?!

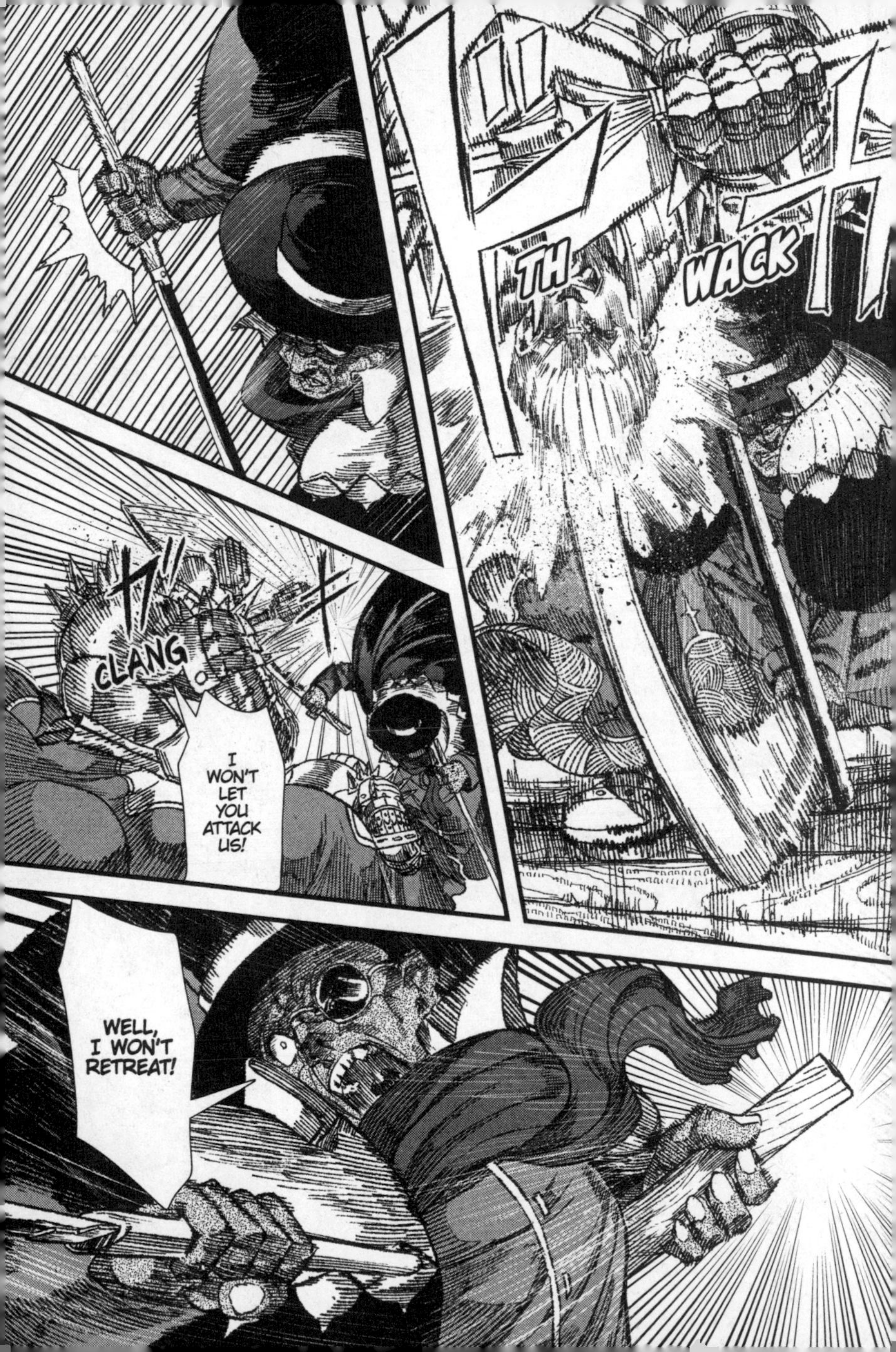
TH
WACK
CLANG
I WON'T LET YOU ATTACK US!
WELL, I WON'T RETREAT!

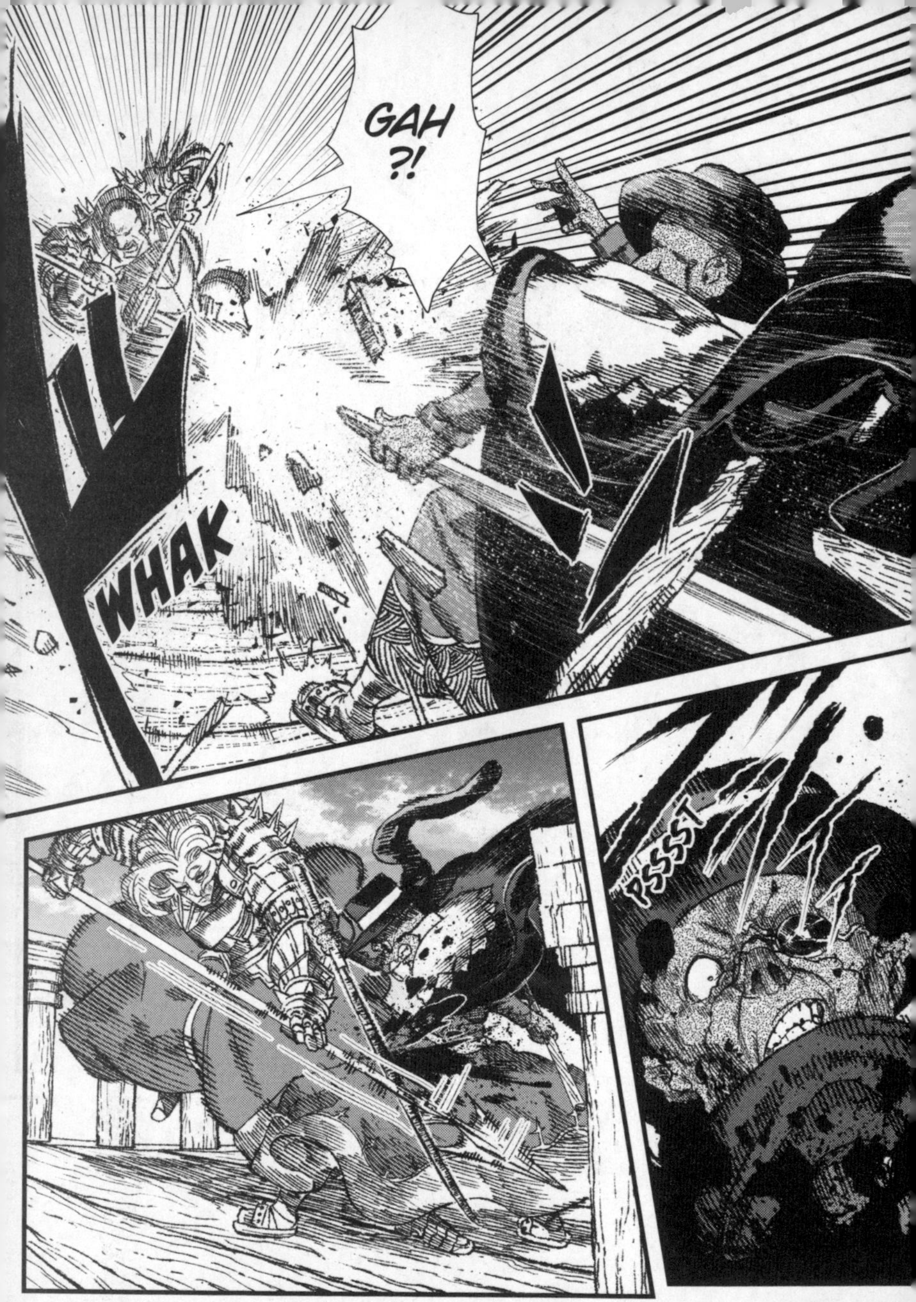
GAH ?!
WHAK
PSSSST

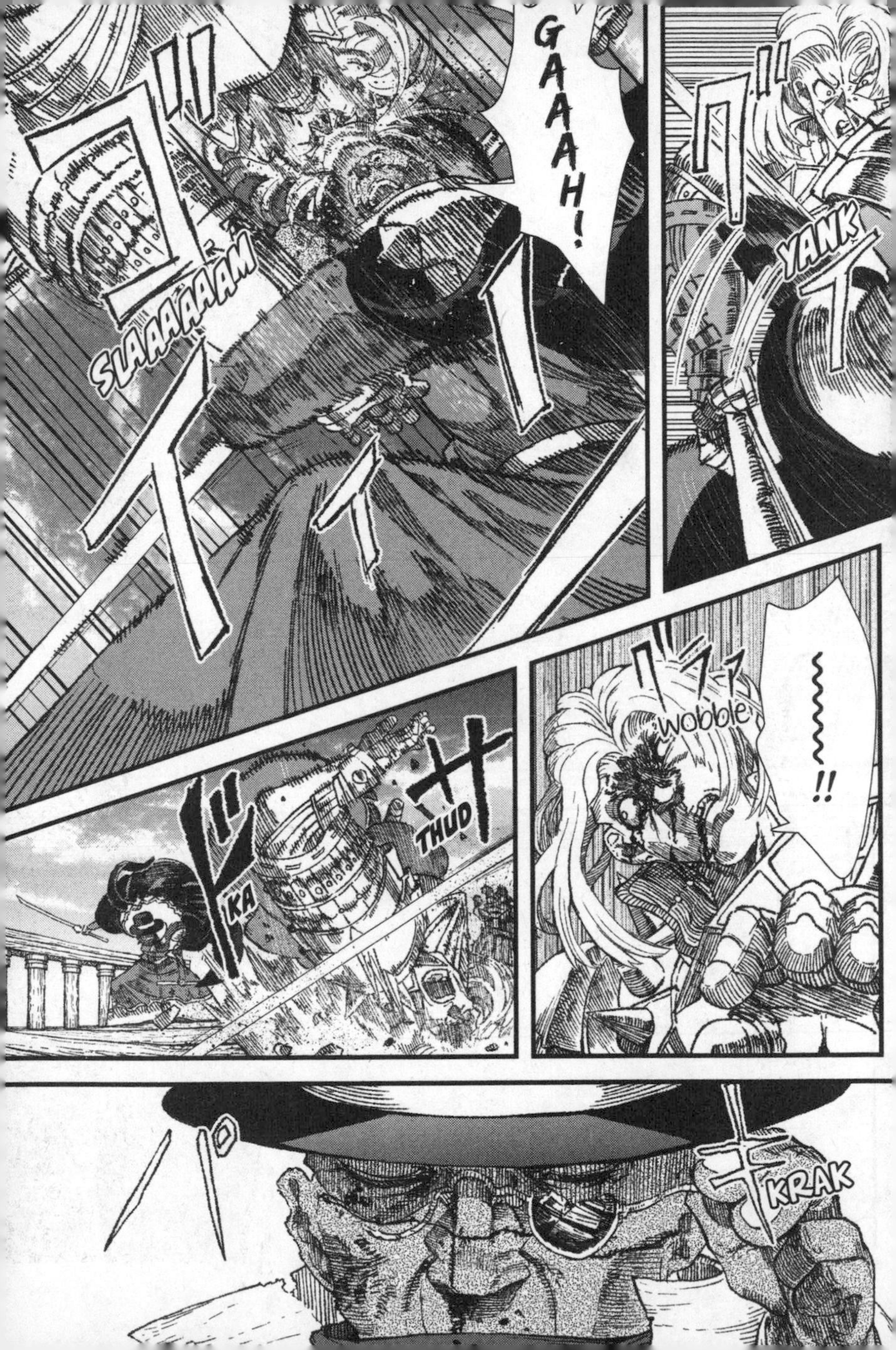
YANK
GAAAAH!
SLAAAAAAM
wobble
~~~~~!!
THUD
KA
KRAK
~~~~~

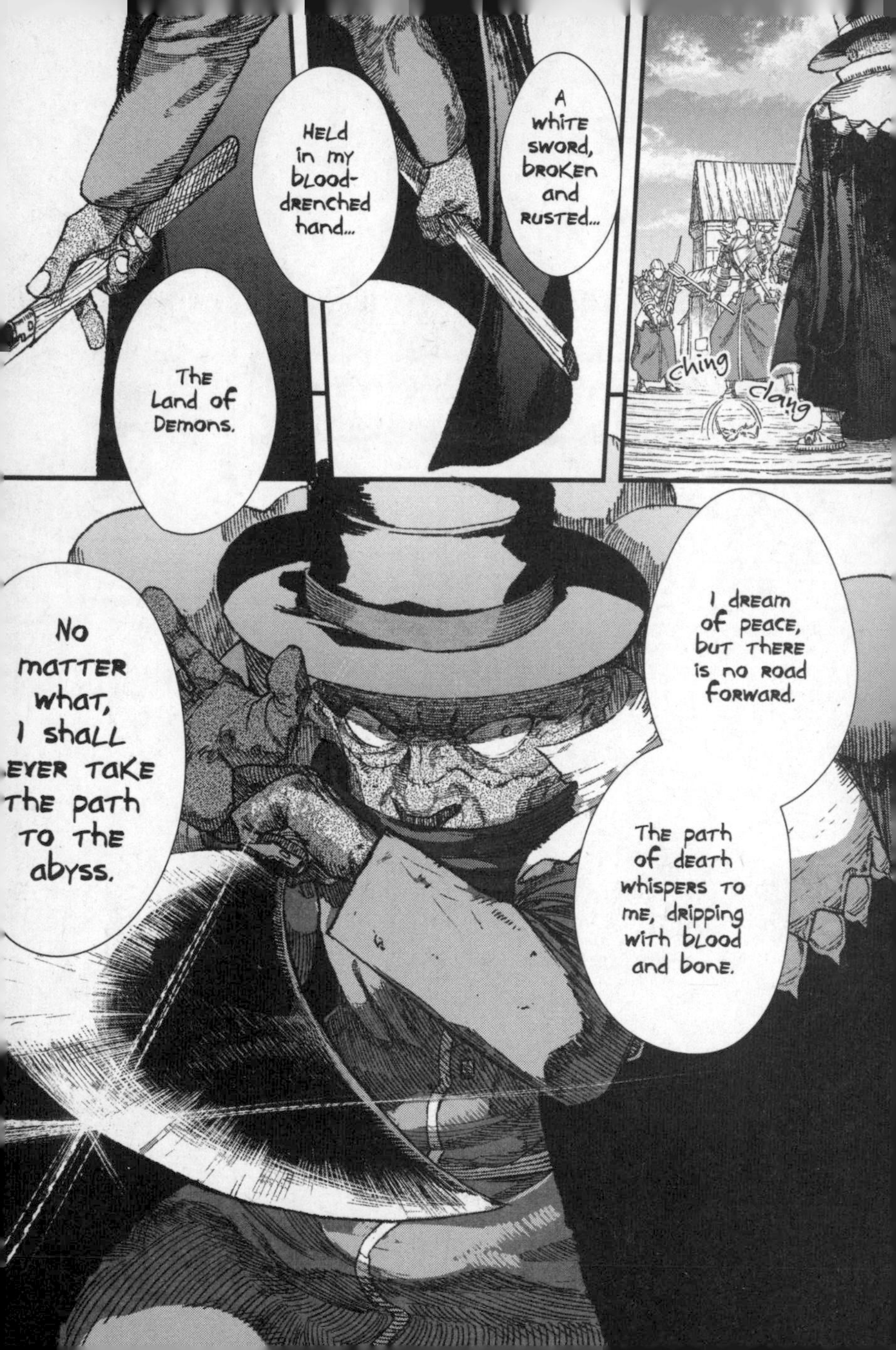

ching
clang
A white sword, broken and rusted...
Held in my blood-drenched hand...
The Land of Demons.
I dream of peace, but there is no road forward.
The path of death whispers to me, dripping with blood and bone.
No matter what, I shall ever take the path to the abyss.

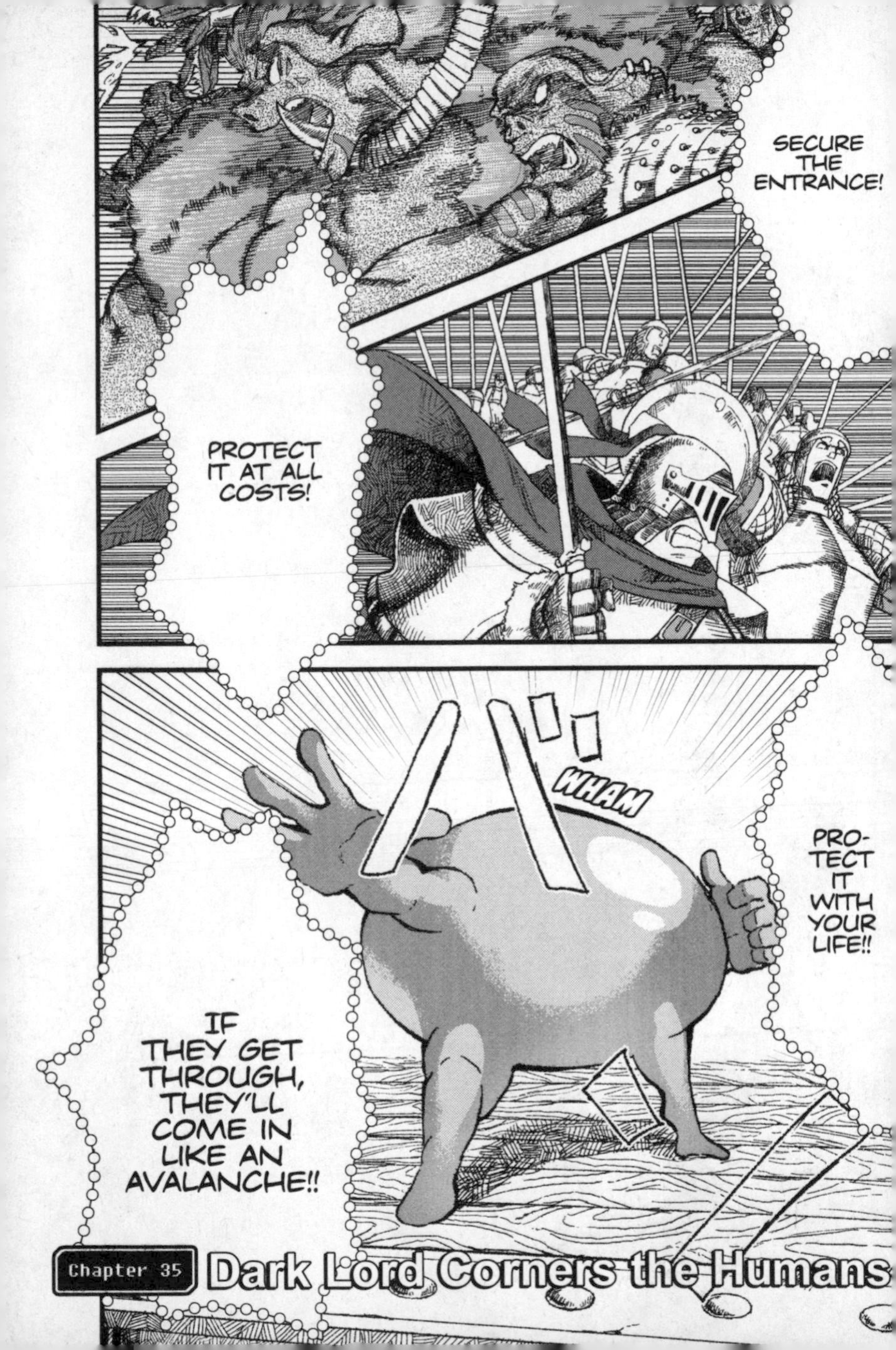
SECURE THE ENTRANCE!
PROTECT IT AT ALL COSTS!
PROTECT IT WITH YOUR LIFE!!
WHAM
IF THEY GET THROUGH, THEY'LL COME IN LIKE AN AVALANCHE!!

Chapter 35 Dark Lord Corners the Humans

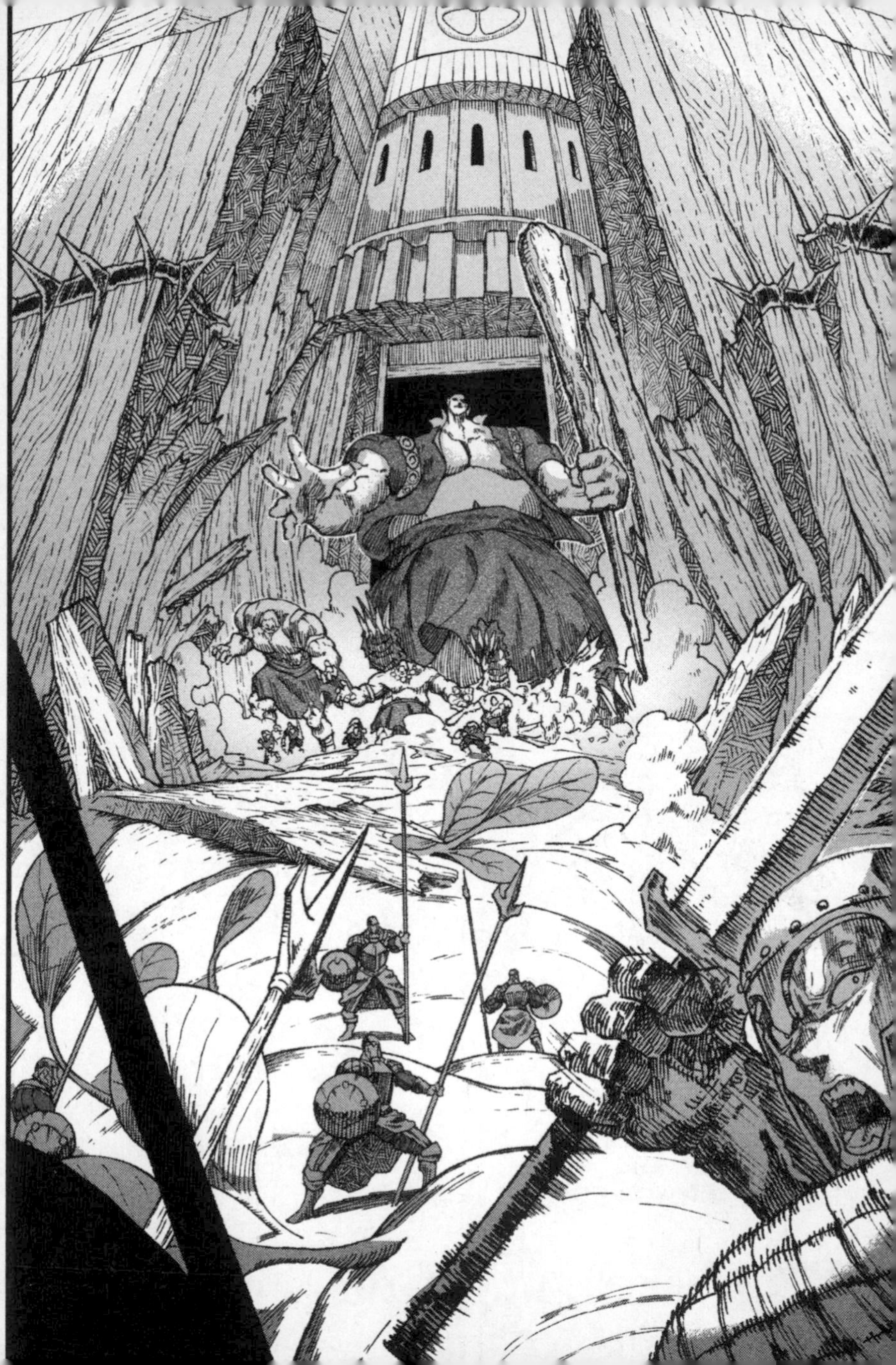

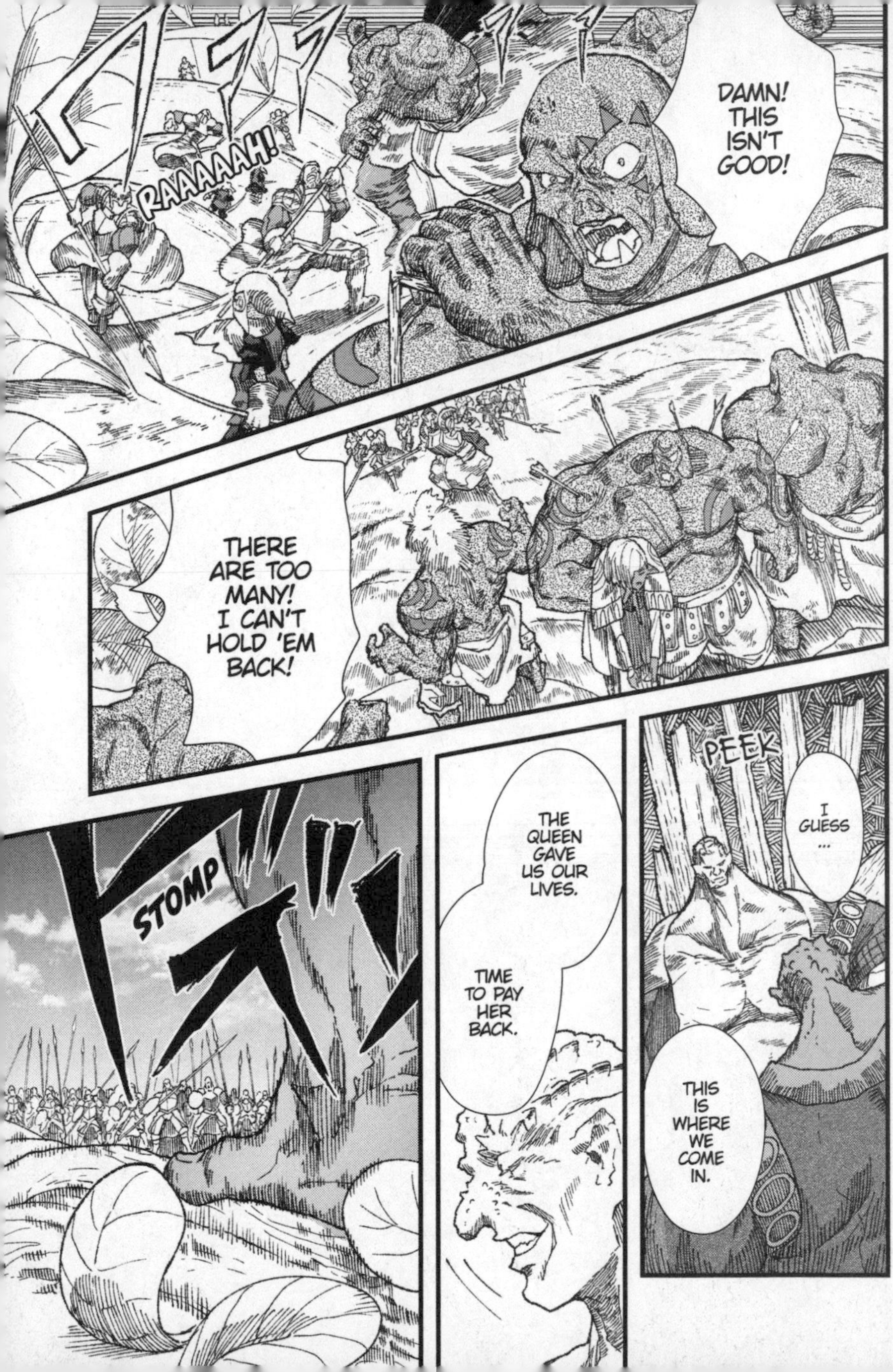
DAMN! THIS ISN'T GOOD!
RAAAAAH!
THERE ARE TOO MANY! I CAN'T HOLD 'EM BACK!
PEEK
I GUESS...
THIS IS WHERE WE COME IN.
THE QUEEN GAVE US OUR LIVES.
TIME TO PAY HER BACK.
STOMP

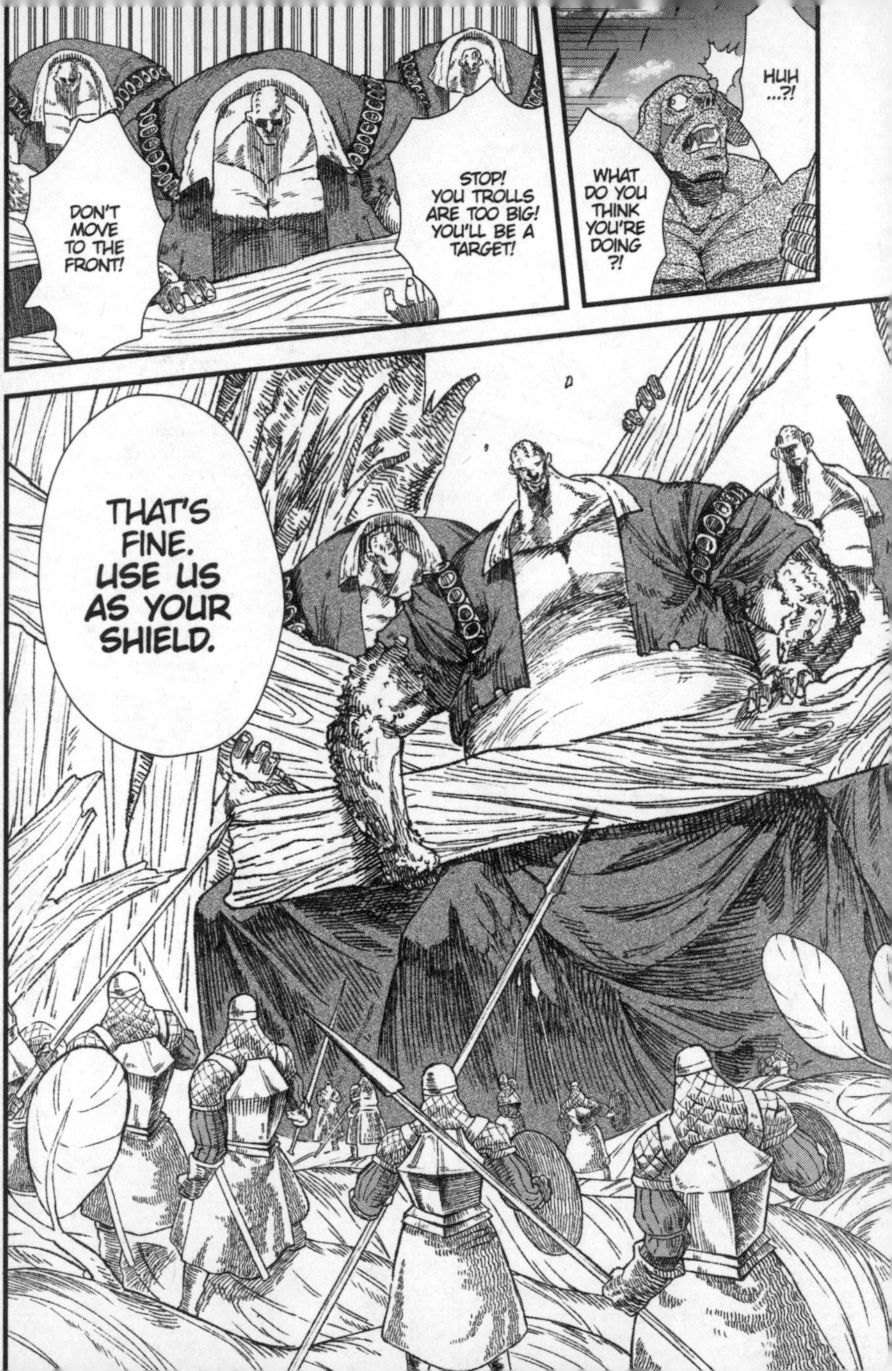
HUH ...?!
WHAT DO YOU THINK YOU'RE DOING ?!
STOP! YOU TROLLS ARE TOO BIG! YOU'LL BE A TARGET!
DON'T MOVE TO THE FRONT!
THAT'S FINE. USE US AS YOUR SHIELD.

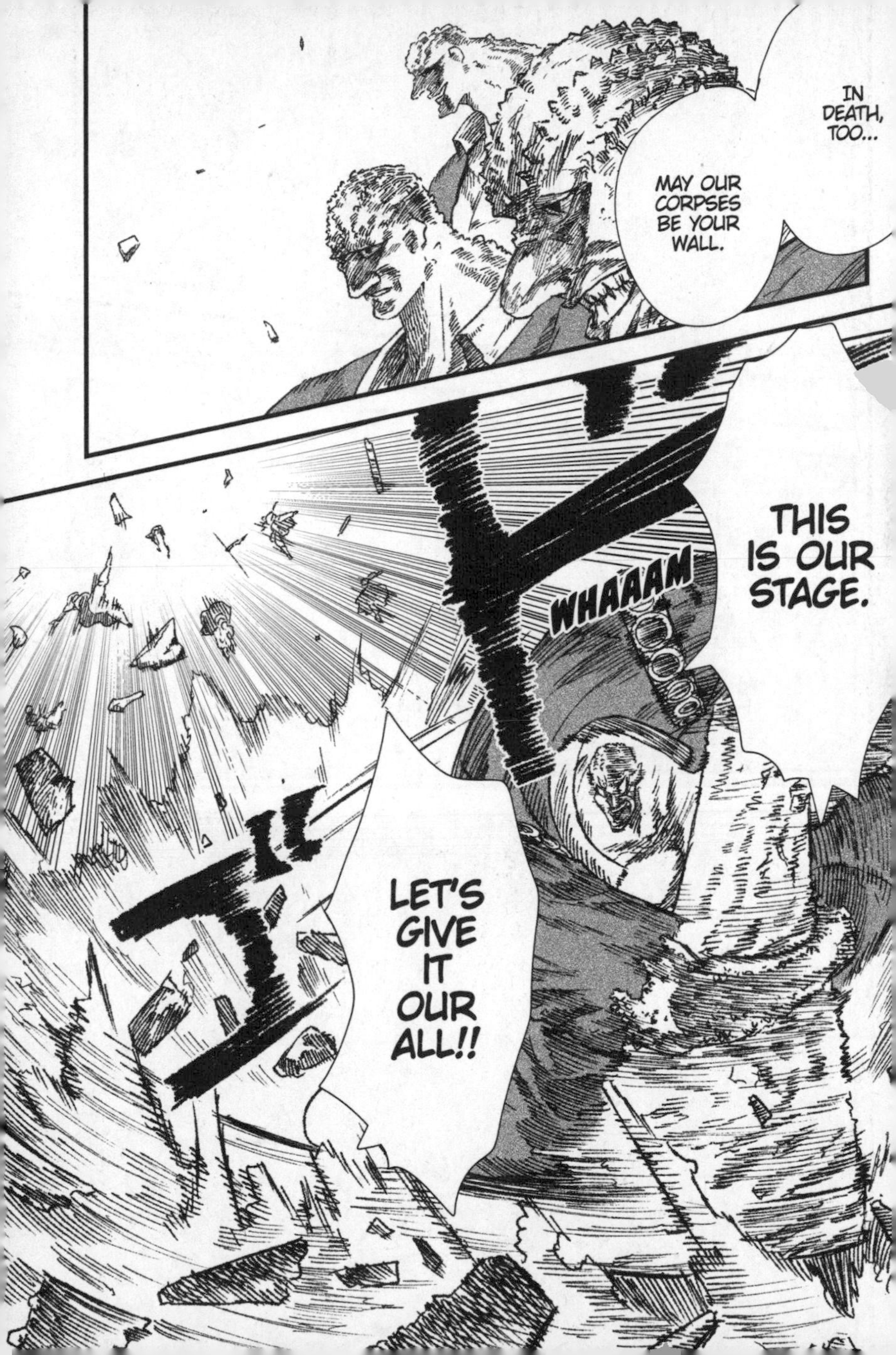
IN DEATH, TOO...
MAY OUR CORPSES BE YOUR WALL.
THIS IS OUR STAGE.
WHAAAM
LET'S GIVE IT OUR ALL!!

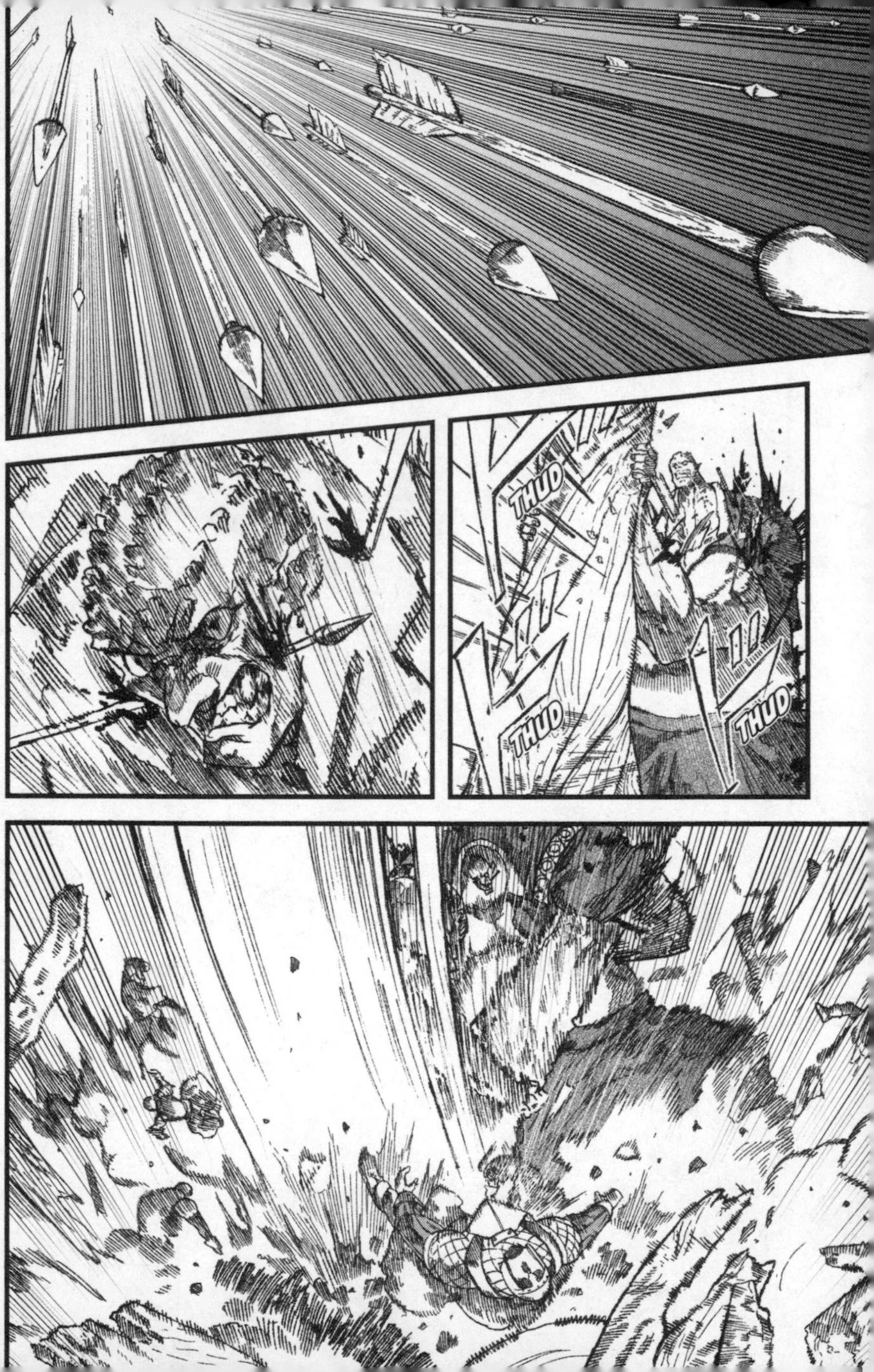
THUD
THUD
THUD

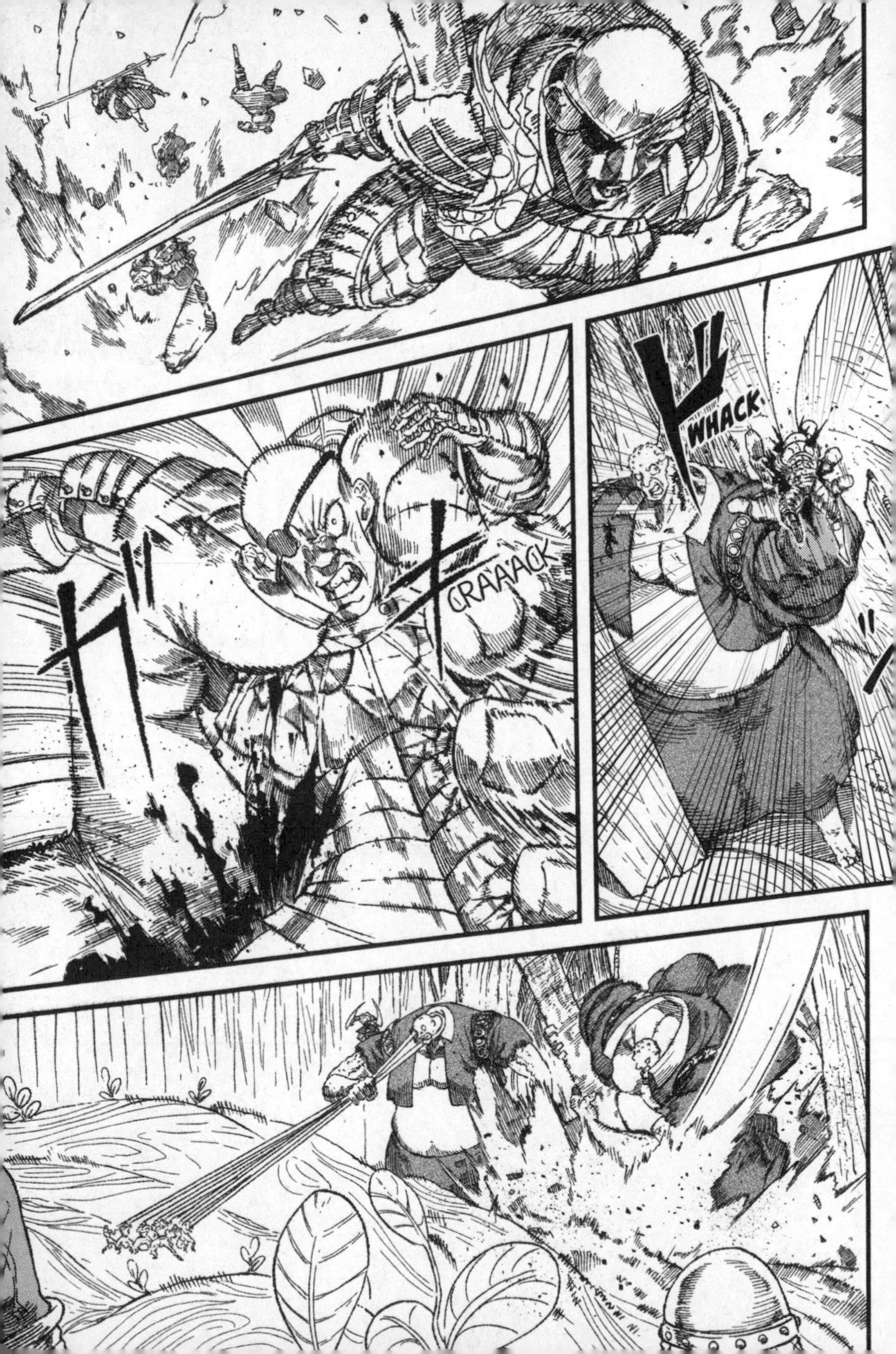
WHACK
CRAAACK

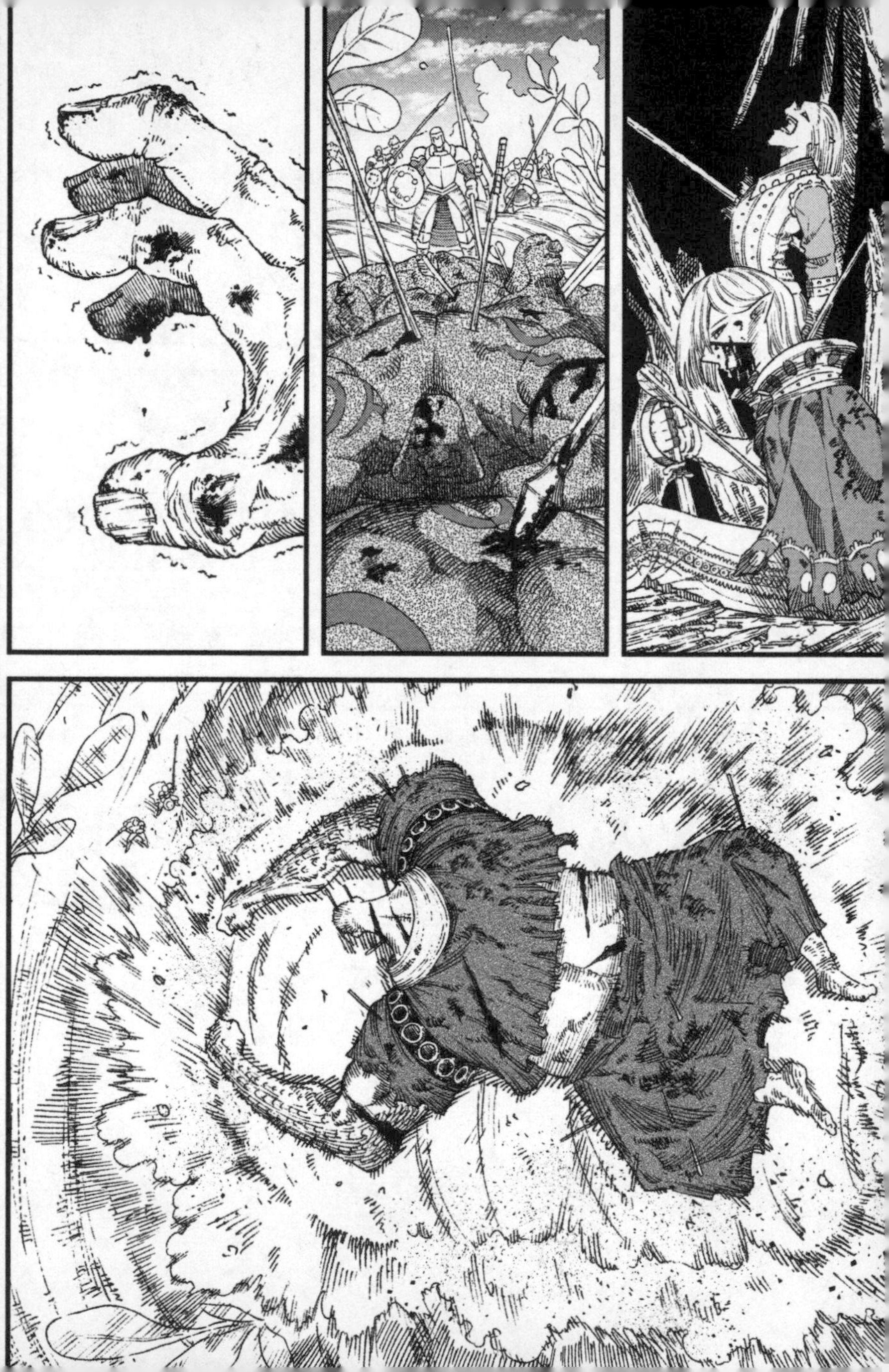

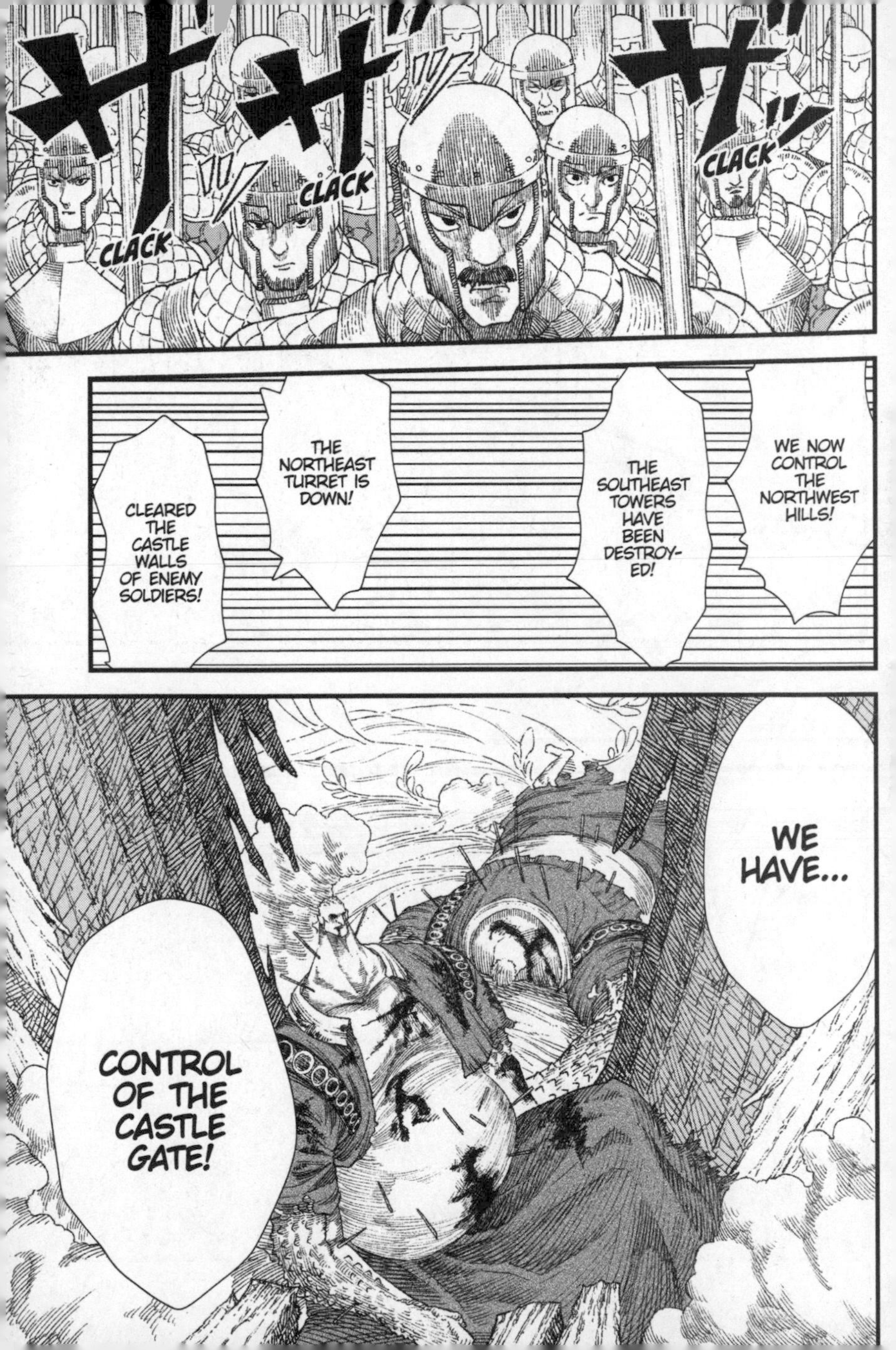
CLACK
CLACK
CLACK
WE NOW CONTROL THE NORTHWEST HILLS!
THE SOUTHEAST TOWERS HAVE BEEN DESTROYED!
THE NORTHEAST TURRET IS DOWN!
CLEARED THE CASTLE WALLS OF ENEMY SOLDIERS!
WE HAVE...
CONTROL OF THE CASTLE GATE!

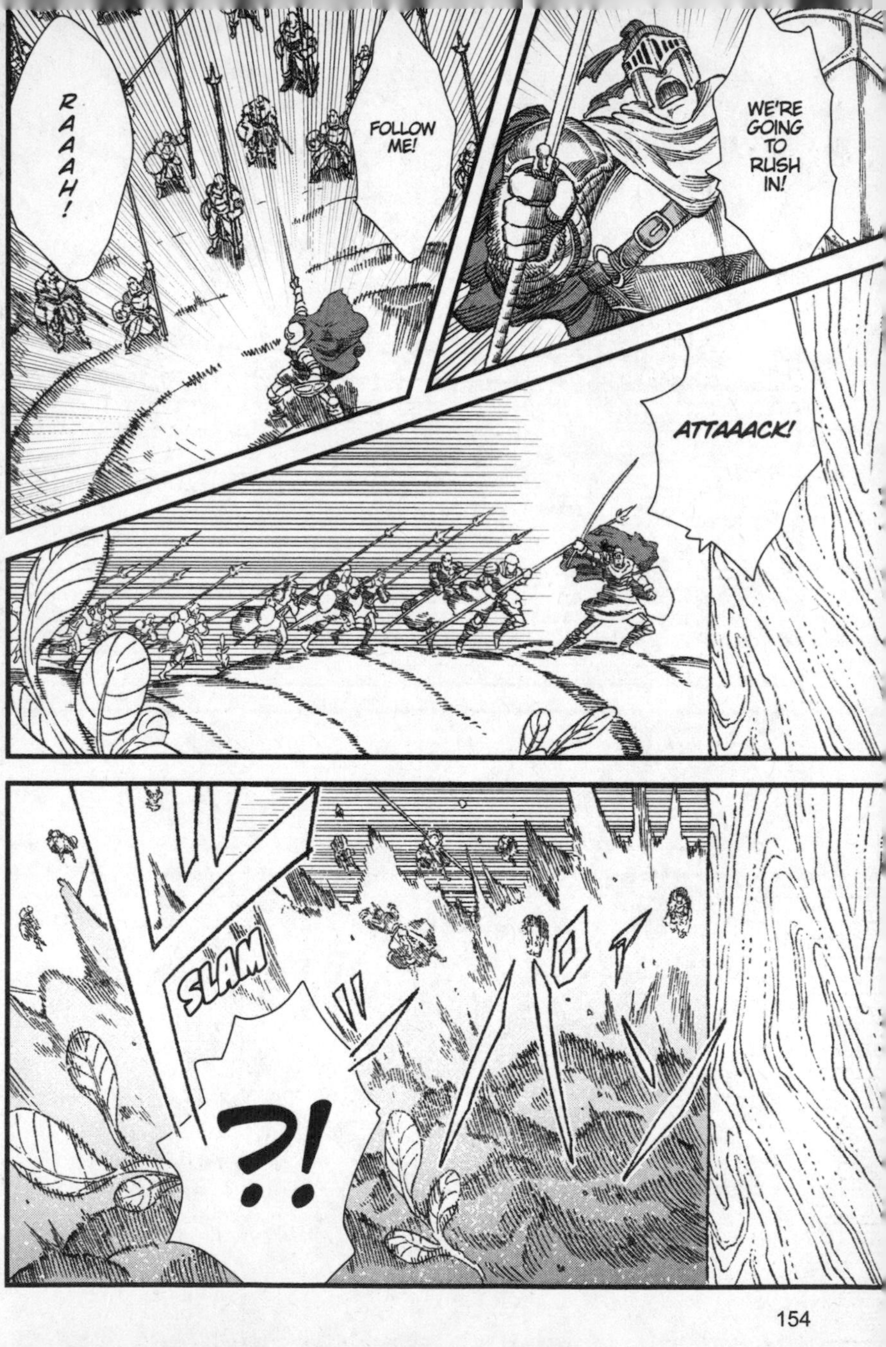
WE'RE GOING TO RUSH IN!
FOLLOW ME!
RAAAH!
ATTAAACK!
SLAM
?!

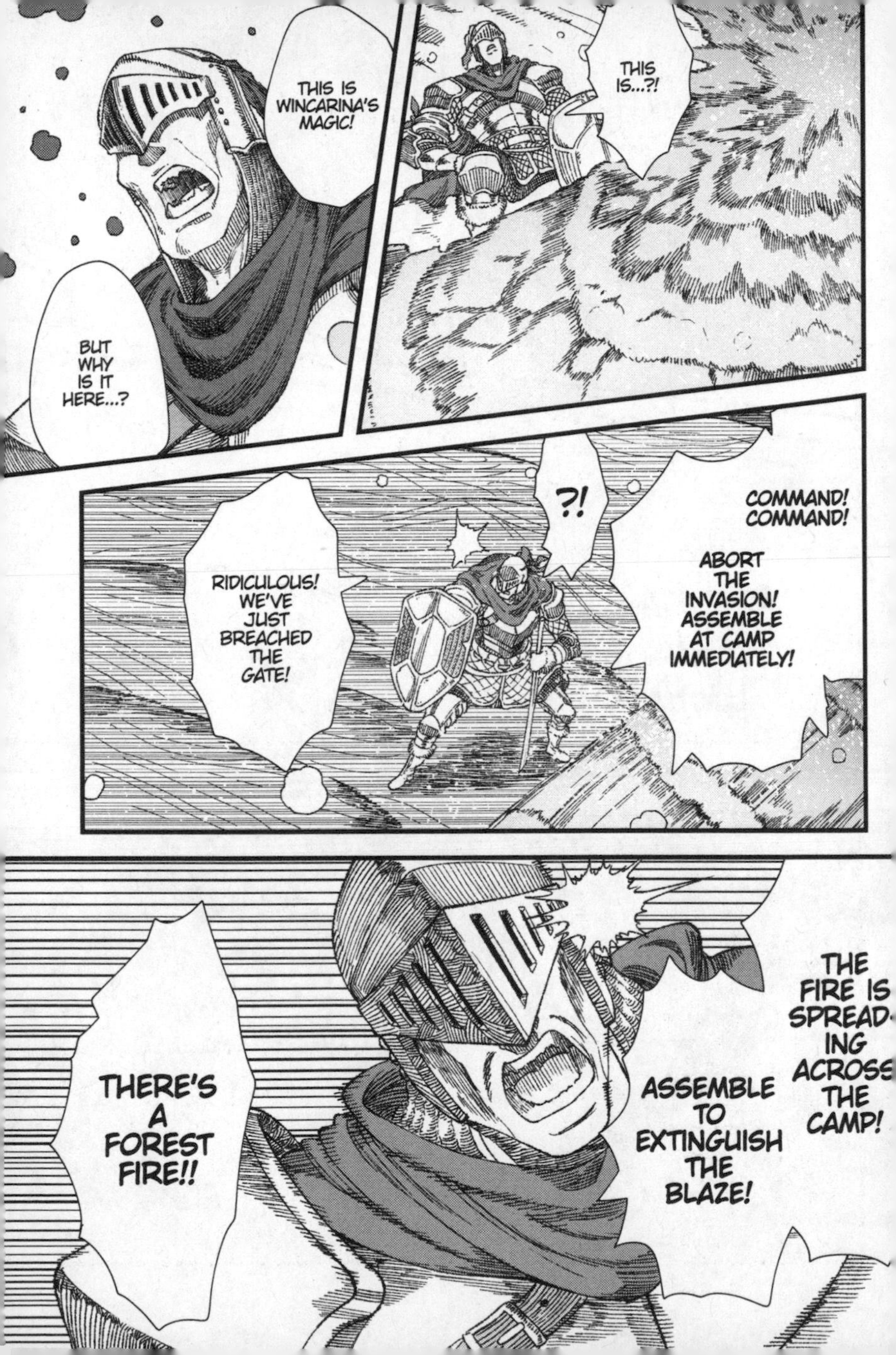
THIS IS...?!
THIS IS WINCARINA'S MAGIC!
BUT WHY IS IT HERE...?
COMMAND! COMMAND!
ABORT THE INVASION! ASSEMBLE AT CAMP IMMEDIATELY!
?!
RIDICULOUS! WE'VE JUST BREACHED THE GATE!
THE FIRE IS SPREADING ACROSS THE CAMP!
ASSEMBLE TO EXTINGUISH THE BLAZE!
THERE'S A FOREST FIRE!!

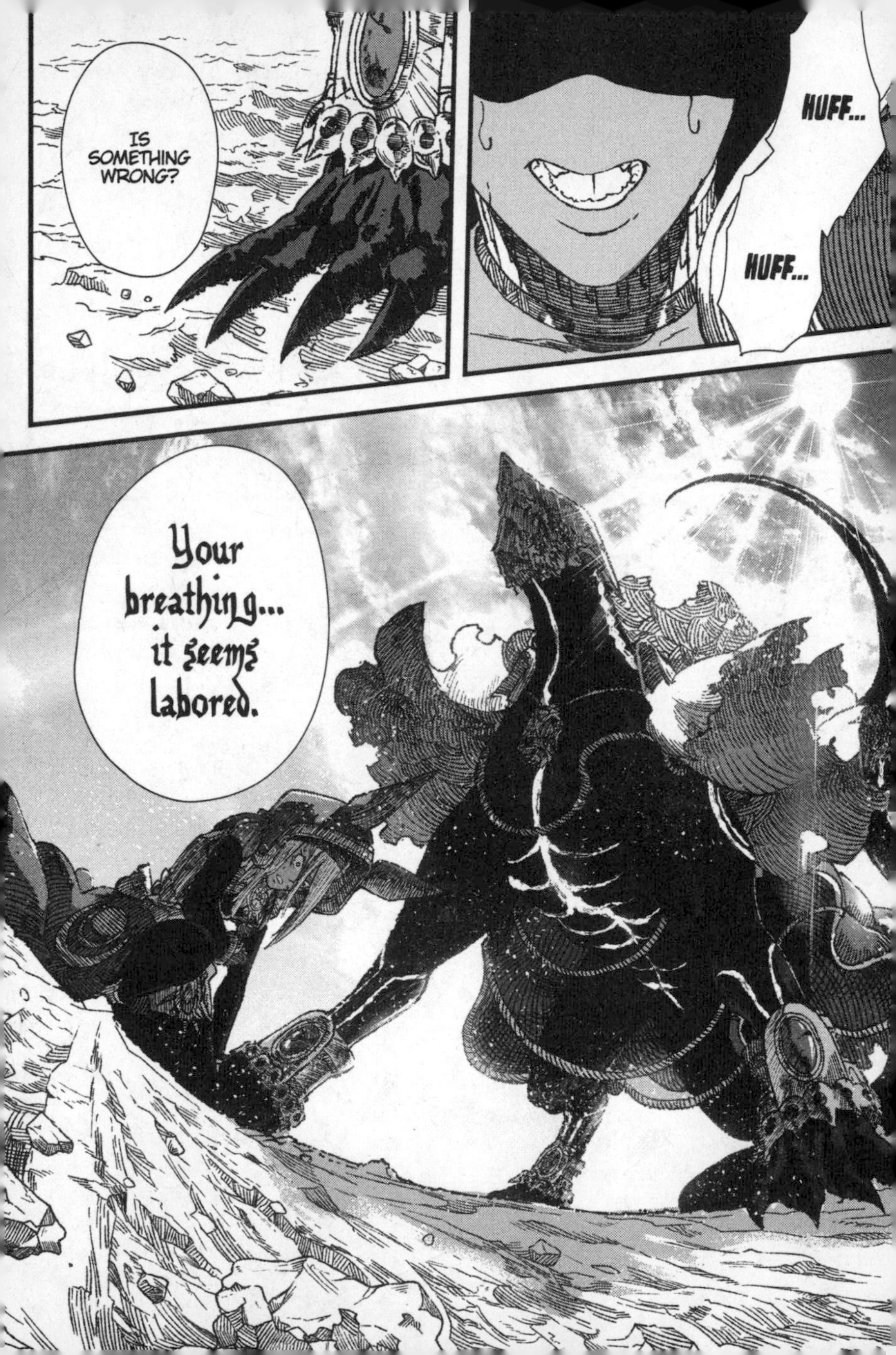
HUFF...
HUFF...
IS SOMETHING WRONG?
Your breathing... it seems labored.

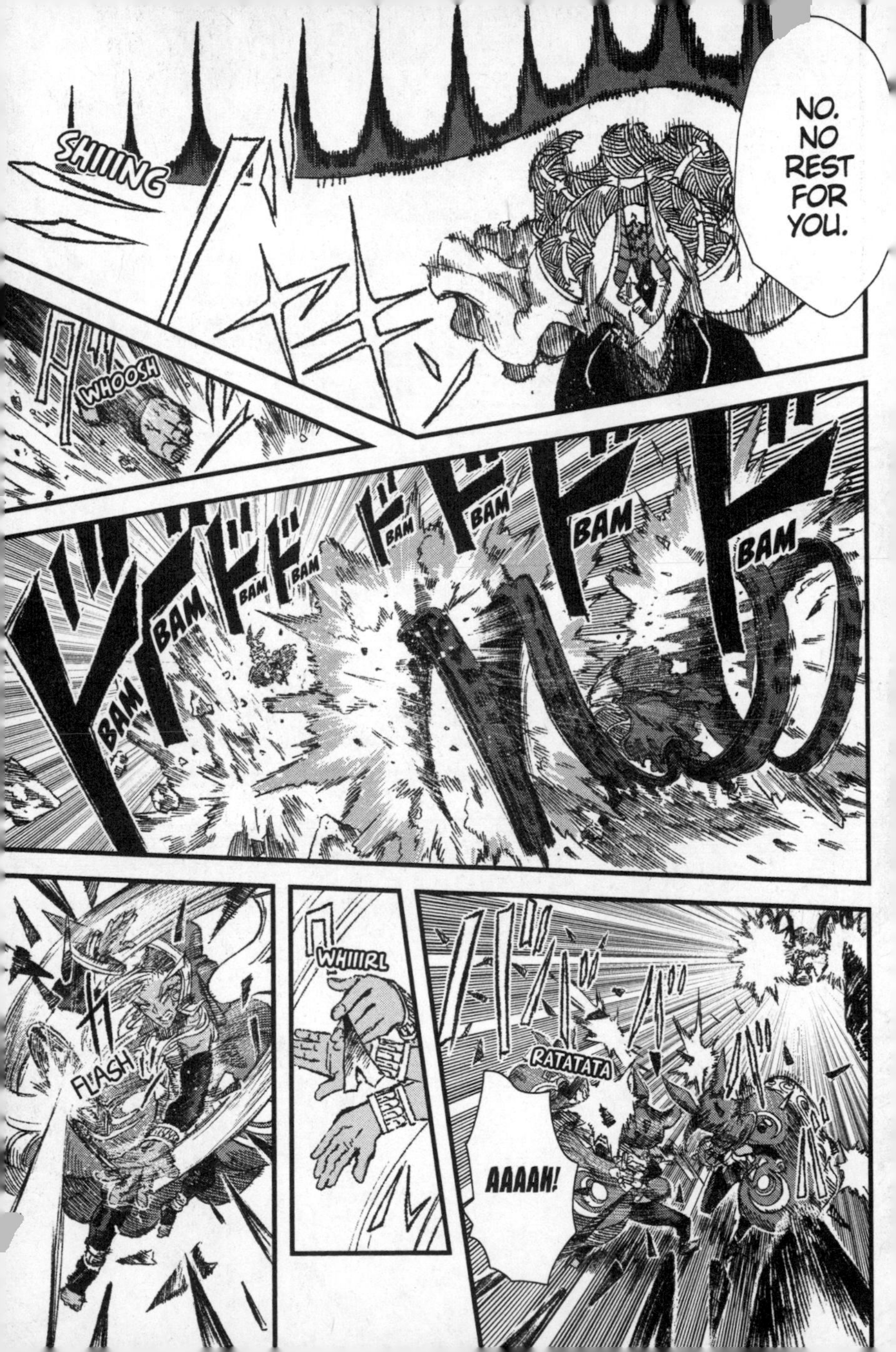
NO. NO REST FOR YOU.
SHIIING
WHOOSH
BAM
BAM
BAM
BAM
BAM
BAM
BAM
BAM
RATATATA
AAAAH!
WHIIIRL
FLASH

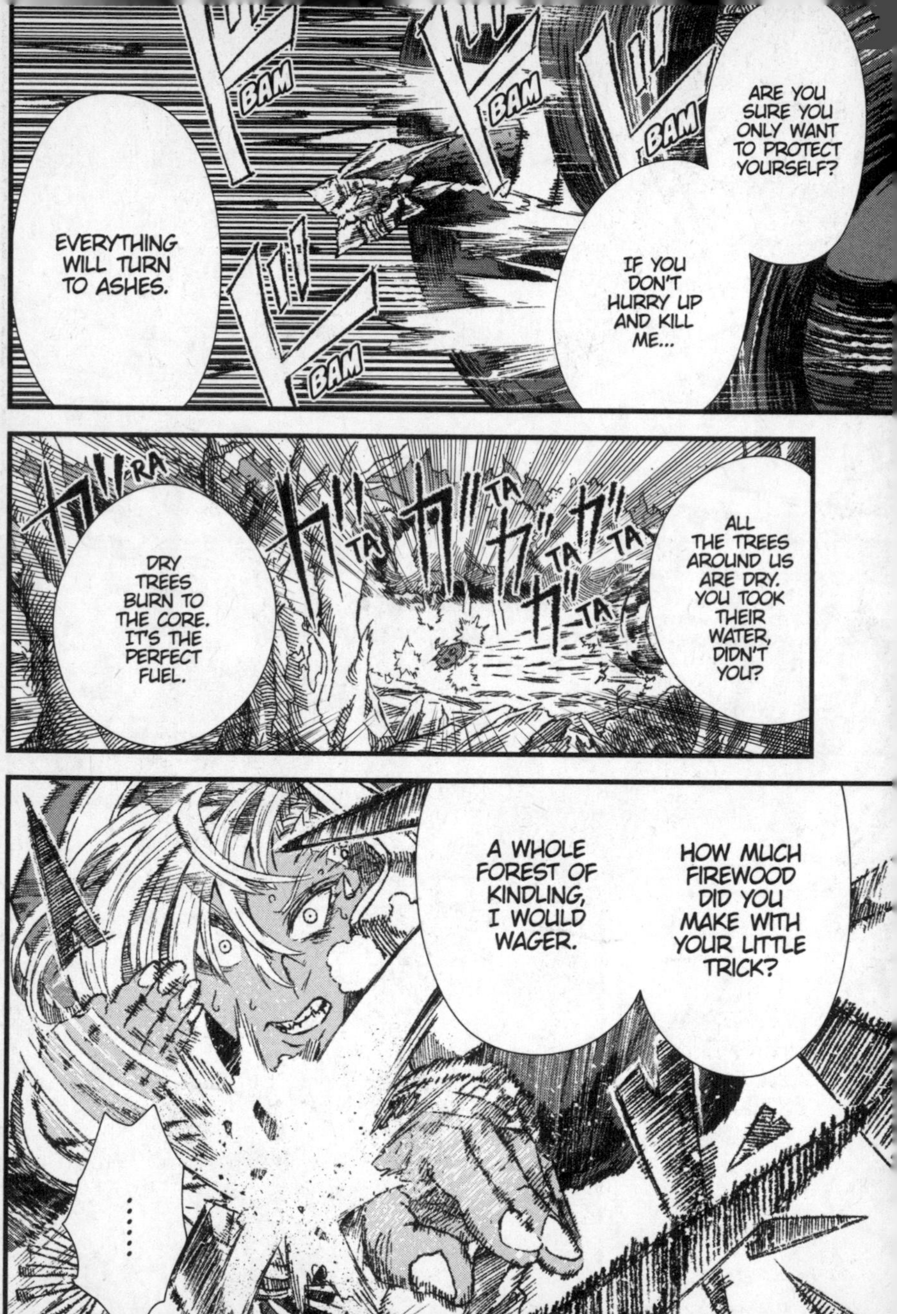
ARE YOU SURE YOU ONLY WANT TO PROTECT YOURSELF?
IF YOU DON'T HURRY UP AND KILL ME...
BAM
BAM
BAM
BAM
EVERYTHING WILL TURN TO ASHES.
ALL THE TREES AROUND US ARE DRY. YOU TOOK THEIR WATER, DIDN'T YOU?
TA
TA
TA
TA
TA
RA
DRY TREES BURN TO THE CORE. IT'S THE PERFECT FUEL.
HOW MUCH FIREWOOD DID YOU MAKE WITH YOUR LITTLE TRICK?
A WHOLE FOREST OF KINDLING, I WOULD WAGER.
......

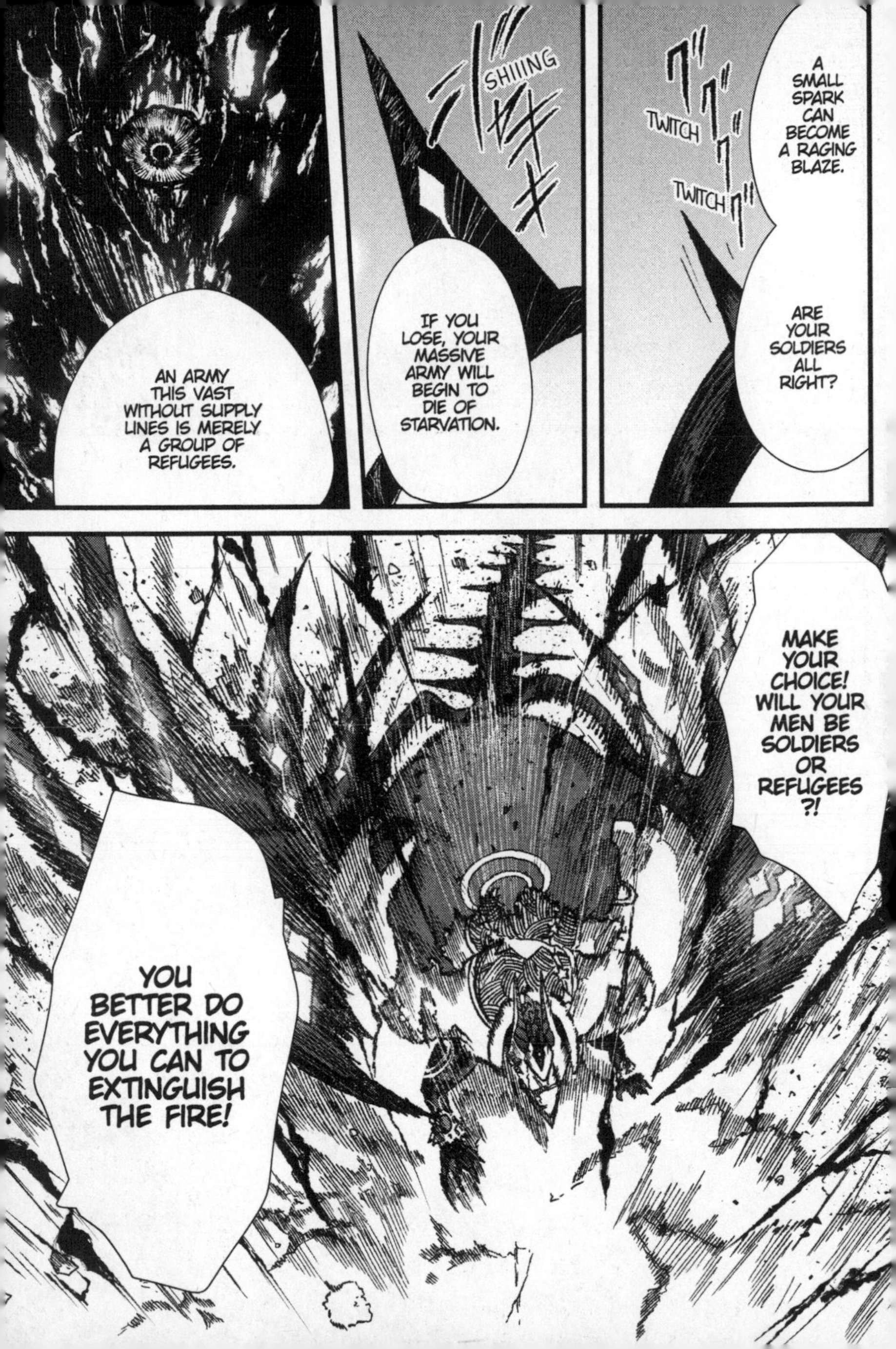

A SMALL SPARK CAN BECOME A RAGING BLAZE.
TWITCH
TWITCH
ARE YOUR SOLDIERS ALL RIGHT?
SHIIING
IF YOU LOSE, YOUR MASSIVE ARMY WILL BEGIN TO DIE OF STARVATION.
AN ARMY THIS VAST WITHOUT SUPPLY LINES IS MERELY A GROUP OF REFUGEES.
MAKE YOUR CHOICE! WILL YOUR MEN BE SOLDIERS OR REFUGEES ?!
YOU BETTER DO EVERYTHING YOU CAN TO EXTINGUISH THE FIRE!

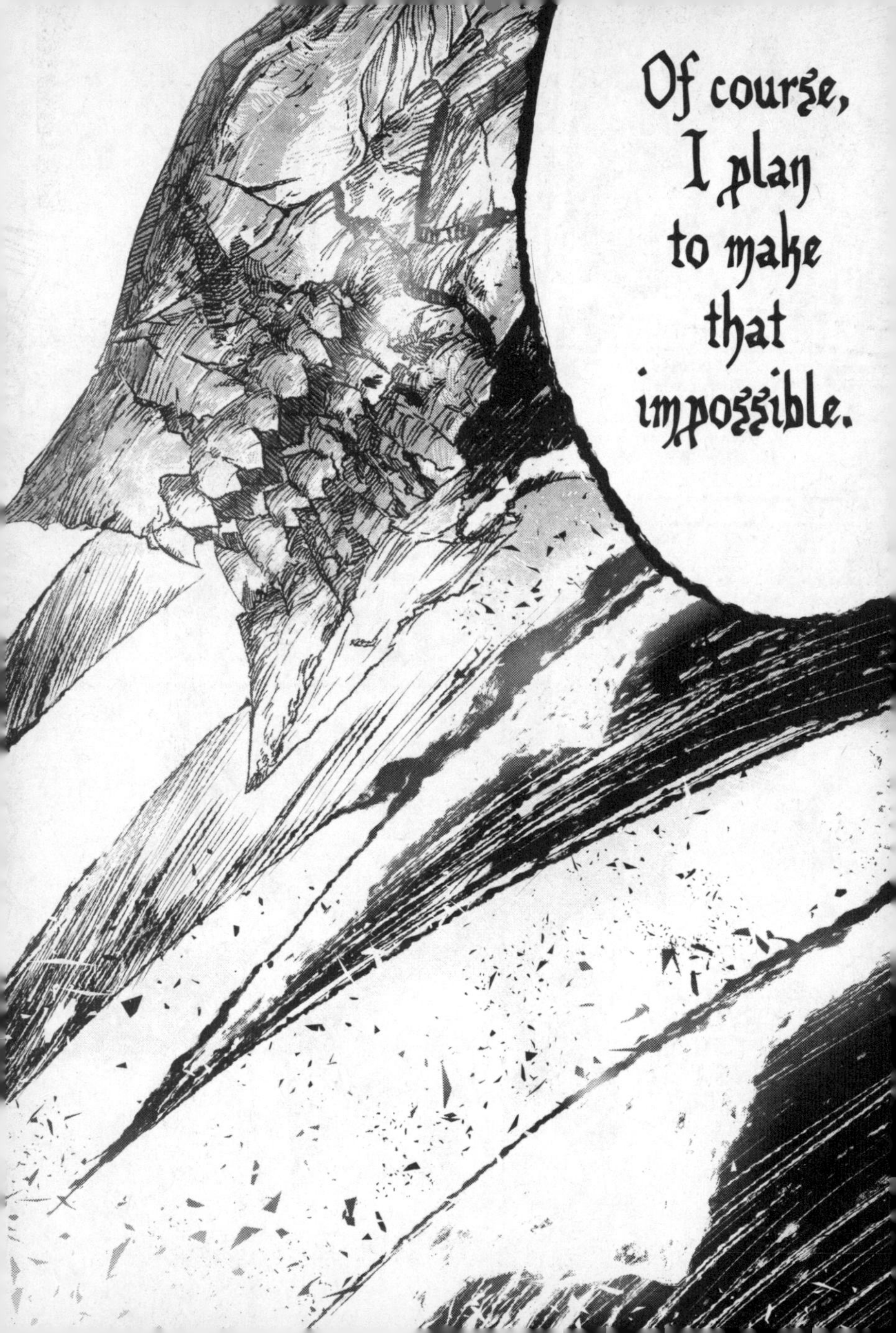
Of course, I plan to make that impossible.

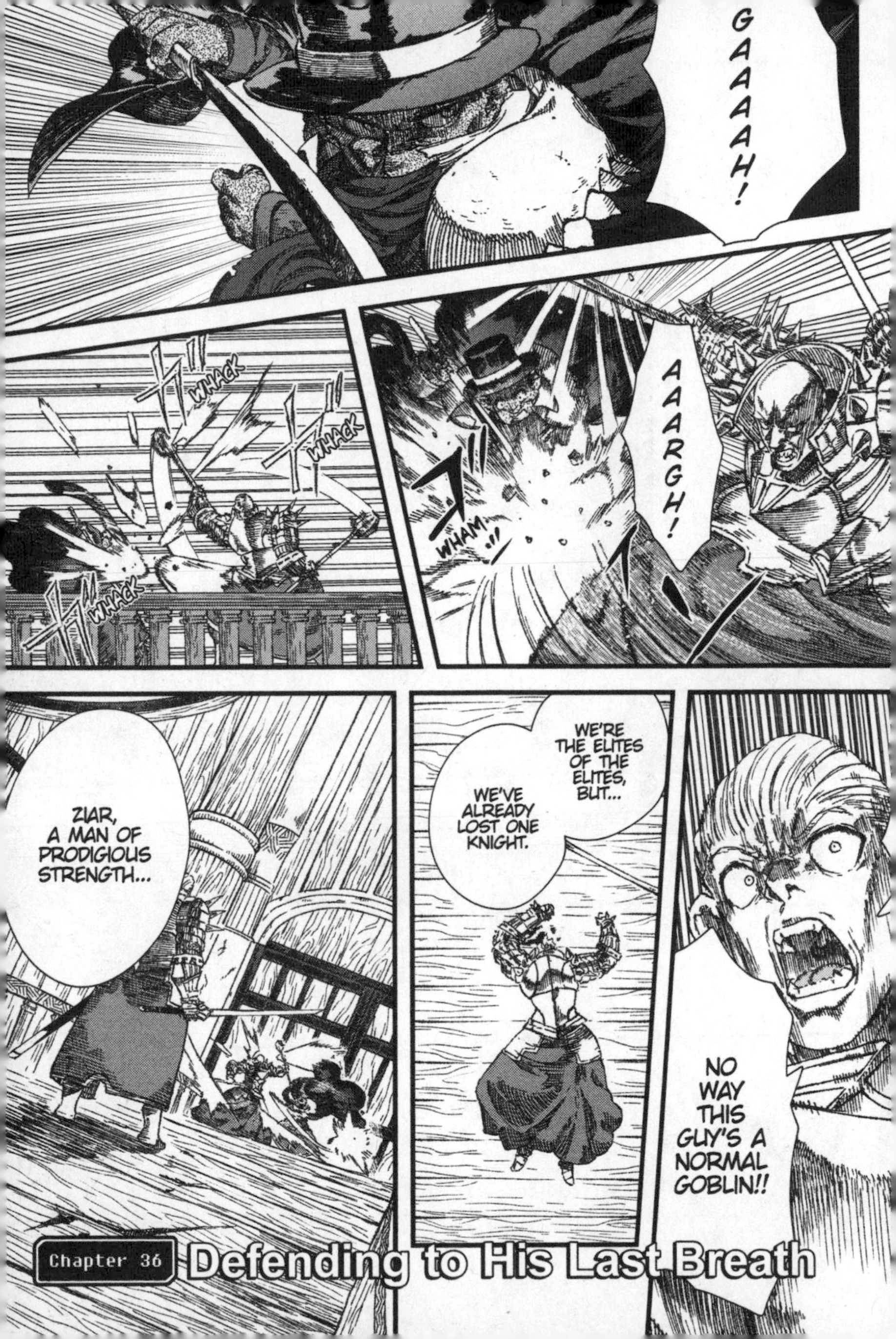
GAAAAAH!
AAAARGH!
WHAM
WHACK
WHACK
WHACK
NO WAY THIS GUY'S A NORMAL GOBLIN!!
WE'RE THE ELITES OF THE ELITES, BUT...
WE'VE ALREADY LOST ONE KNIGHT.
ZIAR, A MAN OF PRODIGIOUS STRENGTH...
Chapter 36
Defending to His Last Breath

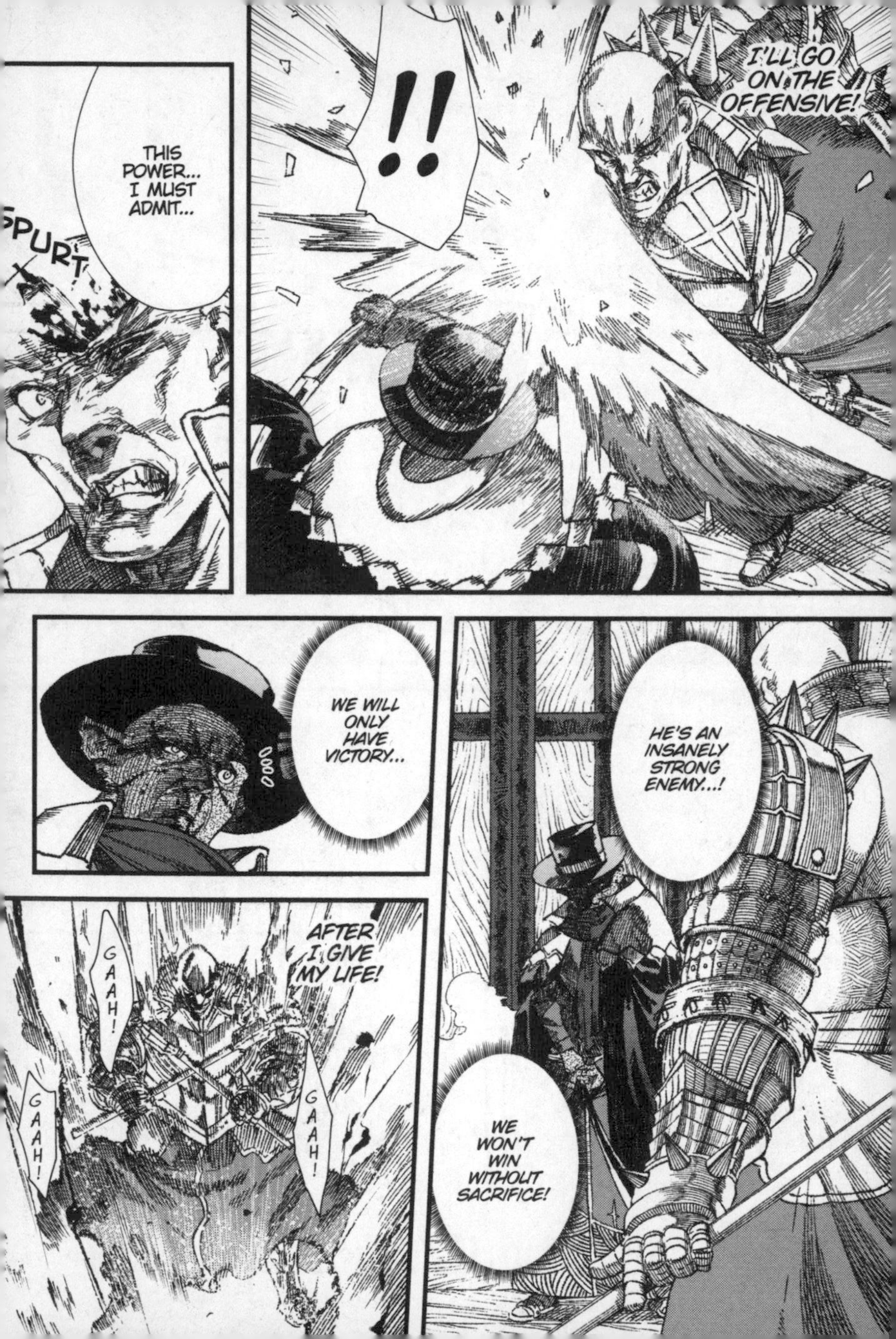
I'LL GO ON THE OFFENSIVE!
!!
THIS POWER... I MUST ADMIT...
SPURT
HE'S AN INSANELY STRONG ENEMY...!
WE WON'T WIN WITHOUT SACRIFICE!
WE WILL ONLY HAVE VICTORY...
AFTER I GIVE MY LIFE!
GAAAH!
GAAAH!
GAAAH!

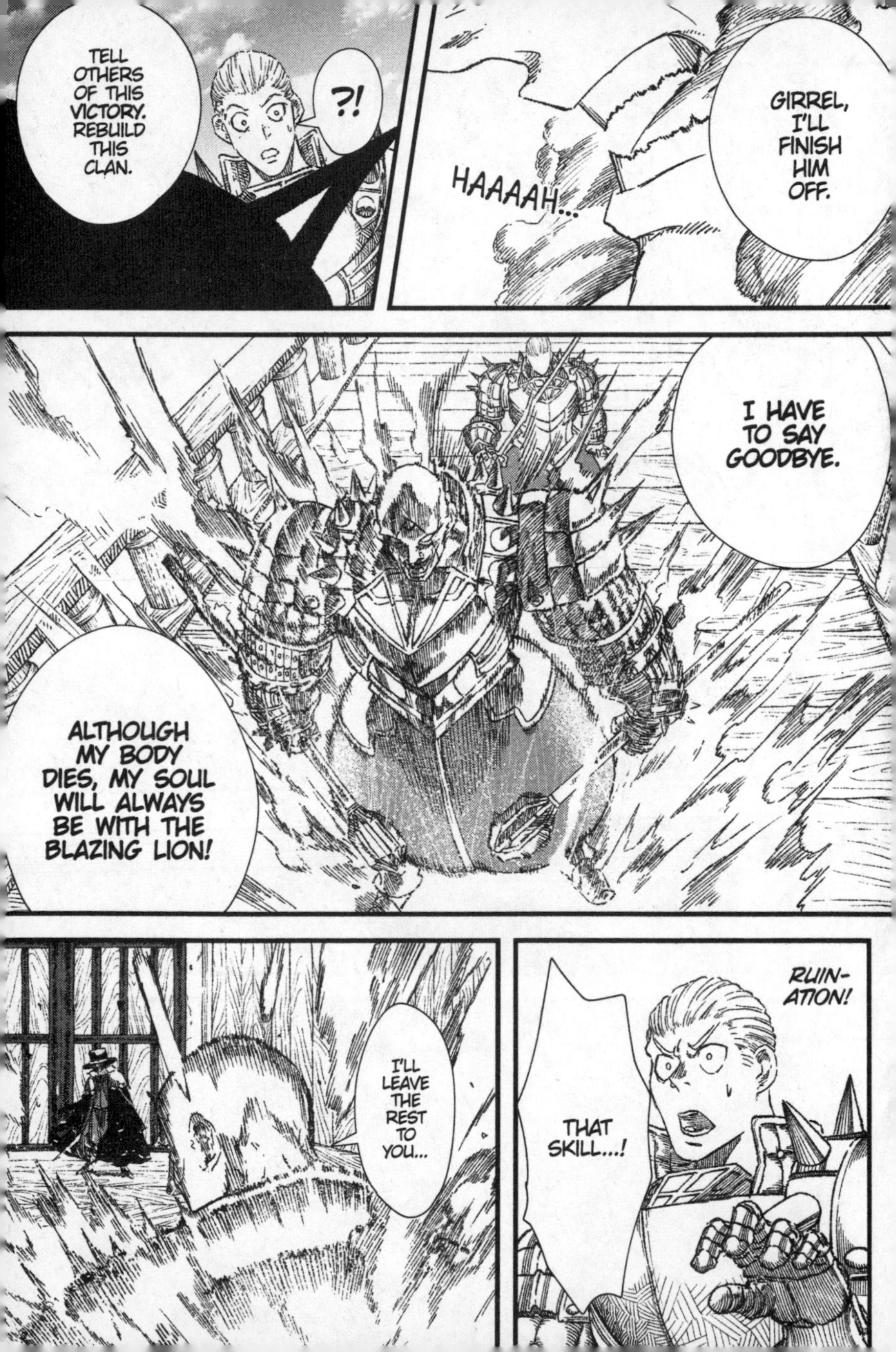
GIRREL, I'LL FINISH HIM OFF.
HAAAAH...
TELL OTHERS OF THIS VICTORY. REBUILD THIS CLAN.
?!
I HAVE TO SAY GOODBYE.
ALTHOUGH MY BODY DIES, MY SOUL WILL ALWAYS BE WITH THE BLAZING LION!
RUIN-ATION!
THAT SKILL...!
I'LL LEAVE THE REST TO YOU...

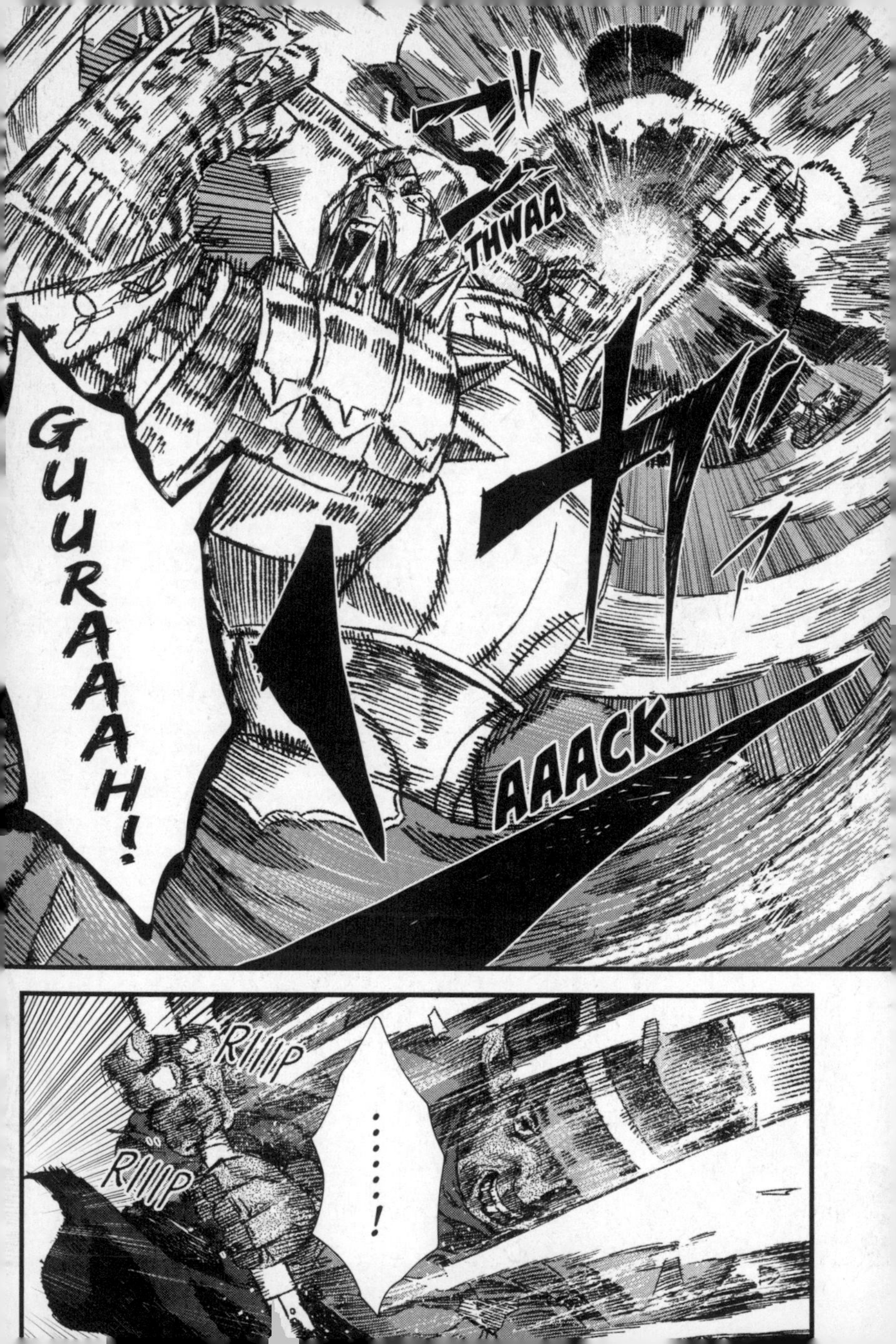
THWAA
AAACK
GUURAAAH!
......!
RIIP
RIIP

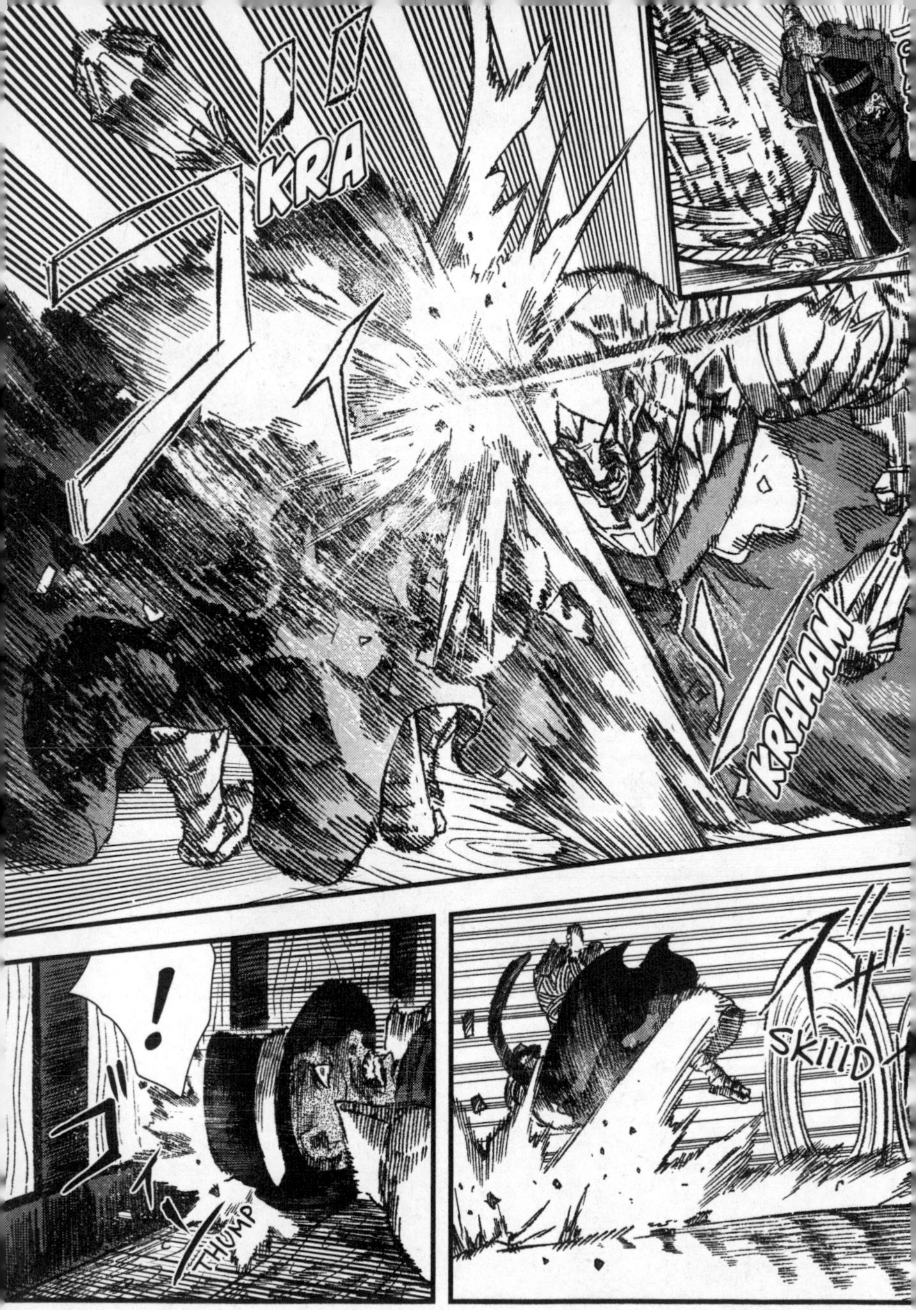
KRA
KRAAAAM
SKIIID
!
THUMP

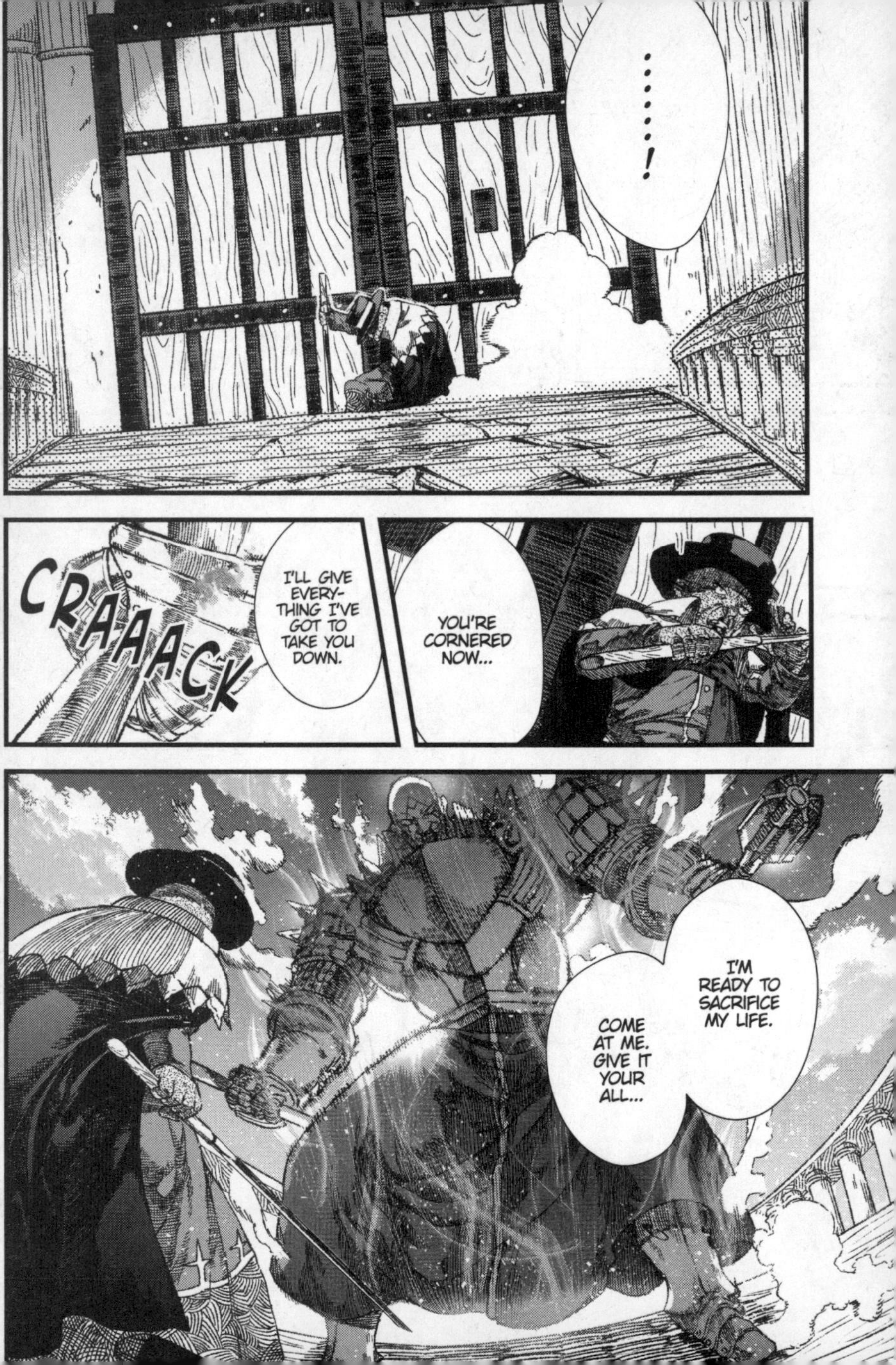
......!
YOU'RE CORNERED NOW...
I'LL GIVE EVERYTHING I'VE GOT TO TAKE YOU DOWN.
CRAAACK
I'M READY TO SACRIFICE MY LIFE.
COME AT ME. GIVE IT YOUR ALL...

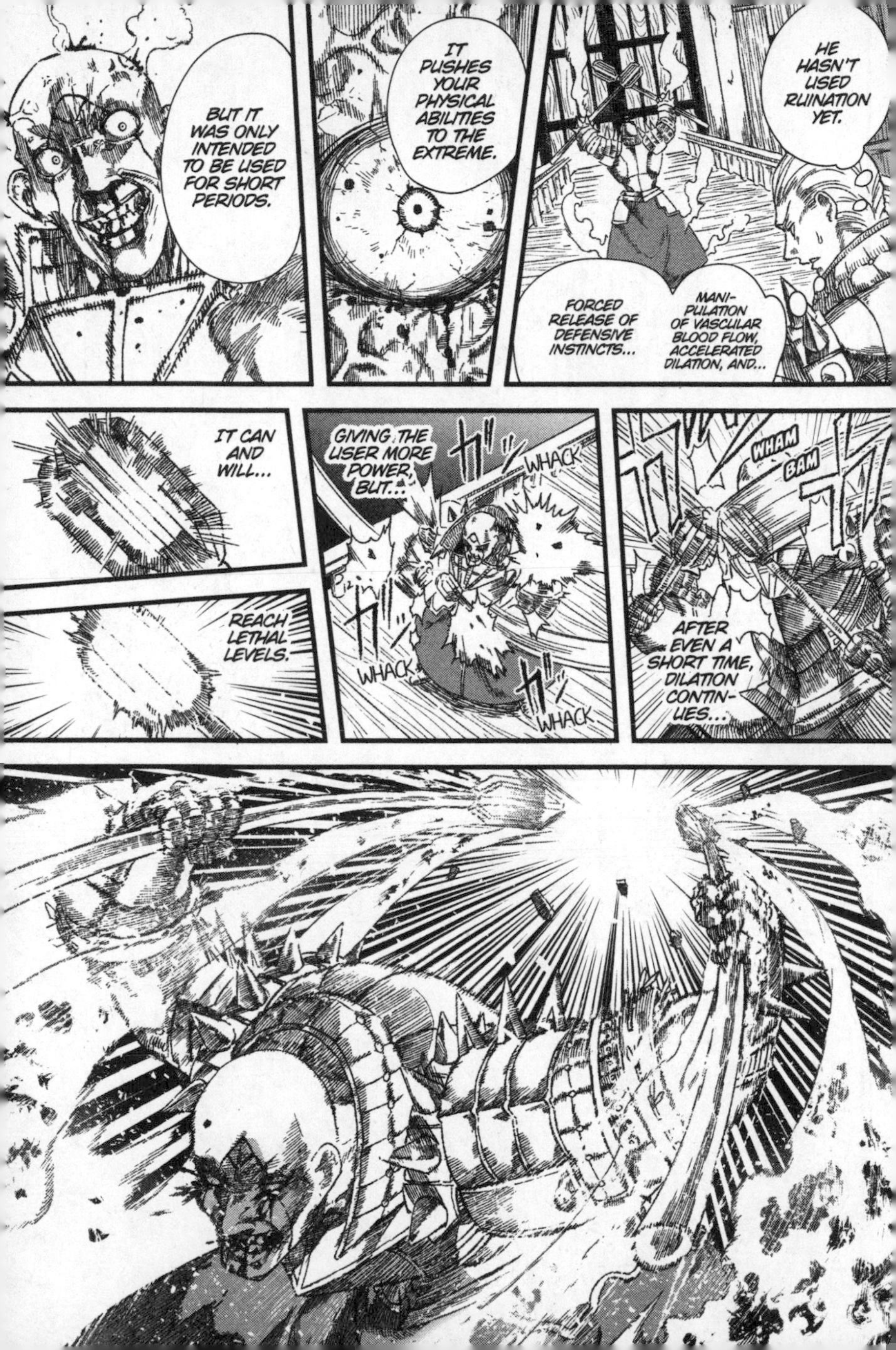
HE HASN'T USED RUINATION YET.
MANIPULATION OF VASCULAR BLOOD FLOW, ACCELERATED DILATION, AND...
FORCED RELEASE OF DEFENSIVE INSTINCTS...
IT PUSHES YOUR PHYSICAL ABILITIES TO THE EXTREME.
BUT IT WAS ONLY INTENDED TO BE USED FOR SHORT PERIODS.
WHAM
BAM
AFTER EVEN A SHORT TIME, DILATION CONTINUES...
GIVING THE USER MORE POWER, BUT...
WHACK
WHACK
WHACK
IT CAN AND WILL...
REACH LETHAL LEVELS.

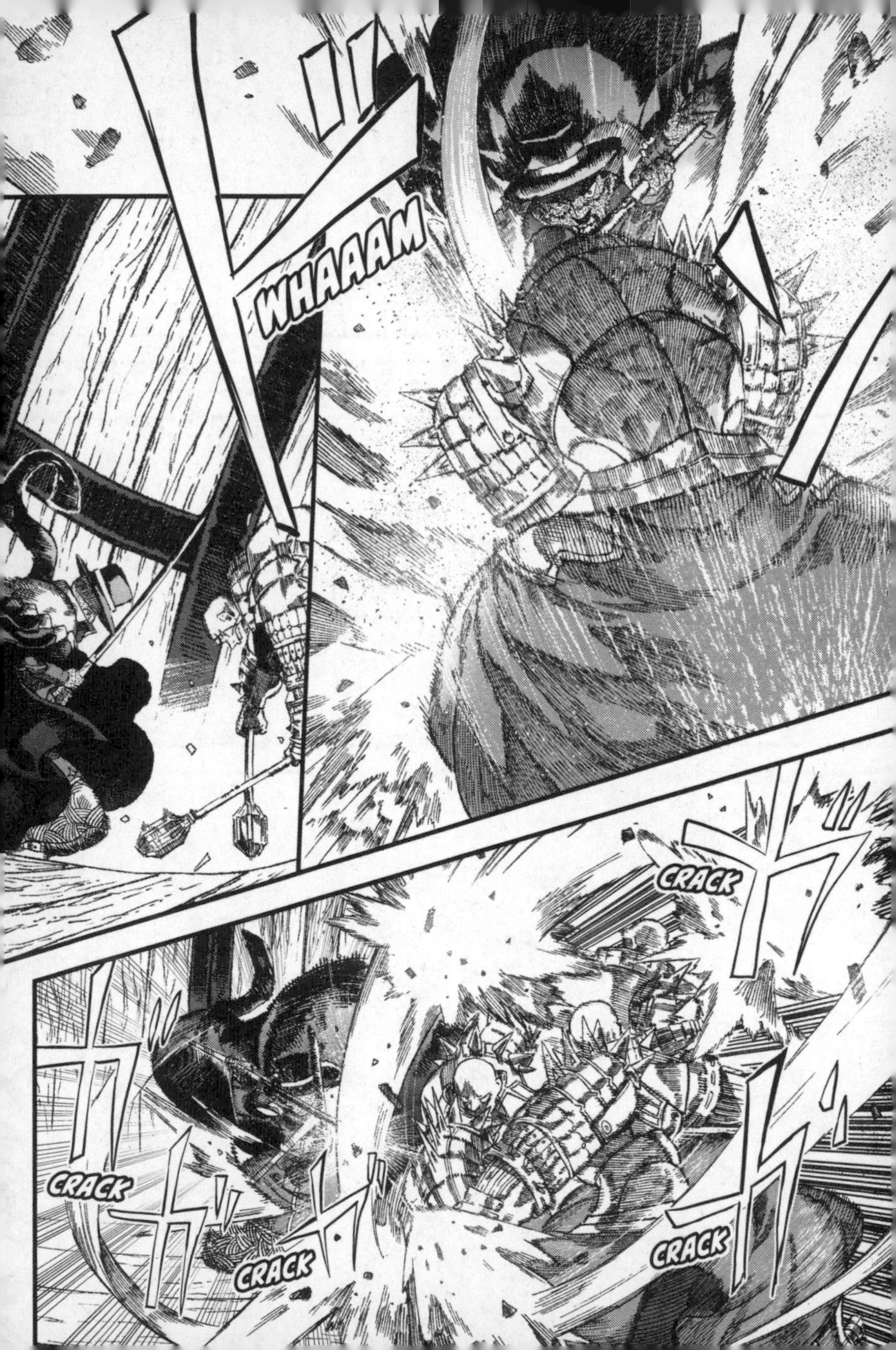
WHAAAM
CRACK
CRACK
CRACK
CRACK

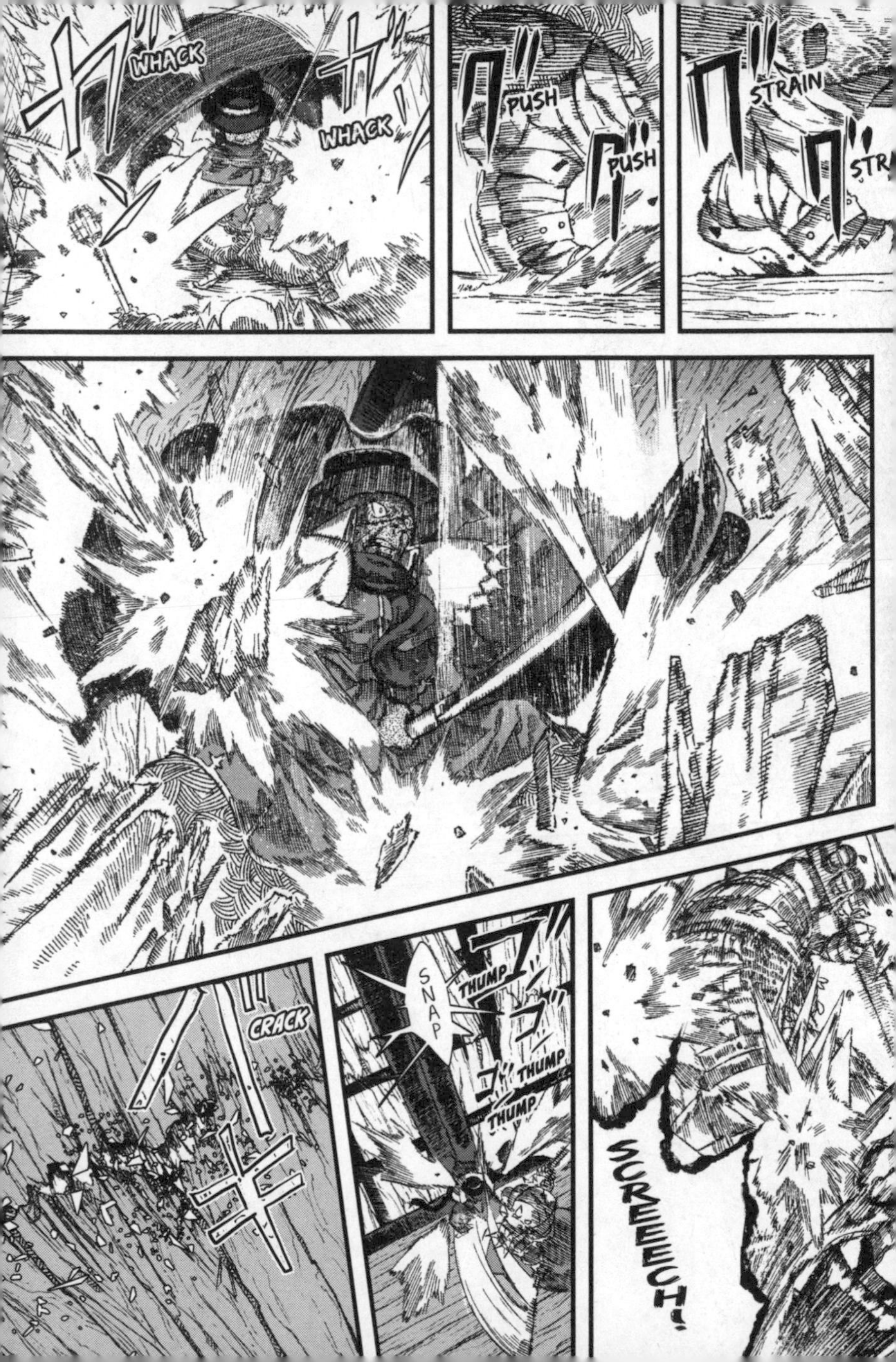
STRAIN
STRA
PUSH
PUSH
WHACK
WHACK
SCREEECH!
SNAP
THUMP
THUMP
THUMP
CRACK

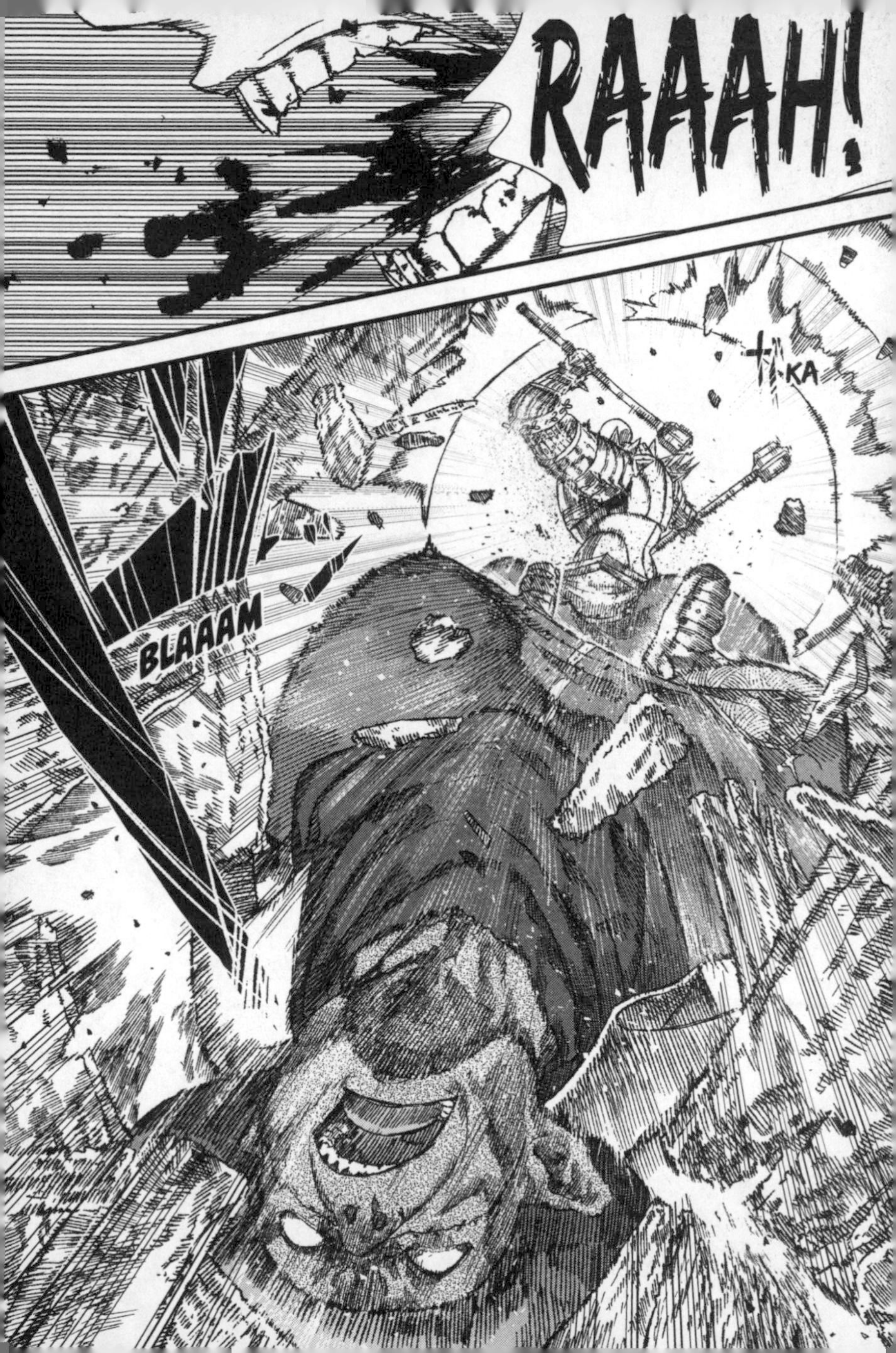
RAAAH!
KA
BLAAAM

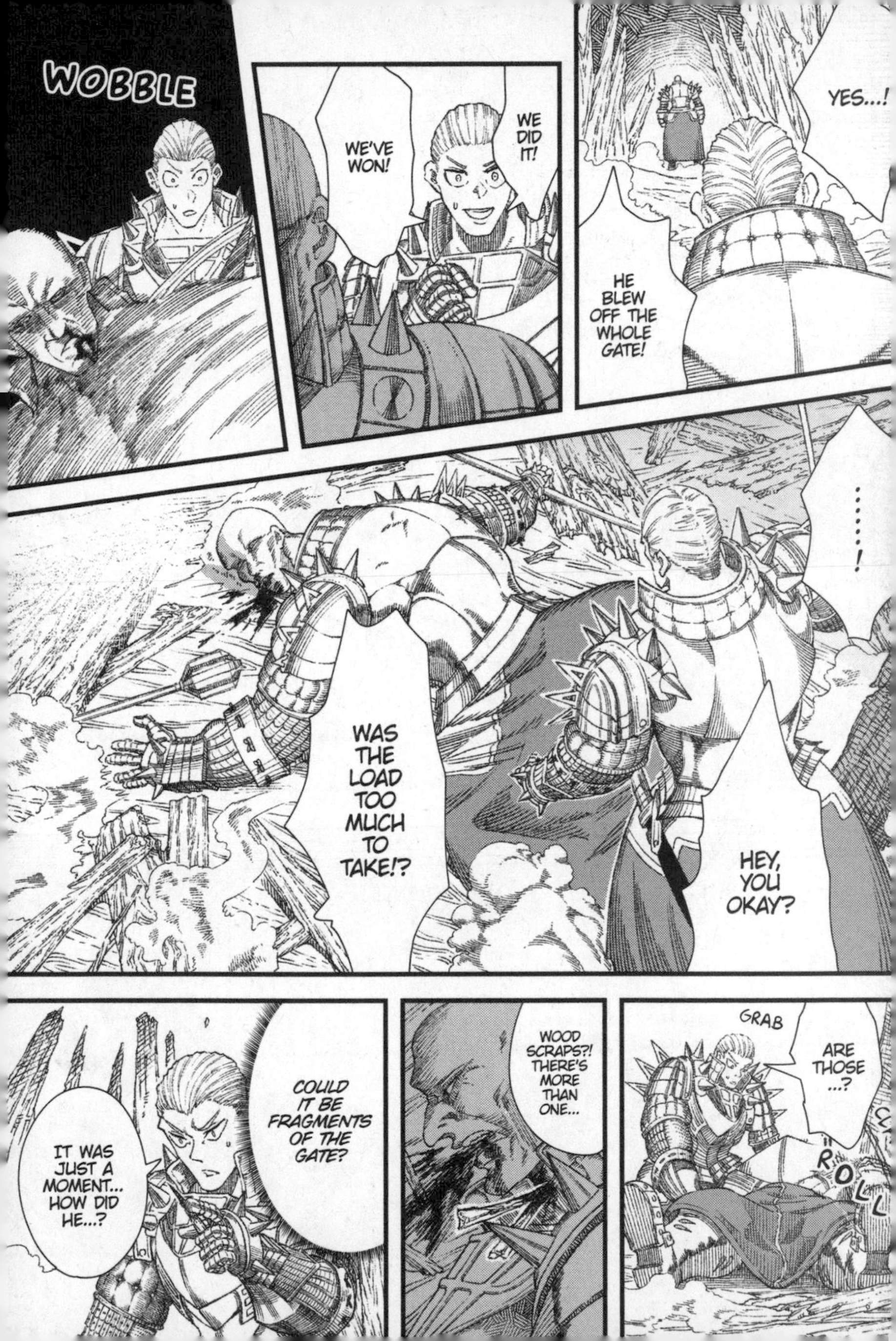
YES...!
HE BLEW OFF THE WHOLE GATE!
WE DID IT!
WE'VE WON!
WOBBLE
......!
HEY, YOU OKAY?
WAS THE LOAD TOO MUCH TO TAKE!?
GRAB
ARE THOSE ...?
ROLL
WOOD SCRAPS?! THERE'S MORE THAN ONE...
COULD IT BE FRAGMENTS OF THE GATE?
IT WAS JUST A MOMENT... HOW DID HE...?

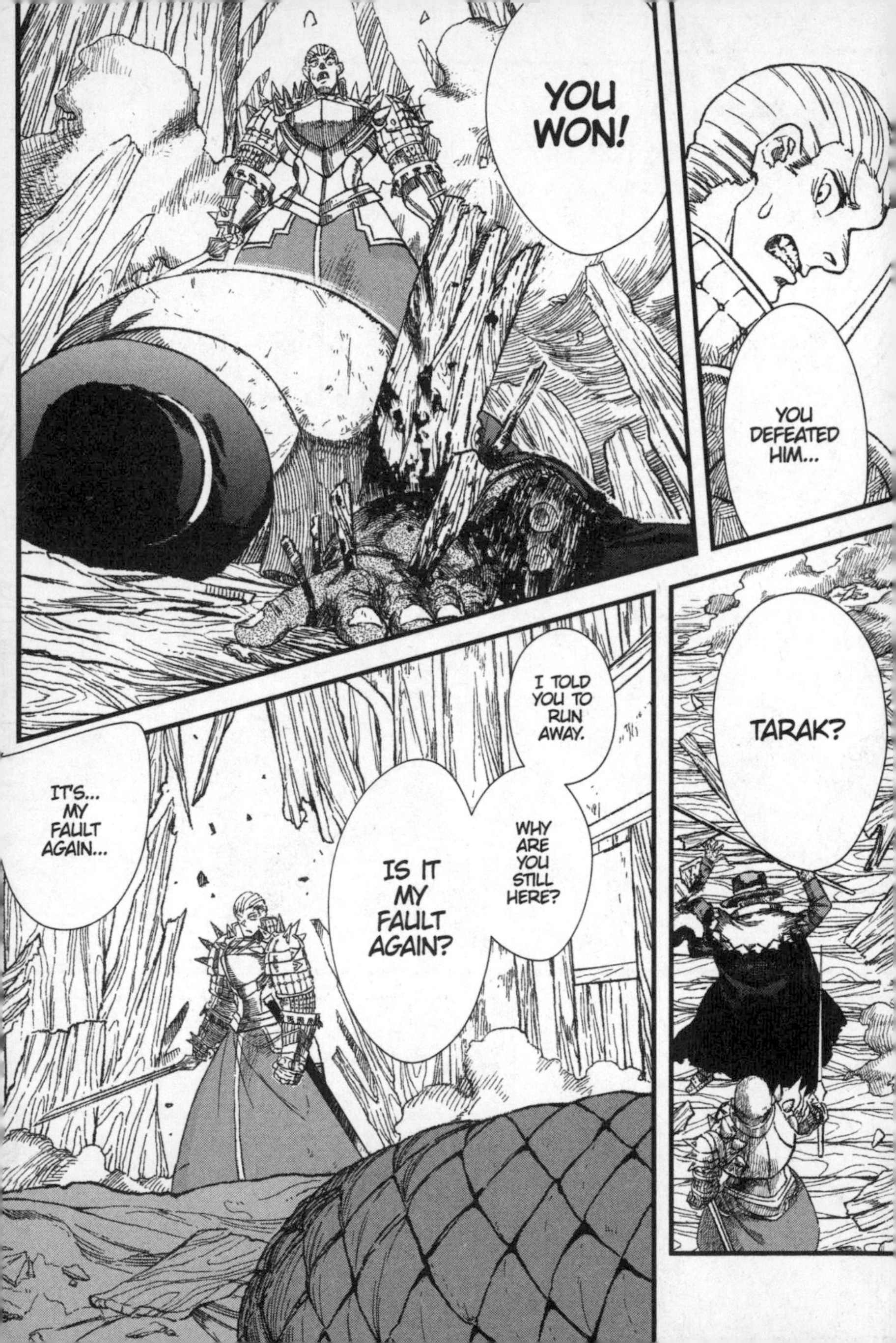
YOU DEFEATED HIM...
YOU WON!
TARAK?
I TOLD YOU TO RUN AWAY.
WHY ARE YOU STILL HERE?
IS IT MY FAULT AGAIN?
IT'S... MY FAULT AGAIN...

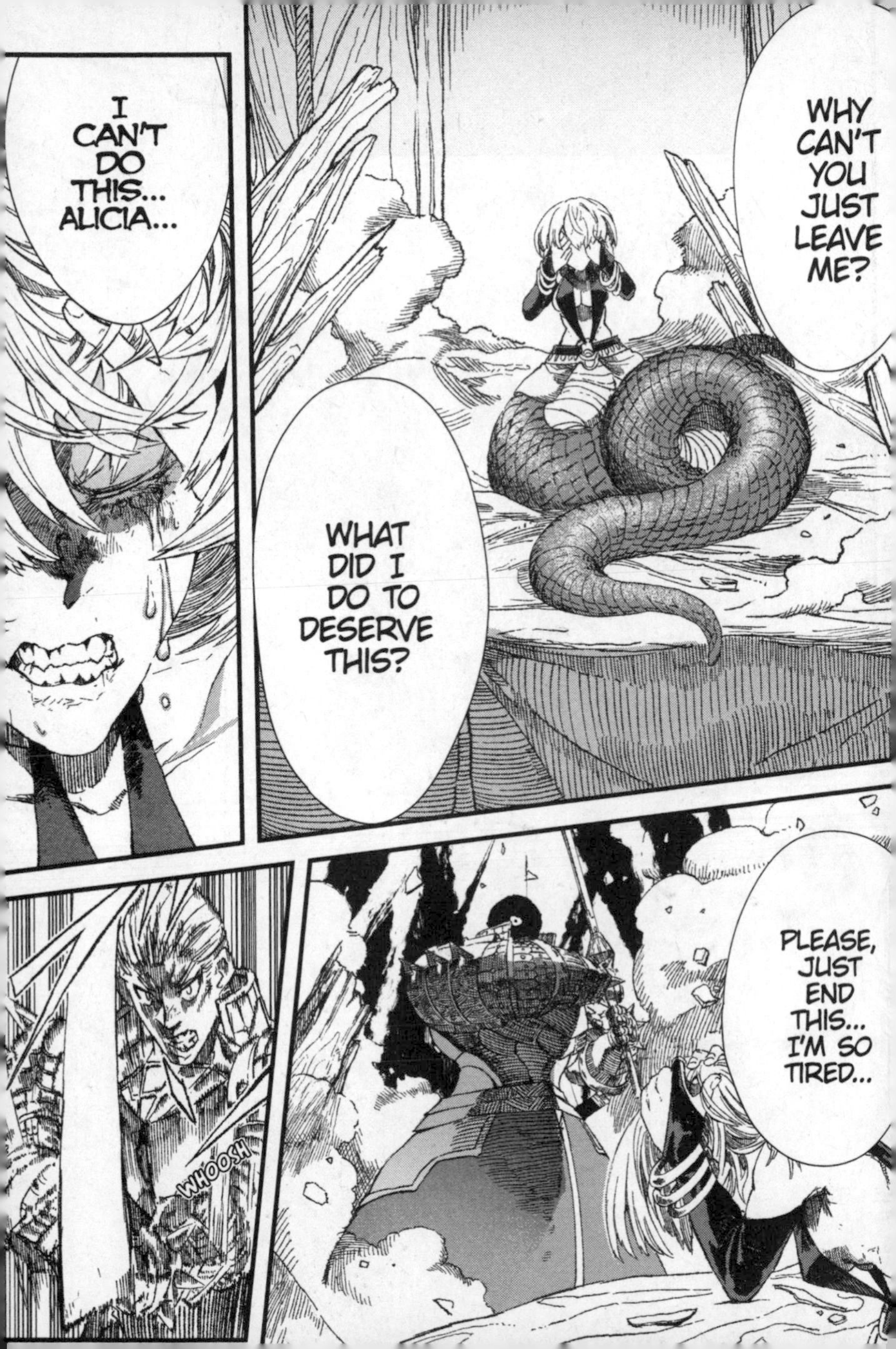
WHY CAN'T YOU JUST LEAVE ME?
WHAT DID I DO TO DESERVE THIS?
I CAN'T DO THIS... ALICIA...
PLEASE, JUST END THIS... I'M SO TIRED...
WHOOSH

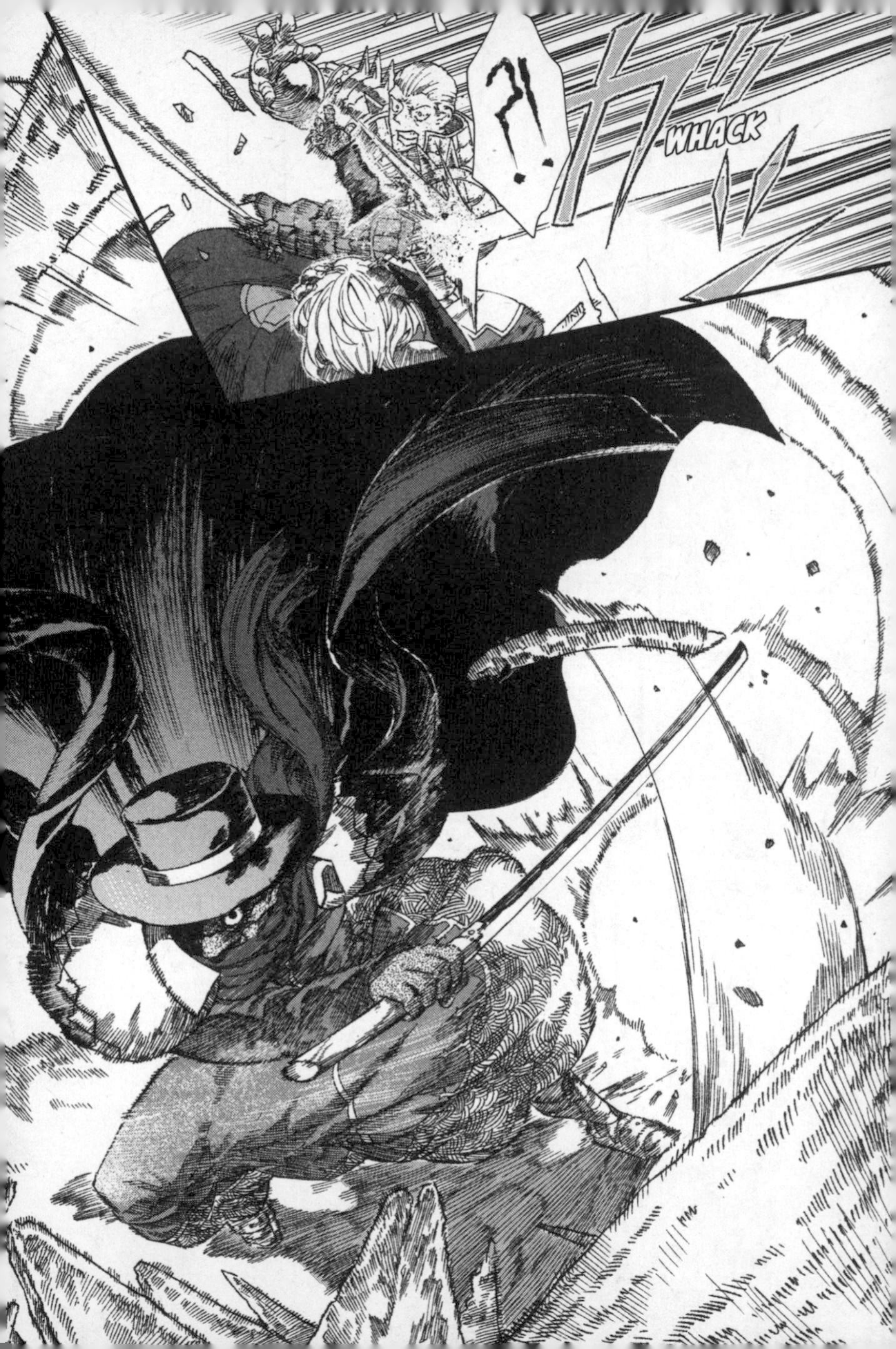
?!
WHACK

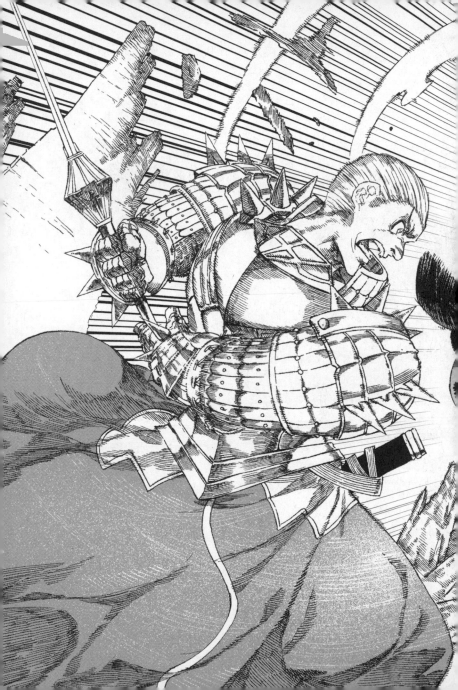

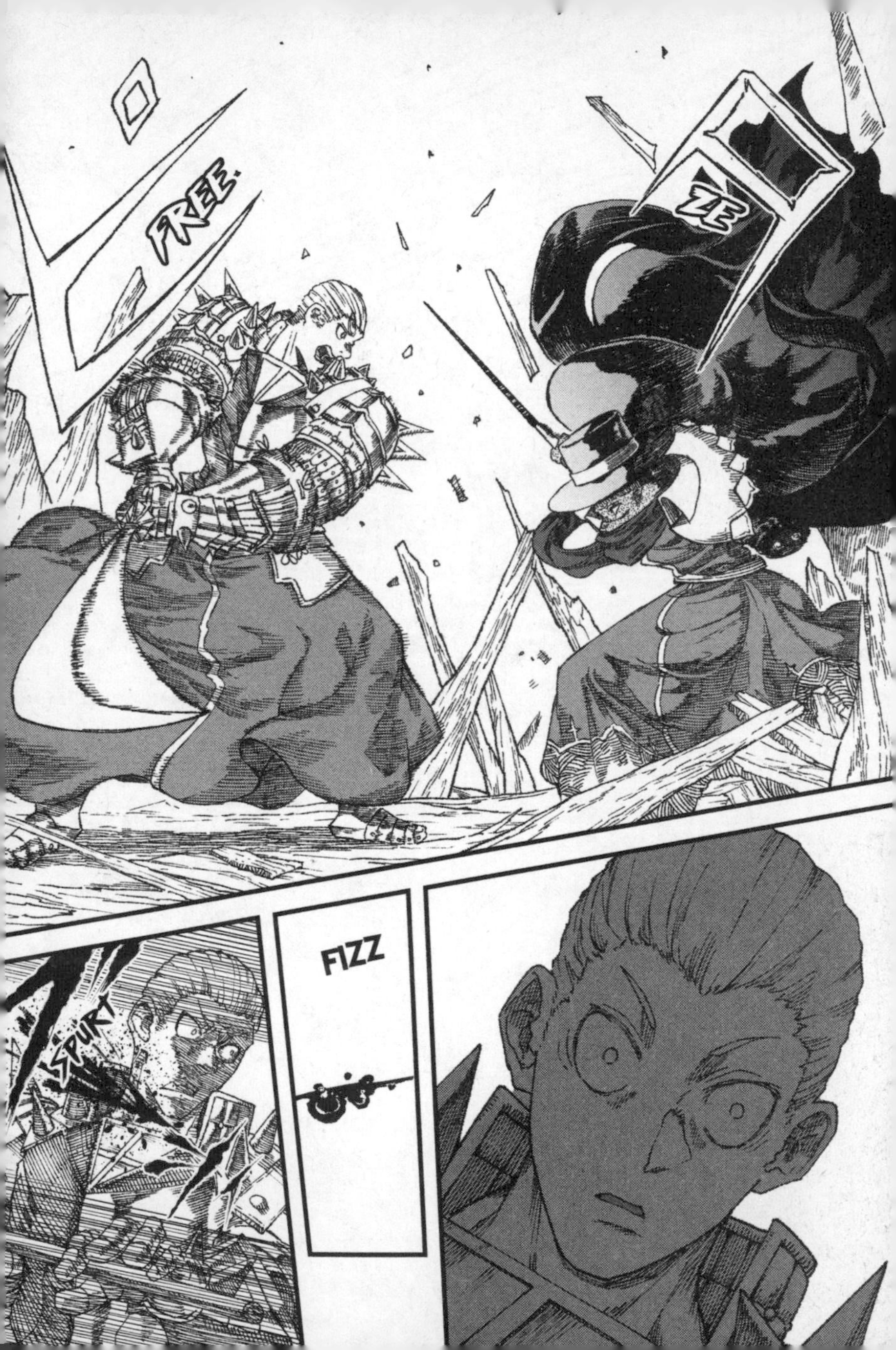
FREE.
ZE
FIZZ
SPURT

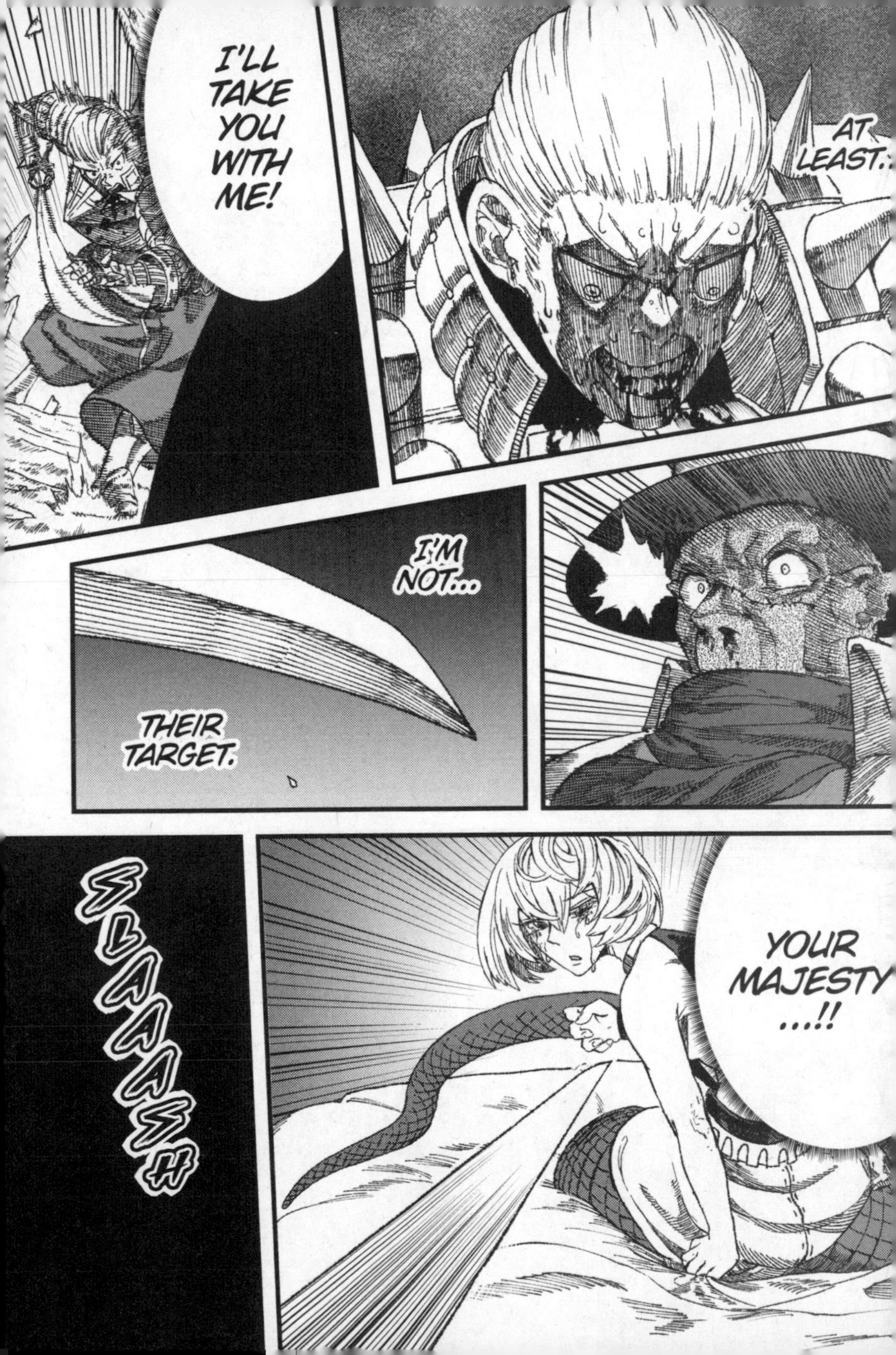
AT LEAST...
I'LL TAKE YOU WITH ME!
I'M NOT...
THEIR TARGET.
YOUR MAJESTY ...!!
SVAAASH

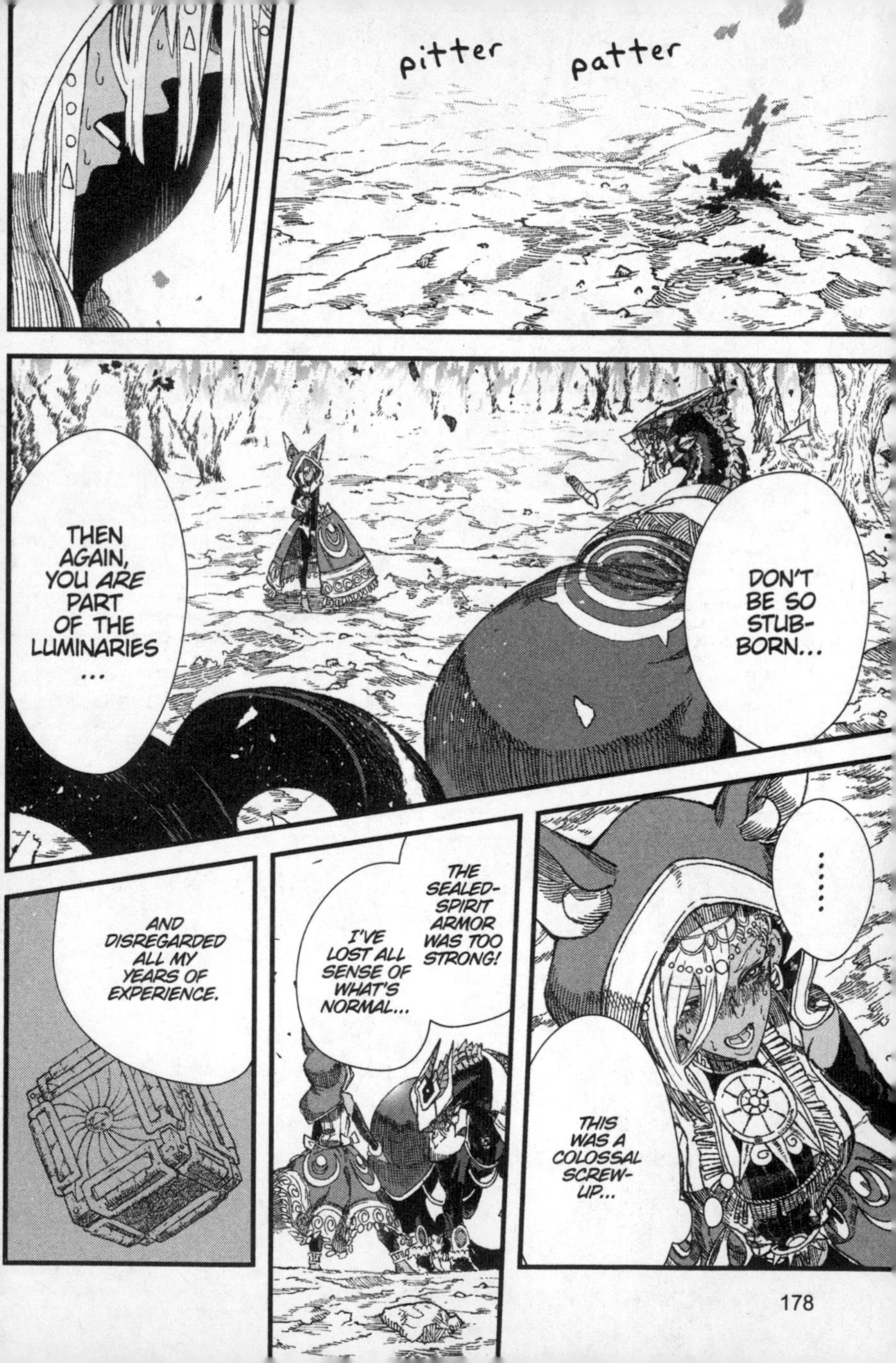
pitter patter
DON'T BE SO STUBBORN...
THEN AGAIN, YOU *ARE* PART OF THE LUMINARIES...
......
THIS WAS A COLOSSAL SCREW-UP...
THE SEALED-SPIRIT ARMOR WAS TOO STRONG!
I'VE LOST ALL SENSE OF WHAT'S NORMAL...
AND DISREGARDED ALL MY YEARS OF EXPERIENCE.

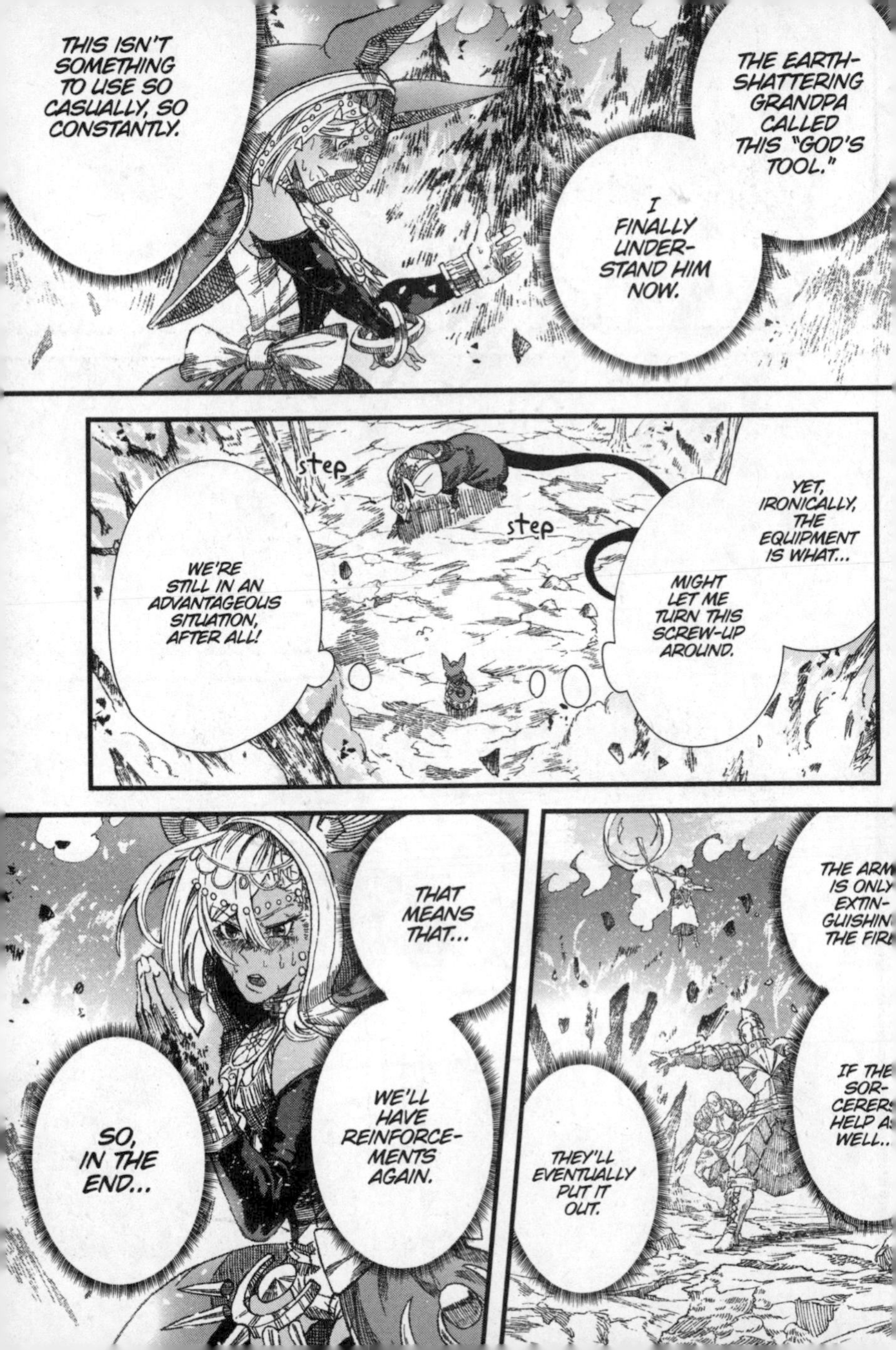
THE EARTH-SHATTERING GRANDPA CALLED THIS "GOD'S TOOL."
I FINALLY UNDER-STAND HIM NOW.
THIS ISN'T SOMETHING TO USE SO CASUALLY, SO CONSTANTLY.
YET, IRONICALLY, THE EQUIPMENT IS WHAT...
MIGHT LET ME TURN THIS SCREW-UP AROUND.
step
step
WE'RE STILL IN AN ADVANTAGEOUS SITUATION, AFTER ALL!
THE ARM IS ONLY EXTIN-GUISHIN THE FIR
IF THE SOR-CERERS HELP A WELL...
THEY'LL EVENTUALLY PUT IT OUT.
THAT MEANS THAT...
WE'LL HAVE REINFORCE-MENTS AGAIN.
SO, IN THE END...

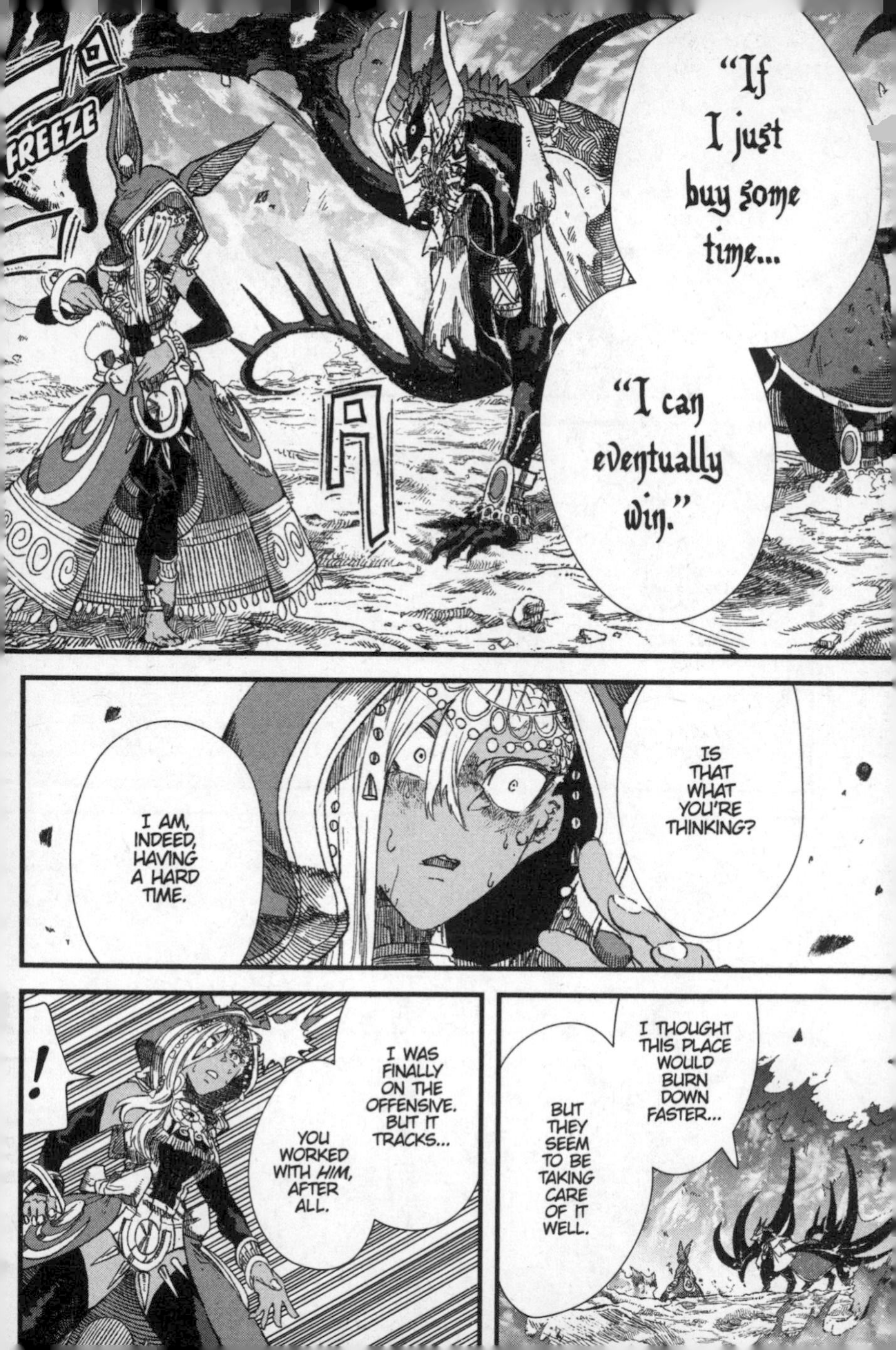
"If I just buy some time...
"I can eventually win."
FREEZE
IS THAT WHAT YOU'RE THINKING?
I AM, INDEED, HAVING A HARD TIME.
I THOUGHT THIS PLACE WOULD BURN DOWN FASTER...
BUT THEY SEEM TO BE TAKING CARE OF IT WELL.
I WAS FINALLY ON THE OFFENSIVE. BUT IT TRACKS...
YOU WORKED WITH *HIM*, AFTER ALL.
!

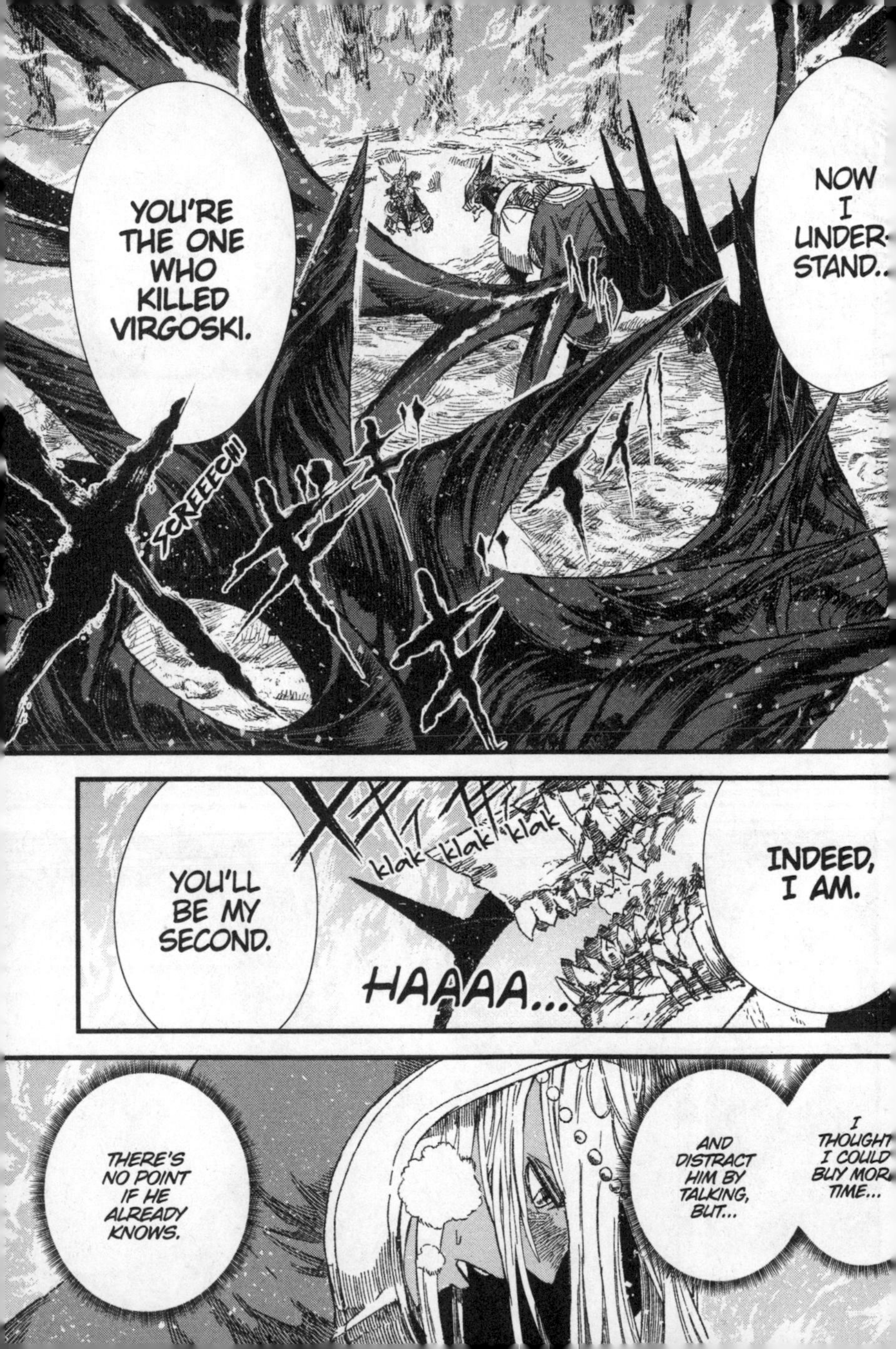
NOW I UNDERSTAND..
YOU'RE THE ONE WHO KILLED VIRGOSKI.
SCREEECH!!
INDEED, I AM.
klak klak klak
HAAAA...
YOU'LL BE MY SECOND.
I THOUGHT I COULD BUY MOR TIME...
AND DISTRACT HIM BY TALKING, BUT...
THERE'S NO POINT IF HE ALREADY KNOWS.

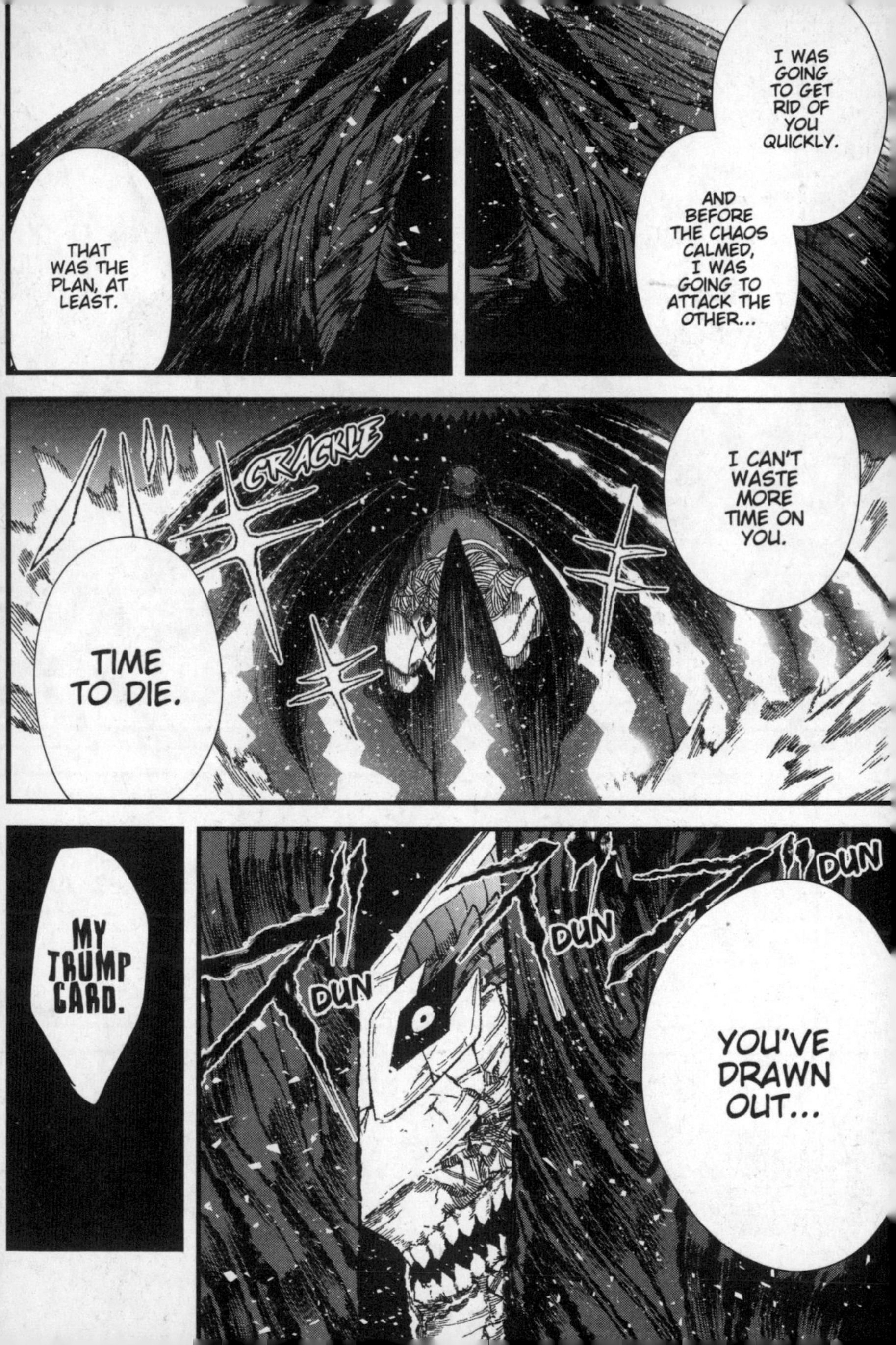
I WAS GOING TO GET RID OF YOU QUICKLY.
AND BEFORE THE CHAOS CALMED, I WAS GOING TO ATTACK THE OTHER...
THAT WAS THE PLAN, AT LEAST.
I CAN'T WASTE MORE TIME ON YOU.
CRACKLE
TIME TO DIE.
DUN
DUN
DUN
YOU'VE DRAWN OUT...
MY TRUMP CARD.

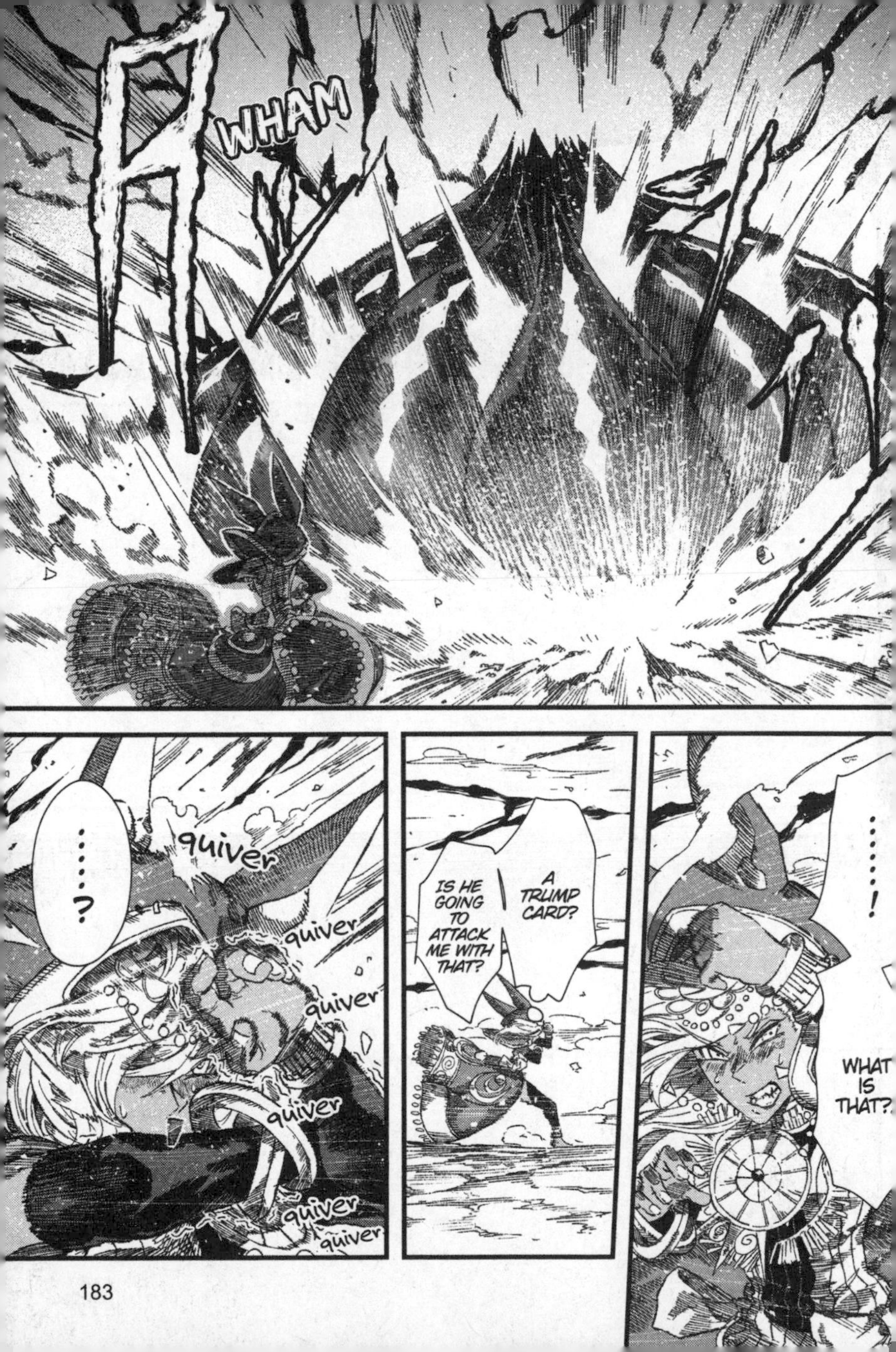
WHAM
......!
WHAT IS THAT?
A TRUMP CARD?
IS HE GOING TO ATTACK ME WITH THAT?
......?
quiver
quiver
quiver
quiver
quiver
quiver

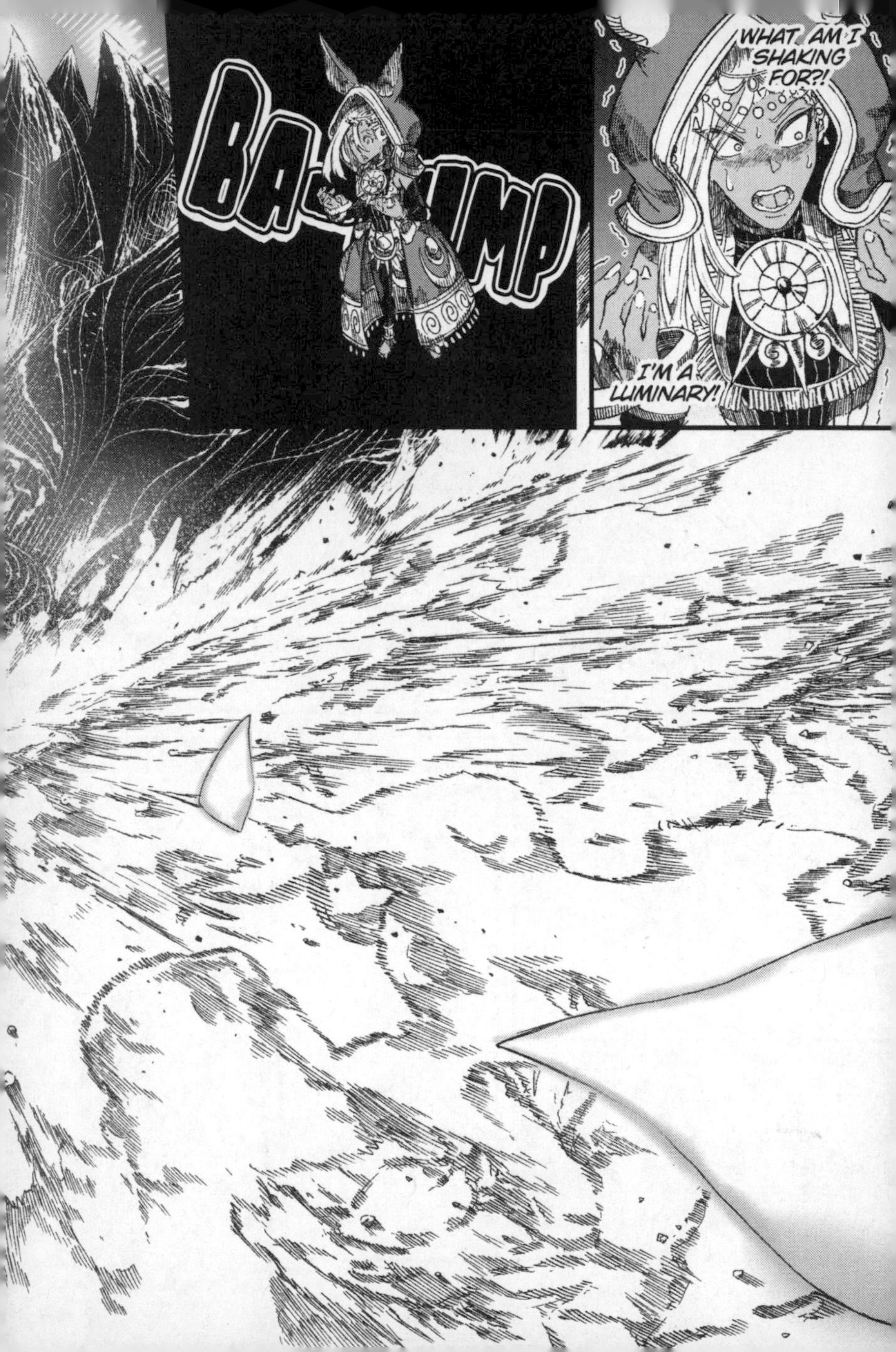
WHAT AM I SHAKING FOR?!
I'M A LUMINARY!

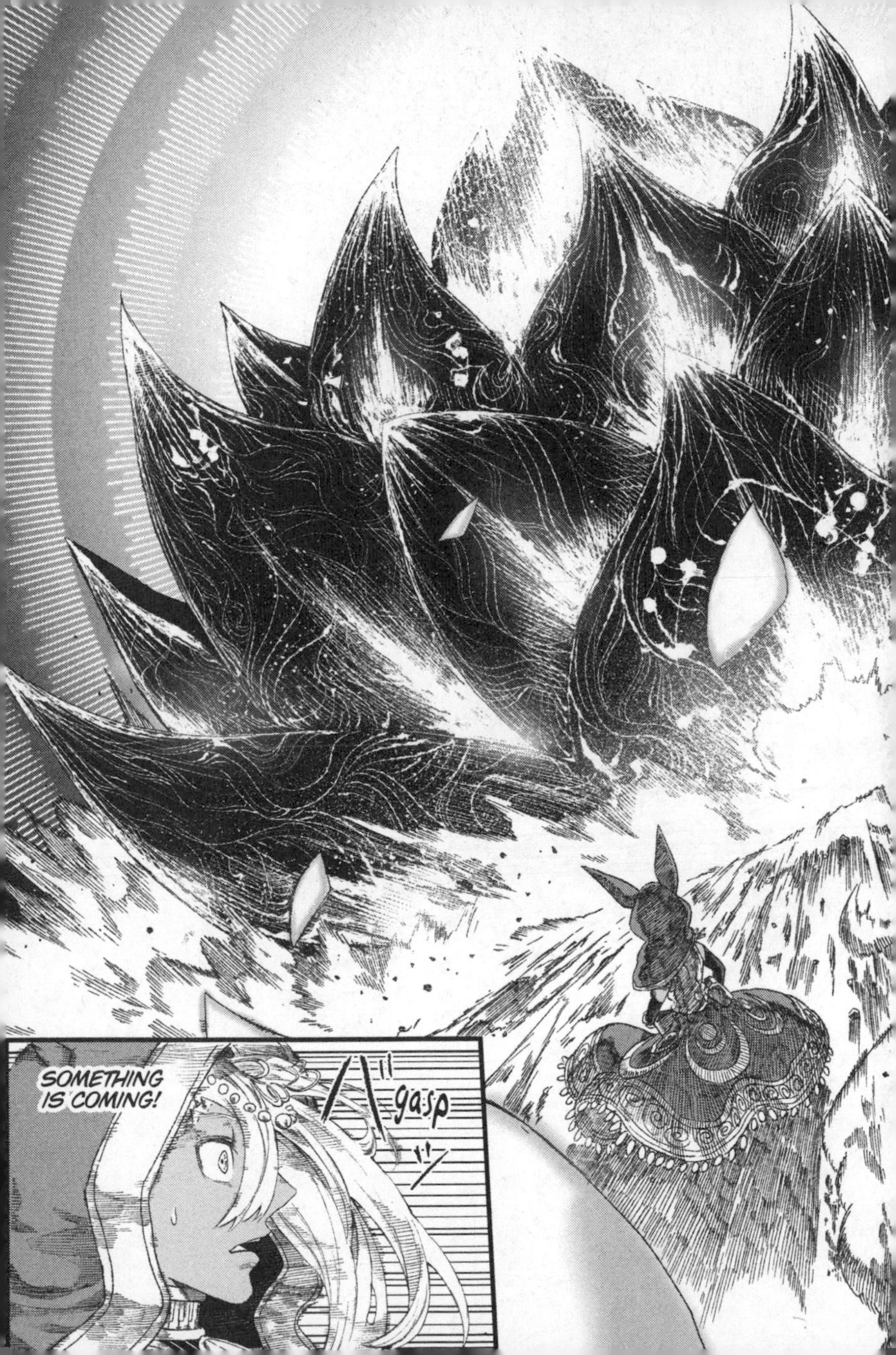
SOMETHING IS COMING!
gasp

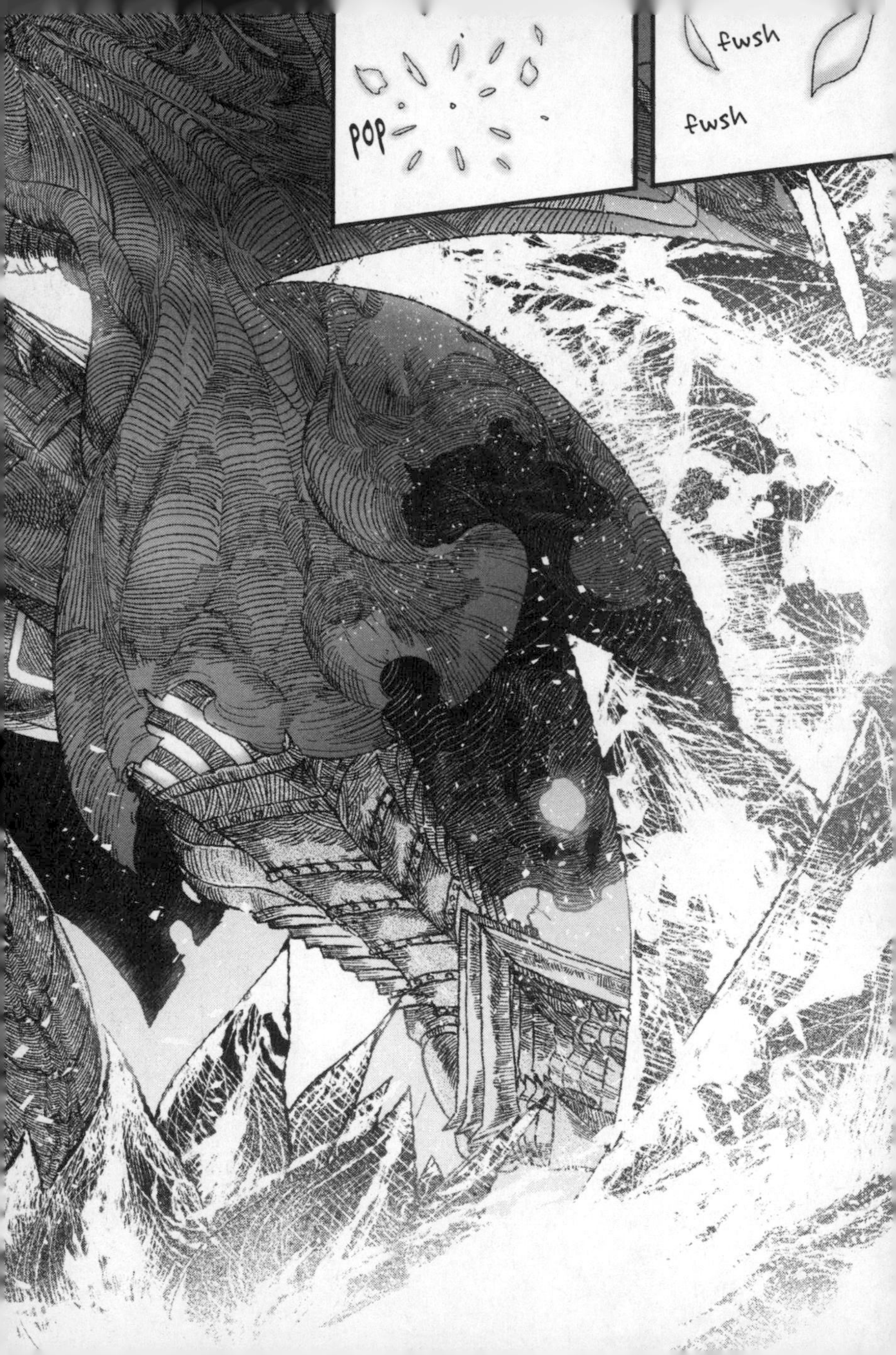
fwsh
fwsh
POP

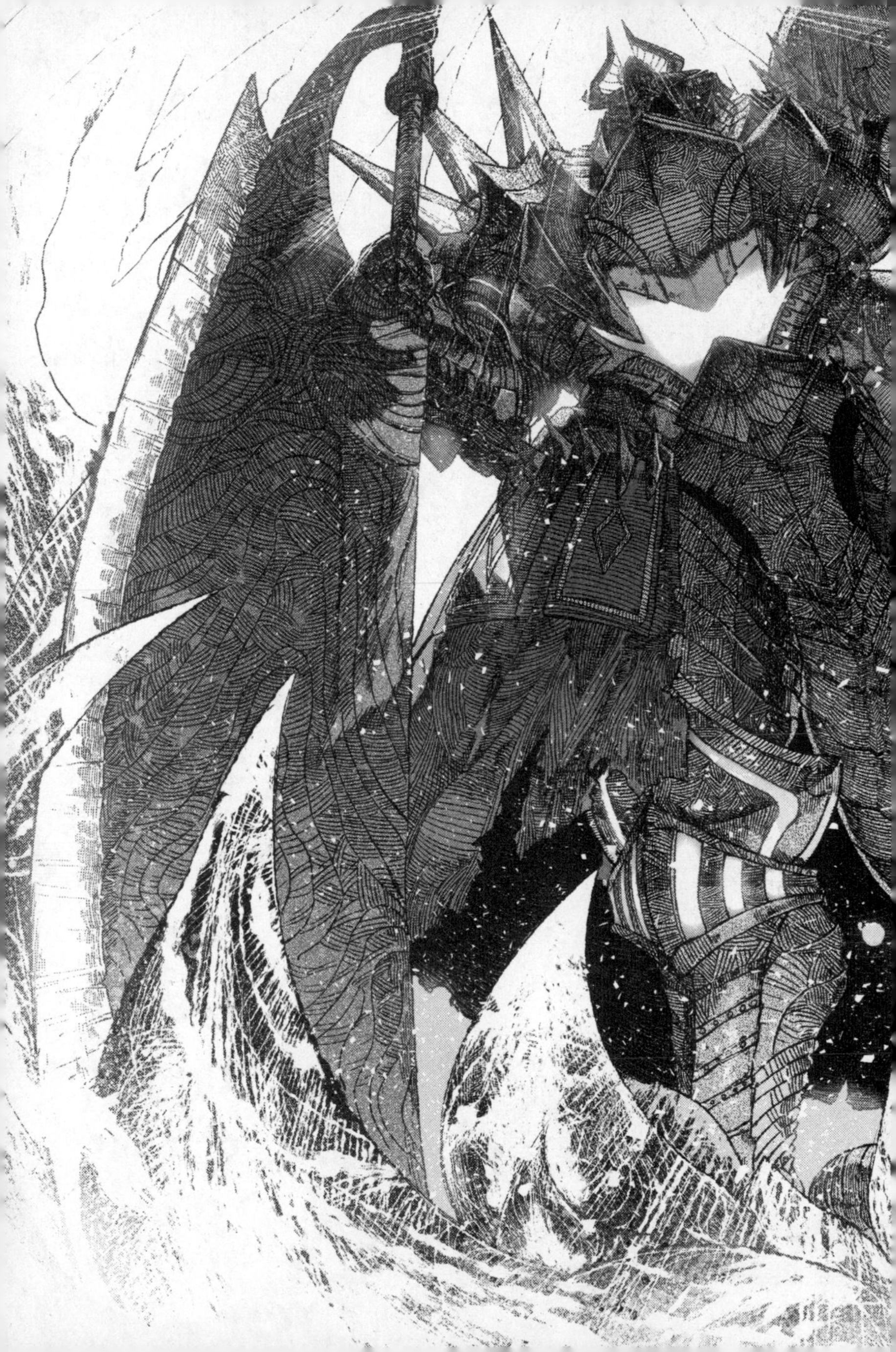

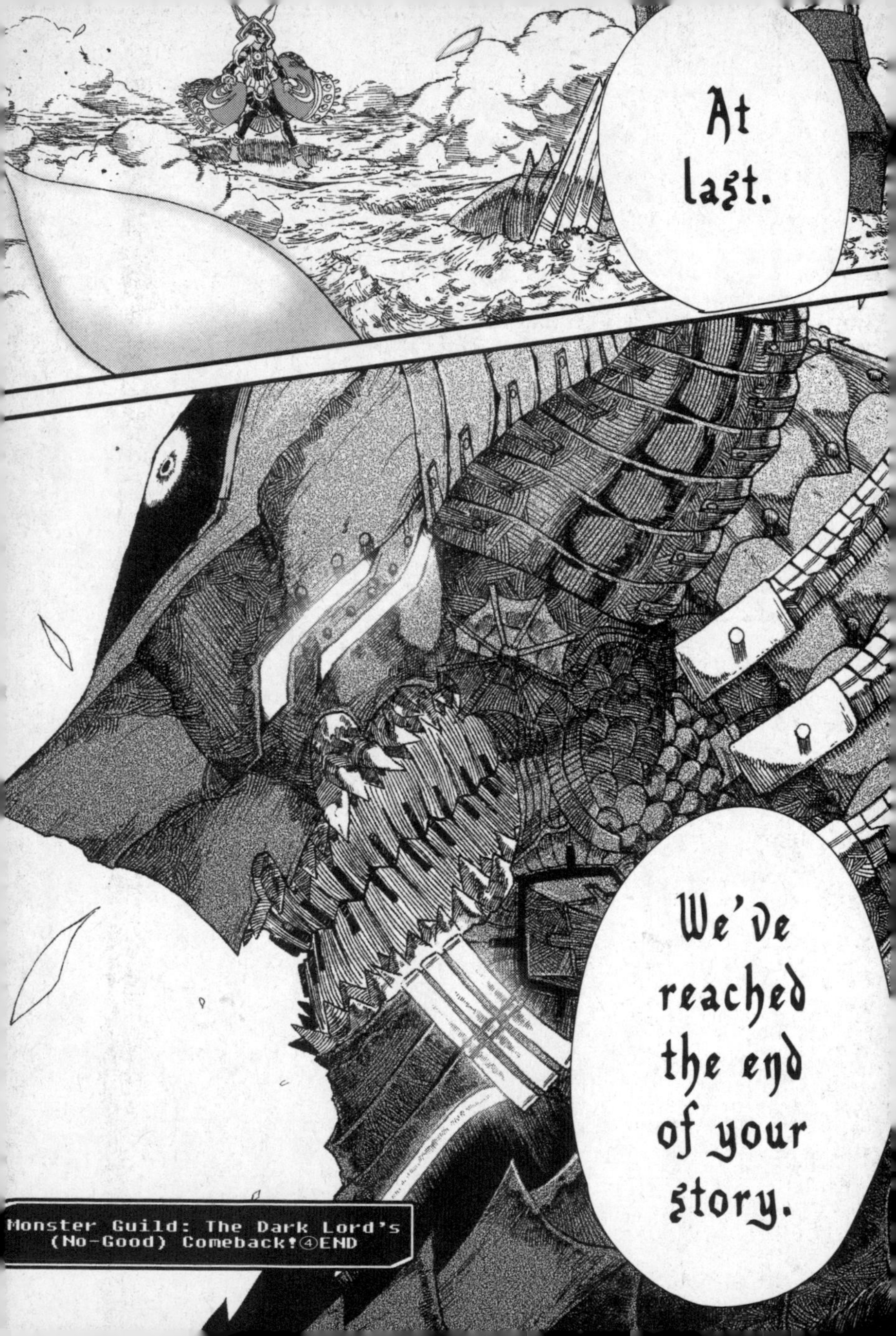
At last.
We've reached the end of your story.
Monster Guild: The Dark Lord's (No-Good) Comeback! ④ END

MONSTER GUILD
The Dark Lord's (No-Good) Comeback!

SPECIAL THANKS

I'd like to use this opportunity to express my deep gratitude to all the people who helped me.

ASSISTANT

Hikaru Sato
Hitoshi Isamu
Wataru Yamashiro
Moto
Shirasu Pendragon

Materials Provided by

Ramu Arata
Takashi Ino

Next Volume--

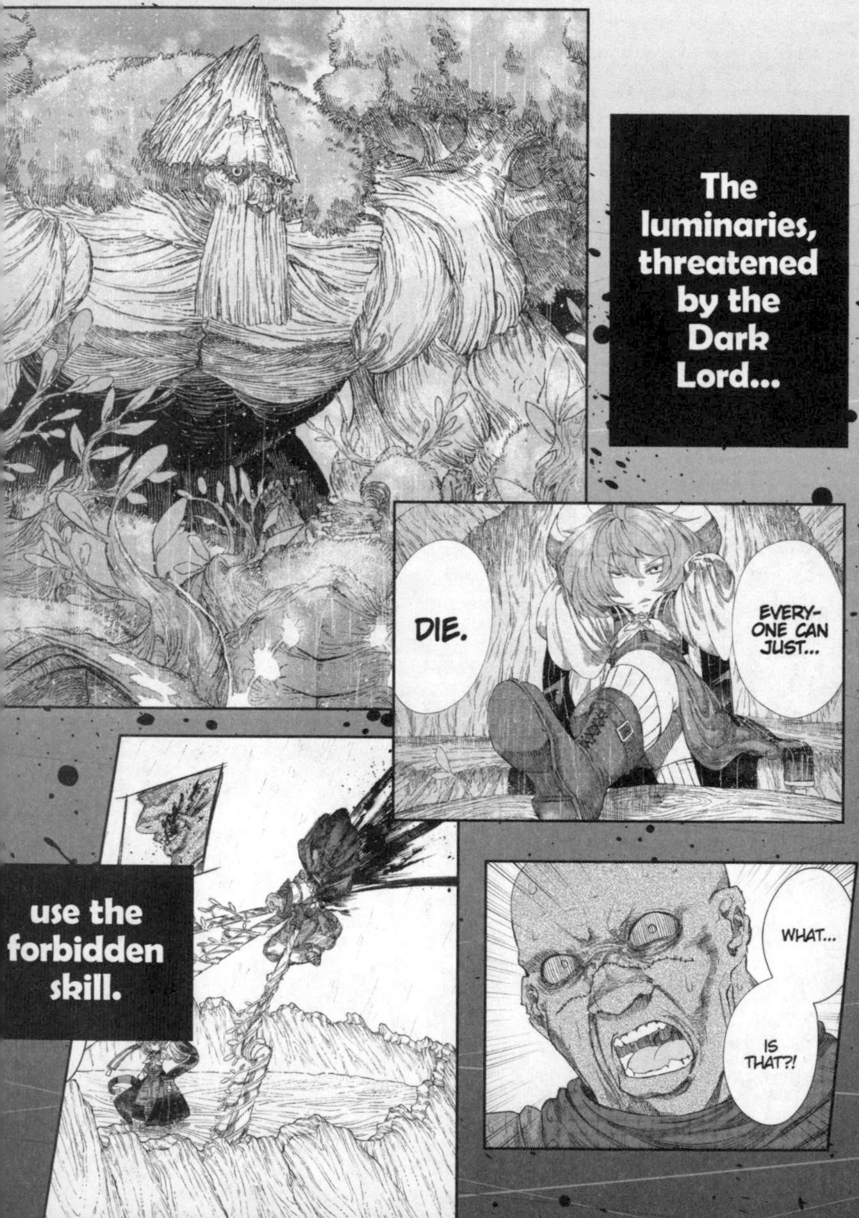
The luminaries, threatened by the Dark Lord...
EVERY-ONE CAN JUST...
DIE.
WHAT...
IS THAT?!
use the forbidden skill.

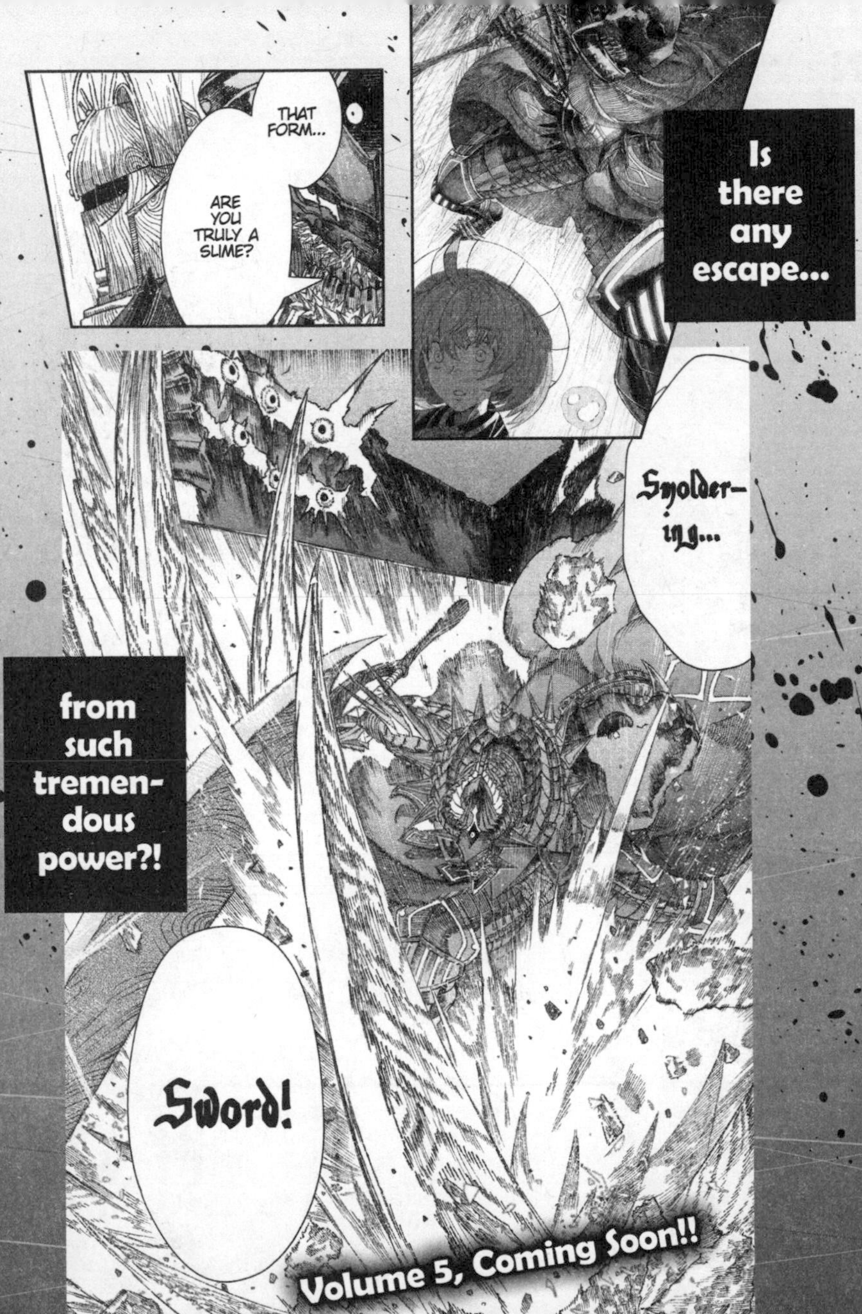
Is there any escape...
THAT FORM...
ARE YOU TRULY A SLIME?
Smolder-ing...
from such tremen-dous power?!
Sword!
Volume 5, Coming Soon!!

SEVEN SEAS ENTERTAINMENT PRESENTS

MONSTER GUILD

The Dark Lord's (No-Good) Comeback!

story and art by TOUROU VOLUME 4

TRANSLATION
Hana Allen

ADAPTATION
Matthew Birkenhauer

LETTERING
Alexandra Gunawan

COVER DESIGN
Kris Aubin

LOGO DESIGN
George Panella

PROOFREADER
B. Lana Guggenheim

COPY EDITOR
Leighanna DeRouen

EDITOR
Kristiina Korpus

PRODUCTION DESIGNER
Eve Grandt
Christa Miesner

PRODUCTION MANAGER
Lissa Pattillo

PREPRESS TECHNICIAN
Melanie Ujimori
Jules Valera

EDITOR-IN-CHIEF
Julie Davis

ASSOCIATE PUBLISHER
Adam Arnold

PUBLISHER
Jason DeAngelis

YUUSHANI HAIBOKUSHITA MAOUSAMAWA KAERIZAKUTAMENI MAMONOGIRUDOWO TSUKURUKOTONI SHIMASHITA. volume 4

Seven Seas press and purchase enquiries can be sent to Marketing Manager Lianne Sentar at press@gomanga.com. Information regarding the distribution and purchase of digital editions is available from Digital Manager CK Russell at digital@gomanga.com.

ISBN: 978-1-63858-781-1
Printed in Canada
First Printing: February 2023
10 9 8 7 6 5 4 3 2 1

READING DIRECTIONS

This book reads from ***right to left***, Japanese style. If this is your first time reading manga, you start reading from the top right panel on each page and take it from there. If you get lost, just follow the numbered diagram here. It may seem backwards at first, but you'll get the hang of it! Have fun!!

1
2
3
4
5
6
7
8
9

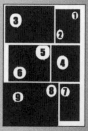

Follow us online: www.SevenSeasEntertainment.com